Tax Planning
To and Through
Early Retirement

Cover design by Carolline Holanda and Sofia Nikssarian
at CobaltSapphire.com

Pearland, TX
ISBN: 979-8-9998415-9-9 (Paperback)
ISBN: 979-8-9998415-2-0 (eBook)
Library of Congress Control Number: 2025918048

Table of Contents

Foreword

If you're holding this book, there's a good chance you know that you don't have to follow the conventional script when it comes to money and retirement.

You might be planning an early retirement. You might already be living one. Or maybe you're just trying to figure out how to make the most of the dollars you do earn so you can buy back more of your time.

Wherever you are on that journey, I want you to know that taxes don't have to be the villain we all fear. In fact, once you understand how the system works, tax planning can become one of your most powerful tools in building a life of freedom and intention.

That's what makes this book so remarkable.

Cody Garrett and Sean Mullaney have created something that's never existed in quite this form: a comprehensive guide to navigating the tax landscape specifically for people pursuing early retirement. And they do it in a way that's empowering, easy to follow, and refreshingly jargon-free.

They've also become two of my most frequent guests on the ChooseFI podcast—and for good reason. They're not just insightful professionals and top-tier educators; they're also the first people I turn to when I need help with a particularly difficult financial or tax question of my own. Sean and Cody are incredible resources, thoughtful thinkers, and, most importantly, wonderful human beings who genuinely care about helping others succeed on this path.

This book won't overwhelm you. It won't try to scare you into action with worst-case scenarios or fearmongering. Instead, it invites you to see tax planning for what it really is—a thoughtful, lifelong puzzle with tremendous upside if approached with just a little strategy and awareness.

When I first encountered these concepts on my own FI journey, I was blown away by how much of an impact small tax decisions could make over a lifetime. But there's a big gap out there between that realization and knowing what to do next.

This book fills that gap.

Whether it's Roth conversions, drawdown strategies, or optimizing for Affordable Care Act subsidies, Cody and Sean guide you through it all with clarity and insight. They even tackle advanced topics like gifting, RMDs, and the Widow's Tax Trap, all in a tone that makes you feel like you're chatting with a (brilliant and extremely knowledgeable) friend over coffee.

At ChooseFI, we talk a lot about reclaiming agency in your financial life. That means learning the levers you can pull and not outsourcing your future to someone else's plan. This book gives you those levers. And it teaches you how to use them, ethically, effectively, and with an eye toward designing the life you want.

So don't treat this like a one-time read. Highlight it and come back to it year after year. Let it be the quiet, confident voice in your corner reminding you that tax planning isn't about fear, it's about freedom.

And with that, enjoy this incredible resource.

Brad Barrett
Richmond, Virginia
August 2025

Introduction

Thank you for joining us on this journey: a journey of tax planning to and through early retirement. This book serves as your guide to navigating retirement tax strategies, especially for those retiring early by conventional standards. Our goal is to help you reduce your total lifetime income tax while effectively building up and spending down your investments.

This book stands out from other retirement tax planning content. Your authors aren't driven by fear. We don't believe retirees will get crushed by taxes. In fact, when it comes to retirement planning, the tax code is more likely to be your friend than your foe. We'll provide detailed examples throughout this book.

Why We Wrote This Book

"Taxes are too complicated!"

"Taxes will crush me in retirement!"

"I'll never be able to retire!"

Are these statements true? From our experience and the available data, it seems many Americans believe they are—often to their own detriment.

Vanguard's 2023 data on median employer retirement account balances paints a sobering picture:

Ages 45 to 54: $60,763

Ages 55 to 64: $87,571

Even assuming the typical American has several retirement accounts, perhaps two or three with former employers and an IRA, millions aren't financially prepared for a successful retirement—let alone an early one.

We wrote this book to cut through the complexity, anxiety, and fear. Tax planning that reduces lifetime income taxes and builds retirement savings can be a powerful and confidence-building tool, no matter when you plan to retire.

We also wrote this book in response to the tax law changes in 2025. July brought with it the passage of the 2025 reconciliation bill, commonly referred to as the One Big Beautiful Bill (the "OBBB" as we refer to it later in the book). This book offers our perspective on OBBB changes and how they shape retirement planning.

Finally, we wanted to explore more advanced retirement planning strategies. We cover complex topics without skipping over the foundational concepts.

Who This Book Is For

We wrote this book for Americans planning to retire in the United States, as well as for the advisors who serve them. Can we speak meaningfully to both professionals and everyday readers? Yes! This book doesn't require a finance degree, and tax planning is not complex surgery or rocket science. The concepts are accessible and practical. We start with the fundamentals and explore more advanced tactics for those seeking deeper insight.

Our focus is especially, but not exclusively, on those considering early retirement or who have already retired early. Most working Americans should at least consider the possibility of early retirement, whether voluntary or involuntary. We live in unpredictable times. Will your job still exist in five or ten years? If it does, will you still want it?

There's little downside to preparing for an early retirement. Why not be ready if life doesn't go according to plan?

That said, this book isn't only for early retirees. We believe that most working Americans can benefit from our thoughts and analysis, even if they're not (yet) planning on an early retirement. If you're already early retired, don't worry: this book includes plenty of insights on drawdown tactics, tax-efficient withdrawals, and more.

Of course, to write a coherent book, we had to draw lines. For example, we don't address situations involving current or future expatriates. These individuals have distinct tax and retirement planning needs that fall outside the scope of our day-to-day professional experience.

Finally, while we cover a wide range of tax planning considerations, we don't attempt to address every possible tactic. Those excluded or only briefly mentioned tend to apply to individuals at the far ends of the wealth spectrum.

What is Early Retirement?

In theory, you get to be the judge and jury as to what an "early" retirement is. That said, we generally define early retirement as any time before Medicare eligibility, typically the first of the month of your 65th birthday. Since around 70% of Americans report retiring before then, early retirement is more common than you might think.

This book offers insights that benefit future and current retirees of any age. Whether you plan to retire early, late, or somewhere in between, we believe you'll find valuable strategies and perspectives that apply to your plan.

Drawdown

The book places particular emphasis on the drawdown years—what some call the decumulation phase. Why?

First, tactics used during our working years must be evaluated based on their eventual tax impact in the drawdown years. We can't assess them in isolation based on what benefits the tax return *this* year.

Second, in our conversations with clients, members of the financial independence community, and readers like you, we've noticed a particular desire to discuss the drawdown tactics in detail. Many have noted that existing personal finance content does not adequately address drawdown in early retirement planning, and we aim to fill that gap.

That said, don't worry if you're not yet close to retirement. We have plenty of tax planning to consider for those building up wealth during their working years.

No Fear

We made a clear decision: we are not going to sell books based on fear. We won't rely on imagined "boogeymen" threatening to "ruin your retirement."

Is high taxation in retirement a legitimate concern? Absolutely.

Is it something to fear? Absolutely not.

The next time you come across personal finance content, ask yourself, "Is this trying to evoke a fear response?" In our experience, too much personal finance content leans on fear-based messaging to generate page views, video clicks, and product sales. We reject that approach.

Taxes in retirement are not something to fear emotionally. They're something to understand and plan for rationally.

We approach retirement tax planning as a thoughtful puzzle: What strategies, applied at the right time, help you get to and through early retirement while reducing your total lifetime income taxes?

Knowledge and Judgment Are Power

When it comes to tax planning, knowledge and judgment are more powerful than fear. Are the **tax laws** complicated? Yes! But does that mean **tax planning** must be complicated? No!

Think of it like driving a modern car. Today's vehicles are packed with complex electronics and computerized systems. Could you explain all the inner workings of that car if your life depended on it? Probably not. But can you drive to the grocery store? Of course.

Tax planning is similar. You don't need to memorize hundreds of pages of tax regulations. You need to understand fundamental tax planning concepts and develop the judgment to apply them to your unique situation.

This book provides you with that knowledge and helps you develop the judgment needed to navigate tax planning in your own life.

Cody's Take and Sean's Take

One unique advantage of this book is that it has two authors. You get two perspectives for the price of one!

It probably won't surprise you to learn that we don't always agree. As football executive Michael Lombardi once recalled, legendary coach Bill Walsh said, "If we are all thinking alike, then no one is thinking."

Throughout the book, you'll see occasional callouts labeled *Cody's Take* and *Sean's Take*. These may highlight a strong personal opinion or respectful disagreement between us.

While we're fundamentally aligned when it comes to tax planning to and through early retirement, we bring different perspectives to certain strategies and nuances. Our hope is that by reading both viewpoints, you'll sharpen your own knowledge and judgment.

Of course, you get to be the judge and jury in your own mind regarding each of our takes. Ultimately, our goal is to help you make informed decisions based on your own values, variables, and desired outcomes.

Tax Rules

At its core, this book is about tax planning. A necessary evil of writing a tax planning book is that we must discuss tax rules, which can be complicated and occasionally frustrating. We can't cover every nuance, nook, and cranny of a particular tax rule, but we aim to present planning concepts clearly and engagingly.

We present tax rules not to overwhelm you, but to help you understand how they shape planning strategy. Just as you don't need to be a mechanic to drive to the grocery store, you don't need to be a tax expert to understand and apply planning concepts.

That said, a basic grasp of how our tax system works is essential. We hope our book helps you build that foundational understanding.

Examples

The book is full of examples of various length and complexity. We provide examples for two main reasons. First, to justify and support our assertions and conclusions. Second, because for some readers, examples help illuminate the concepts we discuss.

However, not every example will help every reader understand the concepts. For some, certain examples may—at first glance—confuse rather than inform. That is a natural consequence of writing a book about a sometimes complex topic like tax planning.

Our recommendation is to avoid getting bogged down by examples. If reading one helps you understand a concept, great—keep reading it. If the example proves difficult to comprehend, skip it for the time being and focus on the narrative discussion. You can always return to the example later to help digest the material presented.

Technical Review

We are honored that Denise Appleby, MJ, APA, CISP, CRC, CRPS, *The IRA Whisperer*, helped us with the technical review of the IRA and qualified plan rules presented in this book. Some edits were made after the technical review was completed, and any remaining errors are solely the responsibility of the authors, Cody and Sean.

Note: Providing a technical review does not imply Ms. Appleby's endorsement of this book, its interpretations, or its conclusions. Her role was limited to reviewing the accuracy of tax rules related to IRAs and qualified retirement plans. Technical reviewers offer input on drafts, and it is ultimately the authors' decision whether and how to incorporate that input into the final version.

Future Reference

We wrote this book not only to be read today, but also to serve as a reference you can revisit in the future. That's why the chapters are written with a level of detail that may, at times, feel repetitive if you read the book from start to finish. Our goal is for each chapter to stand on its own, so you can revisit specific topics later without needing to restart from the beginning. The occasional repetition reinforces important lessons and augments the book's usefulness as a future reference.

Future Tax Changes

We wrote this book in 2025, a year marked by major tax law changes. Will the tax laws change after the publication of this book? Of course. Does that invalidate this book the moment Congress moves a single comma in the Internal Revenue Code? Absolutely not.

Please be aware that tax laws and figures (contribution limits, tax brackets, etc.) change over time. While those changes may affect some of the specific numbers referenced, they do not undermine the core principles and strategies discussed throughout this book.

In Chapter 20, we share how we approach the ever-evolving nature of tax laws. This perspective guides how we believe most Americans can navigate retirement tax planning, even without knowing the exact contours of future tax law changes.

The Final Word

Tax planning involves one constant: continuous learning. No one engages in tax planning without learning along the way. Thus, neither this book—nor any other commentary—can offer "the final word" on the subject.

We encourage readers to consider the principles and arguments in this book while also considering ways to improve upon them for their unique situations. As authors, we refined and expanded our own tax planning knowledge while writing this book. As the saying goes, "When you teach, you learn twice." We plan to keep learning and improving after its publication—and we hope our readers will, too.

Disclaimers

Before we dive into tax planning, here are a few important caveats to keep in mind as you read this book.

First, this book is for educational and entertainment purposes only. It does not constitute tax, legal, financial, or investment advice for you or any other specific person. The book's examples illustrate potential tax or financial outcomes but consider only limited slices of a hypothetical person's financial picture. None of the examples account for the full range of relevant tax or financial details for any particular person or couple, yourself included.

Second, this book is not a substitute for your and your advisors' own research and judgment regarding tax matters. We endeavor to present accurate information, but given the complexity and volume of federal and state tax laws, regulations, cases, and other authorities, we cannot guarantee that this or any other publication discussing tax laws will always be entirely accurate. Tax law also contains many gray areas, and readers should keep that in mind.

Third, implementing the concepts from this book does not guarantee financial success in retirement. As with any planning effort, results will vary based on individual circumstances, decisions, and external factors beyond our control.

Neither Cody Garrett nor Sean Mullaney shall have any liability or responsibility to any person or entity with respect to any damage or loss caused (directly or indirectly) by the information contained in this book.

As a general convention, we've rounded most figures to the nearest whole dollar. Examples should be read in light of the rounding employed. Since some examples build on previous calculations, there can be some rounding on rounding.

All examples in the book involve hypothetical individuals who are U.S. citizens living, working, and retiring in the United States, with calendar-year tax years.

All illustrations of tax returns in the book are presented to show the general direction of taxation for a theoretical individual or couple. They are not intended to illustrate federal tax liabilities to the precise dollar or penny.

Lastly, the opinions expressed herein are solely those of the authors, and they do not represent the opinions of the authors' current or former employers.

Now let's get started with Tax Planning To and Through Early Retirement!

1 – The Federal Income Tax Formula

The following federal income tax formula applies to U.S. citizens. This book's concepts assume residency within the United States, with all income, deductions, and credits reported on the U.S. individual income tax return (Form 1040). It is helpful to review the 2024 Form 1040 as we go through the federal income tax formula line by line.

Income (Lines 1-15)

We begin by totaling gross income from a variety of common sources:

Line 1: Employee wages, tips, and other compensation are reported on Form W-2. The amount in Box 1 *excludes* traditional (pre-tax) employee contributions to workplace retirement plans and other pre-tax Cafeteria Plan deductions (see Box 12). Amounts excluded from W-2 income cannot be deducted again on your income tax return—no double dipping!

Line 2: Taxable interest is reported on Form 1099-INT, including interest from bank accounts, certificates of deposit (CDs), and taxable bonds (including U.S. Treasury securities). Interest earned within retirement accounts is generally excluded from gross income, as it is tax-deferred.

Line 3: Ordinary dividends reported on Form 1099-DIV are distributions from a corporation's earnings and profits to its stockholders. Qualified dividend income (QDI) receives preferential long-term capital gains tax treatment but must meet specific criteria, including being paid by a U.S. or qualified foreign corporation and meeting a holding period—generally at least 61 days during the 121-day period surrounding the ex-dividend date. All dividends that are not QDI are taxed as ordinary income.

Many equity index funds distribute a combination of ordinary dividends and QDI.

Lines 4–5: Taxable distributions from retirement plans, pensions, and annuities are included in gross income and reported on Form 1099-R. Taxable distributions from IRAs, 401(k)s, 403(b)s, 457(b)s, and the federal government's Thrift Savings Plan (the "TSP") are reported here.

Line 6: The taxable portion of Social Security benefits, as reported on Form SSA-1099, is included in gross income. This includable percentage is determined by calculating provisional income (½ of Social Security benefits plus other income, including tax-exempt interest) and applying it to threshold amounts based on filing status. Up to 85% of Social Security benefits may be included in gross income.

Taxpayers can use Worksheet 1 in IRS Publication 915 to determine how much of their Social Security benefits are taxable.

Line 7: Sales of capital assets (e.g., stocks or bonds) held in a taxable brokerage account are reported on Form 1099-B. Realized capital gains or losses are categorized as short-term (held one year or less) or long-term (held more than one year). Capital losses offset capital gains, and any remaining gain or loss (based on its holding period) is included in gross income. Net short-term capital gains are taxed at ordinary income rates, while net long-term capital gains benefit from preferential tax treatment. Up to $3,000 of net capital loss may be used to offset other income in the current year, with unused losses carried forward indefinitely.

If that felt like a lot, don't worry—we'll walk through an example in the next chapter.

Line 8: Additional Income (Schedule 1, Part I) includes sources such as net self-employment income (Schedule C) and net rental real estate or pass-through entity income (Schedule E).

Line 9: The sum of all taxable income sources equals total (gross) income, but we're not ready to calculate income taxes just yet.

Line 10: Adjustments to Income (Schedule 1, Part II) are subtracted from total income. These commonly include Health Savings Account (HSA) contributions not made through payroll withholding, the deductible half of self-employment tax, self-employed retirement plan contributions, the self-employed health insurance deduction, and deductible traditional IRA contributions.

Line 11: The result is **adjusted gross income (AGI)**—a key figure for determining eligibility for various tax deductions, credits, and other benefits. When you see **modified adjusted gross income (MAGI)**, keep in mind that modifications to AGI vary depending on the specific tax program or provision.

Line 12: Before applying the respective tax rates, income is then reduced again, this time by the higher of the standard deduction or combined itemized deductions (Schedule A). Itemized deductions commonly include state and local taxes (capped at $40,000 in 2025), home mortgage interest, charitable gifts, and unreimbursed medical and dental expenses (above 7.5% of AGI). Most taxpayers claim the standard deduction.

Lines 13–15: The Qualified Business Income (QBI) deduction (Form 8995 or Form 8995-A) provides an additional reduction (generally 20% of QBI) for eligible pass-through business owners and real estate investment trust (REIT) investors. The 2025 Form 1040 will need to be updated to include a new schedule or additional lines for the new tips deduction, overtime income deduction, and senior deduction. We discuss the new senior deduction in Chapter 19.

After these deductions, we finally arrive at **taxable income**.

Tax and Credits (Lines 16–24)

It's important to note that federal income tax rates (both ordinary and long-term capital gains) apply to taxable income—not AGI. The standard/itemized and QBI deductions are essential in retirement planning calculations.

Although taxable income appears as a single value, it must be divided into two components before applying their respective federal income tax rates:

1. **Long-Term Capital Gains:** Net long-term capital gains and qualified dividends.
2. **Ordinary Income:** All other taxable income.

These are the two **characters** of taxable income. Throughout this book, you'll see how character counts to and through early retirement.

Line 16: Ordinary income and long-term capital gains are taxed at their respective rates. Taxable income is divided into brackets, with each portion taxed at progressively higher rates. A portion of ordinary income is taxed at 10%, the next at 12%, then 22%, and so on. Your highest tax rate for ordinary income is referred to as your **marginal** tax rate, but the average rate across all income is your **effective** tax rate. We prefer to use total income as the denominator to understand the impact of Adjustments to Income—not just benefits below AGI.

Here is an example of a tax calculation using 2025 numbers:

Melinda, a 40-year-old single taxpayer, earns $140,000 in wages. After applying the standard deduction of $15,750, her ordinary taxable income is $124,250. The first $11,925 of taxable income is taxed at 10% ($1,192.50), the next $36,550 at 12% ($4,386), the next $54,875 at 22% ($12,072.50), and the remaining $20,900 at 24% ($5,016).

Beyond Melinda's ordinary taxable income of $124,250, let's say she also has $25,750 in net long-term capital gains (LTCG). Her combined taxable income (including both ordinary and LTCG) is $150,000, with the entire $25,750 of LTCG taxed within the 15% LTCG tax bracket ($3,862.50).

Melinda's ordinary income tax ($22,667) and long-term capital gains tax ($3,862.50) combine to equal **tentative tax** of $26,529.50.

Although Melinda's marginal (highest) income tax rate is 24%, her tax of $26,529.50 on total income of $165,750 is an effective (average) tax rate of 16%.

Lines 17–18 and 23: Additional Taxes (Schedule 2) are added, such as repayments of the Premium Tax Credit (PTC) (Form 8962), the 10% early withdrawal penalty for retirement account distributions (Form 5329), self-employment tax (Schedule SE), the Additional Medicare Tax (Form 8959), and the Net Investment Income Tax (NIIT) (Form 8960)—an extra 3.8% tax on investment income for high-income taxpayers.

Lines 19–22: Nonrefundable tax credits are subtracted next. These include the Foreign Tax Credit (Form 1116), the Credits for Qualifying Children and Other Dependents (Schedule 8812), and the Credit for Qualified Retirement Savings Contributions (Form 8880). "Nonrefundable" means the tax credit can reduce your tax liability to zero, but it will not generate a refund beyond that.

Line 24: After applying additional taxes and subtracting nonrefundable tax credits, we arrive at **total tax**.

Payments (Lines 25–33)

Lines 25–26: Federal income taxes withheld and paid throughout the tax year are subtracted here. These include withholdings reported on Form W-2 and Form 1099, and any estimated tax payments.

Lines 27–33: Refundable tax credits are then subtracted. These include the Additional Child Tax Credit (Form 8812), the Earned Income Tax Credit (EIC), a portion of the American Opportunity Tax Credit for education expenses (Form 8863), and the net Premium Tax Credit. "Refundable" means these tax credits *can* reduce your tax liability below zero and result in a refund.

Refund or Amount Owed (Lines 34–38)

Lines 34–38: After subtracting tax credits and payments from total tax, we arrive at either a refund or an amount owed, plus an estimated tax penalty (if applicable). We'll cover how retirees make payments and avoid underpayment penalties in Chapter 14.

Federal Income Tax Formula

Congratulations! You now have a fundamental understanding of how the federal income tax system works.

Here's a visual version of the federal income tax formula for future reference:

All Income Sources
− Exclusions from Income
Total (Gross) Income
− Adjustments to Income
= Adjusted Gross Income
− Standard or Itemized Deductions
− Qualified Business Income (QBI) Deduction
= Taxable Income
× Applicable Ordinary and Long-Term Capital Gains Tax Rates
= Tentative Tax
+ Additional Taxes
− Nonrefundable Tax Credits
= Total Tax
− Tax Payments
− Refundable Tax Credits
= Amount Refunded or Owed

Computing the Tax

There are seven progressive ordinary tax brackets: 10%, 12%, 22%, 24%, 32%, 35%, and 37%. Each year, the IRS publishes the specific taxable income thresholds for these brackets based on filing status (single and head of household, married filing jointly and qualifying surviving spouse, and married filing separately).

Long-term capital gains (LTCGs) are taxed separately using three progressive LTCG tax brackets: 0%, 15%, and 20%. The IRS also publishes these brackets annually. Notably, in 2025, the 0% LTCG bracket applies to taxable income up to $48,350 for single filers, $64,750 for head of household, and $96,700 for married filing jointly.

As we'll explore in this book, the lower an early retiree can keep their taxable income, the more of it may be taxed in the lower ordinary and LTCG brackets—including possibly the 0% LTCG tax bracket.

Later in this chapter, we walk through four additional examples to demonstrate how federal income tax is calculated in practice.

Planning for Tax Deductions Versus Tax Credits

You may have heard the phrase, "A tax credit is worth more than a tax deduction." While that's generally true—credits directly reduce taxes owed and deductions reduce income taxed—a tax deduction is often more impactful from a tax planning perspective.

Consider a married couple, Serena and Sam, with $300,000 in taxable income after claiming the standard deduction. This falls squarely within the 24% marginal federal income tax bracket. They're deciding between contributing to a traditional 401(k) or a Roth 401(k). As we'll explore in this book, traditional 401(k) contributions are excluded from taxable income. While technically this is an exclusion (not a deduction), its effect is functionally the same. Throughout this book, we'll refer to it as a **tax deduction**.

From a planning standpoint, the availability of this tax deduction is very impactful and should be carefully considered when making the "traditional versus Roth 401(k)" decision.

Now imagine Serena and Sam are also the parents of 10-year-old twins. Using 2025 rules, they qualify for a $4,400 Child Tax Credit ($2,200 per child). While that's a valuable benefit, it doesn't reduce their marginal tax rate or materially influence their decision to contribute to a traditional or Roth 401(k). For many taxpayers, even a large tax credit like the Child Tax Credit does not change their planning.

There is, however, one notable exception to this general rule for those planning to and through early retirement: the Premium Tax Credit. This credit does not reduce income tax. Rather, it can meaningfully reduce the cost of health insurance coverage in early retirement. We'll explore it in greater detail later in the book.

Income Stacking

"If I have two types of income—ordinary and long-term capital gains (LTCGs)—how do I apply the different tax brackets to them?"

Good question!

The tax rules provide for **income stacking**. Ordinary income is taxed first, and then LTCGs are stacked on top and taxed second.

Here is an example: Margaret, age 50, is single. She has a total ordinary income of $102,000 from a W-2 and a Form 1099-INT (interest income). She also has qualified dividend income (QDI) of $3,000. Her adjusted gross income (AGI) is $105,000. How is that taxed?

The first $15,750 of ordinary income is applied against her standard deduction (effectively taxed at 0%). The next $11,925 is taxed at 10% ($1,192.50), and the next $36,550 is taxed at 12% ($4,386). That leaves us with $37,775 of remaining ordinary income, which is taxed at the 22% bracket ($8,310.50).

Margaret has $89,250 of taxable income (AGI of $105,000 less the standard deduction of $15,750). Dollars $86,251 through $89,250 are her long-term capital gains (in this case, QDI). That portion of her income is applied against the LTCG tax brackets. For single filers in 2025, this income falls within the 15% LTCG bracket, resulting in $450 of tax.

We see how income stacking applies to Margaret. It puts her long-term capital gains in the 15% LTCG bracket, separate from her ordinary income. Margaret's total federal income tax for 2025 is **$14,339** ($1,192.50 + $4,386 + $8,310.50 + $450).

How does income stacking apply to a retired married couple?

Meet Eddie and Elizabeth. Both are 67 and retired in 2025. They distribute $50,000 from traditional retirement accounts, have $5,000 of combined interest income and nonqualified dividends, and have $60,000 in long-term capital gains and qualified dividends. How is that AGI of $115,000 taxed?

The first $46,700 of their $55,000 of ordinary income is soaked up by the standard deduction ($31,500), the additional standard deduction ($1,600 × 2 = $3,200), and the senior deduction ($6,000 × 2 = $12,000). The remaining ordinary income of $8,300 is taxed at 10% ($830).

What about Eddie and Elizabeth's $60,000 of LTCG income? Those dollars—$8,301 through $68,300 of their taxable income—fall entirely within the 0% LTCG bracket for married couples filing jointly in 2025. As a result, Eddie and Elizabeth's total federal income tax is just $830 on $115,000 of gross income. *Wow!*

Did you notice that the retirees do much better in the tax calculation than Margaret? That's because, in addition to larger deductions, character counts! We'll explore that phenomenon next.

Character Counts

While the amount of taxable income is the primary driver of how much tax a taxpayer pays, as you will see frequently throughout the book, character counts!

In fact, character counts so much that **there are situations where taxpayers with lower taxable income pay more taxes than those with higher taxable income.**

Let's consider two married couples, Carl & Connie and Debbie & Don, all age 66 in 2025:

Carl and Connie distribute $53,000 from a traditional IRA, earn $1,000 in interest income, and realize $40,000 in long-term capital gains. Their total deduction, like Eddie and Elizabeth's deduction, is $46,700, leaving **$47,300** in taxable income.

Debbie and Don, on the other hand, distribute $32,000 from a traditional IRA, earn $1,000 in interest income, and realize $81,000 of long-term capital gains. Their total deduction is also $46,700, resulting in **$67,300** in taxable income — **$20,000 more than Carl and Connie.**

So, which couple owes more in federal income taxes in 2025?

It's Carl and Connie! How can that be, given that their "taxable" income is $20,000 lower? The answer is: character counts!

Carl and Connie owe $730 in federal income tax. Let's add it up. The first $46,700 of ordinary income is wiped out by the $31,500 standard deduction, the $3,200 additional standard deduction, and the $12,000 senior deduction. The next $7,300 is taxed at the 10% bracket, resulting in a tax liability of $730. Their $40,000 in LTCGs falls within taxable income from $7,301 to $47,300, which is taxed in the 0% LTCG bracket.

Debbie and Don's $33,000 of ordinary income is completely wiped out by the combined deductions. In fact, those deductions also wipe out $13,700 of their LTCGs. Their remaining LTCGs fall within taxable income from $0 to $67,300, which is taxed in the 0% LTCG bracket.

Despite having a higher taxable income than Carl and Connie, **Debbie and Don paid $0 in federal income tax in 2025!**

These examples highlight that taxable income alone does not determine tax liability; its character (ordinary vs. LTCG) can be just as important. Since character counts, many early retirees will want LTCGs showing up on their tax returns instead of ordinary income.

As you've seen, tax planning isn't always intuitive, but this complexity can work to your advantage if you understand how to optimize your income sources — which we'll explore throughout this book.

2 – Taxable Accounts

Introduction

A taxable account—which includes checking, savings, and taxable brokerage accounts—is a non-retirement account where investment income is taxed in the year it is earned, regardless of whether cash is withdrawn. Unlike tax-advantaged retirement accounts, taxable accounts do not offer tax-deferred contributions or growth. Instead, think of these accounts as "taxable along the way."

Although taxable accounts lack tax deferral, they still provide valuable advantages:

Unlimited Contributions: There are no annual contribution limits, making them ideal for saving and investing beyond retirement accounts.

Tax-Free Cash Withdrawals: While earnings (interest, dividends, and capital gains) are taxed when received within the account, cash withdrawals themselves are excluded from gross income, regardless of age or purpose.

No Age-Based Rules: Unlike traditional retirement accounts, taxable accounts have no early withdrawal penalties or Required Minimum Distributions (RMDs).

Investment Availability: Unlike workplace retirement plans, which often have limited fund options, taxable brokerage accounts offer access to individual stocks and bonds, mutual funds, exchange-traded funds (ETFs), and alternative investments such as commodities, cryptocurrencies, and private equity.

Gifts to Others: Taxable assets may be transferred in-kind (without liquidation) to other people or qualified charitable organizations during life without adverse income tax consequences.

Step-Up in Basis: Upon an investor's death, assets within a taxable account may receive a step-up (reset) in cost basis to their fair market value as of the date of death. This means beneficiaries may sell inherited assets with little or no capital gains tax. More details are covered in Chapter 30.

Account Titling: Unlike retirement accounts, which are individually owned, taxable assets allow for multiple ownership structures, such as Joint Tenants with Rights of Survivorship (JTWROS), Transfer-on-Death (TOD), and revocable living trusts, which can be beneficial for estate planning. Learn more in Chapter 31.

Capital Gains

When an investor sells an asset within a taxable account for more than its cost basis (purchase price), the realized gain is subject to capital gains tax. The applied tax rate depends on the holding period before the sale:

Short-Term: If an investment is held for 1 year or less, the short-term capital gain (STCG) is taxed as ordinary income.

Long-Term: If an investment is held longer than 1 year, the long-term capital gain (LTCG) is taxed at preferential rates of 0%, 15%, or 20%, depending on taxable income. LTCGs taxed at 0% are covered in more detail in Chapter 23.

Extra Credit: Although LTCGs and qualified dividends receive preferential treatment at the federal level, states generally tax them as ordinary income.

Capital Gain Distributions

Mutual funds and ETFs may generate gains from the sale of assets within the fund, known as "capital gain distributions." When held within a taxable account, these distributions are typically taxed as long-term capital gains.

What generates capital gain distributions inside a mutual fund or ETF? There are two main causes:

1. **Active Management:** Actively managed funds tend to sell investments more frequently, triggering realized capital gains distributed to investors.

2. **Outflows Exceeding Inflows:** This primarily affects mutual funds, which issue and redeem shares directly with the fund company. If redemptions exceed new purchases, the fund may need to sell underlying assets to raise cash—potentially triggering taxable capital gains that are passed on to all shareholders. ETFs generally avoid this issue because they trade on an exchange; when an investor sells shares of an ETF, the sale is matched with a buyer without requiring the fund to sell securities.

In Real Life: Review Schedule D, Line 13 (Capital Gain Distributions) on your recent tax return. If there is a number there—especially one in the four figures or higher—it's worth investigating which assets generated it. While we cannot provide specific investment advice, we can note (from a tax perspective) that index funds (mutual funds and ETFs) typically produce minimal capital gain distributions. Reallocating to index funds may reduce or eliminate future capital gain distributions. However, investors should consider the unrealized gains on current holdings before making changes. If reallocating would trigger substantial taxable gains, it might not be worth it.

Dividends & Interest Income

Similarly, dividends received in taxable brokerage accounts are categorized as either nonqualified (taxed as ordinary income) or qualified (taxed at LTCG rates).

Interest income received from taxable bonds (including bond funds), CDs, and savings accounts is taxed as ordinary income. Municipal bond interest is generally exempt from federal income tax and may also be exempt from state and local taxes.

Since taxable accounts generate ongoing tax liabilities ("taxable along the way"), investors may prioritize owning tax-efficient investments, such as low-turnover stock funds, to minimize distributions and benefit from preferential tax rates.

Extra Credit: High-income taxpayers may be subject to the 3.8% Net Investment Income Tax (NIIT) on capital gains, dividends, and interest. Fortunately, even many affluent early retirees can keep their taxable income low enough to avoid NIIT entirely.

Dividend Reinvestment

"Should I automatically reinvest my dividends?"

Often, yes. During the accumulation years, we generally favor dividend reinvestment. Most accumulators fund their living expenses with earned income—not investment income. This approach helps maximize compound growth within investment accounts on the path to early retirement.

In early retirement, some may consider turning off dividend reinvestment. As we'll discuss later, early retirees often prioritize funding their living expenses by selling investments within taxable brokerage accounts—typically triggering capital gains. Taking dividends in cash can reduce the amount of securities that need to be sold, thereby minimizing realized capital gains.

Cody's Take: Since I prefer refilling retirement cash needs every six months, I generally prefer to continue automatically reinvesting dividends in retirement and manually select which shares to sell—using the Specific Identification (Spec ID) disposal method. Each reinvested dividend creates a new tax lot with its own cost basis and holding period, which may offer more flexibility to sell shares with minimal tax consequences, including for tax loss harvesting. When dividends aren't reinvested and instead settle in the money market fund, they may create cash drag and generate ordinary interest income—depending on how long they sit there.

Capital Losses

When an investor sells an asset in a taxable account for less than its cost basis, the resulting realized loss can be used to offset capital gains (but not qualified dividends).

Losses are first used to offset gains of the same holding period—long-term losses offset long-term gains, and short-term losses offset short-term gains. If losses exceed gains within a holding period, the excess can then be applied to the other.

If total capital losses exceed capital gains in a given tax year, up to $3,000 of the net loss can be used to offset other income, including ordinary income. Any unused losses carry forward to future years, where they continue to offset capital gains and up to $3,000 of other income annually—rinse and repeat until the loss is fully used. We explore this strategy and its important considerations in Chapter 23.

Here's a step-by-step example of how capital losses offset capital gains:

Step One – List realized capital gains and losses by holding period:

- **Long-Term Gain:** $10,000
- **Long-Term Loss:** –$1,000
- **Short-Term Gain:** $3,000
- **Short-Term Loss:** –$20,000

Step Two – Offset gains by holding period:

- **Long-Term Gain:** $9,000 ($10,000 – $1,000)
- **Short-Term Loss:** –$17,000 ($3,000 – $20,000)

Step Three – Net gains and/or losses across holding periods:

- **Short-Term Loss:** –$8,000 ($9,000 – $17,000)

Step Four – Offset other income (up to $3,000):

- **Capital Loss Offsetting Other Income:** –$3,000
- **Unused Short-Term Capital Loss Carryover:** –$5,000 (–$8,000 + $3,000)

Measure Twice: When switching tax preparers or tax software, verify that capital loss carryovers are accurately applied to the following year. Confirm your numbers on Schedule D and Form 8949.

Recent History and Taxable Accounts

Five relatively recent developments have made taxable accounts significantly more attractive—especially for early retirees.

First, the introduction of qualified dividend income (QDI) in 2003. Prior to that, all dividends were taxed as ordinary income, just like interest. The QDI concept helped reduce or eliminate the federal income taxation of many dividends. Later in the book, you'll see this is particularly beneficial for early retirees.

Second, the creation of the 0% long-term capital gains (LTCG) tax rate in 2008. This provision can be especially powerful for early retirees, who often have years with relatively low taxable income. Much of their income may come from LTCG and qualified dividends—both potentially taxed at 0% federally.

Third, the higher standard deduction, effective in 2018. While it benefits both workers and retirees, retirees often benefit more since they are more likely to (a) no longer have mortgage interest to itemize, and (b) use Qualified Charitable Distributions (QCDs) starting at age 70½, which allow charitable giving to bypass itemized deductions while still being beneficial from a tax perspective.

Fourth, shifts in asset placement due to the growth of traditional retirement accounts. In our experience, early retirees often hold at least half of their investable assets in traditional retirement accounts and prefer to keep no more than half of their portfolio in taxable bonds. As discussed later in the book, this setup often allows retirees to place their entire bond allocation within traditional retirement accounts—keeping bond interest income off their tax returns. This ability to hide interest income helps reduce taxable investment income and overall federal income tax liability for early retirees. This concept is called **Asset Location**, and we'll cover it in detail in Chapter 18.

Fifth, reduced asset yields. With bond and dividend yields declining over recent decades, taxable accounts now generate less investment income subject to tax. This results in remarkably low tax drag for early retirees—especially when bond income can be sheltered in tax-deferred retirement accounts.

It has not been all peaches and cream for taxable accounts over the past few decades. Since 2013, taxable interest, dividends, and capital gains have been subject to the 3.8% Net Investment Income Tax (NIIT). However, the NIIT only applies to those with adjusted gross income (AGI) above $200,000 (single or head of household) or $250,000 (married filing jointly). As we'll show throughout the book, even many affluent early retirees can keep AGI below those thresholds.

Could all five of these favorable factors disappear? It's possible, but unlikely. Still, aspiring and current early retirees should stay alert to future tax law changes.

3 – Tax-Advantaged Accounts

Pre-Tax Accounts

A pre-tax (traditional) retirement account is a tax-advantaged investment account where contributions reduce taxable income, either by an exclusion from wages or as a tax deduction. Investment earnings—including capital appreciation (asset price growth), interest, dividends, and realized capital gains—are tax-deferred, meaning they are *not* taxable along the way. These accounts incentivize workers to save for retirement while reducing their current tax liability.

The Catch

So, if pre-tax accounts provide immediate tax savings for contributions and tax-deferred growth along the way, what's the downside?

Contributions reduce taxes upfront, but future distributions are included in gross income and taxed at ordinary rates. The tax rules do not allow indefinite deferral of these accounts. Thus, owners must begin Required Minimum Distributions (RMDs) (based on life expectancy) from pre-tax accounts in their 70s.

There are several types of pre-tax accounts, each with its own contribution limits and rules. We highlight the most prevalent here:

Traditional 401(k), 403(b), 457(b), and Thrift Savings Plan (TSP): These employer-sponsored retirement plans allow employees to exclude contributions from taxable wages.

Solo 401(k), SEP IRA (Simplified Employee Pension IRA), and SIMPLE IRA (Savings Incentive Match Plan for Employees IRA): These retirement plans are designed for self-employed individuals and small businesses. They allow tax-deferred contributions but have different contribution and participation rules.

Traditional IRA: These Individual Retirement Accounts may allow tax-deductible contributions depending on income thresholds and workplace plan participation.

You'll learn much more about these in the following Chapters 4 through 6.

Tax-Free Accounts

A tax-free account is an investment account where contributions are generally funded with after-tax dollars. Although contributions are not deductible in the year made, investment earnings—such as capital appreciation, interest, dividends, and realized capital gains—are tax-deferred and may be withdrawn tax-free if certain conditions are met.

There are several types of tax-free accounts, each with specific rules and limits:

Roth 401(k), 403(b), 457(b), and TSP: These employer-sponsored retirement plans allow after-tax contributions and tax-free qualified withdrawals.

Roth IRA: This Individual Retirement Account is funded with after-tax dollars (subject to income limits). The withdrawal of Roth contributions, conversions, and earnings follows specific distribution rules, covered in Chapter 4.

Health Savings Account (HSA): This account offers triple tax benefits: tax-deductible contributions, tax-deferred growth, and tax-free withdrawals for qualified medical expenses. Learn more in Chapter 22.

529 Plan: These education savings accounts offer tax-deferred growth and tax-free withdrawals for qualified education expenses. These details are explored in Chapter 33.

4 – The Basics of IRAs

The individual retirement account (IRA) was established under the Employee Retirement Income Security Act of 1974 (ERISA) and first became available to the public in 1975.

IRAs allow individuals to fund their own retirement savings independent of an employer. One of their key advantages over workplace retirement plans is flexibility—individuals can choose the financial institution and the specific investments. In today's environment, a wide range of financial institutions offer IRAs to the public, many providing low-cost access to investments such as stocks, bonds, mutual funds, and exchange-traded funds (ETFs).

There are two types of IRAs: traditional IRAs and Roth IRAs. Each comes with its own tax advantages and disadvantages. Generally, traditional IRAs offer a potential upfront tax deduction, but withdrawals are taxable. Roths are the reverse: no upfront tax deduction, but qualified withdrawals are tax-free.

We will explore both types in more detail later in the chapter.

Purpose

Why might someone contribute to an IRA? Here are several reasons:

- To build up retirement savings.
- To control investments and expenses by selecting the financial institution and investment options.
- Potential tax deduction for traditional IRA contributions.
- For low-income taxpayers, to qualify for a tax credit (available for both traditional and Roth IRA contributions).
- To benefit from potential tax-free withdrawals from Roth IRAs.
- To benefit from tax-deferred growth in traditional IRAs and either tax-deferred or tax-free growth in Roth IRAs (depending on when the growth is withdrawn).
- To receive creditor protection: IRAs enjoy varying (often substantial) degrees of protection from the claims of creditors under state law, as well as significant federal bankruptcy protection.
- To serve as a retirement home for workplace retirement plans. IRAs have a secondary function: they often become the destination for rollovers from old 401(k) plans and other qualified retirement plans.

Investments

As an IRA owner, the world is your oyster. Dozens of financial institutions across the United States are willing to hold your IRA and offer a wide range of investment options.

IRA investments often consist of financial assets such as stocks, bonds, mutual funds, and ETFs—though other types of investments are possible.

Contributions

There are two primary types of IRA contributions:

1. Annual contributions, made from current year earnings, and
2. Rollover contributions, which involve redepositing distributions from other retirement accounts—such as IRAs or qualified plans like 401(k)s—into IRAs.

Annual Contributions

There are only three types of annual IRA contributions:

1. Traditional deductible contributions
2. Traditional nondeductible contributions
3. Roth contributions

That's it!

Let's briefly review the qualifications to make each type of contribution.

Traditional Deductible Contributions

A deductible traditional IRA contribution reduces adjusted gross income (AGI) on the annual tax return, lowering the taxpayer's income tax for that year. Under current rules, the deductible contribution is reported as an Adjustment to Income on Schedule 1, Part II, which is filed alongside Form 1040.

The ability to **deduct** a traditional IRA contribution depends on two factors:

1. Whether the individual or their spouse is covered by a workplace retirement plan, such as a 401(k), and
2. The household's income level.

If neither the taxpayer nor their spouse is covered by a workplace retirement plan, there is no income limit on the ability to deduct a traditional IRA contribution.

However, if the taxpayer or their spouse is covered by a workplace plan, income limits apply.

For 2025, the deduction for individuals covered by a workplace plan begins to phase out and is eliminated at the following modified adjusted gross income (MAGI) ranges:

- **Single Filer:** $79,000–$89,000
- **Married Filing Jointly:** $126,000–$146,000
- **Married Filing Separately:** $0–$10,000

For individuals not covered by a workplace plan but married to someone who is, a separate MAGI phaseout range applies:

- **Married Filing Jointly:** $236,000–$246,000
- **Married Filing Separately:** $0–$10,000

In practice, many working Americans pursuing early retirement are unable to deduct traditional IRA contributions due to higher income and workplace plan coverage. As a result, they may turn to either traditional *nondeductible* IRA contributions or Roth IRA contributions instead.

Traditional Nondeductible Contributions

This one is simple: there is no income limit on the ability to make a nondeductible traditional IRA contribution, and it is not restricted by workplace retirement plan coverage.

In today's environment, there are two primary reasons to make nondeductible contributions to traditional IRAs:

1. **Backdoor Roth IRA:** This tactic—covered in more detail in Chapter 9—involves two steps. First, the taxpayer makes a nondeductible contribution to a traditional IRA. Second, shortly thereafter, the taxpayer converts the entire amount from the traditional IRA to a Roth IRA. This is typically done when income exceeds the limit for making direct Roth IRA contributions. Note that not all taxpayers have the right profile to make a Backdoor Roth IRA a desirable tactic—because of the Pro-Rata Rule. We'll cover that later in this chapter.

2. **Holding Bonds:** For taxpayers who cannot make direct Roth IRA contributions or efficiently execute a Backdoor Roth IRA, a nondeductible traditional IRA contribution may be a sensible way to hold taxable bonds or bond funds. These assets generate ordinary income in the form of interest payments.

Holding bonds in a taxable brokerage account is inefficient from a tax perspective. Instead, holding them in a traditional IRA allows the interest to grow tax-deferred. Additionally, the nondeductible traditional IRA contribution creates basis, which can later be recovered ratably when the taxpayer withdraws money from the traditional IRA.

Traditional nondeductible contributions are reported on Form 8606, filed with the taxpayer's annual federal income tax return.

Roth Contributions

One key factor governs the ability to make an annual contribution directly to a Roth IRA: the taxpayer's annual MAGI. Despite these income limits, many workers still qualify to contribute each year.

For 2025, the ability to contribute to a Roth IRA begins to phase out and is eliminated at the following MAGI ranges:

- **Single Filers:** $150,000–$165,000
- **Married Filing Jointly:** $236,000–$246,000
- **Married Filing Separately:** $0–$10,000

In Real Life: Many Americans find themselves near the Roth IRA income thresholds. Year-end bonuses, for example, can be highly variable. What should they do? We generally favor waiting until the following year to draft the federal income tax return before making the contribution. This helps clarify whether the taxpayer falls under the applicable MAGI threshold. At that point, a Roth IRA contribution for the prior year can be made (by April 15), or alternatives—such as a Backdoor Roth IRA or investing in a taxable brokerage account—can be considered.

Rollover Contributions

The second type of IRA contribution is a rollover contribution—the transfer of funds from another retirement account. For example, an employee might retire from a large company and want to roll their 401(k) to an IRA for a variety of reasons.

As a practical matter, we generally recommend structuring rollovers from workplace plans as "direct trustee-to-trustee" transfers. This means the account owner completes paperwork, but ideally never handles a check. The current institution simply transfers the funds to the receiving institution. For example, the 401(k) provider transfers the assets directly to an IRA custodian.

Another variation is when the current institution sends a check to the account owner that is payable to the new IRA custodian, rather than to the individual personally.

Cody's Take: Moving money from a 401(k) at one custodian to an IRA at another can be an onerous process. One helpful approach is to break it into two steps:

1. *Request a direct rollover (via trustee-to-trustee transfer) from a 401(k) to an IRA within the same custodian (if allowed).*
2. *Initiate a direct IRA-to-IRA transfer to your preferred custodian. The second step is initiated by the receiving firm.*

The direct trustee-to-trustee transfer is preferred to an indirect rollover, where the owner receives a check made payable to themselves and must deposit it into the desired retirement account within 60 days. Missing the 60-day deadline could result in the amount being treated as taxable income–and, for those under age 59½, a 10% early withdrawal penalty may also apply.

Some custodians issue a rollover check made payable to the receiving custodian FBO (for the benefit of) the account owner, but mail the check to the owner. In this case, the owner should forward the check to the receiving firm to complete the transfer. A growing number of custodians now allow mobile deposits of rollover checks using their official app.

We discuss rollovers in much greater detail in Chapter 6.

Contribution Limits

Limits on Annual Contributions

As of 2025, the annual contribution limit is $7,000, or $8,000 for individuals who turn age 50 or older during the year. This additional $1,000 is called a **catch-up contribution**. The annual contribution limit is occasionally adjusted by the IRS to account for inflation.

To make an annual IRA contribution, the individual must have earned income—generally defined as W-2 wages or net self-employment income. For example, if a teenager earns $3,000 in W-2 income from a summer job, that's the maximum amount they can contribute to an IRA (likely a Roth IRA), since the contribution is limited to the lesser of the annual contribution limit or earned income.

It's also important to note that traditional IRAs and Roth IRAs share the annual contribution limit. If a taxpayer contributes $7,000 to a Roth IRA for 2025, they cannot contribute anything to a traditional IRA—and vice versa.

In Real Life: A spouse without their own wages can "borrow" earned income from their working spouse for IRA contribution purposes. For example, imagine Francisco earns $125,000 in W-2 wages in 2025, while his spouse, Ana (age 35), works inside the home and has no W-2 or self-employment income. Ana can use a portion of Francisco's earned income to support a $7,000 contribution to a traditional or Roth IRA. While earned income is required to make IRA contributions, the contributed funds do not need to come directly from that income—spouses don't actually need to borrow from each other.

Limits on Rollovers

None!

There are no limits on rollover contributions. If you have $10 billion in a 401(k), you can roll it over into an IRA. You don't need earned income to do so, and your eligibility isn't affected by whether you or your spouse are covered by a workplace retirement plan.

Contribution Deadlines

Annual IRA contributions must be made by the tax return filing deadline—typically April 15 of the following year.

There is no deadline for rollover contributions, except in the case of an indirect rollover. In that scenario, the funds must be deposited into the new retirement account within 60 days of receiving the distribution.

Traditional IRA Distributions

Distributions from traditional IRAs are generally taxable. At first glance, this sounds terrible: "Why would it make sense to hold money in a traditional IRA during retirement if everything I withdraw is going to be taxable?"

The answer lies in the combination of progressive tax rates we have in the United States and the large standard deduction. As of 2025, the standard deduction based on tax filing status is:

- **Single:** $15,750, plus $2,000 if turning age 65 or older during the year
- **Head of Household:** $23,625, plus $2,000 age 65+
- **Married Filing Separately:** $15,750, plus $1,600 age 65+
- **Married Filing Jointly:** $31,500, plus $1,600 per spouse age 65+

Now, consider how traditional IRA withdrawals are taxed in retirement. Those withdrawals may first be offset by the standard deduction. Then, any remaining amount is taxed progressively—at 10%, then 12%, then 22%, and so on. It can be surprisingly difficult for even very affluent retirees to generate significant taxable income, particularly since they're no longer commuting to work or paying W-2 payroll taxes. Many also have a paid-off home, which reduces their housing expenses.

Beyond the Scope: Some states offer partial or full exemptions for retirement plan distributions. Be sure to review your state's unique rules.

We'll explore the desirability of traditional retirement accounts in greater detail later in the book. For now, it suffices to say that retirement can be an excellent time to generate taxable income—often taxed at much lower rates than during one's working years.

Early Distributions

Withdrawals from a traditional IRA before age 59½ are generally subject to both income tax and a 10% early withdrawal penalty. If you're like Sean and live in California, you can tack on an additional 2.5% state early withdrawal penalty. *Ouch!*

At first, this seems daunting: "Have I locked up my money until age 59½ by putting it in a traditional IRA?" Hardly. There are several ways to access traditional IRA funds before age 59½ without incurring the 10% early withdrawal penalty. We'll explore those exceptions in more detail later in the book.

Required Minimum Distributions

Tax deferral is a great party. You invest in growing assets within a traditional IRA, and as long as you don't withdraw the money, the interest, dividends, and capital gains generated inside the account aren't taxed.

But tax deferral that never ends becomes tax avoidance. To prevent this, retirement account rules require owners to begin withdrawing money from traditional IRAs through **required minimum distributions (RMDs)**.

RMDs are determined based on two factors:

1. A life expectancy factor from the IRS Uniform Lifetime Table, based on the owner's birthday age for the year.
2. The traditional retirement account balance as of the end of the prior year.

For those born from 1951 through 1959, RMDs begin in the year the account owner turns age 73. With the exception of the first RMD, which can be delayed until April 1 of the following year, all subsequent RMDs must be taken by December 31 each year.

For example, let's say Igor has $2,000,000 in a traditional IRA on December 31, 2024, and turns 73 on July 13, 2025. To calculate his 2025 RMD, he divides $2,000,000 by 26.5—the factor for age 73 from the IRS Uniform Lifetime Table (Publication 590-B). Igor's first RMD is $75,472, and he must withdraw it by April 1, 2026.

In 2026, let's say Igor's traditional IRA balance on December 31, 2025, is $2,100,000. He turns 74 that year, so he uses the 25.5 life expectancy factor. His 2026 RMD is $82,353, and he must withdraw it by December 31, 2026.

People often worry about RMDs, but they typically require modest distributions—especially considering the account owner's age. That's because the Uniform Lifetime Table assumes the account owner has a beneficiary who is 10 years younger and calculates a joint life expectancy, resulting in relatively low required withdrawal rates.

If we take Igor's age, 73, and add it to his life expectancy factor of 26.5, we might believe the IRS expects Igor to live to age 99.5. But that's not the case—the IRS expects the combined life expectancy for Igor and a beneficiary 10 years younger to extend to age 99.5.

This turns out to be highly beneficial for married couples. Suppose Jack and Erica are married and turn 82 and 76, respectively, in 2025. Jack uses an RMD factor of 18.5, and Erica uses 23.7—both benefiting from assuming a beneficiary 10 years younger. If Jack passes away in 2026 and names Erica as the sole beneficiary, she can treat his IRA as her own. From 2026 onward, the RMDs on Jack's former IRA will be based on Erica's age. At age 77, Erica's 2026 RMD factor would be 22.9.

We'll explore how RMDs impact planning in more detail in Chapter 15.

Extra Credit: An account owner's first RMD is due by April 1 of the year following the year the account owner reaches RMD age. However, delaying the first RMD means taking two RMDs in a single tax year, which may not be desirable.

Sean's Take: Congress has managed to make a mess of the RMD beginning date rules. Under SECURE 2.0, enacted in December 2022, RMDs start at age 73 for those born from 1951 through 1959 and start at age 75 for those born January 1, 1960 or later. However, in my opinion, which I expressed in a comment letter to the IRS and Treasury, there is doubt about the validity of SECURE 2.0. If it were to be overturned, RMDs would start at age 72 for everyone without further Congressional action. While this seems messy, earlier RMDs would not meaningfully impact the vast majority of Americans' financial success in retirement.

Account Aggregation

Now is a good time to introduce an important IRA concept: account aggregation. The tax rules, generally speaking, treat all of your traditional IRAs (including traditional SEP IRAs and traditional SIMPLE IRAs) as a single traditional IRA. Likewise, all of your Roth IRAs are treated as a single Roth IRA.

This is generally a taxpayer-friendly rule. In the context of traditional IRAs, it means you have flexibility in how you satisfy RMDs.

For example, say Peter has two traditional IRAs. One was worth $300,000 on December 31, 2024, and the other was worth $1,700,000 on the same date. If Peter turns age 76 during 2025, his RMD life expectancy factor is 23.7. His RMD from the first account is $12,658 ($300,000 ÷ 23.7), and his RMD from the second account is $71,730 ($1,700,000 ÷ 23.7), for a total RMD of $84,388. Peter is allowed to withdraw this amount from either or both traditional IRAs in any proportion he chooses. He could take the full amount from one account, split it evenly, or take any other combination—since the tax rules aggregate these two traditional IRAs into a single traditional IRA.

Basis Recovery

Remember those nondeductible traditional IRA distributions? They create what is known as **basis** in the traditional IRA.

Basis in a traditional IRA is a good thing—at least to an extent. It means that a portion of distributions from the traditional IRA will not be taxable, since that part represents a return of after-tax dollars. That said, basis is hurt by inflation.

For example, say Tammy made $30,000 of nondeductible traditional IRA contributions during her working career. In retirement, she will gradually recover that basis when she takes withdrawals from her traditional IRA. But due to inflation, that $30,000 won't go as far as it once did—and there's no mechanism to adjust basis for inflation.

Basis is recovered under the **Pro-Rata Rule**. Let's say Tammy distributes $40,000 from her traditional IRA this year. At the end of the year, it is worth $200,000, and she had $30,000 of basis going into the year.

Under the Pro-Rata Rule, Tammy must allocate a percentage of the basis to the $40,000 distribution. To calculate the tax-free portion of her withdrawal, Tammy divides the $40,000 distribution by the total of the year-end balance plus the distribution—$240,000 in total. $40,000 divided by $240,000 is 16.67%. She multiplies 16.67% times the $30,000 of basis and gets $5,000.

So, of Tammy's $40,000 distribution, $5,000 is a tax-free return of basis, and $35,000 is taxable. Her remaining basis going into the next year is $25,000.

Basis calculations are done individually—spouses' IRAs are not combined for purposes of calculating the Pro-Rata Rule. Each spouse tracks and recovers their own basis separately.

Income Tax Withholding

The default federal income tax withholding rate on traditional IRA distributions is 10%. However, the account owner may elect a different withholding percentage if desired—though some custodians cap withholding at 99% due to internal policies.

It turns out that IRA withholding is a convenient and effective way to pay taxes in retirement for those at least age 59½. IRA withholding is treated as if it occurred evenly throughout the year, regardless of when the distribution actually takes place. In contrast, estimated tax payments are due quarterly and are credited based on the actual payment period. Many retirees may consider using their traditional IRAs to pay federal and state income taxes by taking a late-year distribution and electing a high withholding percentage. This allows more time for the funds to remain invested and under the owner's control.

For those under age 59½, IRA withholding is not recommended—unless the distribution qualifies for a penalty exception (such as through a 72(t) payment plan). We explore these exceptions in detail in Chapter 12.

An inherited IRA can also be a great vehicle for paying federal and state income taxes in retirement. This holds true even if the inherited IRA beneficiary is under age 59½, since the 10% early withdrawal penalty never applies to inherited IRA distributions. We cover this in more detail in Chapter 14.

Roth IRA Distributions

Qualified Distributions

A qualified distribution from a Roth IRA is tax-free.

How does an account owner qualify to take a qualified distribution? In most cases, two requirements must be met:

1. The account owner is age 59½ or older at the time of the distribution, and
2. The owner has established (opened and funded) any Roth IRA at least five years prior to the distribution.

If both conditions are satisfied, any Roth IRA distribution to the account owner is a qualified distribution—and therefore entirely tax- and penalty-free.

Nonqualified Distributions

If a Roth IRA distribution is not a qualified distribution, how is it taxed? In most cases, very favorably to the owner. Let's take a closer look.

The tax rules say a Roth IRA is composed of three layers:

1. Annual contributions
2. Roth conversions (distributed on a first-in, first-out basis)
3. Earnings

When a nonqualified distribution occurs, these layers are distributed in order. Only after the entirety of a layer has been distributed can the next layer be distributed.

The first layer, annual contributions, is always withdrawn tax- and penalty-free, at any time for any reason! There's no age or holding period requirement to access your regular contributions.

And don't forget about Roth IRA account aggregation. For example, if someone contributes to a Roth IRA at Schwab for three years and then to a Roth IRA at Fidelity for the next three years, they now have six years of annual contributions that can be withdrawn from either account (or both) at any time for any reason.

The second layer is Roth conversions. These also come out tax-free. However, if the conversion is less than five years old and the account owner is under age 59½, the distribution may be subject to the 10% early withdrawal penalty.

The third and final layer is earnings. They are subject to income tax if withdrawn before the distribution becomes qualified. They may also be subject to the 10% early withdrawal penalty if the owner is under age 59½ at the time of the distribution, though exceptions may apply.

These layers matter, but they become entirely academic once the owner turns 59½ and has held any funded Roth IRA for at least five years. At that point, all distributions are qualified, and no further analysis is needed.

Nonqualified distributions from Roth IRAs are reported on Form 8606, Part III.

Extra Credit: *The 5-year rules are based on tax years, not calendar years. For example:*

- *If someone completes a Roth conversion on December 31, 2025, its 5-year clock for taxable Roth conversions starts on January 1, 2025.*
- *If someone opens and funds their first Roth IRA on the April 15, 2025 deadline for the prior tax year, their 5-year clock for Roth earnings starts on January 1, 2024.*

Required Minimum Distributions

None!

There are no RMDs from a Roth IRA during the owner's lifetime.

Under current rules, RMDs do not apply to Roth IRAs except in the case of certain inherited Roth IRAs. We will cover inherited retirement accounts later in the book.

Roth Conversions

Amounts inside a traditional IRA can be converted to a Roth IRA—but not the other way around. Once funds are in a Roth IRA, they cannot be converted to a traditional IRA.

Tax-deferred amounts converted from a traditional IRA to a Roth IRA are taxable as ordinary income in the year of the conversion.

Having the option to convert has tremendous benefits. For example, many early retirees experience several years of relatively low taxable income. Those years may present an ideal opportunity to create taxable income at low rates—potentially even against the standard deduction!

We will cover Roth conversions in much more detail later in the book. For now, understand that the ability to convert to a Roth IRA can be a beneficial planning tactic.

Note that there are no income or other restrictions on the ability to do Roth conversions.

Inherited IRAs

We will also cover inherited retirement accounts later in the book. For now, it's important to understand the value of having a beneficiary designation form on file that clearly reflects your wishes for who should inherit the account. From a tax perspective, spouses are generally the most favored beneficiaries. In many cases, it makes the most sense to name a spouse as the 100% primary beneficiary of the IRA.

Key Differences from Qualified Plans

IRAs share similarities with qualified plans, but there are also important differences.

Both IRAs and qualified plans allow for tax-efficient retirement savings that offer some level of creditor protection.

One advantage of IRAs is that the account owner controls which financial institution holds the account and which investments are available. IRAs also tend to be more user-friendly regarding distributions, since the financial institution works directly with the account owner—not through an employer, as is the case with qualified plans.

However, IRAs have much lower annual contribution limits. In addition, the account owner's annual MAGI affects their ability to deduct traditional IRA contributions or make Roth IRA contributions. In contrast, income usually does not limit the ability to make pre-tax, after-tax, or Roth contributions to qualified plans.

It's important to remember that contributing to an IRA and contributing to a qualified plan are not mutually exclusive. Each is a valuable tool in the toolbox for workers striving to get to and through early retirement. As you'll see, both IRAs and qualified plans play significant roles in the Compelling Three tactics reiterated throughout this book.

Lastly, as a practical matter, many qualified plan accounts are eventually rolled into IRAs. This can make sense for a variety of reasons, including the ability to choose the financial institution and investments, as well as greater flexibility and ease of use when it comes to taking withdrawals.

5 – The Basics of 401(k)s and Other Qualified Plans

Workplace retirement plans—which we will refer to as qualified plans—have a long history. The most popular qualified plan today, the 401(k), was created by legislation in 1978 and became available to employees in 1980.

Qualified plans come in two main flavors. **Defined benefit plans**—the classic pension plans—guarantee a specific retirement benefit in retirement, typically based on salary and years of service. These plans have declined in popularity and are often of modest value to those pursuing early retirement, as they usually require long tenures to earn substantial benefits.

This book focuses on **defined contribution plans**, which are now the more common type of qualified plan. These include 401(k)s, 403(b)s, and 457(b)s. The Thrift Savings Plan (TSP) is the federal government's version of a 401(k). While other qualified plans exist, these "numbered" plans are the most widespread. Their names reflect their location in the Internal Revenue Code.

Qualified plans allow employees to invest in a selection of investment options chosen by the employer. They provide employers with tax deductions and offer a tax-favored way to compensate employees. For employees, these plans are a powerful tool for building retirement savings while reducing tax liability during working years.

Qualified Plan Tax Types

Qualified plans can include both traditional and Roth components. Each offers its own distinct tax advantages and trade-offs. Generally speaking, traditional qualified plans provide an upfront tax benefit—contributions are excluded from taxable income—but withdrawals are fully taxable. Roths are the flip: there's no upfront tax break, but qualified withdrawals are received tax-free.

We'll explore these two types in more detail later in the chapter.

Purpose

Why would someone contribute to a qualified plan? Here are several reasons:
- To build up retirement savings.
- To reduce current taxes through traditional pre-tax contributions.
- For low-income taxpayers, the potential to qualify for a tax credit (for both traditional and Roth contributions).
- To enable tax-free withdrawals from Roth qualified plans, if done correctly.
- To benefit from tax-deferred growth in traditional qualified plans—or tax-deferred or tax-free growth in Roth plans, depending on the time of withdrawals.

- To receive creditor protection—generally speaking, qualified plans governed by ERISA enjoy significant protection.

Investments

Employees can invest their contributions in a menu of investment options offered by the employer. These menus vary, and many employers partner with a financial institution to provide a selection of 10 to 30 mutual funds.

It works a bit like a restaurant: the kitchen designs the menu, and the patron chooses what to order. In a qualified plan, the employer designs the investment menu, and the employee decides which options to invest in from that list.

Contributions

There are several types of contributions to qualified plans. Unless otherwise noted, each contribution has both traditional and Roth versions. While not all employers offer the Roth option, we've found that an increasing number of 401(k), 403(b), and governmental 457(b) plans now offer both. The TSP— the federal government's qualified plan—also includes both traditional and Roth options.

Not all plans allow every type of contribution listed below. To confirm what's available, refer to the plan's **Summary Plan Description (SPD)**, usually provided as a PDF file.

Employee Deferral Contributions

These are contributions employees make to a qualified plan through payroll deductions. They're called deferral contributions—whether traditional or Roth—because the employee chooses to defer receiving a portion of their wages, directing it instead to their 401(k) or other qualified plan account.

As of 2025, the contribution limit for employee deferrals is $23,500. This limit applies to the combined total of traditional and Roth employee deferral contributions. Employees can allocate that amount in any mix between traditional and Roth, up to the $23,500 limit. The IRS adjusts this limit annually for inflation.

Naturally, there's one more constraint: W-2 income. You can't defer income into a qualified plan if you didn't earn it.

Catch-Up Contributions

Employees who turn age 50 or older during the calendar year are eligible to make additional employee deferral contributions, known as **catch-up contributions**. As of 2025, the catch-up contribution limit is $7,500. This means that individuals turning 50 or older in 2025 can contribute up to $31,000 in total employee deferrals for the year.

SECURE 2.0 introduced two notable updates to catch-up rules. First, individuals ages 60 through 63 can make an additional annual catch-up contribution of $3,750 (2025 amount). Second, starting in 2026, employees age 50 and older with prior-year W-2 income above a certain threshold (from the same employer) will be required to make all catch-up contributions as Roth contributions.

Tax Treatment

Traditional employee deferral contributions are generally excluded from taxable income. While this **exclusion** is different from a tax **deduction**, the effect is essentially the same. People often refer to these contributions as deductions, which is correct in principle but not technically precise.

However, traditional employee deferrals are not excluded from income for payroll tax purposes—known as FICA taxes.

An example helps clarify these concepts:

Evan earns a $120,000 W-2 salary. During the year, he contributes $20,000 to his traditional 401(k) through payroll deductions. As a result, Box 1 of his W-2 will show $100,000 of taxable income ($120,000 minus $20,000), which is what he'll report on his income tax return. He doesn't need to claim a deduction—the $20,000 was already excluded from his taxable wages.

However, Evan still pays FICA taxes on the full $120,000, which will appear in Boxes 3 and 5 of his W-2.

Now, let's assume Evan instead contributes $20,000 to a Roth 401(k). In that case, his full $120,000 salary will be reported as taxable income in Boxes 1, 3, and 5 of his W-2—because Roth contributions are not excluded from taxable income.

Employer Contributions

Employers can contribute to 401(k)s and other qualified plans in several ways: matching contributions, nondiscretionary contributions, and discretionary contributions (often called profit-sharing contributions).

In our experience, matching contributions are the most common. These are typically structured as a percentage of employee contributions, up to a certain percentage of salary. For example: Jason works at Pundit Publishing and earns a $100,000 W-2 salary. Pundit's 401(k) plan offers a 50% match on contributions up to 6% of salary. If Jason contributes 6% of his salary ($6,000), he'll receive a $3,000 employer match. He'd be wise to contribute at least that amount to take full advantage of the match.

Subject to vesting, employer matching contributions offer an essentially guaranteed, instantaneous return on investment—hard to pass up if you're aiming for early (or any) retirement.

Cody's Take: A 4% employer match equals more than two weeks of additional pay in the current year. Over multiple decades, that portion could compound into months or even years of retirement income!

Some qualified plans offer nondiscretionary contributions. For instance, a plan might provide that the employer contributes 1% of salary annually, regardless of whether the employee contributes. In Jason's case, that would mean a $1,000 employer contribution.

Some plans include discretionary employer contributions, often referred to as profit-sharing contributions. These allow employers to contribute additional funds—often during strong economic years—as a way to reward and retain employees.

Tax Treatment

Traditional employer contributions are excluded from income for both income tax and FICA (payroll tax) purposes. Continuing with Evan as our example:

Suppose Evan earns $120,000 in W-2 wages, contributes $20,000 to a traditional 401(k) through employee deferrals, and his employer contributes $5,000 to his traditional 401(k) during the year.

- Box 1 of Evan's W-2 will show $100,000 of taxable income for income tax purposes. Both the $20,000 of traditional employee deferral contributions and the $5,000 of employer contributions are excluded from Box 1.
- Boxes 3 and 5 will show $120,000 of wages for FICA tax purposes. The $20,000 of employee deferral contributions are not excluded from FICA wages, but the $5,000 of employer contributions *are* excluded from FICA wages.

Under SECURE 2.0, employers may now make Roth contributions. These are included in the employee's income for federal income tax purposes but are still excluded from income for FICA tax purposes.

Vesting

Employers want to attract and retain talent—and they don't want employees leaving shortly after joining. One way to encourage retention is by subjecting employer contributions (and their associated growth) to a vesting schedule.

The basic idea: to keep the full value of employer contributions and investment growth, the employee must stay with the company for a certain period. Vesting is often gradual over time (e.g., 20% per year over five years), though some plans use a three-year cliff vesting schedule, where the employee becomes 100% vested all at once after three years of service.

Some employers offer immediate vesting, meaning all employer contributions and growth are fully vested from the start.

In our view, workers should understand how vesting works in their plan—but in most cases, it's not a major planning consideration. Why? Because many employer matching programs are based on modest salary percentages—typically 4%, 5%, or 6%. Those seriously planning for early retirement usually contribute well beyond the match amount, regardless of the vesting schedule.

Note: Employee deferral contributions, after-tax contributions, and rollover contributions are generally not subject to vesting. Vesting also doesn't apply to retirement plans for self-employed individuals, such as Solo 401(k)s.

Forfeitures

When employees leave before becoming fully vested, they may forfeit unvested amounts in their qualified plan. So, what happens to that money?

It depends on the plan's rules. In some cases, forfeited amounts are used to help pay plan expenses. In others, they may be reallocated as employer contributions to the accounts of remaining employees.

Forfeitures allocated to a traditional retirement account are not currently taxable to the receiving employee and are not subject to FICA taxes.

After-Tax Contributions

After-tax contributions are another form of employee contribution. Before we dive in, it's important to note that many 401(k) and other qualified plans do not offer after-tax contributions, making this section more academic for many readers.

After-tax contributions have only one tax treatment and can only be made to one type of account.

First, the tax treatment: they are not excluded from taxable income for either income tax or FICA tax purposes.

Second, the account type: they can only be made to traditional accounts. After-tax contributions cannot be made directly to Roth accounts.

At first glance, you might ask, "Why would I contribute to a traditional account if I don't get an upfront tax exclusion?"

The answer lies in a powerful planning tactic: the **Mega Backdoor Roth**. This is a two-step process:

1. The employee makes an after-tax contribution to the traditional 401(k) (or similar qualified plan).
2. That contribution is then quickly converted—either via an **in-plan Roth conversion** to a Roth 401(k) or, in some cases, through an **in-service rollover** to a Roth IRA.

This allows money that would otherwise be invested in a taxable brokerage account to be moved into a Roth account—where it can grow tax-free.

Example: Melvin contributes $23,500 in employee deferrals to his traditional 401(k) in 2025. In addition, every pay period (24 total), he contributes $500 in after-tax dollars to his 401(k), totaling $12,000 for the year. Shortly after each $500 contribution, he converts it to his Roth 401(k). Melvin incurs no material additional income tax for this strategy, though he will receive a Form 1099-R. On his tax return, he reports the gross amount of conversions (approximately $12,000) on Line 5a of Form 1040 and $0 (or close to it) on Line 5b. His after-tax contributions create basis, which he immediately uses to avoid tax on the Roth conversions.

You might be thinking, "That sounds too good to be true." Fortunately, IRS Notice 2014-54 explicitly permits the Mega Backdoor Roth.

Some employers offer a **401(a)** qualified plan with after-tax contributions. These may not be readily convertible to a Roth account during employment—unless the plan has a Roth feature and permits in-plan Roth conversions. However, when the employee leaves or retires, the after-tax contributions can be rolled directly to a Roth IRA. Notice 2014-54 allows a qualified plan owner with basis from after-tax contributions to roll only the basis in a traditional qualified plan directly to a Roth IRA and everything else to a traditional IRA.

Example: Teresa participates in a 401(a) plan that allows her to contribute 4% of her salary after-tax. At retirement, her account is worth $500,000, of which $150,000 represents her after-tax contributions. Teresa can roll the $150,000 after-tax amount directly to a Roth IRA and the $350,000 pre-tax portion to a traditional IRA—both without triggering current-year taxes. This is generally the best use of her after-tax basis, as it moves the funds into a Roth IRA where they can grow tax-free for the rest of Teresa's life, and possibly beyond for her beneficiaries.

Incoming Rollover Contributions

These are contributions from another qualified plan or retirement account. For example, an employee who leaves one employer might choose to roll over their old 401(k) into their new employer's 401(k).

As discussed in Chapter 4, we generally recommend structuring rollovers as "direct trustee-to-trustee" transfers. In this process, the account owner completes paperwork but never receives a check. The current institution transfers the money directly to the receiving institution. This helps avoid issues with the 60-day rule for indirect rollovers. If the account owner receives a check made payable to themselves, they must deposit it into a retirement account within 60 days to avoid taxes and a potential 10% early withdrawal penalty.

And here's a quirky rule: Roth IRAs cannot be transferred into Roth 401(k)s or other Roth qualified plans. Don't ask us—we didn't make the rule.

Contribution Limits

Employee Deferrals

As mentioned, the employee deferral limit is $23,500 in 2025. Catch-up contributions are limited to $7,500 for those age 50 and older by the end of the year. Additionally, individuals ages 60 to 63 can make an extra catch-up contribution of up to $3,750 (2025 amount). These limits are adjusted annually for inflation by the IRS.

It's important to note that this limit is per person, not per plan. For example, Jacob, age 40, works for Evergray Industries from January through June 2025 and contributes $15,000 to Evergray's 401(k). In July, he begins working for Horizon Technologies. For the remainder of 2025, Jacob can contribute up to $8,500 to the Horizon 401(k), staying within the $23,500 annual limit.

The employee deferral limit is shared across 401(k) plans, 403(b) plans, and the Thrift Savings Plan (TSP). However, it is not shared with 457(b) plans, which have their own separate deferral limit. This means individuals with access to a 457(b) can effectively double up—maxing out their 401(k) or 403(b) and contributing the full amount to a 457(b).

All Additions

All contributions to an employer's qualified plans are subject to an annual limit. This is often referred to as the "415(c) limit," named after the section of the Internal Revenue Code where it appears. We'll refer to it simply as the "all additions limit."

The all additions limit applies to the total of employee deferrals, employer contributions, after-tax contributions, and forfeitures. That total cannot exceed the lesser of (1) the employee's W-2 income from the employer or (2) $70,000 in 2025. This amount is adjusted annually for inflation. For individuals age 50 or older, allowable catch-up contributions are added on top of the all additions limit.

Importantly, the all additions limit applies per employer, per person—not just per person. Returning to Jacob's example above, his all additions limit in the Evergray Industries 401(k) is $70,000, and his limit in the Horizon Technologies 401(k) is also $70,000—assuming he earned at least $70,000 of W-2 income from each employer.

In practice, the all additions limit is irrelevant for many workers. However, it becomes relevant in two situations:

1. **Mega Backdoor Roths** – where the limit restricts how much can be contributed via after-tax dollars.
2. **Self-employed retirement plans** – such as the Solo 401(k), where the business owner is responsible for both employee and employer contributions.

For W-2 employees in plans that do not offer after-tax contributions, the all additions limit rarely comes into play, as typical employer matches combined with employee deferrals don't come close to the limit.

The all additions limit applies to all defined contribution plans offered by the employer. For example, earlier in his career, Sean worked for an employer that offered two defined contribution plans: a 401(k) with a match and a separate employer-funded plan. The all additions limit applied to the combined total of his employee deferrals, employer match, and the contributions to the separate plan.

Reminder: Rollover contributions do not count toward either the employee deferral limit or the all additions limit—they are unlimited.

Contribution Deadlines

W-2 employees only need to worry about one deadline: year-end. For an employee deferral contribution to count for a given year, it must be made during that calendar year. For example, to "max out" employee deferral contributions for 2025, they must occur no later than December 31, 2025. Any contributions made in January 2026 will count toward the 2026 employee deferral limit.

Employers can make employer contributions for the year up to their tax return filing deadline, including extensions.

Traditional Qualified Plan Distributions

Qualified Plans Often Retire to IRAs

Before diving into how distributions work from a 401(k) or other qualified plan, we must acknowledge the reality: in many cases, retirees never take withdrawals for living expenses directly from a qualified plan.

Why?

Because many retirees choose to transfer old 401(k)s and other qualified plans into IRAs. From a distribution standpoint, IRAs are generally much easier to use than employer-sponsored plans. IRAs aren't subject to the distribution restrictions that qualified plans may impose. Plus, IRA owners get to choose their financial institution and aren't limited to an employer-selected investment menu.

We'll cover the pros and cons of moving money between retirement accounts in much more detail in Chapter 6.

Retirement Distributions Prior to Age 59½

The distribution rules for traditional qualified plans are similar to those for traditional IRAs, as discussed in Chapter 4. Withdrawals made before the account owner reaches age 59½ are generally subject to income tax and may incur a 10% early withdrawal penalty.

If you're like Sean and live in California, you can tack on an additional 2.5% state early withdrawal penalty. Ouch!

Rule of 55 Distributions

There are several exceptions to the early withdrawal penalty, and one of the most notable for 401(k)s and other qualified plans is the Rule of 55. This rule allows penalty-free distributions from a former employer's plan if the distribution occurs after a separation from service—and that separation happened during or after the calendar year in which the employee turned 55.

The Rule of 55 is a valuable exception because it's relatively flexible. There's no limit on the number of distributions that can qualify, and no minimum or maximum distribution amounts are required.

However, there are two important caveats:

1. **Plan design matters.** Not all plans offer user-friendly partial distributions before age 59½. Employers aren't required to allow partial withdrawals for early retirees—even if those distributions would qualify for the Rule of 55 exception.

2. **Rolling to an IRA disqualifies it.** Rolling an employer's plan into an IRA loses the ability to use the Rule of 55. To benefit from this exception, the funds must remain in the employer's qualified plan until either the account owner reaches age 59½ or no longer needs access under the Rule of 55.

We'll explore additional ways to access qualified plans before age 59½ without incurring the early withdrawal penalty in much more detail later in Chapter 12.

Plan Rules

Depending on the plan's rules, it may be difficult to take a partial distribution from a qualified plan before age 59½—especially while still employed by the sponsoring employer. However, in most cases, employees will want to avoid taking in-service distributions from qualified plans during their working years.

Each qualified plan's SPD should outline the plan's specific distribution rules.

Distributions At or After Age 59½

Distributions from traditional qualified plans are generally included in taxable income. As discussed in Chapter 4, this isn't as bad as it might sound—many retirees will find their taxable income is lower in retirement than it was during their working years.

We'll explore the benefits and strategic use of traditional retirement accounts in much more detail later in the book.

Income Tax Withholding

One disadvantage of traditional qualified plans is that distributions—including those taken under the Rule of 55—are subject to mandatory 20% federal income tax withholding. The account owner can elect to withhold more, but not less. This 20% withholding applies regardless of the account owner's age.

However, this withholding can be avoided by rolling the funds over directly—via a trustee-to-trustee transfer—to an IRA or another retirement plan.

This mandatory withholding is one reason many retirees choose to roll qualified plan balances to IRAs, which are not subject to mandatory withholding rules. But as a reminder: rolling those funds into an IRA eliminates their access to the Rule of 55. Measure twice before moving money around!

Required Minimum Distributions

We discussed RMDs in Chapter 4. The RMD rules also apply to qualified plans. However, unlike IRAs, qualified plans are generally not aggregated for RMD purposes.

For example, if Sam has a 401(k) at Indy Industries with a $40,000 RMD this year, and another 401(k) at JKL Industries with a $30,000 RMD, he cannot simply take $70,000 from the Indy 401(k) to satisfy his RMDs. Doing so would leave him $30,000 short. He must take at least $40,000 from the Indy 401(k) and at least $30,000 from the JKL 401(k).

This issue can be resolved by rolling 401(k) balances into IRAs. Once the funds are in IRAs, they benefit from the IRA aggregation rules, which allow RMDs to be taken from any one (or more) of the owner's traditional IRAs.

Extra Credit: *403(b) plans are not aggregated with other qualified plans, but they can be aggregated with the owner's other 403(b) plans for RMD purposes.*

Roth Qualified Plan Distributions

Roth Qualified Plans Often Retire to Roth IRAs

As discussed earlier, IRAs—including Roth IRAs—often offer greater investment flexibility and easier access to funds than qualified plans. For this reason, many Roth 401(k)s and similar plans eventually "retire" into Roth IRAs.

As covered in Chapter 4, Roth IRA distribution rules—including the treatment of nonqualified distributions—tend to be very taxpayer-friendly. This is yet another reason an early retiree might consider transferring a Roth 401(k) or other Roth qualified plan to a Roth IRA.

Qualified Distributions

A qualified distribution from a Roth 401(k) or other Roth qualified plan account is entirely tax-free.

How does an account owner qualify for such a distribution? In most cases, two conditions must be met:

1. The owner is at least age 59½ at the time of the distribution.
2. The Roth qualified plan account has been open for at least five years at the time of the distribution.

If both tests are satisfied, the analysis is complete: any Roth qualified plan distribution to the account owner is entirely tax- and penalty-free.

Nonqualified Distributions

If a Roth qualified distribution is not a qualified distribution, how is it taxed?

The key rule to remember is what Ed Slott calls the "cream-in-the-coffee" rule: each nonqualified distribution is a mix of contributions (the coffee) and earnings (the cream). The portion of each is determined based on the ratio of contributions to total account value at the time of distribution.

The recovery of the Roth contribution portion is tax-free. Great! But the distribution of the earnings portion is not so great—it's subject to both ordinary income tax and a 10% early withdrawal penalty.

Example: Nicole, age 53, lives in California and takes a $10,000 distribution from her Roth 401(k). At the time of the distribution, she had previously made $50,000 in contributions, and the account was worth $80,000. That means $6,250 of the $10,000 distribution is a tax-free return of contributions, and $3,750 is earnings—subject to ordinary income tax, the 10% federal early withdrawal penalty, and California's additional 2.5% penalty. Note that a penalty exception may apply.

Here's how the taxable portion is calculated:

Earnings: $30,000
Total Account Value: $80,000
Distribution: $10,000
Taxable Portion: ($30,000 ÷ $80,000) × $10,000 = $3,750

Since the earnings portion of a nonqualified distribution can be hit with both income tax and penalties, anyone considering accessing a Roth 401(k) before age 59½ may want to consider transferring the Roth 401(k) to a Roth IRA.

In that case, the contributions, called investment in the contract, are treated as basis. Under Roth IRA rules, nonqualified distributions always pull from contributions first, making early Roth access more flexible and potentially penalty-free.

Required Minimum Distributions

SECURE 2.0 removed the requirement for account owners to take RMDs from Roth qualified plans.

Self-Employed Retirement Accounts

Self-employed individuals have access to their own retirement accounts. Two commonly used plans are the SEP IRA and the Solo 401(k).

A SEP IRA allows only for employer contributions to a traditional retirement account. In contrast, a Solo 401(k) allows for both employee and employer contributions—making it more attractive for many self-employed individuals from a contribution limit perspective.

In fact, Solo 401(k)s often allow higher total contributions than traditional employer plans. Here's an example:

Leo, age 40, works for Large Corp., which offers a 401(k) with a generous employer match: 100% up to 6% of salary. If Leo earns $110,000, he can contribute $23,500 as an employee deferral, and his employer contributes **$6,600**. Not bad.

Now let's say Leo is self-employed instead, with $110,000 of net income reported on Schedule C, and uses a Solo 401(k). He can still contribute $23,500 as the employee. But as his own employer, he can also contribute up to **$20,446** (approximately 20% of net self-employment income), significantly increasing his total contribution potential. This demonstrates how powerful the Solo 401(k) can be as a retirement savings vehicle.

If Leo were using a SEP IRA instead, he'd only be able to contribute the $20,446 employer portion—missing out on the $23,500 employee deferral. Choosing a SEP IRA over a Solo 401(k) would leave a significant portion of his contribution potential on the table.

Note: The Solo 401(k) and SEP IRA share employer contribution limits. Leo can't use both to double his employer contributions.

Special Rules for Governmental 457(b) Plans

Governmental section 457(b) plans have two special advantages.

First, they have their own employee contribution limit—$23,500 for 2025—which is not shared with 401(k) or 403(b) plans. This means that individuals with access to both a 457(b) and a 401(k) or 403(b) through the same employer can "double up" on contributions if they choose.

Second, distributions from governmental 457(b) plans are never subject to the 10% early withdrawal penalty—regardless of the account owner's age. This is a key reason to avoid rolling a governmental 457(b) into an IRA before age 59½, as doing so eliminates this special penalty exception. An important anti-abuse rule: distributions attributable to roll-ins from IRAs or other qualified plans do not benefit from the 457(b) early withdrawal exception.

Note: There's also such a thing as a "nongovernmental" 457(b) plan. These are essentially a form of nonqualified deferred compensation, which we discuss further in Chapter 9. Note that nongovernmental 457(b) plans generally cannot be rolled over into other types of retirement accounts, including IRAs.

Roth Conversions

We discussed the ability to convert traditional IRAs to Roth IRAs in Chapter 4. A similar option exists for traditional qualified plans—they can be converted to Roth qualified plans.

Even if a qualified plan doesn't offer a Roth option, the Roth conversion opportunity still exists from a planning perspective. Why? Because tax-deferred amounts in a qualified plan can first be rolled over to a traditional IRA, and then converted from the traditional IRA to a Roth IRA.

Key Differences from IRAs

Qualified plans share some similarities with IRAs but also have important differences.

Both qualified plans and IRAs offer tax-efficient retirement savings and provide a degree of creditor protection.

One major advantage of qualified plans is their much higher annual contribution limits compared to IRAs. Additionally, an individual's MAGI generally does not limit their ability to make deductible contributions to a qualified plan or to contribute to a Roth qualified plan—unlike traditional and Roth IRAs, which are both subject to MAGI-based contribution restrictions.

On the other hand, IRAs offer greater control and flexibility. The account owner chooses the financial institution and has access to a broader range of investment options. IRAs also tend to be more user-friendly when it comes to distributions, since the account is held directly with the financial institution—not tied to an employer, as with qualified plans.

It's important to remember that contributing to a qualified plan and contributing to an IRA are not mutually exclusive. Both are valuable tools for workers aiming to get to and through early retirement, and both can be part of what we call the Compelling Three, discussed in detail in Chapter 8.

For those who prefer the investment control and distribution flexibility of IRAs, qualified plan contributions can be the first step toward getting there. The best way to build up large IRA balances is often by first building up large balances in qualified plans—balances that, down the road, can be rolled over into IRAs when an employee changes jobs or retires.

6 – Rollovers of Retirement Accounts

Today's 401(k) might be tomorrow's IRA. Today's IRA might be tomorrow's IRA at a different financial institution. This chapter explores rollovers and other transfers between retirement accounts.

Before we begin, it's important to note that, in general, rollovers between retirement accounts should be tax- and penalty-free—assuming proper and timely execution of the transaction. One key exception, which we'll cover later in this chapter, is a Roth conversion. In that case, money is transferred from a traditional retirement account to a Roth retirement account in a taxable manner.

Purpose

Why might someone transfer money from one retirement account to another? Here are several reasons:

- **Investment Improvements:** To reduce investment expenses or improve investment selection.
- **Simplified Distributions:** To make retirement withdrawals easier to manage.
- **Early Withdrawal Exceptions:** To qualify for a 10% penalty exception.
- **Account Consolidation:** Many workers change jobs multiple times. Rather than juggling accounts from each former employer, they may prefer to consolidate for easier planning and oversight.
- **Sophisticated Tax Planning:** Certain rollovers can support sophisticated tax planning, which we will discuss below.
- **Avoiding 20% Mandatory Withholding:** Rolling over funds can help avoid the 20% federal income tax withholding that applies to certain account distributions.
- **Improved Roth Access:** Rollovers may allow unrestricted access to Roth basis.
- **Qualified Charitable Distributions (QCDs):** Making tax-advantaged charitable contributions possible in retirement.

Timing

In our view, there are three common times people consider rollovers:

Leaving a Job

When leaving a job—unless the employee has a very small balance—the departing employee can usually keep the retirement account where it is. Before making any decision, it's important to consider all the relevant factors, especially those discussed in this chapter.

The classic case for rolling out of an employer 401(k) or other qualified plan is when the old plan has poor investment options, high fees, or both.

Retirement

Retirement raises the stakes for rollovers. Account balances are typically larger, and distributions to fund living expenses are on the horizon.

Distribution logistics often become more important at retirement. While many early retirees don't need to access their retirement accounts immediately, this can still be a great time to think through how distributions will work.

Sometimes the path at retirement is to leave the money in a 401(k) or other qualified plan, then roll it over to an IRA at age 59½. Why might someone wait? As we'll discuss, it may be to preserve eligibility for early withdrawal penalty exceptions. Two such exceptions that hinge on this timing are the Rule of 55 and the rules for governmental 457(b) plans.

When They Want To

Leaving a job or retiring aren't the only times to consider a rollover. Suppose you notice your Roth IRA has high-fee investments. That could be a good reason to transfer the Roth IRA to a different financial institution with better options.

Permissible Transfers

Not all types of tax-advantaged retirement accounts can be rolled over into every other type. The IRS has published a helpful chart outlining which rollovers are allowed between different types of accounts. You can view the IRS Rollover Chart at https://www.irs.gov/pub/irs-tege/rollover_chart.pdf.

Kinds of Transfers

Indirect Rollovers

The world of rollovers includes a variety of terminology. In this book, we use the term "indirect rollover" to describe a situation in which the account owner receives a check—or an "in-kind" distribution—from one retirement account and then chooses to roll over the funds or assets to another retirement account.

This type of rollover is often referred to as a "60-day rollover" because it must be completed within 60 days. If the money is not deposited into another retirement account by the 60th day following the distribution, it generally cannot be rolled over and will be treated as a regular distribution to the owner — potentially both taxable and subject to the 10% early withdrawal penalty.

Why the 60-day deadline? Congress intends retirement accounts to be used for retirement. Without a deadline, individuals could pull money out indefinitely for nonretirement purposes.

Sixty days may feel harsh, but the rule dates back to 1974 with the passage of the Employee Retirement Income Security Act (ERISA). At the time, mortgage interest rates exceeded 9%. High-interest-rate environments can tempt people to tap their retirement accounts as short-term loans to avoid borrowing at prevailing rates. The 60-day deadline curbs such behavior.

We generally disfavor indirect rollovers because they introduce unnecessary risk. The primary concern is timing: if the owner fails to deposit the distributed funds into the receiving retirement account in time, it could trigger significant income taxes and penalties. Fortunately, there's a safer alternative — a direct trustee-to-trustee transfer — which avoids this risk by moving money directly between retirement accounts.

Another reason we disfavor indirect rollovers: IRA-to-IRA indirect rollovers are limited to just one per rolling 12-month period, as we'll explain in more detail below.

Waiver of the 60-Day Deadline

It is possible to obtain relief if the 60-day deadline is missed. While this is not a situation anyone wants to be in, it's reassuring to know that a late rollover may still be allowed under certain circumstances — though approval is not guaranteed.

For more information, visit the IRS webpage titled "Retirement plans FAQs relating to waivers of the 60-day rollover requirement."

The Withholding Problem with Qualified Plans

The 60-day risk isn't the only issue with indirect rollovers. Qualified plans — such as 401(k)s — are required to withhold at least 20% of any distribution to the owner for federal income taxes. In the context of a rollover, this creates a real problem: the owner could be taxed on the 20% that was withheld!

An example helps illustrate this: Jorge, age 40, leaves his employer and wants to roll over his traditional 401(k), worth $100,000, to a traditional IRA. If Jorge chooses an indirect rollover, he'll receive a check for $80,000 — because $20,000 will be withheld and sent to the IRS as income tax withholding. If Jorge only rolls over the $80,000 to the traditional IRA within the 60-day window, he'll be taxed on the $20,000 that didn't make it into the IRA. And because he's under age 59½, he'll also likely owe the 10% early withdrawal penalty on that amount.

The irony isn't lost on us: you are punished for sending money to the IRS!

Jorge could avoid this outcome by depositing the full $100,000 into the traditional IRA within 60 days—including an additional $20,000 from other sources to replace the amount withheld. But that's often easier said than done—not everyone has access to that kind of cash on short notice. Additionally, due to the mandatory withholding, he may have effectively given the IRS a $20,000 interest-free loan until he files his federal income tax return the following year. It's an unnecessarily sticky situation.

A direct trustee-to-trustee transfer avoids this problem entirely. No withholding is required when money moves directly between retirement accounts.

In-Kind Rollovers

A quick note on in-kind indirect rollovers: an in-kind transfer occurs when the owner receives the actual securities held in the retirement account, rather than cash.

An in-kind transfer occurs when the owner receives the actual securities held in the retirement account rather than cash. Rollovers involving in-kind transfers are subject to a special rule: the asset received in the receiving retirement account must be the same asset transferred from the distributing retirement account.

For example, if Milton receives 100 shares of ABC Mutual Fund from his 401(k) and wants to roll over the value to an IRA, he generally must transfer those same 100 shares into the IRA.

There is one exception: if the distribution comes **from** a qualified plan (regardless of whether the destination is another qualified plan or an IRA), the distributed property can be sold and the proceeds rolled into the receiving retirement account. This exception, however, does not apply to transfers from an IRA.

Direct Trustee-to-Trustee Transfers

More terminology! The IRS uses two different terms for what we'll refer to as a "direct trustee-to-trustee transfer." The IRS calls a direct trustee-to-trustee transfer from a qualified plan a "direct rollover." When the transfer is from an IRA, the IRS calls it a trustee-to-trustee transfer.

Direct trustee-to-trustee transfers avoid both mandatory tax withholding and the 60-day deadline risk. The account owner simply coordinates with both the sending and receiving institutions and completes the necessary paperwork for the institutions to transfer the assets directly.

In Real Life: Account owners typically need to work with both custodians—the sending and receiving institutions—to initiate a transfer. We generally recommend starting with a phone call to the receiving institution. Since they're receiving the account, they often have a helpful process and an incentive to guide you through it.

Investments

Investment choice and expense are major drivers of rollover decisions. Many rollovers occur because the account owner believes they can access better investment options and/or pay lower fees in a different retirement account.

The typical direction is from a qualified plan to an IRA, though that's not always the case. Most 401(k)s and other qualified plans offer a relatively limited investment menu—often just a few dozen fund options. In contrast, IRAs can be opened at a wide range of financial institutions, each offering access to hundreds or even thousands of potential investments.

Cody's Take: Don't automatically assume your 401(k) or other qualified plan has undesirable or expensive funds. For example, it's increasingly common for large workplace plans to offer low-cost index funds with institutional share classes—often with lower expense ratios than what's available to individual retail investors.

Distribution Flexibility in Retirement

Qualified plans can present two notable challenges when it comes to taking distributions in retirement.

The first is the portal used to request distributions, which may not be particularly user-friendly. The second involves the plan's distribution rules. For example, partial distributions before age 59½ may be restricted, depending on the specific provisions of the plan.

Rolling 401(k)s and other qualified plans into IRAs can help address both issues. The owner can choose the IRA custodian—often selecting a financial institution with a more intuitive platform. In addition, IRAs offer greater distribution flexibility and are not subject to the same limitations that qualified plans may impose.

RMD Flexibility

An RMD from an Employer A 401(k) must be taken from the Employer A 401(k). This creates rigidity and increases the risk of errors when managing RMDs. For example, if Sal has a $50,000 RMD from his Employer A 401(k) and a $25,000 RMD from his Employer B 401(k), taking a $75,000 distribution from his Employer B 401(k) still leaves him $50,000 short—because he took nothing from Employer A's plan.

IRAs don't have this problem. A taxpayer with five traditional IRAs can satisfy their total RMD by taking it from one, two, three, four, or all five accounts—in any combination. For most distribution purposes, traditional IRAs are treated as a single aggregated IRA. The IRS doesn't care which IRA the RMD comes from, as long as the total RMD is taken by year-end. This flexibility can be helpful for many reasons and reduces the risk of incurring a penalty for failing to distribute the required amount.

Avoid Mandatory 20% Withholding on Distributions

As discussed in Chapter 5, a significant disadvantage of 401(k)s and other traditional qualified plans is that distributions to the participant for living expenses are subject to mandatory 20% federal income tax withholding, regardless of the owners age. Note that the owner can elect a greater withholding percentage.

For many retirees, their effective federal income tax rate is well below 20%. As a result, the mandatory withholding often leads to overwithholding—and significant tax refunds when they file their federal income tax returns.

A direct rollover from a 401(k) or other qualified plan to a traditional IRA avoids this mandatory 20% withholding. Traditional IRA distributions are not subject to mandatory withholding. By default, 10% is withheld for federal income taxes, but the account owner can adjust this amount—including reducing it to 0%—for each IRA distribution.

This withholding flexibility is a key reason many retirees choose to roll over 401(k)s and other qualified plans into IRAs.

Qualification for an Early Withdrawal Penalty Exception

Many early retirees rely on one or more exceptions to the 10% early withdrawal penalty when planning for the first years of retirement.

In some cases, qualifying for a penalty exception may be a reason to roll a 401(k) or other qualified plan into a traditional IRA. However, two key exceptions—the Rule of 55 and distributions from governmental 457(b) plans—require the opposite approach: keeping the funds in the qualified plan. Rolling to a traditional IRA before age 59½ would forfeit eligibility for these exceptions.

72(t) Series of Substantially Equal Periodic Payments (SEPP)

We'll cover 72(t) payments in more detail later in Chapter 12. For now, it's enough to understand that a 72(t) payment plan generally involves taking equal annual payments from a retirement account for the longer of (1) five years or (2) until the account owner reaches age 59½. It's a tactic early retirees can use to access traditional retirement accounts without triggering the 10% early withdrawal penalty.

In practice, 72(t) payments are typically taken from traditional IRAs. The amortization calculation is similar to a mortgage payment calculation and often involves splitting one traditional IRA into two accounts: a "72(t) IRA" and a "non-72(t) IRA."

Qualified plans are generally not split to facilitate 72(t) payments. As a result, most 72(t) arrangements come from traditional IRAs. Early retirees who wish to use this tactic may want to roll their 401(k) or other qualified plan into a traditional IRA to facilitate setting up a 72(t) plan.

Qualified Higher Education Expenses

An early retiree might be paying for a child's college education. There is an exception to the 10% early withdrawal penalty for qualified higher education expenses. In this case, the retiree might consider rolling over a 401(k) to a traditional IRA in order to use the funds to pay for college education before reaching age 59½, since the penalty exception only applies to distributions from IRAs.

Rule of 55 Distributions

There is a special exception to the 10% early withdrawal penalty: distributions from a 401(k) or other qualified plan are penalty-free if the employee separates from service in the year they turn age 55 or later.

This is a limited exception. It does not apply to old 401(k)s or qualified plans from employers you left before the year you turned 55, nor does it apply to IRAs.

The Rule of 55 is a key reason not to roll a 401(k) or other qualified plan into an IRA—at least before reaching age 59½.

Governmental 457(b) Plans

Withdrawals from governmental 457(b) plans are not subject to the 10% early withdrawal penalty, regardless of age or separation from service. That said, most aspiring early retirees who plan to take advantage of this exception will, in practice, wait until separating from service before taking a distribution from their governmental 457(b) account.

It's important to note that money rolled into a governmental 457(b) plan from another account (such as a traditional IRA) does not qualify for the 457(b) penalty exception when distributed. However, those funds may qualify for a different applicable penalty exception.

If the account owner rolls governmental 457(b) funds into another account—such as an IRA—they lose access to the 457(b) early withdrawal penalty exception.

Account Consolidation

Who wants to manage a dozen financial account logins? Account consolidation is a legitimate planning objective. As Americans change jobs, they often leave behind employer-sponsored retirement accounts. Rolling over old retirement accounts into a new employer's 401(k) or other qualified plan—or into an IRA—can help streamline account management and improve oversight. Imagine how many retirees are trying to hunt down old qualified plans!

Sophisticated Tax Planning

In some cases, rollovers can open the door to sophisticated tax planning. Here are a few examples:

Backdoor Roth IRA

The Backdoor Roth IRA is a popular planning technique. It's a two-step process that allows a taxpayer whose income is too high to make a direct Roth IRA contribution to still get money into a Roth IRA.

Step one is a nondeductible contribution to a traditional IRA. Step two is a relatively soon-in-time conversion of that amount—and any minor growth—to a Roth IRA.

There's just one catch: the so-called **Pro-Rata Rule**.

Suppose the taxpayer already has a sizable traditional IRA—say, $100,000. That existing balance complicates doing the Backdoor Roth IRA.

Here's an example: Malik, age 38, earns $270,000 in W-2 income and does not qualify to make a direct Roth IRA contribution for 2025. In January, he makes a $7,000 nondeductible contribution to a new traditional IRA. In February, that IRA has grown slightly to $7,020, and he converts the entire amount to a Roth IRA.

Malik assumes he'll only be taxed on the $20 of growth, since his $7,000 nondeductible contribution created basis in the new traditional IRA. But he overlooked one detail: he also has another traditional IRA worth $92,980 as of December 31, 2025.

Because of the Pro-Rata Rule, his $7,000 basis is spread across both the converted amount and the total year-end IRA balance. The calculation is:

$7,000 × ($7,020 ÷ [$7,020 + $92,980]) = $491 of basis recovered

So, instead of being taxed on just $20, Malik is taxed on $6,529 ($7,020 − $491). *Whoops!*

How could Malik have avoided this?

Before December 31, 2025, he could have rolled the $92,980 traditional IRA into his current employer's 401(k) or another qualified plan. This would have removed the $92,980 pre-tax balance from the Pro-Rata Rule calculation. With no other year-end IRA balance, the calculation becomes:

$7,000 × ($7,020 ÷ $7,020) = $7,000 of basis recovered

Now Malik is taxed on just the $20 of growth.

Note: 401(k)s and other qualified plans can accept IRA roll-ins, but they're not required to.

Qualified Charitable Distributions

Qualified charitable distributions (QCDs) are one of our favorite tactics for retirees age 70½ and older. But QCDs are not available from qualified plans—they can only be made from IRAs. From a planning perspective, QCDs are typically done from traditional IRAs, including inherited traditional IRAs.

For example, say Julie is at least 70½ and wants to give $1,000 per month to her church. A very tax-efficient way to do this is to direct her IRA custodian to send $1,000 each month directly from her traditional IRA to the church. Julie can exclude that otherwise taxable distribution from her gross income. And although she claims the large standard deduction on her tax return, she still receives the benefit of a charitable deduction without itemizing.

We'll explore QCDs in more detail in Chapter 32. For now, it's enough to know that QCDs are a compelling reason to roll a 401(k) or other qualified plan into a traditional IRA.

Isolating After-Tax Basis in Qualified Plans

Some qualified plans allow after-tax (nondeductible) contributions to traditional accounts. These are not Roth contributions, but rather after-tax contributions to traditional tax-deferred accounts. In some plans, these after-tax contributions are "taken care of" through the so-called "Mega Backdoor Roth"— usually involving an in-plan Roth conversion shortly after the contributions land in the traditional retirement account.

That quick Roth conversion isn't always available. The plan must include a Roth feature to allow in-plan Roth conversions. Without that option, the after-tax basis is recovered ratably as the account owner takes distributions from the traditional retirement account. The longer that takes, the more inflation erodes the real value of that basis. Plus, all the growth on those after-tax contributions remains subject to ordinary income tax when withdrawn. Not ideal.

But never fear! Rollovers can turn those not-so-great after-tax contributions into an excellent planning opportunity once the employee separates from service or retires. At that point, the after-tax contributions represent basis in the plan.

IRS Notice 2014-54 clarified the treatment of these rollovers: the basis (after-tax contributions) can be rolled tax-free into a Roth IRA, while the pre-tax amounts in the 401(k) or other qualified plan can be rolled into a traditional IRA. This split treatment can be done without triggering tax at the time of the rollovers.

In Real Life: Transfers of retirement accounts involving after-tax basis can be complicated. In our view, two helpful rules of thumb apply:

1. *Basis in a traditional IRA cannot be rolled into a 401(k) or other qualified plan.*
2. *Basis in a 401(k) or other qualified plan can be rolled into a traditional IRA—but it **almost never should**, because Notice 2014-54 allows that basis to be cleanly rolled into a Roth IRA instead.*

Accessing Roth Basis

Retirees under age 59½ may want to access Roth accounts to help fund spending in early retirement.

As discussed in Chapters 4 and 5, Roth IRA withdrawals follow favorable ordering rules. To refresh your memory: generally, withdrawals from Roth IRAs before age 59½ come first from prior annual contributions. These withdrawals are always tax- and penalty-free, making Roth IRAs particularly attractive to early retirees.

By contrast, the rules for Roth 401(k)s and other Roth qualified plans are not attractive to the early retiree. Before age 59½, distributions from these accounts come out pro-rata—a mix of contributions and earnings. While the contribution portion is withdrawn tax- and penalty-free, the earnings portion is subject to both ordinary income tax and a potential 10% early withdrawal penalty.

For early retirees planning to draw from a Roth 401(k), a rollover to a Roth IRA can make withdrawals much more tax-efficient.

Here's an example: Scott, age 53, wants to use money in his Roth 401(k) to fund part of his early retirement. Over the years, he contributed $120,000, and the account is now worth $300,000. If he withdraws $50,000 directly from the Roth 401(k), the distribution will be treated as:

- $20,000 tax- and penalty-free withdrawal of Roth contributions ($50,000 × [$120,000 ÷ $300,000])
- $30,000 taxed and potentially penalized distribution of earnings ($50,000 × [$180,000 ÷ $300,000])

Ouch!

Scott can avoid that outcome by rolling over the full $300,000 Roth 401(k) to a Roth IRA. Once in the Roth IRA, he can withdraw $50,000. Assuming Scott had never established a Roth IRA before, his new Roth IRA consists of $120,000 of annual contributions and $180,000 of earnings. Because withdrawals from a Roth IRA come first from contributions, Scott's $50,000 withdrawal is now entirely tax- and penalty-free!

Extra Credit: What about those dreaded 5-year rules? They don't apply here! The two separate Roth IRA 5-year rules only apply to:

- *Earnings (Scott didn't withdraw earnings)*
- *Previously taxable Roth conversions (Scott hasn't done any)*

Creditor Protection

As a very general rule, 401(k)s and other ERISA-protected qualified plans offer the strongest protection against the owner's creditors. IRAs also enjoy significant creditor protection, but it depends on a mix of federal bankruptcy law and individual state laws.

In theory, ERISA protection is a reason to keep a 401(k) or other qualified plan account with the employer—particularly in states where IRA creditor protection is more limited. In practice, this concern can often be addressed through affordable personal liability umbrella insurance, which provides coverage above home and auto insurance policies.

From a practical standpoint, we generally prefer rolling over old 401(k)s and qualified plans into new and separate IRAs or Roth IRAs to help document that the funds originated from a qualified plan.

Decision Making

To roll over or not to roll over?

Sometimes, a single factor drives the decision. For example, you might leave a job with a 401(k) that has poor investment options and join a new employer whose 401(k) offers excellent ones. In that case, that one factor alone might justify a rollover.

Other times, it's a combination of factors that need to be weighed. In our view, account owners should carefully consider all relevant facts and circumstances before transferring a retirement account to another.

Dollar Limits on Rollovers

None!

There are no dollar limits on rollovers. That makes sense, given that a rollover is not inherently tax-advantaged. For example, moving money from a traditional 401(k) to a traditional IRA does not improve the owner's tax position—it's simply a transfer between tax-deferred accounts.

Tax Return Reporting

The type of transfer determines how it's reported on the income tax return—though there are plenty of nuances and wrinkles we won't dive into in this book.

Direct Rollovers

Direct trustee-to-trustee transfers of 401(k)s and other qualified plans are reported to the owner on Form 1099-R. Assuming the transfer is not from a traditional account to a Roth, Box 1 of the 1099-R reports the gross distribution, and Box 2a shows a $0 taxable amount.

On the owner's Form 1040, the gross distribution is reported on Line 5a, with $0 reported on Line 5b (assuming no other taxable distributions from qualified plans).

The same treatment applies to direct trustee-to-trustee transfers of IRAs to 401(k)s or other qualified plans, except that the reporting appears on Line 4 instead of Line 5.

Trustee-to-Trustee Transfers

Direct trustee-to-trustee transfers from one IRA to another IRA—whether traditional to traditional or Roth to Roth—are not reported on Form 1099-R. As a result, they do not need to be reported on the owner's tax return.

Indirect Rollovers

Indirect rollovers should always generate a Form 1099-R. Whether the distribution comes from an IRA or a qualified plan, it is reported because it *could* be taxable.

This is where the account owner needs to pay close attention when preparing their tax return. For an indirect rollover, the sending institution has no way of knowing whether the funds were actually rolled over. As a result, the Form 1099-R—viewed in isolation—makes it look like a fully taxable distribution. It's up to the owner to ensure their tax return reflects that the money (or other assets) was, in fact, rolled over within the 60-day window.

Typically, this means reporting the gross distribution on Line 4a or 5a of Form 1040 and then showing $0 on the corresponding Line 4b or 5b. This step requires careful attention. Without it—either on the return itself or in tax software—the taxpayer might end up paying tax on what should have been a nontaxable rollover!

Roth Conversions

Roth conversions are reported to the owner on Form 1099-R and should be reported on the owner's Form 1040.

How much of the conversion is taxable? In many cases, the full amount. But in some situations, none—or only a small portion—may be taxable.

Recall Malik's Backdoor Roth IRA example from earlier. If he moved his traditional IRA balance into a qualified plan before year-end, only $20 of his Roth conversion would be taxable. Accurately reporting that outcome on Form 1040 and Form 8606 requires some skill.

Anyone doing a Backdoor Roth IRA (which includes a Roth conversion) should double- and triple-check the reporting to ensure the transaction is properly reflected and the correct amount of taxable income appears on the return.

Four Rollover Restrictions

Below, we cover the basics of four significant restrictions on rollover transactions.

Sixty-Day Rule

As discussed earlier, indirect rollovers must be completed within 60 days. This deadline is a major reason we generally favor direct trustee-to-trustee transfers, which avoid any issues with the 60-day rule altogether.

While the IRS may waive the 60-day deadline in certain cases, it's best to avoid needing a waiver in the first place.

Once Every Twelve Months Rule

There's a special rule for **IRA-to-IRA rollovers**: they can only be done once every rolling 12-month period. This is a common trap for the unwary and one of the key reasons we strongly prefer direct trustee-to-trustee transfers, which are not subject to this limitation.

The rule applies to all IRA-to-IRA rollovers and aggregates traditional IRAs, Roth IRAs, SEP IRAs, and SIMPLE IRAs for this purpose.

However, the rule does not apply to:

- Any direct trustee-to-trustee transfers (including IRA-to-IRA),
- IRA-to-qualified plan indirect rollovers,
- Qualified plan-to-IRA indirect rollovers,
- Qualified plan-to-qualified plan indirect rollovers, and
- Roth conversions.

What if funds are accidentally withdrawn from an IRA and the owner has already completed an IRA-to-IRA indirect rollover within the past 12 months? There are two potential workarounds:

1. Roll to a qualified plan within 60 days—if the owner has a current employer with a qualified plan that accepts IRA roll-ins (not all do).

2. Rollover to a Roth IRA—assuming the funds came from a traditional IRA, SEP IRA, or SIMPLE IRA. This functions as a Roth conversion done through an indirect rollover. The trade-off? The converted amount is taxable, but this option (1) avoids the 10% early withdrawal penalty (if otherwise applicable) and (2) gets the funds back into a retirement account when returning them to a traditional IRA isn't allowed under the once-per-12-month rule.

Required Minimum Distributions

There are two key rules to consider when you're subject to required minimum distributions (RMDs):

First, the initial distribution from a retirement account in any year the owner is subject to an RMD is considered to satisfy the RMD—up to the required amount. And yes, for this purpose, both indirect rollovers and direct trustee-to-trustee transfers count as distributions!

This creates a problem: under the tax rules, the RMD must be satisfied before any indirect rollovers or direct trustee-to-trustee transfer occur during the year. Failing to clear the RMD first can result in an excess contribution to the receiving retirement account.

Second, RMDs cannot be converted to Roth! If the account owner is subject to an RMD, they must satisfy it before initiating any Roth conversion. The RMD can be met through a combination of normal distributions and/or QCDs.

From a practical standpoint, this means retirees subject to RMDs can't wake up on New Year's Day and immediately do a Roth conversion. It's best to let the dust settle at the start of the year, calculate the RMD amount, and then proceed with any additional tax planning.

Basis

Basis in a traditional IRA cannot be rolled into a 401(k) or other qualified plan. It must either remain in a traditional IRA or be distributed to the owner.

Before initiating any rollover from a traditional IRA to a qualified plan, the owner should ask: "What is my basis in the traditional IRA?" That basis must be left behind in the traditional IRA.

Pensions

Many defined benefit pensions can be transferred to traditional IRAs. The key question for the retiree is whether to keep the pension as a pension or transfer it to a traditional IRA.

This is a highly subjective decision that depends on the individual's particular circumstances.

Pros of transferring a pension to a traditional IRA include:

1. **Flexibility:** IRA distributions are incredibly flexible and can generally be deferred into one's 70s. Pension payments are much less flexible and often must begin well before IRA RMDs start.
2. **Inheritability:** IRAs can be inherited by children. In contrast, annuitized pensions typically do not offer similar inheritance options beyond limited survivor benefits.
3. **Account Control:** With a traditional IRA, the owner controls both the investments and the financial institution. With a pension, the owner has no control over either.
4. **Additional Planning Tactics:** Traditional IRAs allow for Roth conversions and QCDs—options that are not available with pensions.
5. **Reduced Counterparty Risk:** As a current or future pension annuitant, the owner is a creditor of their former employer. While the Pension Benefit Guaranty Corporation (PBGC) provides some insurance, it comes with limitations. Rolling the pension to an IRA removes this employer-related risk.

Cons of transferring a pension to a traditional IRA include:

1. **Longevity Protection:** If the owner and/or their spouse live a long time, the "guaranteed" income stream provided by a pension can be advantageous. By rolling the pension into an IRA, the owner gives up the longevity protection that a lifetime annuity provides.
2. **Investment Risk:** Keeping the funds in the pension avoids the risk of depleting the account due to poor investment performance or spending decisions within a traditional IRA.
3. **Potential Payout Rates:** The higher the pension's annual payout as a percentage of the lump-sum value, the less compelling it may be to transfer the pension to an IRA. Any analysis in this regard should generally consider remaining life expectancy and the time value of money.

Finally, as with all retirement account transfers, we strongly favor direct trustee-to-trustee transfers for those choosing to transfer their pension to a traditional IRA.

Roth Conversions

Roth conversions are transfers between retirement accounts—most often from traditional IRAs to Roth IRAs. They serve as the foundation for some excellent early retirement tax planning tactics, which we'll explore in more detail later in the book.

Roth conversions are a workaround to the once-every-twelve-months rule discussed above. Here is an example of how that could work:

In December 2024, Perry, age 50, takes a $10,000 distribution from his traditional IRA and has 100% of it withheld for federal income tax. In January 2025, he contributes $10,000 back to a traditional IRA as an indirect rollover, preventing the distribution from being taxable in 2024.

In September 2025, Perry buys a brand-new car and withdraws $30,000 from his traditional IRA to help pay for it. His plan is to return the $30,000 to the IRA in early October after receiving a large bonus at work. There's just one problem: he's already completed an IRA-to-IRA indirect rollover within the past 12 months, so he's not eligible to do another.

Perry still wants to get the money back into a retirement account. Since he can't roll it into a traditional IRA, he instead contributes it to a Roth IRA as an indirect rollover contribution. Yes, he'll pay income tax on this conversion, but at least the funds stay within a retirement account—and the conversion avoids the 10% early withdrawal penalty.

Note: We present this example to illustrate how a Roth conversion can serve as an effective mop-up tactic after less-than-optimal traditional IRA distributions. This example is not intended to encourage less-than-optimal IRA distributions.

Inherited Retirement Accounts

Inherited employer plan retirement accounts can be rolled over, but these rollovers are subject to three important restrictions:

First, **inherited workplace plan accounts** can only be moved via direct trustee-to-trustee transfer to inherited IRAs. Indirect rollovers are not permitted. As soon as any amount is distributed to the beneficiary, it cannot be rolled back into an inherited retirement account.

Second, **inherited IRAs** can only be rolled over via direct trustee-to-trustee transfer to another inherited IRA—again, no indirect rollovers allowed.

Third, with one exception, Roth conversions of inherited retirement accounts are not allowed. The exception is this: when directly transferring an inherited traditional qualified plan, the nonspouse beneficiary may elect to transfer the funds into an inherited Roth IRA. This functions as a Roth conversion and is fully taxable to the beneficiary.

Spouses have their own rules when it comes to inherited retirement accounts. In many cases, a spouse can treat the inherited account as their own, at which point it becomes subject to the standard rollover and distribution rules that apply to their retirement accounts.

7 – Pay Tax When You Pay Less Tax

In this chapter, we explore the planning environment in which aspiring early retirees face a key decision: whether to contribute to a traditional or Roth retirement plan at work.

Assessing Tax Rates: Working Years Versus Retirement

When deciding between, say, a traditional 401(k) and a Roth 401(k) contribution, it's tempting to focus on the amount of retirement income rather than the tax rate.

Imagine Jennifer invests $1,000 into Pear, Inc., a company she believes will be the next big tech giant. Jennifer might worry that its explosive growth inside a traditional 401(k) would lead to a huge tax bill later—so she considers making Roth 401(k) contributions instead.

Commentator Nick Maggiulli has illustrated that **if tax rates are the same** at the time of contribution and at the time of distribution, there's no mathematical difference between traditional and Roth retirement accounts. Borrowing from an example he shared on his Of Dollars and Data blog, suppose a tax rate of 30%:

Jennifer earns $1,000 and is deciding whether to contribute to a Roth 401(k) or a traditional 401(k). Imagine that Jennifer is correct in her prediction and Pear, Inc. stock grows 1,000x its current value. Which is better for Jennifer, traditional or Roth?

If she chooses the Roth 401(k), she first pays 30% in taxes on her $1,000 of wages, leaving her with $700 to contribute. That $700 grows tax-free to **$700,000 to spend in retirement**, and she owes no tax on distributions in retirement.

If she chooses the traditional 401(k), she contributes the full $1,000 pre-tax. It grows to $1,000,000, but in retirement, she pays 30% in tax on distributions—leaving her with the same **$700,000 to spend in retirement**.

Thus, if tax rates were always the same, there's no mathematical difference between traditional and Roth accounts.

Cody's Take: Some readers may point out that this isn't an apples-to-apples comparison, since both scenarios assume the same $1,000 of income. But the key is recognizing that a $1,000 Roth 401(k) contribution requires more gross income than a $1,000 traditional 401(k) contribution. For a truly fair comparison, we must account for the tax savings from making the traditional contribution. That additional $300 of take-home pay could be invested in a taxable brokerage account, a Roth IRA, or elsewhere—and grow over time as well.

Tax Rate Arbitrage

We refer to deducting contributions at a higher tax rate than the rate applied when those funds are later withdrawn as **tax rate arbitrage**.

Basic Tax Rate Arbitrage Example

Favorable tax rate arbitrage reduces lifetime tax expense. Here's a simplified example to illustrate how it works:

Gloria earns $1,000 at work in **Year 1** and is subject to a **24%** income tax rate. She expects to retire next year, when her tax rate will drop to **12%**. The tax law where Gloria lives allows her to defer $200 of her income into a traditional retirement account. Assume the investment grows 10% between Year 1 and Year 2, and she withdraws it in **Year 2** to help fund retirement.

Below is a comparison of the tax owed with and without the traditional retirement account contribution:

Item	Traditional Retirement Account		No Traditional Retirement Account	
	Taxable Income	Tax	Taxable Income	Tax
Year 1	$800.00	$192.00	$1,000.00	$240.00
Year 2	$220.00	$26.40	$20.00	$2.40
Total Tax		$218.40		$242.40

This simple illustration shows how tax rate arbitrage saves Gloria $24 in total tax ($242.40 – $218.40).

How did Gloria pay less tax?

By paying tax when she pays less tax!

In Gloria's case, that's in Year 2.

When will you pay less tax?

Tax Rate Arbitrage and Workplace Retirement Accounts

Workers should contribute to traditional 401(k)s and other pre-tax retirement accounts if they expect a reasonable chance of achieving tax rate arbitrage. If an aspiring early retiree deducts traditional 401(k) contributions at a marginal federal tax rate of 24% or higher and later pays tax on distributions within the 10%, 12%, and 22% brackets, they've achieved tax rate arbitrage.

In short, many workers are likely to benefit from favorable tax rate arbitrage when contributing to traditional retirement accounts. Why? Because contributions are deducted at the worker's highest marginal tax rate(s), while distributions in retirement are taxed through progressive tax brackets.

We devote a significant portion of this book to demonstrating how and why this dynamic benefits retirees—particularly early retirees.

Negative tax rate arbitrage occurs when a traditional retirement account contribution is deducted at a lower tax rate than is applied to the resulting retirement distribution. In this scenario, a worker should consider making a Roth workplace retirement contribution instead.

Remember, it's not that traditional is better than Roth or vice versa. The goal is simply to pay tax when you pay less tax.

Asking the Right Questions

We've explored two concepts essential to answering the traditional versus Roth question at work. First, tax rate matters most. The key rates to evaluate are the one at the time of contribution (potentially deducted) and the one at the time of distribution in retirement.

Second, if possible, we should aim to achieve tax rate arbitrage in our favor—and avoid negative tax rate arbitrage.

These two concepts equip us to assess the fundamental question: **When am I most likely to pay the highest income taxes?** The answer depends on two follow-up questions:

1.   When am I likely to have the greatest annual taxable income?
2.   Will taxes go up in the future on retirees?

When Am I Most Likely to Pay the Highest Income Taxes?

When am I most likely to pay the highest income taxes? Is it during my working career? Or is it during my retirement?

Answering this question greatly informs how most Americans—particularly most future early retirees—should approach tax planning during their working careers and beyond. It makes little sense to take a tax break today if you'll pay it back twice over in retirement. The opposite is also true: why pass up a meaningful tax break during your working career if the reward in retirement would be less valuable?

Early retirees have an interesting profile. By definition, they spend less than they earn—because they're saving for retirement. That means their spending isn't a brake on their taxable income. You could spend $120,000 per year, but if your salary is $250,000, you'll pay income tax on the full $250,000—possibly reduced by some retirement contributions, which we'll discuss soon.

What about in retirement? In most cases, spending tends to be a powerful brake on income taxes. Imagine a retiree spending $10,000 a month in retirement. How much taxable income might they have? In many cases, the answer is $120,000 or less.

If all withdrawals come from traditional retirement accounts, then yes—$120,000 of spending could translate into $120,000 of ordinary taxable income. But what if withdrawals come only from Roth accounts? In most cases, that produces no taxable income. What if they only sell taxable assets to support their expenses? They'll benefit from basis recovery, and most of the taxable income will likely be long-term capital gains, taxed at lower rates than a worker's ordinary income.

In short, annual spending is a natural ceiling on taxable income in retirement—a limit that doesn't exist during working years. This gives us a key insight: **if income tax rates remain roughly the same, most early retirees will face their highest income tax rates during their working careers**. Even if tax rates do increase in retirement, many retirees will still pay less in tax than they did while working—because it's spending that drives their taxable income.

Retiree Tax Versus Worker Tax

In many ways, our preferred approach boils down to this: pay tax when you pay less tax. We believe that you are likely to pay less in taxes during retirement—so that's the time to pay tax, rather than paying tax on Roth 401(k) contributions that you cannot deduct.

Why do we believe retirees tend to pay less tax than workers? Here are seven reasons:

1. **Spending Caps Income:** For most born in 1960 or later, personal spending serves as the upper ceiling on taxable income from retirement through their 74th birthday year. This natural ceiling doesn't exist during the working years.

2. **Favorable Income Character:** In retirement, many live for years on tax-preferred long-term capital gains. Workers, by contrast, live on more heavily taxed W-2 ordinary income.

3. **Charitable Advantages:** Starting at age 70½, charitable gifts can be made through qualified charitable distributions (QCDs) directly from IRAs, excluded from taxable income without needing to itemize deductions. On the other hand, many workers—even those with high incomes—receive rather modest tax benefits from charitable giving.

4. **Additional Standard Deduction:** Individuals age 65 and older qualify for an additional standard deduction—$1,600 or $2,000 per person in 2025, depending on filing status. While modest, it's still a meaningful increase over the standard deduction younger workers receive.

5. **Senior Deduction:** Individuals age 65 and older may also qualify for a $6,000 per person deduction. For married couples filing jointly, that's up to $12,000 if both spouses are age 65 or older by year-end. While the deduction phases out at higher levels of modified adjusted gross income (MAGI), many retirees can manage their income to remain eligible.

6. **Lower Exposure to Surtaxes:** Workers are more vulnerable to surtaxes like the 3.8% Net Investment Income Tax (NIIT), which kicks in at AGI thresholds of $200,000 (single) or $250,000 (MFJ). Most retirees can manage income levels to avoid NIIT, while many workers cannot.

7. **No FICA Taxes in Retirement:** Retirees generally don't pay Social Security and Medicare (FICA) payroll taxes, which total 7.65% for W-2 employees. This means retirees need less gross income to support the same level of spending, further reducing their overall tax burden compared to their working years.

Retiree taxation can be so light that many early retirees want to increase their taxable income through Roth conversions. We'll discuss that tactic in more detail later in the book.

Even the dreaded required minimum distribution (RMD) does not significantly increase taxable income above spending for many retirees. For example, the RMD for a 75-year-old is only 4.07% of the account balance. By age 80, it's 4.95%, and by age 85, it's just 6.25%. These levels are well within a safe withdrawal rate for most seniors, given their advancing age. We explore this further in Chapter 15.

Some retirees worry about RMDs combined with the so-called Widow's Tax Trap. We'll cover both later. But in our view, they're not as daunting as they're made out to be. During the accumulation phase, RMDs rarely justify avoiding traditional retirement accounts—especially for those pursuing an early retirement.

The Wrong Question

You may now be asking, "Cody and Sean, will taxes go up in the future?"

If so, you are like many commentators. Sorry to say—you've asked the wrong question. To your credit, you were only two words off.

The question you should be asking is, "Will taxes go up in the future **on retirees**?"

Those bolded words are the rub. We believe there are valid arguments that taxes may rise or fall in the future—other books can make those cases.

But we don't believe, for several reasons, that taxes are likely to increase significantly—if at all—**on retirees**. We'll lay out our reasoning more fully in Chapter 20, but for now, here are our three primary arguments:

1. Recent history shows that Congresses and Presidents from both parties have favored tax cuts—not tax hikes—for retirees. The year 2025 continues that trend.
2. Political motivation supports this status quo. Politicians want to get re-elected, and retirees like to vote. That dynamic doesn't exactly scream "tax hikes for retirees."
3. Alternative revenue sources—other "deep pockets"—can be taxed more heavily instead, as evidenced by developments in 2025.

Summarized Pros and Cons of Maxing Out Traditional Retirement Accounts at Work

Our preference for traditional 401(k) and other traditional workplace retirement accounts goes against the views of many commentators who advocate for Roth 401(k) contributions. Of our favored Compelling Three tactics discussed in Chapter 8, maxing out traditional workplace retirement accounts is easily the most controversial.

So, before we dig deeper in Chapter 8, here are the Pros and Cons of maxing out traditional workplace retirement account contributions.

The Cons are outcomes that (1) can occur because the worker contributed to traditional workplace retirement accounts and (2) are highly unlikely to happen if the worker contributed to Roth workplace retirement accounts instead.

Pros:

1. **Outstanding tax rate arbitrage.** This is essentially our central thesis: deduct traditional retirement contributions at a federal income tax rate that's higher than the rate applied to future distributions. In our view, the math outweighs the five potential Cons below in the vast

majority of cases. We cover this thoroughly in Chapter 8 and throughout the book.

2. **Upfront tax savings can fund other accounts.** The tax savings from traditional contributions can be redirected to Roth IRAs or taxable brokerage accounts—potentially creating tax-free years in retirement or, at the very least, a significant amount of tax-free income later on.

Cons:

1. **Early withdrawal penalty**. For those retiring before age 59½, accessing traditional retirement funds may trigger the 10% early withdrawal penalty. As discussed in Chapter 12 and elsewhere, this can often be avoided with proper planning.

2. **Taxation of Social Security**. Taxable distributions from traditional retirement accounts increase the amount of Social Security benefits subject to income tax. Later we demonstrate that the resulting tax is usually relatively small.

3. **IRMAA**. Some retirees will face Medicare premium surcharges (IRMAA) based on MAGI from two years prior. We unpack IRMAA later in the book and demonstrate that it is a nuisance tax that usually has little impact from a planning perspective.

4. **RMDs and the Widow's Tax Trap**. These factors can reduce—but rarely eliminate—the benefits of favorable tax rate arbitrage. In uncommon cases, they may even result in negative arbitrage for a portion of traditional retirement account distributions. We explore RMDs in Chapter 15 and the Widow's Tax Trap in Chapter 16.

5. **Taxation of some investment income**. Distributions from traditional accounts (instead of Roth accounts) may push some qualified dividends and long-term capital gains from the 0% to the 15% LTCG bracket. That said, many early retirees spend down taxable accounts first, and today's low dividend yields mean this added tax is typically minimal. See Bethany and Estelle's examples in Chapter 15.

Our conclusion: **for most Americans, the two Pros far outweigh the five Cons**. We'll continue to demonstrate why throughout the book.

Premium Tax Credit Considerations

For many early retirees, there's an additional layer to consider: The Premium Tax Credit (PTC).

On balance, we believe contributing to traditional workplace retirement accounts generally helps from a PTC perspective.

First, the tax savings from traditional contributions can be invested in taxable accounts. These taxable assets can then be used to fund early retirement while allowing the retiree to qualify for a PTC. As we discuss later, living off taxable accounts is often one of the most effective ways to optimize PTC eligibility.

Second, some early retirees may have income so low that they don't qualify for a PTC without intentional planning—or even part-time work. Traditional retirement accounts can help here. By converting just enough from a traditional account to a Roth, the retiree can generate sufficient income to qualify for a PTC. If all retirement funds are in Roth accounts going into early retirement, this option isn't available.

That said, traditional accounts aren't always helpful from a PTC perspective. Retirees who rely primarily or exclusively on the Rule of 55, a 72(t) payment plan, or governmental 457(b) distributions may have income that's too high to qualify for a PTC. While it's not impossible to use one of these techniques to qualify for a PTC, relying heavily on taxable income often reduces or eliminates the credit.

Our Central Thesis

The central thesis is that, for most Americans, the marginal tax rate benefit received when contributing to traditional retirement accounts will equal or exceed the tax rate applied to most distributions from those accounts.

To be clear, "most" does not mean "all"—but it still means most.

We believe the majority of Americans benefit from tax rate arbitrage when contributing to traditional 401(k)s and other traditional qualified retirement accounts at work.

Considering Traditional Versus Roth at Work

We believe that, for most Americans, the traditional 401(k) and its cousins— the traditional versions of the 403(b), governmental 457(b), and TSP—are an invitation to pay tax when you pay less tax.

Conversely, we believe that the Roth 401(k) and its cousins—the Roth 403(b), Roth governmental 457(b), and Roth TSP—are an invitation to both **accelerate** and **increase** tax. Choosing the Roth versions accelerates taxation (by definition) and often increases the total tax paid, since the tax is typically incurred during higher-income working years.

A Note On Our Quantitative Analysis

Throughout the remainder of this book, we use various degrees and methods of quantitative analysis to look at the future. All such analysis—by us or by others—is, by definition, subjective and speculative. There is no perfect way to assess an uncertain future from a quantitative perspective.

We focus on the big picture. No single statistic holds "the answer" to whether a traditional or Roth contribution is the better choice, especially over decades of accumulation and retirement. Instead, we aim to combine our qualitative and quantitative assessments to offer insights into favorable and unfavorable paths forward.

In Chapters 8, 11, and 15, we will include tables illustrating how hypothetical retirement account distributions are taxed when retirees receive multiple sources of ordinary income—such as Social Security, interest income, nonqualified dividends, and traditional retirement account distributions. This is our favored quantitative method to assess our preferred path.

Questions often arise about how to assess tax results in retirement when there are multiple sources of ordinary income in the picture. To address this, we "tax" traditional retirement account distributions last when allocating ordinary income across tax brackets. This means those distributions are taxed, for analytical purposes, at the retiree's highest marginal ordinary income tax rates. We explain our reasoning further in Chapter 8.

The hypothetical tables break down each tranche of the traditional retirement account distribution and other income and show how it is taxed—i.e., the applicable tax bracket and resulting federal income tax, using 2025 dollars and numbers.

We generally assume the qualified retirement plan contribution was deducted at a 24% rate and evaluate whether the traditional retirement contribution and resulting distribution represent a win for the owner, a win for the IRS, or a tie. This analysis helps the reader assess the efficacy of our favored path.

When presenting mock tax returns in Chapters 8, 11, and 15, we present three statistics to help readers evaluate the tax picture of a hypothetical future retiree.

One statistic we use is the retiree's "**Overall Effective Tax Rate on Income**," which simply divides total federal taxes paid—including federal income tax, the Net Investment Income Tax, and IRMAA—by the retiree's total income for the year. We believe this is one of several valid ways to assess the tax outcome of prioritizing traditional retirement account contributions at work. We use the overall effective rate because it reflects the retiree's overall financial outcome and lived experience. As a statistic, it is less about "playing with numbers" and more a meaningful reflection of real-life retirement taxation.

A second statistic we present is the "**Effective Income Tax Rate for IRA Distributions**" when there are multiple sources of ordinary income in retirement. This rate simply divides the total computed income tax on each tranche of traditional retirement account distributions by the total traditional retirement account distributions for the year. It can be a helpful metric for evaluating the efficacy of our favored path.

A third statistic is the "**Rate Assigning All Tax to IRA Distributions**," which divides all federal taxes paid—including income tax, Net Investment Income Tax, and IRMAA—by the traditional IRA distribution for the year. While this metric has analytical validity, we find it less useful because it does not reflect a retiree's lived experience as closely as the other tools we employ. Nonetheless, we include it to present our hypotheticals in the worst possible light for the reader to consider.

We believe the taxation of retirement account distributions and other income, as illustrated by the tables, is more informative than any statistic. Statistics lack the depth provided by a granular review of how each tranche of income is taxed. Further, analyzing the tables highlights how the Cons of Social Security taxation, investment income taxation, and potential negative income tax rate arbitrage can impact retirees in ways that statistics alone cannot capture.

Ultimately, you—the reader—get to be the judge and jury on the desirability of our favored approach.

Marginal Contribution Decisions

Our overall approach focuses on **lifetime planning over decades** of work and retirement. Only occasionally can our book speak specifically to marginal contribution decisions.

It could be argued that the final few traditional retirement account contributions of one's career create the highest-taxed account distributions and RMDs in retirement—limiting the usefulness of assessing those specific contributions using an overall effective tax rate. While that's a reasonable argument, for many retirees, those later contributions will benefit from deductions at the owner's highest-ever marginal tax rates, since the owner is at the end of his or her career.

In such cases, the higher deduction of late-career **contributions** may more than offset the marginal tax rate on the resulting retirement **distributions**. This matching—between high marginal tax rates at the time of contribution and comparable rates on eventual withdrawals—helps reduce or even eliminate any material analytical deficiencies from using an overall effective rate to assess marginal retirement contributions.

Still, the overall effective tax rate on income in retirement is just one factor among many when making marginal contribution decisions, as illustrated in the Extra Credit below.

Extra Credit: For those approaching retirement with reduced W-2 income due to ramping down hours and salary, it may be worth considering Roth workplace contributions in the final years of work. If a worker's income drops into the 10%–12% marginal tax brackets, they might use W-2 earnings to fund current living expenses while contributing to a Roth 401(k) to capture any employer matching contributions. If there is extra income and they remain in a low tax bracket, they may consider making additional Roth contributions at work.

A Note on Statistics and the Big Picture

Throughout this book, our analysis relies on the totality of the circumstances—not a few percentage-point swings in any one statistic. We believe your planning should take a similar approach. No single metric is the "be-all and end-all." All tax planning is just that—planning. Focus on the big picture, and avoid getting bogged down in the pursuit of mathematical certitude when planning for the future.

Conclusion

Contributions to traditional 401(k)s and other qualified plans are especially attractive during our highest-earning working years. Since we're more likely to face our highest tax rates during this period, it's an ideal time to take advantage of legal tax reductions—such as contributing to a traditional 401(k).

In the next chapter, we detail our Compelling Three tactics, including traditional 401(k) contributions. We'll illustrate the benefits with detailed examples showing what taxation can look like when workers rely on traditional retirement accounts for retirement saving. This chapter has outlined the theoretical case. Next, you'll see the numbers that make the case.

8 – Moving To Early Retirement: The Compelling Three

In this chapter, we explore our three favorite tactics for aspiring early retirees. We believe these tactics are so compelling that we refer to them as the **Compelling Three**:

1. Traditional workplace retirement account contributions
2. Roth IRA contributions
3. Taxable brokerage account contributions

Max Out Traditional Retirement Account Contributions at Work

For many Americans striving for early retirement, the best way to get there is by making substantial contributions to traditional 401(k)s and other workplace retirement plans.

This tactic offers several advantages. It's one of the fastest, most convenient, and most affordable ways to build wealth for retirement. The tax savings—realized at the worker's highest marginal federal and state income tax rates—can be redirected toward other objectives, including:

- Funding current needs
- Making Roth IRA contributions to help fund retirement
- Investing in taxable brokerage accounts to help fund retirement

From a retirement planning perspective, the best way to double dip is to max out a traditional 401(k) and invest the resulting income tax savings in a Roth IRA and/or a taxable brokerage account.

As we discuss throughout this book, many retirees end up paying modest taxes on withdrawals from traditional retirement accounts.

Traditional Retirement Account Drawbacks

Let's take a closer look at the drawbacks of traditional retirement accounts to see just how bad they really are. In Chapter 7, we made the theoretical case for traditional contributions. In this chapter, we back it up with math.

By examining the numbers, we can decide for ourselves whether the benefits of traditional retirement accounts outweigh the drawbacks.

Imagine Joe and Jane, a married couple in their late 30s with about $300,000 of combined gross W-2 wages in 2025. They both have access to a 401(k) at work, with the option to choose between traditional and Roth contributions.

Which option should they choose? Joe and Jane fall squarely within the 24% marginal federal tax bracket. If each of them contributes $23,500 to a traditional 401(k), their federal income tax benefit is 24 cents on the dollar. If that's the only saving they do for the year, their total consumption—including taxes—in 2025 dollars is roughly $253,000.

To assess whether deducting traditional 401(k) contributions is wise for Joe and Jane, we have to "begin with the end in mind," as Stephen R. Covey put it. While we can't perfectly predict the future, we can model two potential worst-case scenarios.

Imagine Joe and Jane want to replicate their working-career annual spending in retirement. That means they plan to spend $253,000 per year (in 2025 dollars) in retirement. Now imagine they're both 66 years old, fully retired, and all their savings are in traditional retirement accounts. Just how bad is the taxation if they withdraw—and spend—$253,000 per year, **all from those traditional retirement accounts?**

Using 2025 tax numbers and brackets, the first $34,700 of that $253,000 is completely free from federal income tax. Here's how that breaks down:

- **Standard Deduction:** $30,000
- **One Big Beautiful Bill ("OBBB") Increase to the Standard Deduction:** $1,500
- **Age 65+ Additional Standard Deduction:** $3,200 ($1,600 per spouse)
- **Total Deduction: $34,700**

Sean coined a term for this phenomenon: the Hidden Roth IRA. It's the idea that some traditional retirement account withdrawals are tax-free! The Hidden Roth IRA lives inside most Americans' traditional 401(k)s or IRAs.

Deduct at 24%, later include it in income at 0%. That's pretty good. Roth 401(k) contributions never offer an opportunity like that.

"But surely Joe and Jane will eventually get crushed by taxes on that income, right?" Let's see:

- The next $23,850 is taxed at 10%, creating $2,385 of federal income tax. Deduct at 24%, later include it at 10%—still winning!
- The next $73,100 is taxed at 12%, creating $8,772 of federal income tax. Deduct at 24%, later include it at 12%—still winning!

Now for the tougher part:

- The next $109,750 is taxed at 22%, generating $24,145 of federal income tax. Deduct at 24%, later include it at 22%—still a win, though not a blowout. The IRS is finally competitive.

And finally:

- The last $11,600 is taxed at 24%, creating $2,784 in federal income tax. Deduct at 24%, include at 24%—a draw.

Here are the federal income tax results of having Joe and Jane's retirement income be $253,000, all from traditional retirement accounts:

Amount Withdrawn	Deducted At	Taxed At	Federal Income Tax	Win
$34,700	24%	0%	$0	Joe and Jane
$23,850	24%	10%	$2,385	Joe and Jane
$73,100	24%	12%	$8,772	Joe and Jane
$109,750	24%	22%	$24,145	Joe and Jane
$11,600	24%	24%	$2,784	Tie
Total **$253,000**	24%	**Effective Rate** **15.05%**	**Total** **$38,086**	Joe and Jane

We're using 2025 figures simply because that's what we have today. The numbers—including the standard deduction and the tax brackets—are generally indexed for inflation. Since we know Joe and Jane plan to spend roughly $253,000 in 2025 dollars, we're modeling the worst-case scenario using today's brackets to see just how bad the taxes are in retirement.

One final consideration is the **Medicare Income-Related Monthly Adjustment Amount (IRMAA)**—an additional premium that higher-income Medicare recipients pay for Parts B and D. It functions as a de facto income tax. IRMAA is based on the tax return from two years prior, so Joe and Jane's $253,000 of retirement income would trigger this surcharge two years later.

The estimated IRMAA cost in that year would be around $2,200 total. As a share of their $253,000 income, it amounts to **less than 1%**—a minor nuisance rather than a significant planning consideration.

This first scenario fits well with our Central Thesis: The tax rate at which Joe and Jane's traditional 401(k) contributions were deducted (24%) equals or exceeds the tax rates applied to their distributions (0%, 10%, 12%, 22%, and 24%).

In fact, **most of their distributions were taxed at lower rates than the original deduction**. The fact that nearly a quarter-million dollars of annual withdrawals are taxed so favorably is remarkable.

Most early retirees will never report a quarter-million dollars (in 2025 dollars) of taxable traditional retirement account distributions, making this test case quite reassuring when it comes to the value of traditional retirement account contributions.

Second, Joe and Jane are spending—after tax—over $200,000 per year in retirement. That's far from an impoverished lifestyle. Do you expect to spend over $200,000 per year in retirement, measured in 2025 dollars?

Third, notice how hard it was for Joe and Jane to get back to the marginal rate at which they deducted their traditional 401(k) contributions (24%). They had to spend over $200,000 in retirement just to push a single dollar into the 24% tax bracket!

To go further: they would have needed to withdraw over $664,000 from their traditional accounts in a single year to face a 24% **effective** federal income tax rate!

Fourth, the Joe and Jane example makes a deliberately conservative assumption: that their spending in retirement will remain equal to what it was during their working years, adjusted for inflation. Will that be the case for you?

Working Americans often have expenses that retirees don't:

- Payroll taxes
- Mortgage payments
- Commuting costs
- Little League and gymnastics fees for their kids

In reality, retirement spending may very well be lower than it was during the working years—regardless of income taxes.

Fifth, Joe and Jane are great candidates for strategic Roth withdrawals. We modeled this as a worst-case scenario to pressure-test our preferred tactic (saving through traditional 401(k) contributions). But had Joe and Jane withdrawn the last ~$12,000 from Roth accounts instead of traditional accounts, they would have entirely avoided the 24% bracket. We mention this here, in the working years chapter, because it illustrates the potential value of making some Roth contributions during the working years. We'll cover Roth IRAs in more detail shortly.

Lastly, our scenario isn't particularly realistic for couples aiming for an early retirement. Joe and Jane saved only 15.7% of their income. How many couples earning $300,000 per year and planning to retire early are saving just 15.7%?

Let's update the scenario so that Joe and Jane save one-third of their income as follows:

- $47,000 through traditional 401(k) contributions
- $14,000 through Backdoor Roth IRAs
- $39,000 through investments in taxable brokerage accounts

This means their annual consumption, including taxes and measured in 2025 dollars, is $200,000.

What might the taxes look like on $200,000 of retirement spending—again, in 2025 dollars—if Joe and Jane follow the least tax-efficient withdrawal path? Let's assume they fund their entire lifestyle with traditional retirement account withdrawals and have already spent down all of their taxable assets.

We're making this assumption to illustrate a worst-case scenario—one that is intentionally tax-inefficient to test the limits of the traditional retirement account strategy.

Before we show the tax breakdown, we need to account for their available deductions, including the partial senior deduction. Since their AGI is $200,000—halfway between $150,000 and $250,000—they receive half of the available $12,000 senior deduction. Here's their full deduction:

- **Standard Deduction:** $30,000
- **OBBB Increase to the Standard Deduction:** $1,500
- **Age 65+ Additional Standard Deduction:** $3,200 ($1,600 per spouse)
- **OBBB Partial Senior Deduction:** $6,000
- **Total Deduction: $40,700**

Amount Withdrawn	Deducted At	Taxed At	Federal Income Tax	Win
$40,700	24%	0%	$0	Joe and Jane
$23,850	24%	10%	$2,385	Joe and Jane
$73,100	24%	12%	$8,772	Joe and Jane
$62,350	24%	22%	$13,717	Joe and Jane
Total **$200,000**	24%	**Effective Rate** **12.44%**	**Total** **$24,874**	Joe and Jane

By deducting at 24% during their working years, Joe and Jane beat the IRS on every dollar of traditional retirement account withdrawals—up to $200,000 of annual retirement spending!

Why would it make sense for Joe and Jane to pass up a 24% immediate tax deduction to avoid a 12.44% effective tax rate in retirement?

This example fits with our Central Thesis: The tax rate at which their traditional 401(k) **contributions** were deducted (24%) exceeds the tax rates applied to their **distributions** (0%, 10%, 12%, and 22%). That's the benefit of a progressive tax system: retirees climb up the tax brackets gradually, reducing the overall tax burden on retirement account withdrawals.

Of course, Joe and Jane's result is not guaranteed. But directionally, the logic holds: it's often wise to take the tax deduction when the marginal rate is highest—typically during peak earning years—and later include the income when taxable income is lower, as it often is in retirement.

The Widow's Tax Trap

We can see it now—some readers nodding along with everything above, but suddenly shouting at the book, "What about the Widow's Tax Trap?!" *It's all well and good while Joe and Jane are both alive, but come on—one of them will pass away, and then the surviving spouse will get slammed by taxes... right?*

The Widow's Tax Trap refers to the phenomenon where a surviving spouse has a similar level of taxable income as when their partner was alive but is now subject to the single tax brackets and the single standard deduction. This shift results in a higher effective tax rate for the widow or widower. But just how harmful is it?

Let's return to Joe and Jane. Suppose it's two years later, and Joe passes away shortly after turning 68. Household spending often declines after the death of a spouse—but not by half. For example, if Jane visits the grandkids and stays in a hotel, that expense remains the same with or without Joe.

For our illustration, let's assume Jane spends $150,000 annually (in 2025 dollars) after Joe's passing. She receives a Social Security survivor benefit of $36,000 per year ($3,000 per month), so she needs to withdraw $114,000 annually from her retirement accounts to fund the rest of her consumption—including taxes.

Eighty-five percent of Jane's Social Security benefit ($30,600) is taxable. That brings her adjusted gross income (AGI) to $144,600 ($30,600 + $114,000).

She also receives several deductions, calculated as follows:

- **Standard Deduction:** $15,000
- **OBBB Increase to the Standard Deduction:** $750
- **Age 65+ Additional Standard Deduction:** $2,000
- **OBBB Partial Senior Deduction:** $1,824
- **Total Deduction: $19,574**

Her taxable income is $125,026. Here is how she is taxed:

Amount Received	Deducted At	Taxed At	Federal Income Tax	Assessment
$5,400	Excluded Social Security	N/A	$0	
$19,574	Taxable Social Security Against Deduction	N/A	$0	
$11,026	Taxable Social Security Against 10% Bracket	10%	$1,103	Con 2
$899	24%	10%	$90	Jane defeats the IRS
$36,550	24%	12%	$4,386	Jane defeats the IRS
$54,875	24%	22%	$12,073	Jane defeats the IRS
$21,676	24%	24%	$5,202	Jane and the IRS tie
Total $150,000	24%	**Effective Rate 15.24%**	**Total $22,854**	

Despite the concern about the Widow's Tax Trap, it turns out to be a relatively minor issue in Jane's case. Using 2025 numbers, her effective tax rate increases from 12.44% to 15.24%—a modest 2.8% increase. From a lived experience perspective, that small increase has little practical impact.

Note that Jane's other two tax statistics discussed in Chapter 7—Effective Income Tax Rate for IRA Distributions (19.08%) and Rate Assigning All Tax to IRA Distributions (22.50%)—still favorably support the decision she and Joe made to prioritize traditional 401(k) contributions at work.

Taxation of Social Security Due to Traditional Retirement Account Distributions

As you inspect Jane's tax calculation, notice that her total deduction and the 10% bracket were first applied to Social Security income—not to the $114,000 traditional IRA distribution. This ordering is intentional. If Joe and Jane had contributed to Roth 401(k)s instead of traditional 401(k)s, Jane's Social Security benefits would have been completely tax-free.

This is Con 2 of using traditional retirement accounts we discussed in Chapter 7: some portion of Social Security benefits is likely to become taxable.

Maxing out traditional 401(k) contributions comes with this drawback—possibly making up to 85% of Social Security benefits taxable.

How impactful is that?

In Jane's case, the taxation of Social Security is relatively mild. Most of her Social Security retirement benefits are offset by her deduction of $19,574, and the remainder is taxed in the 10% bracket. Even in this scenario—designed to be a worst-case tax outcome—Social Security is taxed lightly. And importantly, the majority of Jane's traditional IRA withdrawal still benefits from tax rate arbitrage: it's taxed across the 10%, 12%, and 22% brackets.

For Jane, the tax rate arbitrage provided from having previously contributed to a traditional 401(k) more than outweighs the trade-off of lightly taxed Social Security. In fact, **her effective tax rate on Social Security income is just 3.06%.**

And remember: Jane and Joe enjoyed years of tax rate arbitrage without any Social Security taxation at all—since they hadn't yet started collecting benefits.

Put another way: If Jane and Joe had used Roth 401(k)s, Jane's Social Security would've been taxed at 0%. Because they used traditional 401(k)s, her benefits are taxed at just 3.06%.

A minor drawback to the traditional 401(k) contribution strategy? Sure.

A drawback that makes it less desirable than Roth 401(k) contributions? Hardly.

Extra Credit: *There's no requirement in the tax code that Social Security income be taxed before traditional retirement account distributions. As we noted in Chapter 1, ordinary income (including both taxable Social Security and traditional retirement account distributions) is taxed first, followed by long-term capital gains income.*

However, for planning and analysis purposes, we believe it makes more sense to think of Social Security as being taxed first. Why? If Jane is deciding whether to take an additional $1,000 traditional IRA distribution before year-end, that amount is layered on top of her existing income. That insight supports our approach: treat traditional retirement account distributions as being taxed last, and therefore most heavily.

IRMAA

Now let's turn to Jane's IRMAA situation. In two years, Jane will face IRMAA due to her $144,600 modified adjusted gross income (MAGI) this year. Her estimated IRMAA surcharge is approximately $2,800. For Jane, IRMAA (Con 3 from Chapter 7) is a 1.9% nuisance tax with minimal impact on her lived experience.

To properly evaluate our favored tactics, we prefer to "bring forward" the IRMAA cost. While Jane won't pay it for two years, it's a direct consequence of this year's income. So, throughout this book, we treat IRMAA surcharges as a current cost of current-year income.

Like the taxation of Social Security, IRMAA is a potential drawback of the traditional 401(k) contribution strategy—but not a significant enough drawback to favor Roth 401(k) contributions over traditional 401(k) contributions.

The Benefits and Drawbacks of Traditional 401(k) Contributions

Will the Widow's Tax Trap always be as mild as it was for Jane this year? No. But we hope this example shows that the so-called "Widow's Tax Trap" is something to be assessed, not feared.

Even in the face of the Widow's Tax Trap, this scenario still aligns with our Central Thesis: The tax rate at which Jane's traditional 401(k) contributions were deducted (24%) exceeded the tax rates at which most of her retirement account distributions were taxed (10%, 12%, and 22%).

We hope the above examples help illustrate—conceptually—just how valuable traditional 401(k) deductions can be during one's working years, even in less-than-ideal retirement scenarios like those Joe and Jane faced.

It's time to move away from fear-based narratives about retirement taxes and toward the kind of quantitative analysis we've presented in this chapter—and will continue to offer throughout the book.

We'll soon explore specific tactics for redeploying income tax savings into additional vehicles for retirement, but for now, the key takeaway is: Prioritize traditional contributions to workplace retirement plans. Retirees are likely to face relatively light taxation on their distributions—especially when compared to the marginal tax rate their contributions saved during their working years.

Of course, not everyone can max out their 401(k) each year—and that's okay. As a starting point, we suggest a simple rule of thumb: "At least 10%." That sets a strong foundation, builds good savings habits, and likely captures the full employer match. As those habits take root, increasing contributions over time becomes much easier.

Cody's Take: As an educator for 401(k) plan participants, I encouraged workers to (at least) start there but increase their contribution rate by 1% or more each year on their birthday. It's a great gift to your future self!

Finally, those considering early retirement should strongly consider investing the tax savings from traditional 401(k) contributions into a Roth IRA or taxable brokerage account—a topic we'll dive into further.

Rules of Thumb

From time to time, you'll hear commentators say things like, "If you're in such-and-such marginal bracket, use Roth; if you're in a different bracket, use traditional."

For the most part, we're not big fans of these kinds of rules of thumb. We believe a better approach is to play out what taxes might look like in retirement—even in a worst-case scenario, as we've done in the three examples above. Modeling the outcome on the back end, as best you can, will inform the traditional vs. Roth decision far more effectively than any general rule.

State Income Taxes

Since we're writing for Americans across our great country, we've chosen to focus primarily on federal income tax planning and analysis. But what about state income taxes?

We generally find that state income taxes tend to be either neutral or slightly favorable to our approach when it comes to workplace retirement plans.

Nine states—including Cody's home state of Texas—have no state income tax. If you both work and retire in one of these states, there's no state income tax analysis to worry about.

But let's say you work in New York and plan to retire in Texas—that plan favors traditional workplace retirement accounts over Roth. You get a state tax deduction while working, and then pay no state income tax on withdrawals in retirement. *Yee-haw!*

In a state with significantly progressive tax brackets, like Sean's California, our approach also works well. For example, a worker might deduct traditional 401(k) contributions at an 8% or 9.3% state income tax rate, then include those withdrawals later at lower brackets—1%, 2%, 4%, 6%, and so on.

It's also worth noting that a small handful of states exempt some or all traditional retirement account distributions from income tax, making traditional contributions even more appealing for those who plan to work and retire in those states. These include Illinois, Iowa, Mississippi, and Pennsylvania.

Roth IRA Contributions

You may find yourself thinking, "Max out the traditional 401(k)—got it. What else? Maxing out my 401(k) alone likely won't be enough to get to early retirement."

We hear you. While we hesitate to prescribe a one-size-fits-all "order of operations," for many workers, the next stop is an annual Roth IRA contribution.

Now you might be asking, "Cody and Sean, you just told us to prioritize **traditional** contributions at work—now you're saying **Roth** contributions in our IRAs?"

At work, there's generally no modified adjusted gross income (MAGI) limit on the ability to deduct traditional 401(k) contributions. And importantly, every dollar contributed to a Roth 401(k) is a dollar you can't contribute to a traditional 401(k). For most Americans, the trade-off profile of Roth 401(k) contributions isn't very appealing—since it means sacrificing a potentially valuable tax deduction.

Outside of work, the rules are different. For those covered by a workplace retirement plan, deducting a traditional IRA contribution is subject to strict MAGI limits. While these limits adjust annually, for 2025, covered taxpayers cannot deduct a traditional IRA contribution if their MAGI is at or above the following thresholds:

- $89,000 for single filers
- $146,000 for married filing jointly
- $10,000 for married filing separately

However, many individuals with MAGI above those levels can still make a **Roth IRA** contribution—either directly or through a Backdoor Roth IRA.

For these Americans, the trade-off profile for a Roth IRA contribution—whether direct or Backdoor—is quite favorable. **There's no sacrificed tax deduction, and the alternative would be to invest that money in a taxable brokerage account.**

We're not opposed to taxable accounts—quite the opposite, actually—but we recognize the advantage of having those dollars in a Roth account.

There are several compelling reasons to build up Roth savings.

First, having a tax-free bucket in retirement can be quite helpful. For example, an early retiree optimizing for a high Premium Tax Credit (PTC) might choose to take some Roth distributions instead of drawing from traditional or taxable accounts to keep income low.

Later in retirement, Roth distributions can help retirees avoid being pushed into higher tax brackets. And of course, keeping money in Roth accounts—rather than taxable accounts—means future dividends and capital gains won't show up on the owner's annual tax return.

Roth IRA Versus Roth 401(k)

We've noticed a common misconception: the Roth 401(k) is better than the Roth IRA simply because its annual contribution limit ($23,500 for those under 50) is so much higher than that of a Roth IRA ($7,000 for those under 50).

But retirement accounts are about much more than just their contribution limits. From a planning perspective, what matters most are the known trade-offs.

Generally, when an aspiring early retiree contributes a dollar to a Roth 401(k), they're giving up a $1 tax deduction—because that dollar can no longer be contributed to a traditional 401(k). That's a real and often overlooked downside of Roth 401(k) contributions.

In contrast, for many aspiring early retirees, Roth IRA contributions don't share that same downside. Many individuals can't deduct a traditional IRA contribution due to income limits, but they can still contribute to a Roth IRA—either through a direct contribution or a Backdoor Roth IRA.

In other words:

- Roth IRA contributions often don't forgo a tax deduction.
- Roth 401(k) contributions generally do.

Which Roth contribution do you think is more attractive?

Taxable Account Investing

For many aspiring early retirees, maxing out a 401(k) and a Roth IRA is a great start—but still not enough to achieve early retirement. So, what comes next? For many Americans, the answer is taxable account contributions.

Some people worry about taxable accounts. "Aren't they... taxable? What about tax drag?"

As it turns out, for many early retirees, taxable accounts might not actually be taxable—at least for a while. Let's look at two examples.

Rich and Pat, both age 56, retire with $1.2 million invested in taxable accounts, all held in a domestic equity index fund. That fund produces a dividend yield of about 1.5%, 90% of which is qualified dividend income. The rest of their financial assets are in traditional and Roth retirement accounts.

The index fund has a cost basis of $720,000, and Rich and Pat plan to withdraw $100,000 annually from it to fund the early years of retirement.

So, how much federal income tax do Rich and Pat owe in the first year of retirement? Using 2025 numbers, the answer is: $0.

"Wait—what? They have $1.2 million in taxable accounts! How can they owe nothing in federal income tax?"

It's actually quite simple. Let's estimate:

- $1,700 in nonqualified dividend income
- $15,000 in qualified dividend income
- $40,000 in long-term capital gains (from selling $100,000 worth of investments with $60,000 in basis)

With a standard deduction of $31,500, they can easily shield the nonqualified dividends from tax. The remainder of their income—qualified dividends and long-term capital gains—is first absorbed by the remaining standard deduction, and the remainder is taxed by the 0% long-term capital gains tax bracket.

Turns out, Rich and Pat need not be too worried about tax drag!

Rich and Pat aren't the only retirees who can live tax-free on taxable accounts. Consider Helen and Morty, both age 67. They also have $1.2 million in a taxable account, fully invested in a domestic equity index fund with a 1.5% dividend yield, 90% of which is qualified dividend income. Their holding in the fund has a cost basis of $600,000, and they plan to fund retirement by withdrawing **$150,000** through sales of the fund.

Surely now they must pay federal income tax, right? Not so fast.

The standard deduction of $34,700 plus the senior deduction of $12,000 easily shields the $1,700 of nonqualified dividend income from federal income tax. The remaining deductions, combined with the generous 0% tax bracket for long-term capital gains and qualified dividend income, protect the rest of their income—approximately $15,000 of qualified dividends and $75,000 of long-term capital gains—from federal tax as well.

Do some retirees pay tax on taxable accounts? Yes. But the next time someone frets about "tax drag," you might share these two examples. The label "taxable account" is a bit of a misnomer.

As we'll discuss in Chapter 18, to the extent tax drag exists during the working years, it's often a good reason to hold only domestic equities in taxable accounts. In the current environment, they tend to pay the lowest dividend yields and the highest percentage of qualified dividend income.

And for those working toward early retirement, tax drag is often minimal in the early years—simply because it takes time to build a significant taxable account balance.

Fortunately, we currently live in a very favorable tax environment for taxable accounts. Many workers pay just 15% federal income tax on qualified dividend income. Those with MAGI above $200,000 (single) or $250,000 (married filing jointly) are subject to an additional 3.8% net investment income tax (NIIT). But, as shown here, it's difficult to generate significant taxable income from a brokerage account entirely invested in domestic equities, especially when those equities yield less than 2% annually.

Taxable Accounts Versus Traditional Retirement Accounts

We favor investing in both taxable accounts and traditional retirement accounts at work.

Some readers may look at the examples of Helen & Morty and Pat & Rich and conclude that taxable account investing is so advantageous that they should stop contributing to traditional retirement accounts at work.

That instinct overlooks some important considerations.

Consider Cameron (51) and Kat (49). They believe they'll be ready to retire in three years but are concerned that almost all of their savings are in traditional retirement accounts. As a result, they're thinking about stopping their traditional 401(k) contributions above the employer match and redirecting that money into taxable accounts instead.

After all, withdrawals from taxable accounts aren't subject to the 10% early withdrawal penalty before age 59½, right?

While that's true, there are two significant problems with relying on that line of thinking.

First, with proper planning, the 10% early withdrawal penalty is rarely a barrier to retiring in one's early to mid-50s. We explore this more fully in Chapter 12.

Second, one of the biggest advantages of planning for early retirement is the opportunity for positive tax rate arbitrage. If you're aiming for early retirement, tax rate arbitrage is one of the best tools at your disposal. Why would Kat and Cameron give that up?

By continuing to max out their traditional 401(k)s, especially late in their careers, they might receive a 22%, 24%, or even 32% federal income tax deduction. When they later withdraw that money to fund early retirement, their effective tax rate will likely be under 10%, with the highest marginal rate possibly no more than 12%. Don't believe us? Justin and Rachel's example in Chapter 11 will show us just how low the taxes can be for early retirees using 72(t) payment plans.

The math doesn't lie. Why would Cameron and Kat pay more tax during their peak earning years to avoid paying less tax in early retirement? **By deferring that income, they're choosing to pay tax when they pay less tax—in early retirement.**

Taxable accounts are great—and they absolutely have their place in early retirement planning. But they don't offer the exceptional tax rate arbitrage that traditional 401(k)s and other qualified plans provide to people like Cameron and Kat. That's why we favor building up taxable accounts in addition to maxing out traditional workplace retirement contributions—not instead of them.

The Compelling Three Complement Each Other

The Compelling Three often complement each other on the path to early retirement.

One example: the federal and state income tax savings from contributing to deductible traditional retirement accounts at work can be used to fund annual Roth IRA contributions and/or taxable account contributions.

Another example relates to the MAGI limit for Roth IRA contributions. Some aspiring early retirees can stay under the thresholds by contributing to deductible traditional retirement accounts at work, thereby reducing their MAGI.

You'll also see how the Compelling Three can complement each other during early retirement. One example is the use of tax-free Roth conversions. Want more money in Roth accounts? Great. One way to get it there is to contribute to traditional 401(k)s or other qualified plans during your working years, then convert amounts from those accounts to Roth IRAs during early retirement—sheltered by the standard deduction.

The Compelling Three and Singles

If you're single, you might be concerned about taxation in retirement. However, consider Jane's example as a widow—it's directly applicable to single retirees. As you can see, the federal income tax burden is quite manageable, even when the majority of spending comes from traditional retirement accounts.

In fact, single accumulators have two additional considerations that may actually enhance the benefits of the Compelling Three.

First, single individuals often benefit from higher marginal tax rates on traditional retirement account contributions. As of 2025, taxable income of $197,301 places a single filer in the 32% marginal federal tax bracket. That means many single readers of this book could receive a 32-cent reduction in federal income tax for each dollar contributed to a traditional 401(k)—increasing the odds of achieving strong tax rate arbitrage in retirement.

Second, consider the possibility of marrying later in life. For example, Sean got married at age 40. During his 30s, he benefited from high marginal tax rates while contributing to a traditional 401(k). In retirement, his account distributions can benefit from the larger standard deduction and wider federal tax brackets for those married filing jointly.

Use Restrictions

The Compelling Three have a significant advantage over other potential tactics: no use restrictions!

Generally speaking, the taxation of withdrawals from traditional retirement accounts, Roth retirement accounts, and taxable accounts is not affected by how the money is used.

While some exceptions to the 10% early withdrawal penalty are tied to specific uses, most of those are not particularly relevant from a planning perspective. As we'll discuss in Chapter 12, the penalty exceptions that are most useful for early retirees—such as the Rule of 55, governmental 457(b) plans, inherited retirement accounts, and 72(t) payment plans—are not use-restricted at all.

Thinking About the Compelling Three As We Age

You've seen the opportunity traditional retirement accounts offer: tax rate arbitrage. The idea is simple—deduct contributions at a high **marginal** rate, and later withdraw those funds (and their growth) at a much lower **effective** rate. That's why traditional retirement account contributions tend to be a smart move at any age for someone planning to retire someday.

Taxable accounts, in our view, are especially valuable for two groups: younger adults and those close to retirement.

1. For younger individuals, financial stability is often still developing. Having money in a taxable account can provide flexibility and security in the event of an emergency or job loss. We especially encourage younger workers to maintain a cash or cash-equivalent emergency fund in a taxable account.

2. For those nearing retirement—particularly early retirement—taxable accounts are a powerful tool. They often serve as the "first-spent" asset in early retirement, offering liquidity and income tax control without triggering penalties. We'll discuss this concept more throughout the book.

Roth accounts can play a particularly useful role early in our careers, when marginal tax rates are lower and our savings capacity is limited. A good strategy for some early-career workers may be to contribute to a traditional 401(k) up to the employer match, then max out a Roth IRA.

Roth IRAs also offer emergency fund flexibility. While tapping a Roth IRA for emergencies isn't ideal, it's an option worth considering—especially for younger working adults who are building their emergency fund but don't want to miss out on their annual Roth IRA contribution opportunity.

Finally, for those in their peak earning years, traditional retirement accounts are likely their most attractive. For example, someone who just received their final promotion might now be in the 32% or 35% marginal tax bracket, after previously being in the 24% bracket. That's a strong signal it may be time to go full throttle on traditional 401(k) contributions.

Road Blocks

Not everyone will have access to all of the Compelling Three—and that's okay. There are alternative paths available.

For example, say you're not covered by a workplace retirement plan, and neither is your spouse—but you have earned income. Good news: you may be eligible to make deductible traditional IRA contributions, regardless of your MAGI. That's one potentially available alternative.

Or perhaps you're self-employed. You may not have access to a large employer-sponsored plan, but you may be able to contribute to a Solo 401(k) or SEP IRA—both of which we'll cover in more detail in Chapter 25.

What if your MAGI is too high to contribute to a Roth IRA, and you have an existing traditional IRA that you can't or don't want to move? That's okay too. You might be eligible for a Mega Backdoor Roth through your workplace plan (more on that in the next chapter), or you could simply invest more in taxable accounts.

Fortunately, taxable account investing is always available to those saving for early retirement. And as we'll discuss next, there are additional tactics—beyond the Compelling Three—that may be available during the working years.

We strongly believe in the value of the Compelling Three—but **none of them are individually required for financial success.**

One lighthearted proof for that assertion: the TV show *Lifestyles of the Rich and Famous* debuted in 1984—nearly 14 years before the January 1, 1998 birth of the Roth IRA. If celebrities in the 1980s could achieve financial success without a Roth IRA, there's a good chance you can too.

Conclusion

For most working Americans, we generally prefer the Compelling Three: making significant contributions to traditional 401(k)s (striving to max them out), Roth IRA contributions, and taxable account contributions. We believe these three tactics offer the most effective path to early retirement for the majority of Americans.

9 – Moving To Early Retirement: Additional Tactics

In this chapter, we go beyond the Compelling Three to explore additional tactics that may be available to those working toward early retirement.

Backdoor Roth IRA

Annual Roth IRA contributions, the second of the Compelling Three, are great—but there's one problem: those with modified adjusted gross income (MAGI) above certain thresholds can't make them. In 2025, taxpayers at or above the following MAGI levels are ineligible to contribute **directly** to a Roth IRA:

- $165,000 for single filers
- $246,000 for married filing jointly
- $10,000 for married filing separately

Fortunately, there's a workaround to the MAGI limits: the Backdoor Roth IRA. This is a two-step transaction generally involving a nondeductible traditional IRA contribution followed by a Roth conversion of that amount (and any growth) to a Roth IRA shortly thereafter.

The Backdoor Roth IRA tactic achieves two planning objectives:

1. It moves money into a somewhat creditor-protected account.
2. It moves money that would have otherwise gone to a taxable account into a Roth account—usually with little to no tax impact.

A single $7,000 Backdoor Roth IRA won't change someone's financial future. But what about 5, 10, or 20 years' worth? Over time, this tactic can be quite valuable—keeping dividends and capital gains off the owner's tax return.

That said, the Backdoor Roth IRA isn't for everyone. As discussed in Chapter 4, those with pre-tax balances in traditional IRAs, SEP IRAs, and/or SIMPLE IRAs should usually avoid this tactic. Due to the Pro-Rata Rule, any Roth conversion is treated as partially taxable. This often makes the conversion step much less favorable.

A few practical tips:

- From a tax—not investment—perspective, it generally makes sense to invest the nondeductible traditional IRA contribution in cash, a cash equivalent, or a money market fund. This approach helps limit any growth between the two steps, which would otherwise be taxed as ordinary income.
- Timing between the two steps is another consideration. Sean explored this nuanced topic in detail in a blog post published in early

2025. In short, his view is that timing generally doesn't matter—but to be extra safe, we generally favor the Roth conversion occurring sometime in the calendar month following the traditional IRA contribution.

- Income tax (federal and/or state) should not be withheld for the Roth conversion step. Since the transaction is usually nontaxable—aside from a tiny tax on any small gain—there's no need to withhold tax.

Those doing the Backdoor Roth IRA should schedule a diligence step, ensuring that as of December 31 (of the conversion year), there are $0 balances in all traditional IRAs, SEP IRAs, and SIMPLE IRAs.

Each owner doing the Backdoor Roth IRA must file Form 8606 with their federal income tax return to report both the nondeductible IRA contribution and the Roth conversion.

No Additional Material Income Tax

Question: How do you pay the tax on a Backdoor Roth IRA?

Answer: You don't! For the most part.

We include this brief subsection because confusion around this point is common. The goal of the Backdoor Roth IRA is to move funds into a Roth IRA for those who can't make direct contributions—without incurring significant additional income tax.

Here's a simple example to illustrate why there's usually no meaningful tax impact:

Matt, 45 and single, earns a $320,000 W-2 salary. He's in the 35% marginal federal income tax bracket in 2025. On January 2, 2025, he contributes $7,000 to a traditional IRA and invests it in a money market fund. Matt has no other traditional IRA, SEP IRA, or SIMPLE IRA. On February 1, 2025, he converts the entire balance in the traditional IRA, then $7,026, to a Roth IRA. On December 31, 2025, he had zero balances in all traditional IRAs, SEP IRAs, and SIMPLE IRAs.

In this case, the Backdoor Roth IRA increases Matt's taxable income by $26, resulting in roughly $9 of federal income tax. For someone earning over $300,000, that $9 tax is negligible from a planning perspective.

Planning To Qualify for a Backdoor Roth IRA

Imagine you have a $100,000 pre-tax traditional IRA but want to take advantage of the Backdoor Roth IRA. What could you do?

One approach—though rarely practical—is to convert the entire $100,000 to a Roth IRA. While this technically clears the way for future Backdoor Roth IRA contributions, it would likely trigger a significant tax liability during high-earning working years. That's a steep price to pay just to unlock $7,000 or $8,000 in annual Backdoor Roth IRA contributions.

A second, more commonly used option is to roll the pre-tax traditional IRA balance into a current employer's 401(k) or other qualified plan by December 31 of the Roth conversion year. This removes the pre-tax IRA balance from the pro-rata calculation. However, this approach comes with a few considerations:

- The employer plan may not accept incoming rollovers—and it's not required to.
- If an indirect rollover is used, this starts a strict 60-day clock to complete the transaction.
- The investment options within the employer plan may be limited or expensive.

Note that existing IRA **basis** cannot be rolled into a 401(k) or other qualified plan. However, this tax rule creates a potential opportunity: roll the pre-tax amounts from the traditional IRA to the qualified plan, retain the basis (rounding up to be safe) in the traditional IRA, and then convert the basis to a Roth IRA. This type of transaction calls for measuring twice—and may warrant consulting a professional.

Relationship to the Compelling Three

The Backdoor Roth IRA is simply a technique for individuals who want to make Roth IRA contributions—the second of the Compelling Three—but whose income exceeds the limits for direct Roth IRA contributions.

Mega Backdoor Roth

The Mega Backdoor Roth is a powerful planning opportunity for those who have access to it. It uses one's workplace retirement plan (usually a 401(k)) to get more money into a Roth account in a tax-free manner.

It's a two-step transaction:

Step 1: Make an after-tax contribution to the traditional 401(k).

Step 2: Convert that amount to Roth, either through an in-plan Roth conversion or a rollover to a Roth IRA.

This approach accomplishes the same objective as the regular Backdoor Roth IRA, but with much higher potential dollar amounts. The Mega Backdoor Roth is constrained by the all-additions limit, not the much smaller annual IRA contribution limit. While most 401(k) plans still don't offer this feature, some do.

Does your workplace retirement plan offer this?

Start by reviewing your **Summary Plan Description (SPD)** and ask:

- "Does my plan allow after-tax contributions to the traditional 401(k) or other qualified plan?" If the answer is no, the Mega Backdoor Roth isn't available. If yes, then ask:
- "Does the plan allow me to convert the after-tax balance to a Roth 401(k) with an in-plan Roth conversion or to a Roth IRA with an in-service distribution?" If the answer is yes, your plan offers the Mega Backdoor Roth!

"But isn't this too good to be true?" Not according to the IRS and Treasury Department. They issued Notice 2014-54, which opened up this sort of planning.

Key points to consider:

- Like the Backdoor Roth IRA, the Mega Backdoor Roth has no income limits.
- With a rapid conversion of the after-tax contribution to a Roth account, there's no material additional tax to worry about.
- In our view, the Mega Backdoor Roth is best considered after workers have maxed out their deductible traditional 401(k) contributions. It's a fantastic add-on to the Compelling Three, but the upfront tax deduction often deserves priority.
- Based on our experience, the Mega Backdoor Roth is most common in the tech sector—thanks to competitive employee benefits and higher salaries—though some employers in other industries offer it as well.
- As discussed in Chapter 25, the Mega Backdoor Roth tends to be less practical for self-employed individuals using Solo 401(k)s.

In Real Life: Many people working for plan administrators may not recognize the term "Mega Backdoor Roth," since it's a colloquial rather than technical term. Consult the SPD before asking your administrator specific, informed questions.

Cody's Take: If your workplace retirement plan doesn't currently offer after-tax contributions and in-plan Roth conversions (the Mega Backdoor Roth language in the SPD), consider asking your plan administrator about the possibility of amending the plan. After all, this feature tends to benefit higher-earning employees—especially those in management—the most.

Mega Backdoor Roth Versus Roth 401(k) Employee Deferrals

You may be asking, "Why bother with the Mega Backdoor Roth when I can contribute up to $23,500 to a Roth 401(k)?"

At first glance, both options achieve the same end goals—getting money into a Roth account. But from a tax planning perspective, they are very different.

Why? Trade-offs.

Assuming it's 2025 and you're under age 50, you can contribute up to $23,500 in total employee deferrals to either a traditional 401(k), a Roth 401(k), or a combination of the two. Choosing to contribute $1 to a **Roth 401(k)** means giving up the ability to contribute that same $1 to a **traditional 401(k)**—and with it, the immediate tax deduction. That's a meaningful trade-off.

In contrast, the trade-off drawback of contributing to a Mega Backdoor Roth is much smaller. Assuming you've maxed out your $23,500 in employee deferrals, each additional dollar contributed to a Mega Backdoor Roth is a dollar that could otherwise go into a taxable account—not a pre-tax retirement account.

In short: with the Mega Backdoor Roth, there's no forgone tax deduction!

From a planning standpoint, the Mega Backdoor Roth often makes more sense than directing employee deferrals into a Roth 401(k)—especially for those in higher tax brackets during their working years.

Relationship to the Compelling Three

The Mega Backdoor Roth is a technique available to some that, from a planning perspective, enhances the second of the Compelling Three: Roth IRA contributions.

Health Savings Account

In Chapter 22, we explore Health Savings Accounts (HSAs) in detail. They can be a valuable tool to support the path to early retirement.

Not everyone qualifies to contribute to an HSA. Eligibility requires that a high deductible health plan (HDHP) be the individual's only health insurance coverage.

HSA contributions are appealing from a tax perspective. They are deducted from taxable income and—if made through payroll withholding—also reduce income subject to payroll taxes. HSA distributions used for current or previously qualified unreimbursed medical expenses (what Sean calls "**PUQME**") are entirely tax- and penalty-free. Since there's no time limit on PUQME reimbursements during life, an HSA can effectively be used to pay for virtually any retirement expense—being treated as a tax-free PUQME reimbursement.

HSAs offer several advantages for those pursuing early retirement—one of which is the typically lower insurance premiums associated with HDHPs.

Sean's Take: There's little point in getting to early retirement only to spend much of it in the doctor's office. Eating right, getting sunlight, exercising, and avoiding over-medicalization of one's problems can save money and help people enjoy retirement. This mentality is part of why I like HDHPs for workers—particularly younger ones.

Relationship to the Compelling Three

The HSA is a hybrid: it shares characteristics with both deductible workplace retirement accounts and Roth IRAs (which allow for tax-free withdrawals).

We believe HSAs are not quite as compelling as the Compelling Three for four reasons:

1. Annual HSA contribution limits are relatively low.
2. Contributions require coverage by specific health plans.
3. Withdrawals before age 65 that are not for qualified medical expenses or PUQME reimbursements are subject to both income tax and a 20% early withdrawal penalty. The penalty no longer applies at age 65, but nonqualified withdrawals remain taxable.
4. HSA PUQME reimbursements require recordkeeping to a degree exceeding that of any other account type.

Governmental 457(b)

The governmental 457(b) has two notable advantages. First, it allows separate employee deferral contributions in addition to any salary deferral contributions made to a 401(k) or 403(b). It's a unique benefit and worth considering if your employer offers it.

Second, governmental 457(b) distributions are never subject to the 10% early withdrawal penalty, making it a great tool for early retirement planning. Because of this, governmental 457(b) contributions often deserve priority over 403(b) contributions (beyond any employer-matching contributions)—assuming they can't both be maxed out.

Note that there is a *nongovernmental* 457(b) plan. That version is essentially a form of nonqualified deferred compensation, which we discuss below.

Nonqualified Deferred Compensation

Some Americans have access to **nonqualified deferred compensation (NQDC)** plans. For high-earning workers, these plans can be attractive. They can significantly reduce taxable income at the height of one's working career. The trade-off from a tax perspective is that the deferred compensation must be distributed after a separation from service, typically over a fixed number of years.

Each person needs to carefully evaluate the trade-offs.

First, NQDC plan balances are not the employee's property in the same way that 401(k) or IRA balances are. Deferred compensation remains subject to the general creditors of the employer, creating risk that doesn't exist with qualified plans.

Second, NQDC plans often require the employee to elect a rigid payout schedule—such as 5, 10, or 15 years. This is essentially the worst kind of required minimum distribution (RMD). Say what you will about 401(k)s and IRAs, but they don't start RMDs before one's 70s—and even then, the RMDs begin at relatively low percentages. In contrast, a sizable NQDC payout may begin immediately after retirement, limiting flexibility and tax planning options.

Relationship to the Compelling Three

The governmental 457(b) plan is a variation of the first of the Compelling Three: deductible workplace retirement plan contributions.

Employer Stock Compensation

Some aspiring early retirees have access to stock-based compensation through their employers. The most common employer stock programs we've seen are **restricted stock units (RSUs)** and qualified **employee stock purchase plans (ESPPs)**.

RSU tax planning is relatively straightforward. Restricted stock units vest on a specific date, creating immediately taxable compensation income and establishing a full fair market value basis in the company stock received. You can think of RSUs as a deferred bonus—paid in company stock instead of cash.

We're fans of diversification. Why not sell the company stock immediately, realize little or no tax gain or loss, and reinvest the proceeds into a more diversified portfolio? The employee is already economically tied to their W-2 employer, making diversification an important consideration.

With qualified ESPPs, which allow you to buy company stock at a discount (up to 15%) through payroll deductions, the key planning question is: *Can you sell the stock immediately at the end of the offering period?* If yes, we generally favor participating, selling the shares right away, paying tax on the discount (bargain element), and reinvesting the proceeds elsewhere.

Some employers offer company stock within a 401(k) or other retirement plan. While these situations are beyond the scope of this book, we suggest carefully considering diversification before allocating funds to company stock.

In your own planning, you may also encounter other types of equity compensation, such as restricted stock awards (RSAs), nonqualified stock options

(NSOs), and incentive stock options (ISOs). Planning for those is beyond the scope of this book and often benefits from professional guidance.

Relationship to the Compelling Three

Employer stock is usually—though not always—a version of the third of the Compelling Three: investing in taxable accounts. It can significantly increase the balance in taxable accounts, helping many reach early retirement sooner.

Taxable Roth Conversions

We've mentioned several tactics that those moving to early retirement should consider during their working years. Now let's turn to one that most full-time employees should set aside: taxable Roth conversions.

Roth conversions do have a place in tax planning to and through early retirement. The most appropriate use cases include:

- Tax-free Roth conversions as part of a Backdoor Roth IRA or Mega Backdoor Roth
- Taxable Roth conversions during specific periods in retirement

Taxable Roth conversions during working years tend to rarely make sense. Why add taxable income at the very time most workers should be focused on reducing it through traditional 401(k) contributions? While it's tempting to get money into a Roth, we argue there's plenty of opportunity to do so—through annual contributions, potential Backdoor Roths, and Roth conversions in retirement when federal income taxes might be shockingly low.

One notable exception is an income disruption. During the accumulation phase, income disruptions—such as mini-retirements, grad school, or layoffs—can create a year of usually low taxable income. These temporary breaks from full-time work may offer a valuable window to execute a Roth conversion at a low tax rate. At a minimum, income disruptions should prompt thoughtful consideration of tactical taxable Roth conversions.

Conclusion

Many of the best tactics that go beyond the Compelling Three are essentially complements to or expansions of the Compelling Three. For some aspiring to retire early, these additional tactics can be very impactful. For others, they may play only a minor role—or none at all.

We like many of the tactics discussed above because they don't require straying too far from the Compelling Three. Most planning for an early retirement should be cautious about strategies that deviate too much from these core principles.

10 – Drawdown Principles

In this chapter, we discuss our favored drawdown principles. Not everyone will be able to follow all of them perfectly—and that's okay. Perfection is rarely required to achieve great tax outcomes in retirement.

Principle 1: Taxable Accounts First

Aspiring early retirees often wonder: What's the ideal order of operations? Which accounts should they draw from first in early retirement?

As a general drawdown principle, we favor spending down taxable brokerage accounts first. This holds true regardless of the retiree's age.

This approach offers a clear advantage for those under age 59½: there's no early withdrawal penalty when liquidating taxable accounts. But even beyond that, we generally favor using taxable assets first until they are depleted.

Spending down taxable accounts has several advantages:

First, it helps future years' tax planning. While we appreciate the benefits of taxable accounts—especially when holding currently low-yielding domestic equity index funds—they still generate some taxable income beyond our control. And since future yields may not remain low, spending down these accounts first reduces exposure to potentially increasing taxable dividend income.

Second, retirement accounts often enjoy strong creditor protection. Taxable brokerage accounts do not. By drawing down taxable assets and preserving retirement accounts, retirees maintain a larger share of their portfolio in more protected vehicles. Yes, retirees should also consider personal liability umbrella insurance to help with asset protection. But there's no reason to rely on insurance coverage alone.

Third—and perhaps most important from a tax planning perspective—is the remarkably favorable tax treatment of **long-term capital gains**, discussed in Chapter 1. First, there's basis recovery: if a retiree sells $100,000 of ABC Mutual Fund in 2025 to fund spending, their taxable income is $100,000 minus their basis in the shares sold. Second, long-term capital gains can qualify for a 0% federal income tax rate. This creates opportunities for early retirees to enjoy years with little or even zero federal income tax, as we'll illustrate later.

Finally, the best way to avoid taxes on dividends and capital gains is to spend taxable assets first. Consider the alternative: spending down traditional IRAs first while letting taxable assets sit. This can push nonqualified dividends into the 10%, 12%, or 22% brackets, and qualified dividends from the 0% to the 15% bracket.

By drawing down taxable accounts first, nonqualified dividends are more likely to be shielded from federal income tax by the standard deduction, and qualified dividends are more likely to fall within the 0% long-term capital gains (LTCG) bracket.

Cats and Dogs

Here, we borrow a term, "cats and dogs," from JL Collins' *The Simple Path to Wealth*. Many will not get to retirement with just one domestic equity index fund in their taxable account. Perhaps they worked for a company that had an employee stock compensation plan. Or perhaps they simply liked the idea of investing in a particular company, or mutual fund or ETF focused on one particular sector or geography.

We agree with JL Collins: the best taxable assets to spend down first in retirement are the "cats and dogs" of the portfolio—those one-off or less diversified holdings.

Here is an example:

Jim and Janice, ages 59 and 57, retire in 2025. At retirement, they hold $800,000 in the DEF U.S. Equity Index Fund—a broadly diversified fund they both like. They also own $100,000 of Acme Anvils, Inc. stock, purchased years ago when Jim believed anvils were the next big growth area of the economy. Our favored tactic is for Jim and Janice to begin retirement by funding expenses through the sale of the Acme Anvils stock—the "cat and dog" of their taxable portfolio.

Extra Credit: When individuals and families incorporate charitable giving into their financial plan, donating appreciated "cats and dogs" from the taxable brokerage account—either directly or through a donor-advised fund—can often be an excellent option. This tactic is covered in Chapter 32.

How Often to Withdraw

Retirees worry about how frequently they should sell assets in their taxable accounts to fund living expenses.

Our view is that retirees should choose a withdrawal frequency and cadence that feels comfortable. That might mean selling assets as needed, monthly, or quarterly. Unless the strategy results in an unusually large cash buildup in taxable accounts, the timing of withdrawals is unlikely to significantly affect financial success in retirement.

What matters more is consistency and awareness. Whatever cadence they choose, retirees should track their withdrawals—specifically, the approximate capital gains or losses triggered—to help with tax planning for the year.

Specific Identification

One helpful tactic is to use "specific identification" or "minimum tax" functionalities when selling securities in a taxable account.

Specific identification allows retirees to select specific lots of securities with a known cost basis when selling. By choosing high-basis lots, they can reduce realized gains and potentially lower the current year's tax liability.

Each financial institution handles specific identification differently. A quick internet search combining the institution's name with "specific identification" usually leads to instructions for how to apply it when placing trades.

Keep in mind that specific identification has limited long-term value—eventually, low-basis lots may still be sold to fund retirement expenses. But at the margins, it remains a useful tool.

Dividend Reinvesting

Dividends received within the taxable account are taxable to the retiree. If they're taxable anyway, why not use them to fund your short-term spending? The alternative is to reinvest the dividends into the existing holding and later sell the shares to fund living expenses.

For example, imagine a retiree receives a $1,200 dividend from their domestic equity index fund in June. By using the cash from the settled dividends to cover living expenses, they reduce the need for capital gains transactions— thereby lowering their current year's taxable income for the year.

That said, turning off dividend reinvestment has limited value. Like specific identification, it's primarily a timing play. And in today's low-yield environment—especially for those holding domestic equities in taxable accounts— turning off dividend reinvestment is likely going to be of limited value.

Living on Taxable Accounts Example

Frank and Dana both turn 56 in 2025. They retired on December 15, 2024. In 2025, they plan to spend $160,000, funded entirely by sales of taxable assets. Those sales will generate $80,000 of long-term capital gains. Their dividends total $13,000 in qualified dividends, $1,000 in Section 199A dividends from REITs, and $1,000 in other nonqualified dividends—all of which they choose to reinvest automatically. They also keep $50,000 in a savings account, earning $2,500 in taxable interest.

How much federal income tax do you think Frank and Dana owe in 2025?

Item	Amount
Long-Term Capital Gains	$80,000
Qualified Dividends	$13,000
199A Dividends	$1,000
Nonqualified Dividends	$1,000
Interest Income	$2,500
Adjusted Gross Income	$97,500
Standard Deduction	$31,500
Taxable Income	$66,000
Federal Income Tax	**$0**

See why we are so fond of spending from taxable accounts first in retirement?

Frank and Dana's example—much like the examples of Rich & Pat and Helen & Morty in Chapter 8—validates the "invest in taxable accounts" leg of the Compelling Three. These scenarios are repeatable until the early retiree depletes their taxable accounts, potentially resulting in years of federal income tax–free living in the early phases of retirement.

These examples show that the term "taxable accounts" might be somewhat misleading—at least in early retirement. Dividends and capital gains might end up being entirely tax-free!

Making Dividends Taxable In Early Retirement

We generally favor spending down taxable accounts first in early retirement. Failing to do so can result in unnecessarily paying the IRS a 15% tax on qualified dividends.

Picture Larry, a single 60-year-old who retires at the beginning of 2025. He has $800,000 in a domestic equity index fund held in a taxable account, with a $500,000 basis. However, Larry decides not to draw from this account because he's concerned about future RMDs. Instead, he funds his $80,000 of living expenses entirely through traditional IRA distributions.

Now imagine that Larry's domestic equity index fund generates $8,000 in qualified dividends in 2025. Because his IRA distributions create $80,000 of taxable income, the dividends are pushed into the 15% long-term capital gains bracket. As a result, Larry pays $1,200 in federal income tax on those dividends.

Our favored approach would have avoided these taxes. If Larry had instead funded his expenses by selling shares of the index fund, his taxable income would have been much lower due to basis recovery. In that case, his qualified dividends and long-term capital gains would have remained within the 0% LTCG bracket (up to $48,350 of taxable income for single filers in 2025)—received completely tax-free!

Sequence of Returns Risk

Sequence of returns risk refers to the danger that a retiree experiences poor stock and bond market returns early in retirement. One or more bad years at the start of retirement can present a risk to the retiree.

One way to mitigate this risk is to reduce expenses early in retirement. The lower the expenses are, the fewer sales the early retiree needs to make during a market downturn—reducing the damage caused by withdrawing from a declining portfolio.

Our favored approach—spending taxable accounts first—helps mitigate sequence of returns risk. Compare Frank and Dana, who pay no federal income tax early in retirement because they draw from taxable accounts, to Larry, who draws from traditional retirement accounts instead. Assuming Larry takes the standard deduction, portions of his $80,000 traditional IRA distribution fall into the 10%, 12%, and 22% tax brackets—and he also pays a 15% tax on his $8,000 of qualified dividends.

From a sequence of returns risk perspective, it is better to delay paying taxes until later in retirement. That's what Frank and Dana do. In contrast, Larry's drawdown strategy increases his vulnerability by incurring higher income tax expenses early in his retirement.

Inherited Traditional IRAs

One exception to the general principle that early retirees should draw from taxable accounts first arises when retirees inherit a sizable traditional IRA or other traditional retirement account.

In many cases, beneficiaries must empty an inherited traditional IRA within 10 years. This makes it essential to manage distributions carefully over that period to minimize the tax impact. As a result, some or all of the early years of retirement may be funded—partially or entirely—by the inherited IRA rather than taxable accounts.

This can be good news. In the hands of an early retiree, distributions from an inherited traditional IRA may benefit from what we call "Hidden Roth

IRA" treatment on a significant portion of the income. We explore that concept in more detail in Chapter 11.

Principle 2: Keep Ordinary Income Low

One of the key ways to maintain flexibility in retirement is to keep ordinary income low. Doing so offers several benefits:

- Lowers current-year federal and state income taxes
- Opens the door to Roth conversion opportunities
- Helps maximize Premium Tax Credits
- Reduces the tax burden on traditional retirement account distributions, including RMDs

We've explored ways to keep ordinary income low throughout this book. One approach is to hold bonds—and potentially cash or money market funds—in traditional retirement accounts.

Principle 3: Roth Conversions Sheltered by the Standard Deduction and Other Available Deductions

As a general principle, **we favor Roth conversions up to the level that keeps total ordinary income at or below the standard deduction and any other available deductions.** While conversions beyond that threshold can still be beneficial, the conversions we're referring to here are often—though not always—a slam dunk for retirees.

Here's an example:

Paul and Jessica both turn 66 in 2025. That year, they plan to spend $100,000, entirely funded by sales of taxable assets. Their sales will trigger $60,000 of long-term capital gains. They also keep $50,000 in a savings account, which earns $2,500 of taxable interest income. Their dividends total $6,000 in qualified dividends, $500 in Section 199A dividends, and $400 in other non-qualified dividends—all of which they choose to reinvest.

Notice that, at least initially, their ordinary income is $3,400—made up of $2,500 in interest income, $500 in Section 199A dividends, and $400 in other nonqualified dividends. Keep that in mind as you consider their tax planning opportunities.

Without any further planning, here's what their 2025 federal income tax return would look like:

Item	Amount
Long-Term Capital Gains	$60,000
Qualified Dividends	$6,000
199A Dividends	$500
Nonqualified Dividends	$400
Interest Income	$2,500
Adjusted Gross Income	$69,400
Standard Deduction	$31,500
Additional Standard Deduction for Seniors	$3,200
Senior Deduction	$12,000
Total Deductions	$46,700
Taxable Income	$22,700
Federal Income Tax	**$0**

Paul and Jessica have a significant opportunity on the table. Before year-end, they could complete a **$43,300** Roth conversion—though we often favor rounding down when planning conversions. That $43,300 is calculated as their total deductions ($46,700) minus their current ordinary income ($3,400).

By doing this $43,300 Roth conversion, Paul and Jessica would still owe $0 in federal income tax for 2025. *Wow! Hard to pass that up.*

Paul and Jessica's $43,300 Roth conversion is what we call a Tailored Taxable Roth Conversion (a "TTRC"), which is discussed in detail in Chapter 17.

Are there situations where it might make sense to skip a Roth conversion against the standard deduction? Yes. Two factors could tip the scales:

1. If the conversion pushes long-term capital gains or qualified dividends into the 15% capital gains tax bracket.
2. If the retiree is on an ACA health plan, the conversion could reduce or eliminate their Premium Tax Credit (PTC).

That said, both considerations need to be assessed. A Roth conversion triggering one or both of these drawbacks could still be well worth it. Some subjective judgment is required.

Principle 4: Take from the Older Spouse's Traditional Retirement Accounts First

Roth conversions, qualified charitable distributions (QCDs), and regular distributions from traditional retirement accounts should generally come first from the older spouse's accounts.

The older spouse becomes subject to required minimum distributions (RMDs) sooner. Thus, it is usually preferable to reduce the older spouse's traditional retirement accounts first. Additionally, the older spouse can access traditional retirement accounts penalty-free sooner and becomes eligible to make QCDs earlier as well.

Principle 5: Rebalance Using Tax-Advantaged Accounts

Consider a retiree who is living off taxable accounts first—and who, like us, prefers holding domestic equities in those accounts.

As a reader, you might be wondering: "Are Cody and Sean suggesting that retirees reduce their exposure to domestic equities by spending down taxable accounts first?"

We're not. To be clear, this book does not offer investment advice to you or anyone else.

We favor retirees selling domestic equities in taxable accounts first to fund living expenses. But that doesn't necessarily mean we favor reducing overall exposure to domestic equities. Retirees following any form or degree of the Compelling Three are likely to hold both traditional and Roth retirement accounts. These tax-advantaged accounts are ideal for rebalancing or reallocating the portfolio to match the retiree's desired asset mix.

In theory, a retiree could fund living expenses by selling domestic equities in taxable accounts while simultaneously increasing domestic equity in their retirement accounts—without changing the overall allocation of their total portfolio. This concept of asset location is covered in Chapter 18.

*Cody's Take: I prefer to view asset **allocation** across three levels to help uncover asset **location** opportunities:*

1. *The total portfolio*
2. *Per tax location (taxable, pre-tax, and tax-free)*
3. *Per account*

Principle 6: Delay Claiming Social Security

We generally favor delaying Social Security benefits until age 70 for single retirees and for the higher-earning spouse of a married couple. The benefits of this approach include:

- Increased annual Social Security benefits
- Greater longevity protection
- Spending down volatile assets in one's 60s to increase nonvolatile income in one's 70s and beyond
- Tax planning: keeps Social Security income off a retiree's income tax return in their 60s

Keeping Social Security off the tax return in the mid-to-late 60s opens the door to valuable planning opportunities, which we'll explore in more detail in Chapter 11.

That said, there are situations where "wait to 70" can be less than optimal:

1. **The person needs the money**. If someone needs their Social Security benefits to meet living expenses, they should claim them. In these cases, there is usually little tax downside to claiming before age 70, and tax planning necessarily goes to the back burner.

2. **The lower-earning spouse**. There are many reasonable approaches to deciding when a lower-earning spouse should claim benefits. Often, if the lower earner is younger, it may make sense for them to claim when the higher-earning spouse reaches age 70, which can support overall tax planning. Alternatively, it might be optimal for the lower-earning spouse to claim as early as age 62 to maximize projected lifetime benefits based on their own earnings record.

3. **The death of a spouse**. When one spouse dies, the surviving spouse often claims either their own benefit or a survivor benefit prior to age 70. In many cases, not claiming would be equivalent to leaving free money on the table. A surviving spouse should carefully evaluate their options and consider working with a professional to determine the best path forward.

The Taxation of Social Security

Delaying Social Security can reduce the portion of benefits that is subject to income tax.

Depending on household income, anywhere from 0% to 85% of a person's annual Social Security benefits may be included in gross income. The more

other income one has, the more likely it is that up to 85% of those benefits will be taxable.

In Real Life: Curious as to how much Social Security benefits will be taxed? IRS Publication 915, Worksheet 1 can help you calculate the amount of Social Security benefits subject to federal income tax.

Delaying Social Security until age 70 typically means drawing more from taxable assets before 70. Once Social Security begins, retirees often rely less on taxable and traditional retirement accounts to fund living expenses.

For example, say Ed and Betty are both considering claiming Social Security at age 69. Based on their respective earnings records, their combined annual benefits at that age would be approximately $70,000. To meet their $120,000 spending goal, they would need to withdraw around $50,000 from their traditional IRAs.

Alternatively, they could wait until age 70 to claim benefits, increasing their annual Social Security to about $76,000. That would reduce the future amount they need from traditional IRAs to roughly $44,000.

In the first scenario, about **58.4%** of their Social Security ($40,850) would be subject to federal income tax. In the second scenario—claiming at age 70— **50.4%** ($38,300) would be taxable.

Delaying Social Security can be another way to **pay tax when you pay less tax!**

You might be thinking, "But if they wait until 70, don't they have to withdraw the full $120,000 from their traditional IRAs at age 69?" Yes—and we say that's a feature, not a bug. By withdrawing around $50,000 more from their traditional IRAs before RMDs begin, they reduce future required distributions. While that money won't be available for future spending, their annual Social Security benefit increases by 8% by delaying.

Principle 7: Consider Tactical Roth and HSA PUQME Distributions

Imagine a retiree considering their final living expense distribution for the year in November. Prior to that distribution, they may be near the top of the 0% LTCG tax bracket. Triggering additional capital gains could push them into the 15% bracket. In such cases, it might be advantageous to take that final distribution from a Roth IRA or from an HSA PUQME (previously unreimbursed qualified medical expense) distribution.

This type of planning can also apply later in retirement when someone is primarily living off traditional retirement account distributions. For example, perhaps they take their last distribution for the year from a Roth or from HSA PUQME to avoid going from the 12% tax bracket to the 22% tax bracket.

Roth distributions and HSA PUQME can also be used to help maximize Premium Tax Credits. Recall Frank and Dana from earlier: while they paid no federal income tax, under 2026 rules, they would not qualify for a PTC.

What could they do to qualify? Among other options, they could take Roth IRA distributions or HSA PUQME distributions to fund living expenses.

By avoiding capital gains from taxable accounts or ordinary income from traditional retirement accounts, these distributions reduce modified adjusted gross income (MAGI)—potentially helping them qualify for a PTC.

Major Purchases in Retirement

Retired and thinking about buying a new car? A Roth IRA might be an excellent source to fund that purchase!

Significant expenses funded by gains from taxable asset sales or traditional retirement account distributions can create one-time tax hits—such as pushing a retiree into a higher marginal tax bracket. In many cases, a tax-free distribution from a Roth account can be a smart alternative for covering major purchases while managing federal income tax liability and preserving eligibility for PTCs.

Principle 8: Blending Distributions

Some early retirees won't have enough in taxable assets to fully fund living expenses through the month they enroll in Medicare at age 65.

Consider a hypothetical couple, Raj and Priya. They retire at age 58 and plan to use an ACA health insurance plan. At retirement, they've saved approximately three years' worth of living expenses in a taxable brokerage account.

If they simply spend down taxable assets until they run out, they may face three or four years before Medicare enrollment in which they must rely primarily on traditional retirement account distributions. In those years, Raj and Priya might not qualify for any PTCs.

To optimize PTCs over the entire seven-year period before Medicare, Raj and Priya choose a different approach. Each year, they fund a little more than half of their living expenses from traditional retirement accounts, with the rest coming from the sale of taxable assets. This blended strategy results in a more moderate MAGI each year—helping them qualify for PTCs until they enroll in Medicare.

Raj and Priya's alternative would be to use only taxable assets for the first three years—maximizing PTCs in those years—but likely forgoing the credits entirely in the final four years.

Those entering early retirement with insufficient taxable assets to bridge the gap to Medicare should evaluate whether a blended strategy makes sense, and how important PTCs are to their overall financial picture.

Blending doesn't need to be limited to taxable and traditional retirement accounts. Roth IRA and HSA PUQME distributions can also be part of the mix.

Another consideration is COBRA coverage at retirement. Since COBRA often lasts for 18 months, some retirees will have a full calendar year covered under COBRA. That "COBRA year" may present an opportunity: the retiree could draw entirely from traditional retirement accounts during that year—allowing taxable accounts to keep growing—and then shift to taxable accounts or a blended strategy once COBRA ends.

Conclusion

We've outlined eight principles to help guide the drawdown phase.

In the next chapter, we divide the drawdown journey into five distinct time periods—from retirement to death. Using examples, we illustrate key planning concepts and what the federal income tax burden can look like during each phase of retirement.

11 – Moving Through Retirement

In this chapter, we discuss drawdown strategies in retirement.

Everyone's drawdown journey is different. Each retiree brings a unique tax and investment history, so there's no one-size-fits-all "Compelling Three Drawdown Strategy."

That said, there are guiding principles we can turn to with the goal of reducing total lifetime taxation in retirement. We detailed those principles in the previous chapter.

We begin this chapter with a theoretical ideal: the optimal strategy for funding retirement from early retirement through the end of life. From there, we explore the five primary time blocks of an early retiree's retirement, along with the drawdown and tax considerations we generally favor from a somewhat idealized perspective.

Of course, we recognize that many retirees don't fit the "ideal." That's okay. We use the ideal as an anchor—once that anchor is firmly rooted, we can better explore practical approaches for less-than-ideal circumstances.

This chapter also shows our work. We include sample tax returns and tables illustrating the types of income retirees might have and the taxes owed on that income. We hope you study those tables. While somewhat complex, they offer a clear picture of how income is—and isn't—taxed during retirement. There's real power in understanding that!

One helpful approach: read this chapter twice. The first time, focus on the narrative and skip the tables. On your second pass, read both the text and the tables. With the context already in mind, you're more likely to learn from the numbers.

Ideal Funding of Retirement

Before diving into the five phases of retirement in detail, we present an idealized version of how a retiree might fund their retirement.

We approach this from a **"practical ideal"** perspective—a case that's at least somewhat achievable in the real world.

We offer this framework as an anchor. By starting with the ideal, you'll be better equipped to evaluate the variations and exceptions we explore throughout the chapter.

In our "practical ideal" world, just four "rules" guide the funding of retirement:

1. **From retirement through age 65**, live primarily or exclusively on taxable accounts.
2. **From age 66 onward**, live primarily or exclusively on traditional retirement accounts.
3. Claim Social Security at age 70.
4. Use Roth and HSA withdrawals selectively—for example, to increase a Premium Tax Credit (PTC), fund a major purchase, or avoid a spike in marginal federal income tax rate.

That's it! Very few retirees will follow this path exactly—and that's okay!

Some retirees may need to rely on traditional retirement accounts well before age 66. As we demonstrate in Justin and Rachel's example later in this chapter, these retirees can still achieve excellent tax outcomes.

Others may continue living on taxable accounts beyond age 65. As we'll discuss in the Golden Years section, they may unlock additional tax planning opportunities by doing so.

Ideal Compelling Three Drawdown By Age

Below, we review tax tactics for the five main phases of retirement for early retirees. Once again, we approach this from a practical ideal perspective. While many retirees won't be able to follow the ideal exactly, that's okay. In fact, many "suboptimal" tax planning situations in retirement can still lead to very favorable outcomes.

Phase 1: Retirement Through Age 65

The ideal from retirement through the year one turns 65 is to live off taxable accounts.

As you saw with Rich & Pat in Chapter 8, and Frank & Dana in Chapter 10, living off taxable accounts during this phase can often result in paying no federal income tax.

See why we like deducting traditional 401(k) contributions and investing the resulting tax savings in taxable accounts?

Let's take a closer look at Frank and Dana's example. Sure, a tax-free year in early retirement is a great outcome. But suppose they're enrolled in an ACA medical insurance plan and hoping to qualify for a PTC. There are several tactics they can use to reduce their adjusted gross income (AGI).

In their case, their AGI was $97,500—above the $84,600 threshold for a two-person household, which represents 400% of the federal poverty level for PTC eligibility in 48 states (excluding Alaska and Hawaii) in 2026.

Here are a few ways they could reduce their AGI and potentially qualify:

- Take dividends in cash instead of reinvesting them, reducing the need to realize capital gains.
- Use tax-free Roth IRA distributions and/or tax-free HSA distributions of previously unreimbursed qualified medical expenses (PUQME) to fund some living expenses instead of realizing capital gains.
- Choose a Bronze Plan and contribute to an HSA. Under current rules, they could deduct up to $10,750 in 2026 by maxing out their HSA contributions, thereby reducing AGI.

Roth Conversions When Living On Taxable Accounts

The pre-Medicare years can be a good time for Roth conversions—especially when keeping ordinary income at or below the standard deduction. However, it's important to weigh potential downsides, such as reducing or eliminating PTCs or causing long-term capital gains and qualified dividends to be taxed at 15% instead of 0%.

These years tend to be both conservative and opportunistic when it comes to Roth conversions, primarily due to PTC considerations. Keep in mind that the years from age 66 through 69 are particularly favorable for conversions, since PTC eligibility is no longer a concern.

Interestingly, some early retirees may have income so low during the years prior to their 66th birthday year that they need to do some Roth conversions in order to qualify for a PTC.

Implications of the Effectiveness of Taxable Accounts

The examples of Rich & Pat and Frank & Dana show that if you enter retirement with enough taxable assets to fund your living expenses until Medicare enrollment, you can potentially avoid federal income taxes during those years. *Wow!*

This highlights just how powerful taxable accounts can be when built up during the accumulation phase. Why not maximize the tax benefits of traditional 401(k) contributions and invest the resulting tax savings into taxable accounts?

A related takeaway: "tax-free" concepts and products—like "buy, borrow, and die," index universal life (IUL) insurance, and cash value whole life insurance—are often less compelling for early retirees. Why rely on expensive tax-free vehicles when taxable accounts can function as tax-free for several years?

Mega Backdoor Roth Alternative

Some people have access to the Mega Backdoor Roth strategy through their workplace plan and have made significant contributions over the years. We discuss this in Chapter 9.

Although uncommon, at least in theory, an early retiree could enter retirement with $1.7 million in a traditional 401(k) and $1 million in Roth accounts (Roth 401(k) and Roth IRA), largely thanks to the Mega Backdoor Roth. They could roll the Roth 401(k) into a Roth IRA and then use Roth IRA funds to cover living expenses (though basis recovery or qualified distributions).

In this scenario, Roth basis distributions—and eventually qualified Roth IRA distributions—replace taxable account withdrawals during the years the retiree is covered by an ACA medical insurance plan. The retiree could still implement Roth conversions from the traditional account to generate enough income to qualify for a PTC, often keeping those conversions within the standard deduction and avoiding federal income tax altogether.

Roth Conversion Ladders

In some circles, the term "Roth conversion ladder" has become popular. Roughly speaking, the idea is to reach early retirement and use taxable accounts to fund the first five years of living expenses. During those five years, the retiree implements annual Roth conversions intended to fund living expenses five years later. For example, the Year 1 conversion covers Year 6 expenses, the Year 2 conversion covers Year 7 expenses, and so on. Starting in Year 6, the retiree begins living off the five-year-old Roth basis. Depending on how early they retired, Roth conversions may continue well into the "living on Roth" years.

Roth conversion ladders are great in theory. They are much less desirable in practice.

First, these ladders typically require large Roth conversions during years the retiree may be enrolled in an ACA health insurance plan. These conversions can significantly reduce or even eliminate the PTC before Medicare eligibility begins.

Second, Roth conversion ladders require non-strategic conversions. Ideally, Roth conversions should be guided by relevant tax attributes—such as how much room is left within the standard deduction or what future RMDs might look like. But with a ladder, the retiree converts enough to cover living expenses five years down the line. This approach risks overpaying federal (and possibly state) income tax on those Roth conversions.

Third, the alternatives to Roth conversion ladders are excellent. In Chapter 12, we discuss various penalty exceptions, including the Rule of 55, governmental 457(b) distributions, existing Roth basis, and 72(t) payment plans. Later in this chapter, we show just how favorably a married retired couple can be taxed while living on a 72(t) payment plan. Why lock into a rigid Roth conversion ladder when excellent alternatives exist?

For these reasons, we rarely favor Roth conversion ladders for early retirees.

There are Other Paths to Success

Please don't mistake our fondness for necessity. Too often we hear, "Almost all my wealth is tax-deferred, so I can't retire yet."

Yes, we believe the ideal path involves having significant taxable accounts to spend down first in retirement.

That said, the ideal path is not the only excellent option for funding the early years of early retirement.

As we explore in Chapter 12, penalty exceptions make it feasible to rely on traditional retirement account distributions before age 59½.

Below, we present a 72(t) payment plan starting at age 55. You may be surprised at how light the tax burden can be for a married couple living solely on traditional retirement account distributions in their 50s.

While living off taxable accounts before the 66th birthday year is "ideal," living off traditional retirement accounts during those years can also result in excellent tax outcomes.

Phase 2: The Golden Years: Ages 66 through 69

The four birthday years from ages 66 through 69 present a particularly promising window for retirement tax planning. During this period:

- PTC eligibility is no longer a factor,
- Social Security benefits can still be delayed (and therefore increased), and
- Required Minimum Distributions (RMDs) have not yet begun.

In short, the tax planning world is your oyster during these four years!

Keep in mind that for married couples, this window may look different — unless both spouses share the same birth year. In those cases, the opportunities discussed below may still apply, but may be different in scope and scale.

There are two main paths during the Golden Years:

1. **The Roth Conversion Path** – for those still living off taxable accounts.
2. **The Hidden Roth IRA Path** – for those living on traditional retirement accounts.

Golden Years Roth Conversion Path

Recall from the previous chapter the example of Paul and Jessica, both age 66, living on $100,000 from their taxable accounts. Their income level puts them in a great position to complete sizable Roth conversions while paying no federal income tax. As long as they continue living off taxable accounts, they can repeat this strategy each year until they begin collecting Social Security retirement benefits.

Roth Conversion Beyond the Standard Deduction

Should Paul and Jessica consider Roth conversions that create ordinary income beyond the standard deduction?

The answer: absolutely maybe!

The larger their traditional retirement accounts, the more likely it is that Roth conversions will be beneficial. But retirees need to ask additional questions. Most importantly, they should compare the upfront tax cost of Roth conversions to the expected taxes on future RMDs. Chapter 15 explores what future RMD taxation might look like, and Chapter 17 dives deeper into evaluating the desirability of Roth conversions.

One wrinkle: taxable Roth conversions can increase income enough to push some long-term capital gains and qualified dividends from the 0% LTCG tax bracket to the 15% LTCG bracket. In that case, the effective federal income tax rate on the conversion could be as high as 25% or even 27%—due to a combination of the conversion being taxed at 10% or 12%, plus the bump in LTCG income taxation.

Our favorite type of Roth conversion during the Golden Years is the Tailored Taxable Roth Conversion (the "TTRC"). We'll cover that strategy in much more detail in Chapter 17.

Golden Years Hidden Roth IRA Path

If a retiree has run out of taxable accounts by January 1st of their 66th birthday year, it's usually time to begin drawing from traditional retirement accounts.

Oh no! That's all taxable, right? Not exactly.

Generally speaking, if the retiree has no basis in their traditional retirement accounts, the distributions are fully taxable. However, a significant portion of those distributions can be offset by the standard deduction and the senior deduction—meaning they are not subject to federal income tax. Sean coined a term for this phenomenon: the **Hidden Roth IRA**.

If you receive a retirement account distribution and pay no federal income tax on it, isn't it a Roth IRA distribution? Technically, no—it came from a traditional IRA or 401(k). But when that distribution ends up being tax-free, it behaves a lot like a Roth IRA. Hence, the name Hidden Roth IRA.

The Hidden Roth IRA disguises itself as a future taxable amount inside a traditional retirement account. But since you're reading this book, you've pulled off the mask!

Let's look at an example. Vinny and Mona Lisa turn 66 in 2025. They've exhausted their taxable accounts and are now living solely on traditional retirement accounts. During their working years, they deducted traditional 401(k) contributions at a 24% marginal federal tax rate. In 2025, they withdraw $140,000 from traditional IRAs (with no basis) and receive $2,500 in interest from their savings account.

Here's what Vinny and Mona Lisa's federal income tax return looks like:

Item	Amount
Traditional IRA Withdrawals	$140,000
Interest Income	$2,500
Adjusted Gross Income	$142,500
Standard Deduction	$31,500
Additional Standard Deduction for Seniors	$3,200
Senior Deduction	$12,000
Total Deductions	$46,700
Taxable Income	$95,800
Federal Income Tax	**$11,019**
Overall Effective Tax Rate on Income	7.73%
Effective Income Tax Rate for IRA Distributions	7.87%
Rate Assigning All Tax to IRA Distributions	7.87%

Here's how their federal income tax breaks down:

Amount Received	Type of Income	Deducted At	Taxed At	Federal Income Tax	Assessment
$2,500	Interest Income Against Deduction	N/A	0%	$0	
$44,200	IRA Distribution Against Deduction	24%	0%	$0	**This is the Hidden Roth IRA.**
$23,850	IRA Distribution Against 10% Bracket	24%	10%	$2,385	Vinny and Mona Lisa defeat the IRS.
$71,950	IRA Distribution Against 12% Bracket	24%	12%	$8,634	Vinny and Mona Lisa defeat the IRS.
Total $142,500			**Effective Rate 7.73%**	**Total $11,019**	

A few observations about Vinny and Mona Lisa's tax situation:

First, Vinny and Mona Lisa pay no federal income tax on nearly a third of their $140,000 "taxable" traditional IRA distribution. The Hidden Roth IRA can be surprisingly large.

Second, take note of the size of their 2025 Hidden Roth IRA: $44,200! And they can replicate this each year at ages 67, 68, and 69.

Third, notice what reduces the size of the Hidden Roth IRA: interest income — or, more broadly, any other form of ordinary income. This is one of the main reasons we favor keeping ordinary income low in retirement. Higher ordinary income reduces opportunities like the Hidden Roth IRA.

This also supports our general preference for delaying Social Security until age 70. Vinny and Mona Lisa benefit from both spouses delaying, which preserves room for large Hidden Roth IRA distributions. In their case, the Hidden Roth IRA is a compelling argument for both spouses to wait until age 70 to claim benefits.

Fourth, Vinny and Mona Lisa illustrate why we generally prefer reviewing the granular tax results in retirement rather than statistics. Statistics hide the Hidden Roth IRA, while the tax table reveals it clearly.

Roth Conversions When Using the Hidden Roth IRA

For those utilizing the Hidden Roth IRA path during the Golden Years, Roth conversions are generally not a planning consideration. There are two reasons for this.

First, using traditional retirement account distributions to fund living expenses during the Golden Years helps reduce future RMDs, significantly reducing any need for Roth conversions.

Second, any Roth conversions would be stacked on top of the income already generated from the normal distributions to fund the retiree's living expenses — making them more likely to be taxed at higher federal income tax rates.

The Golden Age of the Golden Years: The New Senior Deduction and the New Charitable Deduction for Non-Itemizers

The 2025 One Big Beautiful Bill made the Golden Years (ages 66 through 69) even more golden by introducing a $6,000 per person senior deduction. Thanks to this new provision, Vinny and Mona Lisa's Hidden Roth IRA was $12,000 larger.

Keeping income low helps maximize the benefit of the senior deduction. Our favorite technique for doing so? Delaying Social Security until age 70. This allows more traditional retirement account withdrawals to be sheltered by the senior deduction as a Hidden Roth IRA—while also increasing future Social Security benefits.

For those on the Roth Conversion Path during the Golden Years, the senior deduction increases the amount of Roth conversions that can be completed tax-free.

And it gets even better starting in 2026: taxpayers taking the standard deduction will also be able to deduct $1,000 per person in cash charitable contributions. Many financially successful retirees who aren't particularly charitably inclined still give $1,000 per year in cash to charities, making this a practical benefit for many.

From 2026 through 2028, a married couple in their Golden Years can benefit from:

- $31,500 standard deduction (2025 figure, indexed for inflation)
- $3,200 additional standard deduction (2025 figure, indexed for inflation)
- $2,000 charitable deduction ($1,000 per person, non-itemized, not indexed for inflation)
- $12,000 senior deduction (not indexed for inflation)

Before we began writing this book in early 2025, the relevant Golden Years deduction total for a married couple in 2025 was $33,200. After the One Big Beautiful Bill, the relevant deduction for 2026 will be at least $48,700—and likely more, as two of the components are indexed for inflation!

Could the senior deduction go away in 2029? Sure—there's a risk. As we explain in Chapter 20, we believe that risk is small. But even if it disappears, a married couple would still have access to:

- $31,500 standard deduction
- $3,200 additional standard deduction
- $2,000 charitable deduction

And most of that will continue to be adjusted for inflation.

This is the Golden Age of the Golden Years!

Do the Golden Years Include the 65th and 70th Birthday Years?

The tax laws give those of us born in January and in December a fifth full Golden Year. Those born in January begin Medicare coverage on January 1 of their 65th birthday year. As a result, the PTC is irrelevant for that year.

The mirror image is for those born in December. They get the 70th birthday year as a full Golden Year, since they can delay Social Security until 70 and thus will get their first Social Security payment in January of the year they turn 71.

Everyone else—those born in months other than January or December—receives two partial additional Golden Years instead. For example, if you're born in February or November, one of those partial years will be 11 months long—making it nearly as beneficial as a full Golden Year.

Phase 3: Age 70 to the Start of RMDs

By age 70, most readers will have started receiving Social Security benefits. At this point, both the Hidden Roth IRA strategy and the opportunity for tax-free Roth conversions against the combined standard and senior deduction are typically off the table. But there's still meaningful planning to be done, and the tax picture can remain quite favorable—even for retirees with little or no taxable account assets remaining.

Let's look at an example:

Mike and Christine are both 71 in 2025. They want to live on $12,000 per month in gross income, through a combination of traditional retirement account withdrawals and Social Security. They receive $80,000 in annual Social Security benefits. They also give $1,000 per month to their church using qualified charitable distributions (QCDs). Their savings account generates $2,000 in interest income in 2025.

During their working years, Mike and Christine made traditional 401(k) contributions at a 24% marginal federal tax rate.

Here's what their 2025 federal income tax return looks like:

Item	Amount
Traditional IRA Withdrawals	$64,000
Interest Income	$2,000
Taxable Social Security Income	$58,700
Adjusted Gross Income	$124,700
Standard Deduction	$31,500
Additional Standard Deduction for Seniors	$3,200
Senior Deduction	$12,000
Total Deductions	$46,700
Taxable Income	$78,000
Federal Income Tax	**$8,884**
Overall Effective Tax Rate on Income	5.62%
Effective Income Tax Rate for IRA Distributions	9.85%
Rate Assigning All Tax to IRA Distributions	11.69%

Here's how Mike and Christine's income is taxed:

Amount Received	Type of Income	Deducted At	Taxed At	Federal Income Tax	Assessment
$21,300	Excluded Social Security	N/A	0%	$0	
$12,000	Excluded QCD	24%	0%	$0	Mike and Christine defeat the IRS
$46,700	Taxable Social Security Against Deduction	N/A	0%	$0	
$12,000	Taxable Social Security Against 10% Bracket	N/A	10%	$1,200	Con 2
$2,000	Interest Income Against 10% Bracket	N/A	10%	$200	Con 5
$9,850	Traditional IRA Distribution Against 10% Bracket	24%	10%	$986	Mike and Christine defeat the IRS
$54,150	Traditional IRA Distribution Against 12% Bracket	24%	12%	$6,498	Mike and Christine defeat the IRS
Total $158,000			Effective Rate 5.62%	Total $8,884	

After paying federal income taxes, Mike and Christine are living on over $11,000 per month. Despite relying primarily on "taxable" sources of income, they're doing very well.

For a couple receiving $158,000 from primarily taxable sources—which some might say is inefficient—they end up paying surprisingly little in federal income tax.

Of their Social Security benefits, 26.6% (**$21,300**) is excluded from income. By comparison, many affluent retirees have only 15% of their Social Security excluded. What is the planning tactic that increases Mike and Christine's tax-free Social Security portion? Their QCD. If that **$12,000** had been distributed as ordinary income instead, 85% of their Social Security would have been taxable.

If you're planning to give to charity in your 70s and beyond, why not do it with a QCD? You received a tax deduction when contributing to the traditional retirement account, and now, in retirement, that same money can be bailed out of a traditional IRA tax-free. Further, QCDs reduce future RMDs. Great planning!

Finally, Mike and Christine benefit from a **$46,700** deduction, made up of the standard deduction ($31,500), the additional senior deduction ($3,200), and the new senior deduction ($12,000).

Altogether, this affluent couple paid 0% federal income tax on **$80,000** of their $158,000 gross income!

Why do we fear taxes in retirement? Mike and Christine certainly don't!

It's interesting to see the drawbacks of using traditional retirement accounts play out in Mike and Christine's situation. Had all of their withdrawals come from Roth accounts instead of traditional ones, they would have paid no federal income tax in 2025.

That said, because their traditional IRA withdrawals were taxed in the 10% and 12% brackets, they still achieved favorable tax rate arbitrage. In a vacuum, deducting contributions at a 24% marginal rate during their working years and later withdrawing at 10% or 12% is better than Roth treatment. But that is not the end of the analysis.

Using traditional instead of Roth retirement accounts caused Mike and Christine to incur some tax on both their interest income (Con 5 from Chapter 7) and their Social Security income (Con 2 from Chapter 7) in 2025.

- Con 5 (taxation of interest income in retirement) cost them just $200.
- Con 2 (partial taxation of Social Security) cost them just $1,200.

Together, these drawbacks amount to a 0.89% nuisance tax on their $158,000 of gross income. For this affluent couple, these relatively minor drawbacks do not come close to outweighing the 24 cents-on-the-dollar tax benefit they received for traditional retirement account contributions during their working years.

Extra Credit: Mike and Christine are squarely in the so-called Tax Torpedo. The last dollars they withdrew from their traditional IRAs are taxed at 12% and also cause 85 additional cents per dollar of Social Security income to be taxed at the 12% bracket. That creates an effective 22.2% marginal tax rate on that dollar.

But even within the Tax Torpedo, their overall effective federal tax rate is just 5.62%. This illustrates an important point: while the Tax Torpedo is relevant for marginal decisions (such as whether to add a Roth conversion), it's not significant enough to derail overall tax and retirement planning.

This situation highlights the usefulness of the "Overall Effective Tax Rate on Income" statistic. Paying less than six cents on the dollar of gross income to the IRS is the outcome they want to maintain from a financial planning perspective.

Additional Tactics

We saw the power of QCDs in Christine and Mike's example. They provide a tax-free way to access traditional retirement accounts, reduce future RMDs, and potentially lower the amount of Social Security income subject to income tax.

Other tactics worth considering include tactical Roth withdrawals and HSA PUQME withdrawals. These can help lower taxable income, reduce the amount of Social Security subject to taxation, and help retirees stay within a lower marginal federal income tax bracket.

Another useful tactic is using HSA funds to pay Medicare Part B and Part D premiums, as well as other current medical expenses.

Roth Conversions

The years between age 70 and the start of RMDs are typically not ideal for Roth conversions—though limited opportunities may exist. If a retiree is still covering living expenses beyond Social Security through taxable accounts, there might be some room for tax-efficient Roth conversions.

However, in most cases, by this phase, retirees have exhausted their taxable accounts and are relying on traditional retirement distributions. In such situations, Roth conversions are often a nonstarter because of the additional taxable income they generate.

Phase 4: RMD Years

For those born in 1960 or later, RMDs begin in the year they turn 75.

But just how bad are RMDs? In Chapter 15, we share two examples—including one that's quite extreme. In this chapter, we start with a more typical case: an affluent retired couple living on sizable traditional retirement accounts and Social Security.

Ted and Elaine turn 79 in 2025. They receive $80,000 in Social Security and hold $2.2 million in traditional IRAs. During their working years, they made traditional 401(k) contributions at a 24% marginal federal income tax rate. Their 2025 RMD is $104,265, and they also receive $2,000 in interest income.

Here's what their 2025 federal income tax return looks like:

Item	Amount
RMDs	$104,265
Interest Income	$2,000
Taxable Social Security Income	$68,000
Adjusted Gross Income	$174,265
Standard Deduction	$31,500
Additional Standard Deduction for Seniors	$3,200
Senior Deduction	$9,088
Total Deductions	$43,788
Taxable Income	$130,477
Federal Income Tax	**$18,533**
Overall Effective Tax Rate on Income	9.95%
Effective Income Tax Rate for IRA Distributions	15.22%
Rate Assigning All Tax to IRA Distributions	17.77%

Here's how their federal income tax breaks down:

Amount Received	Type of Income	Deducted At	Taxed At	Federal Income Tax	Assessment
$12,000	Excluded Social Security	N/A	0%	$0	
$43,788	Taxable Social Security Against Deduction	N/A	0%	$0	
$23,850	Taxable Social Security Against 10% Bracket	N/A	10%	$2,385	Con 2
$362	Taxable Social Security Against 12% Bracket	N/A	12%	$43	Con 2
$2,000	Interest Income Against 12% Bracket	N/A	12%	$240	Con 5
$70,738	RMD Against 12% Bracket	24%	12%	$8,489	Ted and Elaine defeat the IRS
$33,527	RMD Against 22% Bracket	24%	22%	$7,376	Ted and Elaine defeat the IRS
Total $186,285			**Effective Rate 9.95%**	**Total $18,533**	

Did you notice? For all $104,265 of RMDs, Ted and Elaine "defeat the IRS." Every dollar was taxed at a lower rate than the 24% deduction they received during their working years. RMDs complete the positive tax rate arbitrage they signed up for when making traditional 401(k) contributions.

As Larry David would say on *Curb Your Enthusiasm*—that's "pretty, pretty, pretty, pretty good."

Why do we fear RMDs when an affluent retired couple can take over $100,000 in RMDs and still come out ahead on every dollar?

What to do With An Unneeded RMD

With Social Security benefits coming in—and a natural decline in spending on things like travel, large purchases, and extreme sports—some retirees may find they don't need to spend all of their RMD.

In those cases, we generally favor investing the unspent RMD in a taxable brokerage account, following the asset location principles discussed in Chapter 18. If the retiree wants exposure to domestic equities, a taxable account is often an ideal place to hold them. This helps keep taxable income low and ensures most dividends are taxed at favorable long-term capital gains rates.

Other Tactics

One of our favorite RMD-year tactics is the QCD, which can directly reduce the taxable portion of an RMD.

Additional strategies may be helpful on the margins—typically when a retiree wants to spend more than their RMD. These include:

- Roth IRA distributions
- HSA PUQME distributions
- Using an HSA to pay Medicare Part B and Part D premiums, as well as other current medical expenses

Roth Conversions

Once RMDs begin, Roth conversions rarely make sense. That's because Roth conversion income is stacked on top of Social Security, RMDs, and other income—making the Roth conversion less attractive.

For those still interested in pursuing Roth conversions during an RMD year, two important rules apply:

1. The first dollars withdrawn from a traditional retirement account during the year are deemed to satisfy the RMD.
2. RMDs cannot be converted to a Roth account.

To avoid an excess contribution to a Roth account, the retiree must fully satisfy their RMD—either through regular distributions, QCDs, or both—before initiating a Roth conversion.

Phase 5: Widow(er)'s Years

People worry about RMDs after the first spouse has died. Let's return to Ted and Elaine. Elaine is now an 82-year-old widow with a $2.4 million traditional IRA. She receives $48,000 in Social Security benefits and $2,000 in interest income.

Let's look at those numbers on Elaine's federal income tax return (using 2025 numbers):

Item	Amount
RMDs	$129,730
Interest Income	$2,000
Taxable Social Security Income	$40,800
Adjusted Gross Income	$172,530
Standard Deduction	$15,750
Additional Standard Deduction for Seniors	$2,000
Senior Deduction	$148
Total Deductions	$17,898
Taxable Income	$154,632
Federal Income Tax	**$29,960**
IRMAA (Estimated)	**$4,300**
Overall Effective Tax Rate on Income	19.06%
Effective Income Tax Rate for IRA Distributions	20.97%
Rate Assigning All Tax to IRA Distributions	26.41%

Here's how her federal income tax breaks down:

Amount Received	Type of Income	Deducted At	Taxed At	Federal Income Tax	Assessment
$7,200	Excluded Social Security	N/A	0%	$0	
$17,898	Taxable Social Security Against Deduction	N/A	0%	$0	
$11,925	Taxable Social Security Against 10% Bracket	N/A	10%	$1,193	Con 2
$10,977	Taxable Social Security Against 12% Bracket	N/A	12%	$1,317	Con 2
$2,000	Interest Income Against 12% Bracket	N/A	12%	$240	Con 5
$23,573	RMD Against 12% Bracket	24%	12%	$2,829	Elaine defeats the IRS
$54,875	RMD Against 22% Bracket	24%	22%	$12,073	Elaine defeats the IRS
$51,282	RMD Against 24% Bracket	24%	24%	$12,308	Elaine and the IRS tie
Total $179,730			Effective Rate 16.67%	Total $29,960	

Here we are, right in the heart of the so-called Widow's Tax Trap. There's plenty to say about Elaine's tax results—even the argument that she might have fared better had she and Ted prioritized Roth contributions at work over traditional ones.

But that analysis relies on a single statistic for a single stage of retirement: her estimated widowhood Rate Assigning All Tax to IRA Distributions of 26.41%. It overlooks the broader arc of Elaine and Ted's lifetime tax planning.

- During their working years, they contributed to traditional 401(k)s to receive an immediate 24-cents-on-the dollar benefit.
- If they followed the Compelling Three, they could have spent the early years of retirement with no federal income tax by living off taxable accounts.
- After depleting their taxable accounts, Ted and Elaine—as affluent retirees—could have maintained an effective annual federal tax rate below 10% before RMDs (see Mike and Christine's example for just how lightly taxed they might have been) and around 10% even with RMDs.
- Until Elaine's widowhood, it's a clear win for prioritizing traditional retirement account contributions. In widowhood, it's a close call. Despite all the fears about the Widow's Tax Trap, Elaine doesn't experience negative income tax rate arbitrage—not even on a penny of an RMD of nearly $130,000! Ted and Elaine pay tax when they pay less tax! That's pretty good planning.

In Elaine's case, fears about the Widow's Tax Trap amount to the slightest potential tax inefficiencies after decades of winning the tax planning game.

Other Tactics

QCDs can be especially beneficial for a widow. Elaine would save 24 cents on the dollar for any QCDs she makes. If she's charitably inclined, QCDs are the clear choice.

As discussed earlier, other tactics—such as Roth IRA distributions and HSA distributions—can still be helpful on the margins, particularly if Elaine wants to spend more than her RMD.

It's difficult to recommend that Elaine complete a Roth conversion taxed at 24% this year just to reduce next year's RMD—also taxed at 24%.

Early Retirement 72(t) Drawdown Example

We've presented examples of retirees who followed the Compelling Three. But not everyone follows it perfectly.

Take Justin and Rachel, for example. They didn't implement the Compelling Three—more like the **Compelling 1.2**.

They retired in January of the year they each turned 53 with:

- $140,000 in brokerage accounts (with $70,000 of built-in gains)
- $40,000 in a savings account
- Approximately $2 million in traditional 401(k)s and IRAs
- No Roth accounts

Their plan is to live off taxable accounts for the first two years of retirement. After that, they'll start annual distributions from their traditional retirement accounts with a 72(t) payment plan. In other words, they'll spend briefly from taxable assets (the "0.2") before relying almost entirely on traditional retirement accounts (the "1") for the rest of retirement. Without the full Compelling Three, Justin and Rachel have somewhat limited flexibility.

With that said, how much federal income tax might they pay during those first two years, living on $70,000 annually from taxable assets—half of which ($35,000) is long-term capital gains?

You should know the answer by now: None! Zip! Zilch! Nada!

In fact, they may even add some tax-free Roth conversions to the mix, since they'll likely have plenty of room under the standard deduction before the conversions are considered.

Starting the year they turn 55, Justin and Rachel start one or more 72(t) payment plans to generate $80,000 in distributions from traditional IRAs. For more on setting up a 72(t) payment plan, see Chapter 12.

Oh no, some might think—$80,000 of fully taxable income in early retirement? Isn't that wildly inefficient?

Since you've been reading this book, you know that's not the case. But let's demonstrate it.

Here's what Justin and Rachel's tax return looks like when living on an $80,000 72(t) payment plan (using 2025 numbers):

Item	Amount
Interest Income	$3,600
72(t) Payment	$80,000
Adjusted Gross Income	$83,600
Standard Deduction	$31,500
Taxable Income	$52,100
Federal Income Tax	**$5,775**
Overall Effective Tax Rate on Income	6.91%
Effective Income Tax Rate for IRA Distributions	7.22%
Rate Assigning All Tax to IRA Distributions	7.22%

Here's how their federal income tax breaks down, assuming they deducted traditional 401(k) contributions at a 24% marginal federal income tax rate during their working years:

Amount Received	Type of Income	Deducted At	Taxed At	Federal Income Tax	Assessment
$3,600	Interest Income Against Standard Deduction	N/A	0%	$0	
$27,900	72(t) Payment Against Standard Deduction	24%	0%	$0	**Justin and Rachel have a $27,900 Hidden Roth IRA!**
$23,850	72(t) Payment Against 10% Bracket	24%	10%	$2,385	Justin and Rachel defeat the IRS
$28,250	72(t) Payment Against 12% Bracket	24%	12%	$3,390	Justin and Rachel defeat the IRS
Total $83,600			**Effective Rate 6.91%**	**Total $5,775**	

We have another case where roughly a third of a "taxable" traditional retirement account distribution is free from federal income tax!

Justin and Rachel enjoy the benefits of the Hidden Roth IRA years before the Golden Years begin.

They're locked into the 72(t) payment plan for five years (to age 60), but their plan is to continue withdrawing at a similar rate since nearly all of their assets are in traditional retirement accounts—and Social Security isn't available at age 60.

They have a pretty good plan:

- Retire at 53
- Enjoy two years of tax-free income
- Pay an effective tax rate of around 7% from 55 to 65
- Pay an even lower effective tax rate at 66+ if the senior deduction (enacted in 2025) is extended
- Benefit from the Hidden Roth IRA for 15 years before Social Security

Sure, they'll start collecting Social Security at 70. But as we saw with Mike and Christine, those years can also be tax-efficient. And thanks to two decades of spending down traditional accounts before age 75, Rachel and Justin's RMDs should be very manageable.

We share this example to show how an early retiree—who didn't follow the full Compelling Three—can still achieve very favorable tax results, **primarily by using traditional retirement contributions at work.**

Bonus Note: If Justin and Rachel had access to the Rule of 55 or a governmental 457(b), they could achieve similar tax outcomes with even greater flexibility—without the need for a 72(t) payment plan.

Evaluating the Compelling Three Versus a Roth-Centric Approach

Pay tax when you pay less tax!

We strongly advocate prioritizing traditional retirement account contributions at work. Some commentators, however, recommend a Roth-centric approach—favoring Roth contributions during the working years.

We already know that during the accumulation phase, our preferred approach wins. But how does it hold up in retirement compared to a Roth-centric strategy?

We've seen that prior to enrolling in Medicare, retirees who followed the Compelling Three can often enjoy several years of federal income tax-free living by drawing down taxable accounts. In this phase, both approaches—ours and the Roth-centric one—can lead to similar results, as long as the retiree has sufficient taxable assets.

However, if a retiree enters early retirement with no traditional retirement account balances, they may struggle to generate enough income to qualify for the PTC. Additionally, tax savings from traditional retirement account contributions help build up taxable accounts to efficiently fund living expenses during the PTC years. These two factors tip the scale in favor of our approach, as it better positions pre-Medicare retirees for financial success.

From there, we acknowledge that someone living exclusively on Roth accounts during the Golden Years may pay zero federal income tax—and the Compelling Three doesn't necessarily set that up. But it can set up years of tax-free Roth conversions or Hidden Roth IRA withdrawals.

A Roth-centric approach risks wasting large portions of the annual standard deduction and the senior deduction in retirement. Our favored approach seeks to make the most of these tax rules in retirees' favor.

Our favored approach also achieves something a Roth-centric strategy can't: tax rate arbitrage. Even for retirees relying entirely on traditional retirement accounts during the Golden Years, a sub-10% effective federal tax rate is often achievable.

We've seen even very affluent retirees in their 70s have excellent tax outcomes in retirement when traditional 401(k) contributions were the primary driver of their retirement account contribution strategy. Why would someone pass up traditional 401(k) deductions at 24% or 32% to avoid tax rates on traditional retirement account distributions that can be 12% or 22% in many cases?

It comes back to our Central Thesis: Most Americans—especially early retirees—will pay a lower effective tax rate in retirement than the marginal tax rate at which they deduct traditional 401(k) contributions.

Our preferred approach is to pay tax when you pay less tax.

We're okay paying some tax in retirement, because those years tend to be more lightly taxed. We favor shifting the tax burden from the highest-tax years (accumulation) to the lowest-tax years (retirement).

When would you prefer to pay taxes?

12 – Your Money Isn't Locked Up: The 10% Additional Tax "Penalty"

Many people worry about retiring before age 59½. That's not a magical age, but it is one made especially important by our tax laws—specifically, Internal Revenue Code Section 72(t)(2)(A)(i).

Retirement account distributions made before age 59½ may be subject to the 10% early withdrawal penalty, which the Internal Revenue Code refers to as an "additional tax."

For simplicity, we'll refer to this as the **10% penalty** throughout the rest of the chapter.

It sounds intimidating at first, but as it turns out, the 10% penalty is not much of an obstacle to retiring early.

Before we explore the tactics for avoiding the 10% penalty, **we must acknowledge the role of taxable accounts in early retirement.** Ideally, early retirees begin by living primarily off taxable accounts, as discussed in detail in Chapter 10. One key advantage of using taxable accounts to fund early retirement is that the 10% penalty doesn't apply—regardless of the owner's age.

Below, we outline several tactics that help avoid the 10% penalty for those under age 59½. These are presented in a general order of preference, considering a range of factors. Some will simply not apply to certain readers. Others may choose to use a combination of these tactics to fund retirement prior to age 59½.

This chapter focuses on the penalty exceptions most relevant from a retirement planning perspective, though there are others that can be helpful in specific circumstances. The IRS publishes a full list of penalty exceptions at: https://www.irs.gov/retirement-plans/plan-participant-employee/retirement-topics-exceptions-to-tax-on-early-distributions.

Inherited Retirement Accounts

This is our favorite exception to the 10% penalty: inherited retirement accounts are never subject to the 10% penalty, regardless of the beneficiary's age.

In most cases today, beneficiaries are required to spend these accounts anyway due to the 10-year rule. That is, by the end of the 10th full year following the original account owner's death, the beneficiary must fully deplete the inherited retirement account. While there are exceptions to this rule, they rarely apply in common scenarios—such as an early retiree inheriting from an elderly parent.

In most cases, an early retiree will want to drain an inherited traditional retirement account gradually over the ten-year window. Even setting aside the need to fund living expenses, delaying distributions can be problematic. If the beneficiary lets the account grow untouched (or only takes any required minimum distributions), they could face a tax bomb in year 10—when the entire, potentially much larger, balance must be withdrawn and taxed in a single year.

This consideration alone makes living off inherited traditional retirement accounts in early retirement quite appealing. And the fact that these accounts are never subject to the 10% penalty makes them even more attractive as an early retirement funding vehicle.

Roth Inherited Retirement Accounts

Roth inherited retirement accounts, like their traditional counterparts, are usually subject to the 10-year rule when inherited from an elderly parent during early retirement.

There are two key differences when using inherited Roth accounts from a planning perspective. First, Roth accounts do not create taxable income for the beneficiary—except in the rarest of circumstances, which aren't worth exploring here. Second, there's no need to spread distributions across multiple tax years, since there's no income tax to avoid. So, why not keep the inherited Roth account growing tax-free for the full 10 years and then take a lump-sum distribution in the 10th year?

That said, an inherited Roth account may also be one of the easiest ways to fund years of early retirement. If that's the case, there's no shame in drawing it down before the tenth year after the original owner's death.

In fact, the best path might involve living off inherited Roth IRA distributions while simultaneously doing Roth conversions from the early retiree's own traditional retirement accounts. This creates taxable income to (1) make use of what would otherwise be unused standard deductions and (2) generate the gross income needed to qualify for a Premium Tax Credit (PTC).

Surviving Spouses and Inherited Retirement Accounts

Spouses inheriting retirement accounts before age 59½ have an important decision to make: roll the inherited account into their own IRA or maintain it—as an inherited IRA—until at least age 59½.

Why might a surviving spouse not roll the account into their own IRA right away? The 10% penalty. Most younger surviving spouses can maintain the account as an inherited IRA without being subject to required minimum distributions (RMDs) and with the ability to take flexible distributions without the 10% penalty.

Consider this example: Julia's husband, Chuck, dies when Julia is 52 and already retired. Chuck had not yet reached his required beginning date for RMDs. Julia should evaluate her needs: Will she need to tap into the inherited IRA before turning 59½ to support her living expenses, or are her taxable assets sufficient to bridge the gap?

If Julia suspects her taxable assets may not last through age 59½, she may want to maintain Chuck's traditional IRA as an inherited IRA. This allows her to take penalty-free distributions before 59½. Then, once she reaches that age, she can roll the inherited IRA into her own IRA for simplicity.

By contrast, if she were to immediately roll the inherited IRA into her own traditional IRA, any distributions taken before age 59½ would be subject to the 10% penalty.

If the inherited account is a Roth IRA, there's less downside to rolling it into her own Roth IRA. Doing so would combine Chuck's basis with her own. Since Roth IRA basis can be withdrawn tax- and penalty-free at any age, Julia likely wouldn't face any issues unless she expects to withdraw earnings (above basis) before turning 59½. In that case, she should consider keeping the account as an inherited Roth IRA until she reaches 59½. This would allow her to access Roth earnings tax- and penalty-free, assuming at least five tax years have passed since Chuck first opened and funded a Roth IRA.

Rule of 55 Distributions

The Rule of 55 is one of the most readily available exceptions to the 10% penalty—but it comes with some important nuances.

This exception applies to distributions from the 401(k) or other qualified plan of the employer you separate from on or after January 1 of the year you turn age 55. It does not apply to IRAs or to qualified plans from employers you left before the year you turned 55. If you plan to use the Rule of 55, avoid rolling the account into a traditional IRA before age 59½—since IRA distributions don't qualify for this exception.

Note: For certain qualified public safety employees, this exception may apply at age 50 instead of 55. Thank you for your service!

Pros of the Rule of 55 include significant flexibility. The owner can withdraw varying amounts from year to year—for example, $20,000 one year, $40,000 the next, and $25,000 the year after.

But there are some cons of the Rule of 55 to keep in mind:

1. The employer's plan is not required to allow partial distributions before age 59½, as discussed in Chapter 5.

2. While using the Rule of 55, the investments are limited to the options available within that specific employer's plan.

3. Distributions are subject to 20% mandatory federal income tax withholding, regardless of age. In practice, the owner should be attentive to filing their annual income tax return early to receive a likely refund from over-withholding. **Most early retirees using the Rule of 55 will have a much lower effective tax rate than 20%**, often resulting in a refund.

Additionally, most early retirees using this rule will likely have simple tax returns—typically reporting a Form 1099-R for the Rule of 55 distribution, possibly a 1099-R for any Roth conversions, and perhaps a 1099-INT for a small amount of interest income from bank accounts.

As a practical matter, the 20% withholding rule isn't much of a barrier to using the Rule of 55. It's simply a minor cash flow issue. The mandatory withholding may require larger gross distributions to meet net living expense needs, but the excess withholding is often returned as a tax refund early the following year.

Rule of 55 Example

Praveen celebrates his 55th birthday on July 9, 2025. He retired from Acme Industries on February 1, 2025, and chose to leave his Acme 401(k) in place. On May 18, 2025, Praveen takes a $20,000 partial distribution from the Acme 401(k).

Because Praveen separated from service on or after January 1 of the year he turned 55—and the distribution was taken after his separation from that employer's plan—it qualifies for the Rule of 55 exception. The distribution is fully taxable, but Praveen does not owe the 10% early withdrawal penalty.

Rule of 55 Case Study

Trish turned 56 in October 2024. She lives in Florida. In November 2024, she retired from DEF, Inc. She owns her home outright and has a small checking account, a traditional IRA, a DEF traditional 401(k), and an emergency fund in a savings account. She plans to spend $80,000 per year (after tax) and use the Rule of 55 to fund her early retirement starting in 2025.

To receive $80,000 after the mandatory 20% federal income tax withholding, Trish withdraws $100,000 from her DEF 401(k) in 2025. She calculates this amount by dividing her $80,000 net distribution need by 80% (the percentage of her distribution she actually receives after withholding).

In early 2026, Trish receives a Form 1099-INT from her bank showing $2,000 of interest income and a Form 1099-R from the DEF 401(k) showing $100,000 in distributions and $20,000 withheld for federal income tax. These two forms provide the key information she needs to file her 2025 federal income tax return.

Let's review how much federal income tax Trish owes:

Income	Rate	Tax
$15,750	0% (Standard Deduction)	$0
$11,925	10%	$1,192.50
$36,550	12%	$4,386
$37,775	22%	$8,310.50
Total **$102,000**	**Effective Rate** **13.62%**	**Total** **$13,889**

By this estimate, her federal income tax liability for 2025 is $13,889. Since $20,000 was withheld from her traditional 401(k) distribution, Trish will receive a $6,111 federal tax refund in early 2026.

Assuming she wants to spend $82,000 (after tax) in 2026, she can factor in the $6,111 refund from 2025. That means she only needs to receive $75,889 ($82,000 less the $6,111 federal income tax refund) from her DEF 401(k) in 2026 to meet her spending needs. To calculate the gross amount to withdraw, she divides $75,889 by 80%, resulting in a gross distribution of $94,861.25—using the Rule of 55 again in 2026.

These detailed calculations aren't required, but they help illustrate how Trish can determine her gross distribution amount based on her desired spending and the impact of 20% mandatory federal tax withholding. Note: If Trish lived in a state with income tax, additional withholding could affect these percentages.

Governmental 457(b) Distributions

Before we begin, note that there are also "nongovernmental" 457(b) plans. These are deferred compensation plans that cannot be rolled over into other retirement accounts. While they have their uses, they often require inflexible payout structures, which limit their appeal from a retirement planning perspective.

In contrast, governmental 457(b) plans are much more attractive. These accounts can be rolled over into a traditional IRA—but most early retirees will want to wait until they turn age 59½ to do so.

Distributions from traditional governmental 457(b) plans are taxable but are never subject to the 10% early withdrawal penalty. From a planning perspective, a governmental 457(b) functions much like the Rule of 55 exception—but with two major advantages:

1. No separation from service requirement, and
2. No age requirement for penalty-free access.

In many cases, employees eligible to contribute to a governmental 457(b) also have access to a 403(b) plan. If maximizing both plans isn't feasible each year, it may make sense to prioritize contributions to the 457(b)—after securing any available employer match in the 403(b). Why? Because 403(b) distributions taken before age 59½ are generally subject to the 10% penalty, while governmental 457(b) distributions are not.

Extra Credit: *You can roll a traditional IRA, 401(k), or other qualified plan into a governmental 457(b)—if the plan allows it—but doing so does not provide a 10% penalty advantage. Rolled-in amounts must be kept in a separate account within the plan. Distributions from that portion of the account are subject to the 10% penalty unless another exception applies.*

Roth Basis

The easiest way to take a tax-free Roth distribution before age 59½ is to withdraw from a Roth IRA.

People often worry about tapping their Roth IRAs before reaching the "magic birthday" of 59½. But the rules for these "early" distributions are surprisingly favorable to taxpayers.

Let's take Ernie as an example. He turns 56 in 2025 and decides it's time to retire. He has a mix of traditional retirement accounts, taxable accounts, and a Roth IRA. Over the years, he has contributed $100,000 to his Roth IRA through annual contributions, and the account has grown to $350,000.

Ernie might consider taking some Roth IRA withdrawals before turning 59½. Why? Possible reasons include:

- Keeping income low to qualify for a greater PTC for his ACA health insurance plan

- Avoiding pushing other income into a higher tax bracket later in the year

Suppose Ernie withdraws $10,000 from his Roth IRA in November to cover living expenses. What are the tax consequences of this "nonqualified distribution"?

It's important to remember that, regardless of ownership period, most tax-payers under age 59½ cannot take a "qualified distribution" from a Roth IRA.

Fortunately, the rules are quite favorable. As we discussed in Chapter 4, Roth IRA distributions follow a specific ordering rule before age 59½. Roth IRA distributions are treated as coming out in the following sequence:

1. Roth IRA Annual Contributions
2. Roth IRA Conversions (on a first-in, first-out basis)
3. Roth IRA Earnings

Each layer must be fully withdrawn before the next layer is touched. That means Ernie's annual contributions must be fully distributed before any of his Roth conversions are accessed. And both of those must be fully distributed before any Roth IRA earnings are tapped.

In Ernie's case, his $10,000 withdrawal is treated entirely as a return of annual contributions. That leaves him with $90,000 of remaining contribution basis in the Roth IRA. The entire $10,000 distribution is completely tax- and penalty-free.

As you can see, the Roth IRA rules stack the deck in the owner's favor. The first dollars out are always from contributions—and they always come out tax- and penalty-free!

In Real Life: *Ernie will report the Roth IRA distribution on his 2025 federal income tax return using Form 8606, Part III, indicating it's a nontaxable return of previous annual contributions.*

Extra Credit: *It is possible—though rare—for a Roth IRA owner under age 59½ to take a qualified distribution. This occurs if the owner's first Roth IRA has been open at least five years and either:*

(i) the owner is disabled under Internal Revenue Code Section 72(m)(7), or

(ii) the distribution (up to $10,000) qualifies as a "first-time" homebuyer distribution.

Roth IRA Nonqualified Distribution Tax Treatment

What is the tax treatment of a nonqualified distribution from each of the three Roth IRA layers?

1. **Roth IRA Annual Contributions:** Always fully tax- and penalty-free.

2. **Roth IRA Conversions:** If the conversion is at least five years old, the distribution is tax- and penalty-free. If the conversion is less than five years old and was taxable when converted, the distribution is subject to the 10% penalty, unless an exception applies. Note: Roth conversions are never subject to income tax again—only potentially the penalty.

3. **Roth IRA Earnings:** Nonqualified withdrawals of earnings are always subject to income tax. If the owner is under age 59½, the 10% penalty also applies—unless an exception applies.

When we say "Roth basis," we're using a planning term. Roth basis includes two components:

1. Annual contributions, which are always tax- and penalty-free upon withdrawal.
2. Roth conversions that are at least five years old, which are also always tax- and penalty-free, regardless of the owner's age.

When you add these two together—annual contributions plus five-year-old conversions—you get the Roth basis, which can generally be withdrawn at any time, for any reason, without tax or penalty.

As mentioned earlier, the Roth IRA rules stack the deck in the owner's favor, since Roth basis is distributed first, before any amounts that could trigger income tax or the 10% penalty.

Extra Credit: "Five years old" for Roth IRA conversions has a very particular definition. Each Roth conversion is deemed to have occurred on January 1 of the year it actually happened. For example, if Andy converts $10,000 from a traditional IRA to a Roth IRA on December 15, 2025, that conversion is treated as having occurred on January 1, 2025. It will meet the five-year test on January 1, 2030.

Roth IRA Qualified Distributions

What if, instead of being 56, Ernie were 60 years old and had owned a Roth IRA for at least five years? In that case, the analysis is easy: his $10,000 distribution would be a qualified distribution, fully tax- and penalty-free.

Once Ernie (or anyone else) meets the "59½ and 5" requirements—age 59½ and at least five years since first funding a Roth IRA—every distribution from a Roth IRA is considered qualified. Qualified distributions are always completely tax- and penalty-free.

Roth Basis and Roth Workplace Plans

You might be thinking, "Okay, thanks for the Roth nonqualified distribution rules. I'll retire before age 59½ and just live off some **Roth 401(k)** distributions, since they'll likely be tax-free."

Unfortunately, Roth 401(k)s and other qualified workplace plans have their own, less favorable distribution rules. They do not follow the same ordering rules as Roth IRAs.

With Roth 401(k)s, nonqualified distributions are taken out on a pro-rata basis—a mix of contributions and earnings. The portion representing contributions is tax- and penalty-free, but the portion representing earnings is subject to income tax and possibly the 10% penalty.

Here's an example:

Julio retires from GHI Inc. in March 2025 at age 56. In November 2025, he withdraws $20,000 from his GHI Roth 401(k). Before the distribution, the account was worth $100,000, and Julio had made $60,000 in employee contributions.

Since 60% of the account is contributions, $12,000 of his $20,000 distribution is a tax-free return of contributions. The remaining 40%—or $8,000—is considered earnings and is taxable. Fortunately, because Julio qualifies for the Rule of 55, he avoids the 10% penalty on the $8,000 of earnings.

Still, taking a **taxable** distribution from a **Roth** account is generally bad planning. A "Roth" without "tax-free" is not much of a benefit—especially for early retirees.

So, what can people like Julio do if they retire before 59½ and want to use Roth 401(k) funds to cover early retirement expenses?

The most effective planning technique is to roll the Roth 401(k) into a Roth IRA. This moves the account under the more favorable Roth IRA distribution rules. Recall that nonqualified Roth IRA distributions are deemed to be treated first as tax- and penalty-free withdrawals of contributions. Roth 401(k) contributions are treated as Roth IRA contributions when rolled into an Roth IRA.

Rolling a Roth 401(k) to a Roth IRA creates accessible Roth basis that can be withdrawn in early retirement—without having to worry about pro-rata taxation.

Here's the revised example:

Julio retired from GHI Inc. at age 56 in March 2025. In May 2025, he completed a direct trustee-to-trustee transfer of his Roth 401(k) to a new Roth IRA.

At the time, his Roth 401(k) was worth $100,000, of which $60,000 was from previous employee contributions.

As part of the rollover:

- $60,000 entered the Roth IRA as annual contributions, and
- $40,000 entered as Roth IRA earnings.

In November 2025, Julio withdrew $20,000 from the Roth IRA. Because the distribution came entirely from old Roth IRA annual contributions, the entire $20,000 is received tax- and penalty-free.

In Real Life: When rolling over workplace retirement plans, we generally prefer rolling Roth 401(k)s and other qualified plans into new, separate Roth IRAs via direct trustee-to-trustee transfers.

Extra Credit: You'll notice this example doesn't mention how long Julio has owned a Roth IRA. Why not? Because it doesn't matter! **Withdrawals of Roth IRA annual contributions are always tax- and penalty-free!** *There's no five-year test for accessing Roth IRA contributions.*

72(t) Payment Plans

A series of substantially equal periodic payments is often referred to as **72(t) payments, a 72(t) payment plan, a 72(t) SEPP, or even a SOSEPP.** Don't worry—they all mean the same thing.

Generally speaking, this is the 10% penalty exception available to those who:

1. Have significant traditional retirement account balances, and
2. Do not qualify for one of the other more flexible penalty exceptions.

For early retirees with sizable taxable accounts or access to other penalty-free retirement distributions, a 72(t) payment plan is rarely the first funding source for living expenses. It's typically used when other options aren't available or have been mostly exhausted.

72(t) payments are usually fixed annual payments that do not change. That said, there are planning strategies to effectively increase or decrease those payments over time, which we'll discuss later.

The most common method for calculating a 72(t) payment is the fixed amortization method. This approach uses an IRS-provided life expectancy (typically from the Single Life Table) and an interest rate to calculate the annual payment—similar to how fixed-rate mortgage payments are determined.

Until early 2022, the planning environment for 72(t) payment plans was relatively constrained due to two concerns:

1. **Modification Risk:** If the payment schedule is improperly changed, the IRS imposes the 10% penalty retroactively, plus interest. While we believe this risk is manageable with proper planning, it's still something to consider.

2. **Interest Rate Limits:** Prior to IRS Notice 2022-6, the maximum allowable interest rate for the amortization calculation was limited to 120% of the federal midterm rate from either of the two months preceding the first payment. If interest rates dropped too low, retirees might be stuck with very small annual withdrawals—even if they had large account balances.

The game changed in 2022. The IRS and Treasury issued Notice 2022-6, which allows taxpayers to select an interest rate that is no greater than the greater of:

- 120% of the midterm federal rate (from either of the two preceding months), or
- 5%

This means that no matter how low interest rates go, taxpayers can always use at least 5% when calculating the annual fixed amortization payment. This significantly improves the flexibility and utility of 72(t) plans—and it's our impression that many financial and tax advisors haven't fully caught up with this new planning opportunity.

72(t) Payment Fixed Amortization Payment Calculation

The 72(t) payment plan for an early retiree is based on a three-input present value calculation:

1. **Interest rate** – determined by both the IRS and the taxpayer
2. **Life expectancy factor** – determined by the IRS
3. **Annual payment** – determined by the taxpayer

Retirees use these inputs to solve for the starting size of the 72(t) IRA. Generally speaking, the goal is to keep the 72(t) IRA as small as possible—for reasons we'll explore later. The annual payment comes from the 72(t) IRA.

Interest Rate

The maximum allowable interest rate is set by the IRS. Taxpayers are allowed to use a lower rate if they wish, but we generally prefer using the highest allowable rate to maximize the flexibility of the plan.

As mentioned before, the IRS allows taxpayers to use the greater of:

- 120% of the Applicable Federal Midterm Rate (AFR) for either of the two months preceding the first distribution, or
- 5%

If neither AFR percentage exceeds 5%, taxpayers may simply use 5%. You can find current rates on the IRS website here: https://www.irs.gov/businesses/small-businesses-self-employed/section-7520-interest-rates.

Life Expectancy Factor

The life expectancy factor comes from the IRS Single Life Table, based on the taxpayer's age in the year of the first distribution. While it's possible to use other tables (e.g., Joint Life and Last Survivor or Uniform Lifetime), we disfavor doing so because they result in lower annual payments for the same account balance—working against the goal of minimizing the size of the 72(t) IRA.

Annual Payment

The annual payment amount is determined by how much the taxpayer needs (or wants) to withdraw each year—including the amount needed to cover federal and state income taxes—after accounting for other income sources.

In practice, many early retirees will want to delay starting a 72(t) payment plan until later in early retirement, when other resources (e.g., taxable accounts) have been used up and the plan becomes more necessary.

Let's illustrate with an example:

Audra turned 53 in July 2025. In January 2025, she left her job at JKL Inc. At the time, she owned her home outright, had $40,000 in a savings account earmarked as an emergency fund, and held $2 million in a traditional 401(k). Including income taxes, she wants to live on $6,000 per month, or **$72,000 per year**, with the first distribution scheduled for May 2025.

The IRS-published 120% AFRs for March and April—using annual compounding—are 5.36% and 5.06%, respectively. Audra uses the higher rate, **5.36%**, for her 72(t) payment calculation.

Next, she consults the IRS Single Life Table and finds that the life expectancy factor for age 53 is **33.4**.

With those three inputs—$72,000 annual payment, 5.36% interest rate, and 33.4 life expectancy factor—Audra calculates the present value required to generate that payment. The result: she needs to set up a 72(t) IRA with a starting balance of **$1,108,429.96** to produce a fixed annual payment of $72,000.

Three important notes:

1. The 33.4 years is not the payment term. It's a computational input—not the number of years the payment must be made. The required payment term is the longer of five years or until the account owner (Audra) reaches age 59½.

2. Audra can validate her present value calculation by using a different example. For instance, if she wanted a $30,000 annual payment for 30 years at a 0% interest rate, the present value would be $900,000. If her spreadsheet produces that result, she's likely calculating her actual scenario correctly.

3. The AFR won't always exceed 5%, as it did in Audra's case. If she had used the default 5% rate, her required 72(t) IRA would have been $1,157,746.13. That means her $72,000 annual payment would represent about 6.22% of her 72(t) IRA.

   A 6% withdrawal rate is a good general <u>rule of thumb</u> when designing a 72(t) plan using the fixed amortization method in today's environment, where the interest rate floor is 5%. For those in their 50s, it's reasonable to expect a bit more than 6% as an annual distribution rate.

   If you're thinking, "Maybe in my 50s I'd like a 72(t) IRA producing $100,000 a year," just divide $100,000 by 0.06 to get a **back-of-the-envelope estimate** of the required account size—about $1.67 million.

Having completed her 72(t) IRA calculation, Audra implements the following plan:

Step 1: She arranges a direct trustee-to-trustee transfer of her traditional 401(k) into a traditional IRA.

Step 2: Once the 401(k) funds are fully transferred and settled in the IRA, Audra contacts the financial institution and requests to start a 72(t) payment plan using a $1,108,429.96 IRA. She asks the institution to split the approximately $2 million IRA into two separate accounts:

1. A 72(t) IRA worth exactly $1,108,429.96
2. A "non-72(t)" IRA holding the remaining balance

As a practical step, Audra may choose to invest the 72(t) IRA temporarily in a money market fund—even just for a few days or until the end of the month—to clearly establish the opening account balance.

Step 3: Once the IRA has been divided, Audra saves account statements to fully document the opening balance of the 72(t) IRA. She also saves a copy of her calculation worksheets and any provided by a tax or financial professional. For added confidence, she might use the Florida Retirement System 72(t) online calculator (available at https://www.myfrs.com/calculators/Retire72T.html) to verify her results. Note: While we have not validated the calculator's internal coding, we've never seen it produce results we believe to be incorrect.

Step 4: In May 2025, Audra takes her first annual $72,000 distribution from the 72(t) IRA.

Step 5: She continues taking the same $72,000 payment each year until she reaches age 59½. Ideally, her final payment occurs on or around the anniversary of her first distribution in 2031.

In Real Life: While 72(t) payment plans can be taken from 401(k)s and other qualified plans, they are almost always implemented using traditional IRAs. As tax expert Natalie Choate has pointed out, it's generally not possible to divide a single 401(k) into separate accounts for planning purposes. That's why the preferred technique is to first roll the 401(k) into a traditional IRA, then divide the IRA into two: one for 72(t) distributions and the other non-72(t) IRA for future flexibility.

72(t) Payment Plan Term and Lock Up

A 72(t) payment plan begins with the first distribution and must continue for the longer of:

- Five years, or
- Until the taxpayer reaches age 59½

In Audra's case, she turns 59½ in January 2032. This means her final required 72(t) payment must be taken in 2031, preferably around the last anniversary of her first distribution in 2025.

The 72(t) IRA is locked up for the duration of the plan. In Audra's case, this lock-up period lasts until she turns 59½. During this time, no amounts can be deposited into the 72(t) IRA, and only the required annual payment may be distributed from the 72(t) IRA.

Any additional deposits or distributions—other than the specified 72(t) payment—are likely to be considered impermissible modifications. Such modifications can trigger the 10% early withdrawal penalty on all previously taken 72(t) payments before age 59½ and related interest charges.

In Real Life: From a "best practices" perspective, it's usually best to take the annual 72(t) payment around the same time each year, ideally near the anniversary of the first distribution. That said, the IRS does not require payments to occur on or near the anniversary.

While 72(t) payments can be taken monthly or quarterly, we strongly favor annual payments to reduce complexity, avoid missed distributions, and simplify the underlying calculation.

Increasing 72(t) Payments

Suppose Audra wants to increase her annual withdrawal from $72,000 to $84,000 starting in May 2028. Can she do that?

Not from her 72(t) IRA. Increasing the withdrawal amount would be considered an impermissible modification.

However, Audra can establish a second 72(t) payment plan by dividing her non-72(t) IRA into two parts:

1. A new second 72(t) IRA
2. A remaining non-72(t) IRA

The second 72(t) IRA will provide the additional $12,000 per year she wants to begin withdrawing in 2028.

Assuming low interest rates in March and April 2028, she uses the default 5% interest rate, her desired **$12,000** annual withdrawal, and her age 56 life expectancy from the IRS Single Life Table: **30.6**. This results in a second 72(t) IRA size of **$186,071.46**—from which she will take $12,000 annually for five years.

Here's what Audra's 72(t) payment schedule looks like:

Year	Birthday Age	Required First 72(t) Withdrawal	Required Second 72(t) Withdrawal	Total Required Annual Withdrawal
2025	53	$72,000	$0	$72,000
2026	54	$72,000	$0	$72,000
2027	55	$72,000	$0	$72,000
2028	56	$72,000	$12,000	$84,000
2029	57	$72,000	$12,000	$84,000
2030	58	$72,000	$12,000	$84,000
2031	59	$72,000	$12,000	$84,000
2032	60	$0	$12,000	$12,000

Extra Credit: There are no IRS rules limiting the number of 72(t) IRAs or traditional IRAs a person can have. That flexibility can be incredibly useful in early retirement.

Sean's Take: For those planning to rely on a 72(t) payment plan before age 59½, maintaining a non-72(t) IRA should be considered. Having only a 72(t) IRA limits flexibility. Fortunately, the 6% 72(t) withdrawal rule of thumb is higher than the commonly discussed 4% safe withdrawal rate rule of thumb. That gap essentially creates room to carve out a non-72(t) IRA, giving early retirees additional flexibility.

Decreasing 72(t) Payments

Some early retirees may want to reduce a previously established 72(t) payment plan. For example, someone might retire early, begin 72(t) withdrawals, and later come into additional resources that can support their lifestyle until age 59½.

The most common situation? Receiving an inheritance.

Let's say Dan starts a 72(t) payment plan at age 52 to fund $90,000 per year in living expenses. At age 56, Dan's last surviving parent passes away, and he inherits $300,000 in a taxable brokerage account and $300,000 in a traditional IRA.

With those new assets, Dan no longer needs the full $90,000 annually from his 72(t) plan. He'd rather live off the taxable inheritance (with its step-up in basis) and manage withdrawals from the inherited IRA to control tax exposure.

"But isn't he locked into that $90,000 payment?"

There is one way to reduce the required annual payment. Thankfully, Dan can make a one-time switch from the **fixed amortization method** to the **required minimum distribution (RMD) method**, which often results in a significantly lower annual payment.

Assume Dan's 72(t) IRA was worth $1,300,000 at the end of the prior year. If he switches to the RMD method, he divides that balance by a life expectancy factor—typically from the Uniform Lifetime Table—as provided for in IRS Notice 2022-6.

Since Dan turns 56 this year, his Uniform Lifetime Table factor is 42.6. Dan divides $1,300,000 by 42.6 and gets a required annual 72(t) payment of just **$30,516**. That's a massive reduction from $90,000 per year!

Each year going forward, Dan must repeat the calculation: dividing the prior year-end IRA balance by the updated life expectancy factor for his age. This annual recomputation of the 72(t) payment is a key distinction between the RMD method—which requires it—and the fixed amortization method, which uses a fixed amount for each annual payment.

Importantly, switching to the RMD method does not reset the original 72(t) plan term. Dan must still follow the original schedule—continuing the plan until the later of five years from the first payment or until he reaches age 59½.

The ability—and potential desire—to reduce the annual 72(t) payment is a good reason to keep the 72(t) IRA balance as low as possible.

This is why **we prefer using the highest allowable interest rate** when calculating the initial fixed amortization payment: The higher the interest rate, the smaller the 72(t) IRA needs to be to produce the annual desired payment.

Additionally, it may make sense to invest lower-growth assets in the 72(t) IRA and higher-growth assets in the non-72(t) IRA. That way, most of the growth occurs outside the locked-up account, preserving flexibility and minimizing the size of future taxable 72(t) distributions with a switch to the RMD method.

Managing 72(t) Payment Plan Risk

A 72(t) payment plan presents a risk. If an impermissible modification occurs during the plan's term, all prior 72(t) payments made before the owner reaches age 59½ become subject to the 10% early withdrawal penalty, and interest charge on that penalty.

Impermissible Modifications Include:

- Changing the annual withdrawal amount (outside of an allowed switch to the RMD method)
- Failing to take the required payment during a year
- Adding funds to the 72(t) IRA—such as rolling in assets from another retirement account

To reduce the chance of missing a distribution, we prefer taking the annual 72(t) payment around the same time each year, ideally on or near the anniversary of the first payment.

Once the 72(t) term ends, the 72(t) IRA reverts to a plain old traditional IRA. The account is no longer subject to the restrictions of the 72(t) payment plan.

Bottom Line: Most 72(t) IRA owners should keep it simple:

- Take only the required annual payment—no more, no less
- Make sure nothing is rolled into the 72(t) IRA

That level of vigilance is easy for most early retirees to maintain.

Cody's Take: Some investment custodians allow owners to add "identifiers" (nicknames) to their accounts. I prefer naming them clearly—something like "72(t) IRA" and "Non-72(t) IRA"—to avoid accidentally initiating Roth conversions or withdrawals from the wrong account. Clear account naming is a simple but powerful way to reduce the risk of costly mistakes.

Managing Risk: When to Start a 72(t) Payment Plan

One way to manage risk is to start the 72(t) payment plan as late as possible. This is why we often prefer first exhausting other resources—such as taxable accounts, inherited accounts, qualified plans using the Rule of 55, governmental 457(b) plans, and Roth basis—before initiating a 72(t) plan.

The later in life the 72(t) plan begins, the lower the risk of triggering a retroactive penalty and interest.

72(t) IRA Asset Allocation

In general, we prefer to hold the investment portfolio's lower expected return assets inside the 72(t) IRA and higher expected return assets inside the non-72(t) IRA. As discussed earlier, keeping the size of the 72(t) IRA modest has advantages—particularly if the owner later wants to reduce the annual 72(t) payment by switching to the RMD method.

Changing the portfolio allocation within the 72(t) IRA is allowed. Internal reallocations are fine. The issues arise with in-and-out movements—such as adding funds to the 72(t) IRA or withdrawing amounts other than the required 72(t) payment—which can trigger a violation of the 72(t) plan rules.

72(t) Income Tax Withholding

Retirees taking 72(t) payments should remember to estimate their annual federal and state income tax liability and ensure that an appropriate amount of tax is withheld from each distribution. It's perfectly acceptable to have **a portion of the required distribution** withheld and sent directly to the IRS and any applicable state tax authority.

72(t) Payment Plans and Roth Conversions

In theory, one potential use for the non-72(t) IRA is Roth conversions. In practice, however, this is rarely appropriate.

A significant reason to pursue Roth conversions is to reduce future RMDs.

You know what is already reducing your future RMDs: your in-effect 72(t) payment plan!

Additionally, the annual 72(t) payment often fills up much or all of the lower tax brackets, including the standard deduction and the 10% and 12% brackets. In that case, it can be difficult to justify adding more taxable income through a Roth conversion—since it would be taxed at higher marginal rates.

Roth Conversions and the 72(t) Payment

Let's say you're like Dan—you start a 72(t) payment plan, then later inherit significant assets and no longer need the 72(t) income. You think: "I'll just convert the 72(t) payments to a Roth IRA!"

Unfortunately, that's not allowed. 72(t) payments cannot be converted to a Roth IRA or rolled over to another retirement account.

72(t) Implementation

As Cody is fond of saying: measure twice! That principle absolutely applies before starting a 72(t) payment plan.

Thankfully, today's early retirees have access to several useful resources. One we've already mentioned is the Florida Retirement System 72(t) calculator (available at https://www.myfrs.com/calculators/Retire72T.html). Why not run your numbers through it and other online calculators? The point of this exercise is to provide additional support and validation. As Cody is also fond of saying, "clarity precedes confidence!"

Another helpful resource is a YouTube video by Sean that demonstrates how to use Google Sheets to calculate a 72(t) fixed amortization payment.

Lastly, the IRS has a helpful Substantially Equal Periodic Payments webpage (available at https://www.irs.gov/retirement-plans/substantially-equal-periodic-payments). Q&A 7 on that page includes a sample amortization calculation for "Bob." Anyone creating their own fixed amortization schedule should compare their result with the IRS example. Note: The IRS rounds to the nearest dollar, which we don't recommend for 72(t) calculations. That rounding may result in minor differences (over a dollar), but these won't affect the validity of the calculation.

Further, document, document, document:

- Where you got your inputs (interest rate, life expectancy factor, account balance)
- How the calculation was done
- Where you validated the calculation (e.g., calculators, IRS examples)
- Copies of account statements used to determine beginning balances

72(t) payment plans are absolutely a valid reason to seek professional guidance. Working with a knowledgeable financial planner or tax advisor can add confidence and reduce the risk of costly mistakes. Still, we encourage you to run your own parallel calculation. **An educated client gets the best value out of working with a professional.**

In Real Life: There's very little formal guidance on how to document a 72(t) payment plan. We generally recommend keeping digital records of the entire process.

One formal requirement: An early retiree using a 72(t) plan must file Form 5329 with their annual federal income tax return to report that the distribution qualifies for a 72(t) exception. On Line 2, the taxpayer enters code "02" to indicate that the 10% penalty does not apply due to the 72(t) payment plan exception.

HSA PUQME

Each HSA owner has a potentially valuable resource: previously unreimbursed qualified medical expenses. To make this concept more memorable, Sean coined the acronym PUQME (pronounced puck-me).

PUQME is the cumulative total of all qualified medical expenses (incurred by the HSA owner, their spouse, and their dependents) that:

- Were incurred on or after the date the owner first opened an HSA
- Were paid out-of-pocket by the owner, their spouse, and/or their dependent.
- Have not yet been reimbursed from the HSA

Up to the PUQME amount, the HSA can be accessed tax- and penalty-free to cover living expenses.

Dipping into PUQME can help keep taxable income low and potentially increase eligibility for Premium Tax Credits (PTCs).

In Real Life: HSA distributions should be reported on Form 8889, Part II, and included with the annual federal income tax return.

Paying the Penalty on Retirement Account Distributions

Yes, it's a 10% penalty—and it matters. But would a year or two of paying that penalty derail the financial future of most financially successful early retirees? Probably not.

There may be situations where someone doesn't qualify for one of the "easier" penalty exceptions—like the Rule of 55 or a governmental 457(b)—and the penalty amount is modest. In those cases, the most practical answer may be to simply pay the penalty on a small, targeted distribution (likely taken relatively close to age 59½) and move on.

That said, the full situation should be carefully assessed before knowingly taking a distribution that will trigger the 10% penalty.

Sean's Take: For those just a year or so away from turning 59½, the 72(t) payment plan should be strongly considered before opting to pay the penalty. One potential strategy:

1. *Start a 72(t) plan.*
2. *Let it run for the required five years.*
3. *If needed, reduce the required annual payment after the first year by switching to the RMD method.*

Blending Methods in Early Retirement

In today's environment—where managing for the PTC can be a highly compelling financial planning objective—it may be logical to blend one or more of the early retirement distribution strategies discussed above.

Consider this scenario: A married couple retires at age 55 and plans to rely on ACA health insurance for the next ten years. They have substantial traditional and Roth retirement accounts, along with four years' worth of expenses invested in taxable accounts.

Rather than depleting taxable accounts over the first four years—and potentially facing large traditional account withdrawals in the final six years before Medicare—they might choose a more balanced approach.

They might want to take inherited IRA distributions, Rule of 55 distributions, governmental 457(b) withdrawals, and/or 72(t) payments up to a modest income threshold—say 150%, 200%, or 250% of the federal poverty level (FPL). They could use taxable accounts, Roth IRAs, and HSA PUQME to cover the remaining expenses.

This approach allows them to meet their spending needs while keeping modified adjusted gross income (MAGI) within PTC-friendly limits.

Your Money is Not Locked Up

We firmly believe that for taxpayers age 50 or older with sufficient financial assets, the 10% early withdrawal penalty is not a barrier to early retirement—even if every last dollar is held in traditional retirement accounts.

For those under 50 with most of their financial wealth in traditional retirement accounts, the 10% penalty may not be a barrier either—but early retirement at that age typically requires one of the following:

- A sizable inherited IRA
- Access to a governmental 457(b)
- A carefully constructed 72(t) payment plan alongside a substantial non-72(t) IRA for flexibility

You may hear phrases like "your money is trapped" or warnings to "avoid the trap of having most of your wealth in traditional retirement accounts." We strongly disagree.

72(t) payment plans are reliable and effective, capable of producing sufficient cash flow to support retirement spending needs.

As we saw in Audra's example, setting up a 72(t) payment plan is not especially burdensome. And as shown in Chapter 11, the tax treatment of 72(t) distributions—such as in Justin and Rachel's case—can be surprisingly favorable, especially for married couples.

Yes, the tax rules—including the 10% penalty—must be factored into early retirement planning. But they are hardly a bar to early retirement.

13 – Health Insurance Before Medicare and the Premium Tax Credit

Securing affordable health insurance before becoming eligible for Medicare at age 65 is a concern for many early retirees. Notably, data from the Employee Benefit Research Institute indicates that approximately 70% of Americans retire before reaching Medicare eligibility.

This highlights the importance of understanding available health coverage options, especially since some retirements are involuntary—due to health issues, layoffs, or caregiving responsibilities.

As you'll see, health insurance planning often intersects with tax planning for the early retiree.

Health Insurance Options Before Age 65

Individuals retiring before Medicare eligibility have several health coverage options, each with distinct benefits, costs, and limitations:

1. **COBRA Coverage:** Employers with 20 or more employees are generally required to offer continued participation, at the **employee's** expense, in the employer's health insurance plan under the Consolidated Omnibus Budget Reconciliation Act (COBRA). This allows departing employees to maintain group health coverage for up to 18 months (or up to 36 months in certain situations). While COBRA maintains existing provider networks and deductibles, premiums are typically higher because the employer no longer subsidizes the cost.

2. **Spousal Employer Plan:** If married, a retiree may be eligible to join their spouse's workplace plan.

3. **Retiree Health Coverage:** Some employers offer retiree health benefits, often tied to years of service and age, and typically in conjunction with a pension plan.

4. **Healthcare Sharing Ministries:** These cost-sharing programs are alternatives to insurance, but they often restrict pre-existing conditions, limit provider networks, and require members to meet certain eligibility criteria (such as faith-based conditions).

5. **Private Insurance Market:** Individuals and families may purchase coverage directly from insurers outside the Health Insurance

Marketplace. These plans are not eligible for Premium Tax Credit (PTC) subsidies and usually require medical underwriting, which can pose challenges for those with pre-existing conditions.

6. **Medicaid and CHIP:** Households with income below state-specific thresholds may qualify for Medicaid or the Children's Health Insurance Program (CHIP), offering free or low-cost coverage.

7. **Health Insurance Marketplace (Affordable Care Act Exchange):** This is the most widely used option for early retirees. The Marketplace offers standardized coverage tiers and, for eligible individuals, substantial premium subsidies through the PTC mechanism. Affordable Care Act (ACA) plans do not require medical underwriting and generally provide higher-quality coverage than Medicaid.

Sean's Take: Assuming a prospective early retiree has sufficient assets, it is quite rare that "I can't retire because of medical insurance" is true. In today's environment, medical insurance for early retirees is not perfect. But medical insurance available to early retirees is good enough such that it should not be the decisive factor for most making the decision to retire or not retire.

Throughout the remainder of the book, we will refer to plans offered through the Health Insurance Marketplace as "ACA plans," ACA medical insurance," or "ACA health insurance."

ACA plans are categorized into "metal tiers": Bronze, Silver, Gold, and Platinum. The higher the metal tier, the higher the insurance premiums and the greater the share of medical costs covered by the insurance company. Thus, Bronze plans have the lowest premiums but require patients to pay the highest share of medical expenses. Platinum plans, on the other hand, have the highest insurance premiums but the lowest out-of-pocket costs for the patient.

Catastrophic plans are also available, but only to individuals under age 30 or those who qualify for a hardship or affordability exemption.

The majority of current and future early retirees reading this book are likely to be enrolled in an ACA plan. The remainder of this chapter focuses on reducing insurance premium costs for those covered by ACA plans.

The Cost of an ACA Plan

The cost of an ACA plan boils down to two key factors: the insurance premium and the subsidy the retiree receives for ACA medical insurance. Both variables matter in controlling medical insurance costs in early retirement.

Too often, retirees focus only on the PTC, but that's just one part of the equation.

ACA Plan Insurance Premiums

Think of ACA plan insurance premiums like the price of grass-fed ribeye steak at the supermarket: if it's $23.99 per pound, the richest and poorest shoppers pay the same price.

ACA premiums work the same way: the listed price is identical regardless of a household's wealth or income.

To get an initial estimate of ACA plan premiums, the Kaiser Family Foundation offers a useful calculator at: https://www.kff.org/interactive/subsidy-calculator/. This tool provides an estimate of the second-lowest cost Silver plan (SLCSP) and Bronze plan premiums in your area. The key detail to look for is the section that says, "Without financial help, your silver plan would cost..." — that's the full listed price. The Gold and Platinum plans will cost more than the estimated SLCSP plan cost.

The calculator also estimates Bronze plan costs, though as of this writing, retirees must add their expected cost plus the subsidy noted in the narrative text beneath the Silver estimates to arrive at the Bronze premium.

Premium Tax Credit

The Premium Tax Credit is the subsidy that helps reduce the cost of ACA insurance.

The taxpayer needs two pieces of information to estimate the PTC:

1. The required contribution amount, determined by their household's modified adjusted gross income (MAGI) relative to the prior year's Federal Poverty Level (FPL).
2. The SLCSP premium, which varies based on their age and location.

The PTC equals the difference between the full-price SLCSP premium and the required contribution amount. The required contribution amount is calculated as a percentage of income. This percentage increases as income rises relative to the FPL. In general, early retirees benefit from maintaining modest income levels for PTC purposes: the lower the income, the lower the percentage, resulting in a larger PTC.

Note that the Kaiser Family Foundation calculator referenced above also provides PTC estimates.

We'll cover the mechanics of the PTC calculation in greater detail below.

Total Cost

To determine the retiree's actual medical insurance expense for the year, they subtract the PTC from the full ACA plan premium.

Note: If the PTC exceeds the ACA plan insurance premiums, the retiree does not receive the difference as a payment from the government.

This illustrates that while PTCs are important, they're not the only consideration. Retirees aiming to reduce their insurance costs—a very legitimate planning objective—should pay close attention to both the plan premiums and the PTC.

The PTC functions similarly to a tax (though it's not technically a tax), which means tax planning techniques can be helpful in optimizing it. The remainder of this chapter focuses primarily on those planning techniques.

Premium Tax Credit (PTC) Eligibility and Key Variables

For early retirees covered by an ACA plan, PTC eligibility is generally based on three key factors:

1. No one else can be able to claim the early retiree as a dependent on their tax return.
2. The early retiree must not be eligible for other "minimum essential coverage."
3. The early retiree's MAGI and family size must fall within certain thresholds relative to the FPL.

Let's unpack the latter two factors in more detail:

One is considered eligible for minimum essential coverage if they have access to either (1) affordable employer-provided medical insurance or (2) Medicaid or CHIP. Generally, employer-provided medical insurance is deemed affordable if the employee's share of the premiums does not exceed 8.39% of household income.

Medicaid and CHIP eligibility are mostly based on annual income. In most states, having income below 138% of the FPL qualifies a household for Medicaid, which disqualifies them from receiving a PTC.

The third factor limits PTC eligibility to households with MAGI of at least 100% of the FPL and no more than 400% of the FPL. The upper end of this range (400% of the FPL) is often referred to as the "subsidy cliff," since exceeding it disqualifies a household from receiving any PTC.

The American Rescue Plan of 2021 (ARPA) temporarily suspended the 400% FPL subsidy cliff, extending subsidies to higher-income households. The Inflation Reduction Act extended the suspension through 2025.

The One Big Beautiful Bill (OBBB) did not extend the suspension of this cliff. As of this writing, we do not anticipate that Congress will extend the suspension. While not guaranteed, we anticipate the subsidy cliff will return in 2026.

Within the 100% to 400% range, the amount of the PTC decreases as household income increases. In other words, the higher the income within that range, the lower the available credit.

Later, we discuss ways to reduce income to keep MAGI at or below 400% of the FPL. We will also discuss ways to create income sufficient to (1) avoid Medicaid qualification and (2) meet the 100% of FPL minimum for PTC eligibility.

Advance Payment of the PTC and Form 8962

After you fill out an application with the Marketplace with your household and estimated income information, you'll learn whether you qualify for a PTC.

Insurance premium payments during the year account for the anticipated PTC, referred to as the **advance payment** of the PTC. This amount is calculated using the benchmark SLCSP premium in your area, adjusted for household size and estimated income in the coverage year.

When filing the annual tax return, retirees "true-up" their net premiums using Form 8962, comparing what they actually paid (after the PTC) to what they should have paid based on their actual income. If income is higher than originally estimated, the retiree may owe money back to the government due to a reduced PTC. If income is lower, the retiree may receive additional PTC as a refund.

Federal Poverty Level (FPL) and MAGI Definition

The Federal Poverty Level (FPL) is updated annually and varies based on household size and location.

For the most accurate and up-to-date information, consult the official state resources where you plan to receive coverage. Visit Healthcare.gov/see-plans to find your state-specific Marketplace website, review plans, and calculate estimated PTCs. The Kaiser Family Foundation calculator discussed above may also be helpful.

For most early retirees, MAGI for PTC purposes is simply their adjusted gross income. However, certain amounts must be added back to AGI to determine MAGI for the PTC:

MAGI = Adjusted gross income (AGI) + nontaxable Social Security benefits + tax-exempt interest + foreign earned income

PTC Texas Case Study

Here's an example of how the PTC works in practice:

Leah (57) and Greg (55) plan to retire at the beginning of 2025. In late 2024, they visit the Health Insurance Marketplace website to explore health plan options. They enter their ZIP code (77062) for Harris County, Texas, and provide their household details. The cheapest plan available to them is listed at over $1,100 per month—$13,267 per year—**before factoring in the PTC.** *Ouch!*

But after entering an expected MAGI of $30,000, Leah and Greg qualify for a significant PTC computed as follows (using Form 8962):

- The **2024 FPL** for a household of two is $20,440.
- Their **2025 MAGI** ($30,000) is divided by the **2024 FPL** ($20,440): 147%
- According to the 2024 Form 8962 instructions, the applicable figure for 147% of FPL is 0%.
- MAGI ($30,000) is multiplied by the applicable figure (0%): $0 annual expected contribution
- The **2025 SLCSP premium** based on their location, household size, and age, is $19,176 (provided by the Marketplace website).
- Subtracting their expected contribution ($0) from the SLCSP premium ($19,176), they qualify for a PTC of $19,176.

At this income level, Leah and Greg are eligible for the maximum PTC, equal to the full cost of the benchmark Silver plan. If they choose a plan with premiums at or below $19,176, they pay no health insurance premiums in 2025. If they select a more expensive plan, they simply pay the difference above $19,176.

Extra Credit: If you're curious about your own net premium cost, you can walk through a similar process as we did for Leah and Greg above.

As of this writing, 2026 plan premiums and SLCSPs are not yet available. However, for illustrative purposes, we can estimate Leah and Greg's 2026 PTC using the same income level (MAGI of $30,000) and assuming the SLCSP premium ($19,176) stays the same:

- The **2025 FPL** for a household of two is $21,150.
- Their **2026 MAGI** ($30,000) is divided by the **2025 FPL** ($21,150): 142%

Under Internal Revenue Code Section 36B, beginning in 2026, households with MAGI between 133% and 150% of FPL are expected to contribute between 3% and 4% of MAGI toward premiums on a sliding scale. For Leah and Greg, that percentage comes out to about 3.53%.

- MAGI ($30,000) is multiplied by the applicable figure (3.53%): $1,059 annual expected contribution.
- Subtracting their expected contribution ($1,059) from the SLCSP premium ($19,176), they qualify for a maximum PTC of $18,117.

Extra Credit: Why did we use the 2024 IRS instructions for the 2025 PTC calculation but not for the 2026 calculation? Because the law changes in 2026. The table in the 2024 Instructions reflects the PTC factors applicable from 2021 through 2025. IRS instructions for 2026 won't be available until sometime in 2026 at the earliest. Thus, as of this writing, we must refer to the Internal Revenue Code itself (specifically Section 36B) to determine the applicable factors for estimating the 2026 PTC.

PTC California Case Study

Here's an example of how the PTC works at a higher income level in Santa Barbara, California:

Bernard (53) and Emily (53) retire in late 2024 and look for a 2025 ACA plan. In Santa Barbara (ZIP code 93101), a Bronze plan is priced at over $1,700 per month—$20,846 per year—according to the KFF calculator, before factoring in the PTC. *Oof!*

With a MAGI of $70,000, Bernard and Emily qualify for a 2025 PTC computed as follows:

- The **2025 SLCSP premium** based on their location, household size, and age, is $25,294 (estimated by the KFF calculator).
- Their **2025 MAGI** ($70,000) is divided by the **2024 FPL** ($20,440): 342%
- According to the Form 8962 instructions, the applicable figure for 342% of FPL is 7.05%.
- MAGI ($70,000) is multiplied by the applicable figure (7.05%): $4,935 annual expected contribution.
- Subtracting their expected contribution ($4,935) from the SLCSP premium ($25,294), they qualify for a maximum PTC of $20,359.

For illustrative purposes, like with Leah and Greg, we can estimate Bernard and Emily's 2026 PTC at the same income level, assuming the SLCSP premium remains unchanged:

- The **2025 FPL** for a household of two is $21,150.
- Their **2026 MAGI** ($70,000) is divided by the **2025 FPL** ($21,150): 331%

Under IRC Section 36B, those with income between 300% and 400% of FPL in 2026 use 9.5% to determine the expected contribution.

- MAGI ($70,000) is multiplied by the applicable figure (9.5%): $6,650 annual expected contribution.
- Subtracting their expected contribution ($6,650) from the SLCSP premium ($25,294), they qualify for a maximum PTC of $18,644.

In Real Life: Geography matters! We were shocked by the high SLCSP premium in Santa Barbara for our hypothetical couple. If we drive down the coast to Los Angeles County—the most populous county in the country—the KFF calculator reports an SLCSP premium for the same 53-year-old couple at only $15,693, nearly $10,000 less than in Santa Barbara!

Yes, the PTC essentially smooths out that difference for plans priced at the SLCSP, since the net premium cost after the PTC will be the same when using the SLCSP.

But at a minimum, those considering a move for retirement ought to consult the KFF calculator (or similar resources) if they expect to rely on an ACA medical insurance plan for several years. High premium costs put additional pressure on the PTC issue.

Tactics to Decrease MAGI in Early Retirement

Early retirees may have several tactics available to lower their MAGI and enhance PTC amounts within the FPL ranges:

1. **Living on Taxable Assets First:** Drawing down taxable accounts in early retirement with basis recovery.

2. **Tactical Roth Basis and HSA PUQME Withdrawals:** Using Roth basis and HSA PUQME can provide tax-free funding for some living expenses in early retirement.

3. **Health Savings Accounts (HSAs):** Deducting contributions as Adjustments to Income (no earned income requirement). Starting in 2026, this will be available to all early retirees enrolled in Bronze ACA plans.

4. **Asset Location:** Avoiding fixed income and high dividend stocks within taxable brokerage accounts to reduce recurring investment income.

5. **Tax Loss Harvesting:** Offsetting capital gains and up to $3,000 of other income (annually) with realized capital losses within taxable brokerage accounts.

6. **Traditional Retirement Accounts:** Making pre-tax contributions with part-time or self-employment income.

7. **Living Off Dividends Instead of Reinvesting:** Turning off auto-reinvested dividends in taxable brokerage accounts to potentially reduce the amount of capital gain transactions necessary to fund living expenses.

8. **Delaying Social Security:** Postponing retirement benefits at least until Medicare coverage begins (though in many cases, we favor delaying beyond the beginning of Medicare coverage).

Tactics to Increase MAGI in Early Retirement

Some early retirees may need to increase their income to stay above the 100% FPL threshold for PTC eligibility and/or avoid qualifying for Medicaid or CHIP:

1. **Roth Conversions:** Converting pre-tax retirement funds to Roth accounts as ordinary income.

2. **Selling Securities:** Realizing net capital gains in taxable brokerage accounts.

3. **Part-Time Work or Self-Employment:** Earning income through consulting, freelance work, or seasonal employment. Don't forget the self-employed health insurance deduction!

More Information About the Health Insurance Marketplace in 2025

- Certain life events, such as losing health coverage, moving, getting married, or having a baby/adopting a child, may qualify for a Special Enrollment Period outside the annual Open Enrollment Period.
- All ACA plans must cover treatment for pre-existing medical conditions and include a list of essential health benefits.
- Monthly premiums, including advance payments of the PTC, are paid directly to the insurance company, not to the household.
- ACA plans must have an in-network out-of-pocket maximum for the year, which helps limit total medical costs for early retirees. However, ACA plans are not required to have an out-of-network out-of-pocket maximum.
- Open enrollment for 2026 plans begins November 1, 2025.

Cost-Sharing Reductions

Early retirees who (1) have a MAGI between 100% and 250% of the FPL and (2) enroll in a Silver plan are eligible for cost-sharing reductions (CSRs). These reduce out-of-pocket medical expenses, such as deductibles, copayments, and coinsurance.

PTC and Tax Planning

PTC planning goes hand-in-hand with tax planning. The potential relevance of the PTC in early retirement is a reason to have taxable accounts to help fund retirement until age 65.

From a planning perspective, the goal is to have some household income—but not too much. If an early retiree enters retirement with only Roth IRAs and cash in a checking account, they may face challenges in generating enough MAGI to qualify for the PTC without returning to some level of work.

If there's no MAGI, the retiree won't qualify for a PTC–an obviously unfavorable outcome. This is one reason why having a balance of account types, including traditional retirement accounts, is beneficial in early retirement. With pre-tax assets, the retiree may qualify for the PTC by generating income through Roth conversions.

The New Planning Environment

The planning environment has changed since 2020—the last time the 400% subsidy cliff was in effect. Key developments have occurred since then:

- The Tax Cuts and Jobs Act's (TCJA's) increased standard deduction and lowered tax brackets have been made permanent.
- Required Minimum Distributions (RMDs) now begin at age 75 (not 72) for those born in 1960 and later.
- The new senior deduction has been introduced.

As we discuss in Chapter 15, RMDs are not as harmful as often perceived–especially for early retirees. This makes prioritizing the PTC even more compelling, since the "back end" of retirement taxation has become less treacherous, while the subsidy cliff is most likely to return in 2026.

In the new planning environment starting in 2026, PTC considerations may justify withdrawing Roth IRA basis to fund a portion of early retirement expenses. For many early retirees, the alternatives to withdrawing Roth basis will be either selling taxable assets with capital gains or taking taxable traditional retirement account distributions.

Later in retirement, retirees typically face one layer of tax, the income tax. Before enrolling in Medicare, however, early retirees on ACA plans effectively face two layers of tax: the income tax and the "tax" of a potentially reduced

PTC. Very broadly, each additional dollar of income tends to reduce the PTC by roughly 9.5 to 15 cents. This means a traditional retirement account distribution in this context could result in a 9.5% to 15% "additional tax."

Why not withdraw some Roth basis to fund early retirement expenses instead? Doing so could avoid both a 10%, 12%, or 22% income tax on a traditional retirement account distribution and a 9.5% to 15% reduction in the PTC.

Said differently, Roth IRA distributions may be most valuable when they help avoid two layers of tax rather than one.

Extra Credit: The PTC calculation is based on Section 36B of the Internal Revenue Code. Starting in 2026, it is often–but not always–the case that each additional dollar of income reduces the PTC by roughly 9.5 to 15 cents. However, in some cases, the reduction could be as little as 2 cents per dollar. On the other hand, the one dollar that pushes an early retiree's MAGI above 400% of the FPL could cost thousands in lost PTCs. Yikes!

Bronze is Gold Planning

The OBBB provided early retirees with a new tool to reduce medical insurance costs. Starting in 2026, all Bronze ACA plans will be deemed to be high deductible health plans (HDHPs). With HDHP status comes the ability to make deductible HSA contributions.

For a married retired couple both 55 or older in 2026, this could result in $10,750 in tax-deductible contributions. Even if both spouses are under age 55, the maximum contribution is still a healthy $8,750.

The combination of a Bronze ACA plan and HSA contributions is incredibly valuable to retirees trying to reduce insurance costs and save on federal (and possibly state) income taxes. This pairing can lead to several great planning outcomes for early retirees.

1. Lower insurance premiums
2. Lower taxable income, reducing federal and (in some cases) state income taxes
3. Lower MAGI, increasing PTC amounts and/or bringing income below 400% of FPL to turn on eligibility
4. Tax-free funding of current medical expenses using the HSA

For many early retirees, starting in 2026, *Bronze is gold!*

With the 400% FPL cliff returning, some early retirees are understandably concerned. However, we believe most can still qualify for PTCs in 2026 and beyond. Reviewing the eight "Tactics to Decrease MAGI in Early Retirement" and considering a Bronze plan could make a significant difference.

Concluding Considerations

Lastly, it's important to assess the overall relevance of the PTC in the context of an early retiree's long-term financial plan. For those retiring one, two, or three years before Medicare enrollment, it's worth keeping the value of the few years' worth of PTCs in perspective. While optimizing for the PTC each year makes sense, it shouldn't overshadow the early retiree's tax planning picture.

Navigating health insurance before Medicare is a complex but essential part of early retirement planning. The PTC offers significant financial assistance to those who strategically manage their household income, regardless of their net worth. By understanding available insurance options, planning around MAGI thresholds, and leveraging HSAs and tax-efficient withdrawal strategies, retirees can reduce healthcare costs while maintaining financial flexibility.

14 – Paying Taxes in Early Retirement

Paying income tax changes in retirement. At work, employers withhold taxes from paychecks—covering both income and employment taxes. But in retirement, without a traditional paycheck, the retiree is responsible for managing and paying tax obligations.

In retirement:

1. Instead of wages, income comes from withdrawals from taxable brokerage and retirement accounts, Social Security benefits, pensions and annuities, and/or rental income—each with its own tax treatment.

2. Retirees need to estimate and pay taxes themselves, usually through withholding on retirement account withdrawals or by making estimated tax payments.

3. Income may fluctuate year-to-year—and even within the year—due to strategic account withdrawals, Roth conversions, and asset sales within taxable brokerage accounts.

Avoiding Underpayment Penalties (Safe Harbor Rule)

There are penalties for underpaying taxes throughout the year. To avoid those penalties, taxpayers can rely on the **Safe Harbor Rule** by meeting one of the following conditions:

1. Owe less than $1,000 for the **current year** after subtracting withholding and refundable credits from your total tax liability.

2. Pay at least 90% of the **current year's** tax liability through withholding, timely estimated payments, or both.

3. Pay at least 100% of **last year's** tax liability—or 110% if last year's adjusted gross income (AGI) exceeded $150,000 ($75,000 for those married filing separately)—through withholding, timely estimated payments, or both.

Meeting any of these conditions avoids underpayment penalties, even if income fluctuates throughout the year.

Beyond the Scope: *Don't forget to review your state income tax rules, as safe harbor thresholds and estimated payment deadlines can vary.*

Avoid Withholding Taxes from Roth Conversions in Early Retirement

When implementing Roth conversions before age 59 ½, it's important to avoid withholding taxes directly from the Roth conversion amount. Withholding taxes from a Roth conversion under age 59 ½ is treated as an early distribution and may trigger a 10% penalty on the amount withheld. It also reduces the amount converted into the Roth IRA, limiting its potential for future tax-free growth.

Inherited IRAs

One of the best ways to pay taxes in retirement is by withholding taxes from inherited IRA distributions. With a few exceptions, most people who inherit an IRA or qualified plan account after 2019 must empty the account within 10 full years after the original owner's death. In most cases, that means intentionally spreading out withdrawals over that time to minimize the risk of pushing ordinary income into higher marginal tax brackets—especially in the final year.

If the inherited IRA is drained annually anyway, why not have a portion of it withheld for taxes? This helps manage the tax impact of the inherited IRA withdrawals and ensures the taxes are paid for the current year.

Furthermore, withholding from IRAs is credited as occurring evenly throughout the year, regardless of when it occurs.

Pros:

- It only needs to happen once a year, but it can occur at any time and multiple times throughout the year.
- It can happen late in the year, giving the taxpayer more time to estimate their tax liability and allowing the funds to continue growing in the account (assuming they are invested).
- There's never a 10% early withdrawal penalty on distributions from inherited IRAs, making this a flexible tactic at any age.

Con:

- Inherited traditional IRA distributions create taxable income. However, that taxable income likely needs to be recognized anyway to manage the tax impact of the inherited IRA over the 10-year window.

Traditional IRAs

For those age 59 ½ or older or with access to an exception to the 10% early withdrawal penalty (such as an existing 72(t) payment plan), withholding from the retiree's own traditional IRA distributions can be an effective way to pay income taxes.

As noted earlier, withholding from IRAs is credited as if it occurred evenly throughout the year, regardless of the actual timing of the withholding.

Pros:

- It only needs to happen once per year.
- It can be done late in the year, giving the taxpayer more time to estimate their tax liability and allowing more time for the funds to remain invested.
- Withholding reduces the IRA balance, which may help mitigate future required minimum distributions (RMDs).

Cons:

- Distributions from traditional IRAs create taxable income.
- For those under 59 ½, any taxes withheld are subject to a 10% early withdrawal penalty, unless the distribution qualifies for an exception (such as the Rule of 55, governmental 457(b), or being part of a 72(t) payment plan).

To withhold taxes from an IRA distribution, the retiree requests a distribution and, before completing the process, elects to have a percentage withheld for the IRS and the state tax authority (if applicable).

Estimated Tax Payments (Form 1040-ES)

In addition to withholding, retirees can make estimated tax payments to the IRS. Today, this is often done online at DirectPay.IRS.gov. The rules generally require four equal payments throughout the year. An alternative method—called the annualized income installment method—can be used to reduce or eliminate underpayment penalties when income is uneven across the year.

Although commonly referred to as "quarterly" estimated tax payments, the tax rules do not divide the calendar year into four equal quarters.

General Payment Period Deadlines:

- **Q1: April 15** – for income earned in January through March
- **Q2: June 15** – for income earned in April and May
- **Q3: September 15** – for income earned in June through August
- **Q4: January 15 (of the following year)** – for income earned in September through December

Pros:

- If paid from cash, estimated payments do not create taxable income.
- If paid by selling taxable assets, the sale can recover basis and potentially realize long-term capital gains with preferential tax treatment.

Cons:

- Payment must generally be done four times per year.
- There's less time for savings to remain invested, since generally half of the tax payment must be made by June 15.

The simplest way to approach estimated tax payments is to take the prior year's total tax liability—generally shown on line 24 of Form 1040 or Form 1040-SR—and divide it into four equal payments. In practice, most retirees follow the 100% safe harbor (or 110%, if applicable), whether through withholding or estimated tax payments, as it provides a conservative approach to avoid penalties.

Here's an example of how the 100% safe harbor works when making estimated income tax payments:

Alan and Midge are retirees who primarily fund their retirement by selling taxable assets in their brokerage accounts. They filed their 2024 federal income tax return on April 1, 2025, reporting total tax of $2,800 on line 24.

They expect their 2025 taxable income to be similar to or higher than 2024, and they aren't ruling out a big trip to Australia later this year.

The simplest way for Alan and Midge to avoid an underpayment penalty for 2025 is to divide their 2024 tax liability ($2,800) by four. That gives them $700 per quarter. To satisfy the safe harbor, they should make $700 estimated tax payments by:

- April 15, 2025
- June 16, 2025 (since June 15 falls on a Sunday)
- September 15, 2025
- January 15, 2026

These four equal payments satisfy 100% of their prior year's tax liability, protecting them from underpayment penalties—even if their taxable income increases later in the year.

So, if Alan and Midge decide to fund their big trip by increasing taxable asset sales later in the year, or even if they win a $100 million lottery during 2025, they're still protected from the underpayment penalty under the 100% safe harbor. Of course, they'll still need to pay the balance of their 2025 tax by April 15, 2026.

Note that if Alan and Midge were living off traditional IRA distributions instead, they might choose a different approach: Rather than making four quarterly estimated tax payments, they could simply take a traditional IRA distribution late in 2025 and withhold at least $2,800 to cover their federal tax liability.

For those anticipating lower taxable income than in the prior year, the 90% safe harbor is likely the better choice for paying taxes and avoiding underpayment penalties. Refer to the Federal Income Tax Formula in Chapter 1 to see how income tax liabilities are calculated. When using the 90% safe harbor, we recommend rounding up (not down) the tax payments.

Measure Twice: Don't forget to review your previously paid estimated taxes when gathering documents to prepare your income tax returns.

Beyond the Scope: Those potentially facing an underpayment penalty due to uneven income throughout the year—for example, from a large Roth conversion in December—may need to file Form 2210 (Schedule AI) with their federal tax return. This form allows taxpayers to report income and tax payments by period using the annualized income installment method, which may reduce or eliminate the penalty.

Social Security Income Tax Withholding

Some retirees choose to pay federal income taxes through voluntary withholding from their Social Security benefits once they begin receiving them. To initiate withholding, the retiree fills out Form W-4V and sends it to the payer—in this case, the Social Security Administration.

This method is relatively inflexible, as the retiree must elect a withholding rate of 7%, 10%, 12%, or 22%. Additionally, amounts withheld from Social Security are no longer available for investment, meaning they miss out on potential growth throughout the year.

Withholding income taxes from Social Security benefits is entirely voluntary—not mandatory.

Conclusion

Paying taxes in early retirement requires a shift from passive to active tax management, but you can handle it! For some, working with a professional will be the best way to handle tax payments and returns in retirement.

By understanding your income sources, planning for estimated tax payments, and avoiding common pitfalls—like withholding from Roth conversions in early retirement—early retirees can manage tax obligations effectively and avoid unnecessary penalties and headaches.

15 – Tackling Required Minimum Distributions

Perhaps you've read up to this point and are thinking, "Cody and Sean, I like the Compelling Three. But I still have one lingering concern:

Doesn't maxing out a traditional 401(k) lead to horrible required minimum distributions (RMDs)?

You're not alone in that concern. RMDs worry commentators so much that personal finance legend JL Collins titled Chapter 20 of his newly revised *The Simple Path to Wealth* "RMDs: The Ugly Surprise at the End of the Tax-Deferred Rainbow."

We disagree with that framing. RMDs are not an ugly surprise—they're simply tax rules to be navigated.

Contrary to conventional wisdom, we contend that the RMD rules usually have little harmful effect. After reading this chapter, we think you'll agree: RMDs are not inherently ugly and are rarely problematic from either a tax standpoint or a lived experience perspective.

We'll review the RMD rules and share why they're not a significant issue for those using the Compelling Three to guide tax planning to and through early retirement.

RMD Basics

RMDs make sense when you consider the tax deferral offered by traditional retirement accounts. Without RMDs, tax deferral could effectively become tax exemption during the account owner's lifetime. RMDs ensure the owner withdraws a minimum amount each year, subject to federal and state income taxes.

RMD Computation

How are RMDs computed?

The account owner divides the prior year's year-end account balance by a divisor—typically from the IRS Uniform Lifetime Table. This table provides a life expectancy factor that accounts for both the owner's remaining life expectancy and that of a hypothetical beneficiary who is 10 years younger.

For example, the table says a 75-year-old has a remaining life expectancy of 24.6 years. Does the IRS really believe that 75-year-olds, on average, will live to nearly 100? No.

Instead, the IRS estimates that the joint life expectancy of a 75-year-old and a 65-year-old (in 2025) extends to approximately 2050. Since there are two people in the picture—and one is only 65—it's somewhat reasonable to assume that, on average, the survivor might live that long.

Extra Credit: If your spouse is more than 10 years younger than you and is the sole beneficiary of your traditional retirement account, you get to use the IRS Joint and Last Survivor Table. This table assumes a longer combined life expectancy, which results in a smaller required distribution each year.

The good news? Even the standard IRS Uniform Lifetime Table produces RMDs that fall well within what most commentators would consider a safe withdrawal rate.

Meet Adam, who turns 75 in 2025. On December 31, 2024, Adam's traditional IRA had a balance of $2,040,500. To determine his 2025 RMD, he divides that balance by the age-75 factor from the IRS Uniform Lifetime Table: 24.6. The result? A 2025 RMD of **$82,947**.

Now, take a look at that $82,947—it represents a **4.07% withdrawal rate** ($82,947 ÷ $2,040,500).

Do you think 4.07% is a safe withdrawal rate **for a 75-year-old?**

As one ages, life expectancy decreases—and the required withdrawal percentage increases. Suppose Adam's IRA is worth $2,110,001 on December 31, 2025. To calculate his 2026 RMD, he divides that amount by 23.7, the age-76 factor. The result? A 2026 RMD of **$89,030**.

In Real Life: As JL Collins points out, financial institutions often make it easy to take the current year's RMD amount.

Here are the RMD withdrawal percentages at ages 80, 85, 90, and 95:

Age	RMD Withdrawal Rate
80	4.95%
85	6.25%
90	8.20%
95	11.24%

This supports our first reason for arguing that RMDs are not a significant problem: **the required distributions are relatively modest, considering both the account size and the owner's age.** In fact, many retirees will want to withdraw more than their RMD—despite the tax bill—to fully enjoy life while there's living to be done.

As Dr. Jim Dahle recently said on a podcast, "Your hearse will not have a trailer hitch."

Now compare the IRS Uniform Lifetime Table life expectancies with actuarial life expectancies from the most recent Social Security Trustees' Report (as of this writing):

Age	IRS Uniform Lifetime Table	Trustees' Report Male	Trustees' Report Female
75	24.6	10.92	12.68
80	20.2	8.11	9.49
85	16	5.75	6.76
90	12.2	3.91	4.62
95	8.9	2.63	3.10

Consider an 80-year-old woman, Aretha. Her actuarial life expectancy from the table is around 9 to 10 years. The RMD rules require her to withdraw 4.95% of her traditional retirement account. Is that a safe withdrawal rate? Given Aretha's age, she might choose to spend more than her RMD—to enhance meaningful experiences while she's still in good health.

RMD Beginning Year

RMDs are not required until the year the account owner turns 75—for those born in 1960 or later. In general, RMDs must be taken by December 31 of each year. Failing to take an RMD on time can result in a significant tax penalty, though mitigation techniques (beyond the scope of this book) are available.

Extra Credit: For the first RMD only, the account owner can delay the withdrawal until as late as April 1 of the following year. However, this usually isn't advantageous, since it results in two RMDs being taxed in a single year.

RMDs and Planning During the Accumulation Phase

Picture Christopher, who turns 50 in 2025. He has $2,000,000 in his employer's traditional 401(k) and plans to retire at age 55. Lately, he's heard many personal finance commentators sounding the alarm about RMDs, which has made him uneasy. As a result, Christopher is considering switching all of his 401(k) contributions to Roth for the next five years. He's currently in the 24% marginal federal tax bracket.

How should Christopher approach his uncertainty?

Here's one helpful tactic: **Christopher should consider his remaining life expectancy.** He can refer to the most recent actuarial data from the Social Security Trustees Report, available at https://www.ssa.gov/oact/STATS/table4c6.html. According to the latest report at the time of this writing, a 50-year-old man has a remaining life expectancy of 29.05 years.

According to actuarial science, Christopher and his fellow 50-year-old men are expected to live, on average, a bit beyond their 79th birthday. What does that mean for his traditional 401(k) versus Roth 401(k) decision?

Christopher is expected to have a retirement that lasts about 24 years. Of those, 20 years (ages 55 through 74) come with no RMDs. Only about 4 years (on average) would be subject to RMDs—and those years are less likely to occur than the first 20.

So, what should Christopher prioritize? The tax burden of his five remaining working years and the 20 RMD-free years in retirement—or the (expected) four years of RMDs late in life? Put differently, while RMDs are worth considering, they represent only a small part of his overall tax and retirement landscape. RMDs are expected to affect just four of his 24 retirement years— roughly one-sixth of the total timeframe.

That's why RMDs should be, at most, a minor factor in deciding between making traditional and Roth 401(k) contributions.

Even if Christopher remains concerned about future RMDs, he should remember that he has 20 years (ages 55 to 74) to plan for a problem that may only last a few years.

Why give up what are likely the most valuable tax deductions of his life because of a potential problem that's both distant and time-limited?

For all the commentary about RMDs, few acknowledge that—if they are a problem—**they tend to be a problem of short duration, affecting only a narrow slice of retirement.** That limited timeframe is our second reason that RMDs are not a significant concern.

The Taxation of RMDs

The taxation of RMDs may not be as burdensome as you might have expected before reading this book. In fact, RMDs often benefit from **tax rate arbitrage**— they're frequently taxed at lower federal income tax rates than the marginal rates that applied when the original 401(k) contributions were made.

We'll walk through two examples to help you see how RMDs are actually taxed—and whether the outcome is better or worse than expected.

First, meet Estelle. She's a widow who turns 85 in 2025. On December 31, 2024, her traditional IRA was worth $1 million. Using the age-85 factor of 16 from the IRS Uniform Lifetime Table, her 2025 RMD is $62,500.

Estelle also holds a domestic equity index fund worth $250,000 in a taxable account. It generates $3,400 of qualified dividend income (QDI), $200 of Section 199A dividends (ordinary income eligible for the 20% deduction), and $200 of other nonqualified dividends. She also has $50,000 in a bank account, producing $2,500 of interest income.

Estelle's 2025 Social Security income is $36,000. Assume she and her late husband made their traditional 401(k) contributions at a 24% marginal federal income tax rate.

Here's what Estelle's 2025 federal income tax return looks like:

Item	Amount
Social Security	$30,600
Qualified Dividends	$3,400
199A Dividends	$200
Other Nonqualified Dividends	$200
Interest Income	$2,500
RMD	$62,500
Adjusted Gross Income	**$99,400**
Standard Deduction	$15,750
Additional Standard Deduction	$2,000
Share of Senior Deduction	$4,536
Qualified Business Income Deduction	$40
Total Deduction	**$22,326**
Taxable Income	**$77,074**
Federal Income Tax	$11,632
Net Investment Income Tax	$0
IRMAA (Estimated)	$0
Total Tax	$11,632
Overall Effective Tax Rate on Income	**11.10%**
Effective Income Tax Rate for IRA Distributions	16.01%
Rate Assigning All Tax to IRA Distributions	18.61%
Marginal Federal Income Tax Rate	22%
Percent of Traditional IRA Paid in Federal Income Taxes	**1.16%**

Here's a breakdown of Estelle's federal income tax in 2025:

Amount Received	Type of Income	Deducted At	Taxed At	Federal Income Tax	Assessment
$5,400	Excluded Social Security	N/A	0%	$0	
$22,326	Taxable Social Security Against Deduction	N/A	0%	$0	
$8,274	Taxable Social Security Against 10% Bracket	N/A	10%	$827	Con 2
$2,900	Non-RMD Ordinary Income Against 10% Bracket	N/A	10%	$290	Con 5
$751 RMD	RMD Against 10% Bracket	24%	10%	$75	Estelle defeats the IRS
$36,550 RMD	RMD Against 12% Bracket	24%	12%	$4,386	Estelle defeats the IRS
$25,199 RMD	RMD Against 22% Bracket	24%	22%	$5,544	Estelle defeats the IRS
$3,400 QDI	QDI Against 15% LTCG Bracket	N/A	15%	$510	Con 5
Total $104,800		24%	Effective Rate 11.10%	Total $11,632	

In Estelle's case, her RMD is taxed across the 10%, 12%, and 22% federal income tax brackets. This illustrates a core benefit of tax rate arbitrage: although she and her late husband deducted their contributions at a 24% marginal rate, the distributions are now taxed at lower rates.

Few commentators mention that some or all of an RMD might actually result in favorable tax rate arbitrage for the retiree. Estelle's example shows that the so-called "ugly surprise" of RMDs may not be so ugly after all.

Estelle is in the so-called Widow's Tax Trap, and her RMD is based on her turning 85. Still, her RMDs are only lightly taxed.

Further, the two drawbacks we previously discussed in Chapter 7—light taxation of Social Security (Con 2) and light taxation of investment income (Con 5)—together added just **$1,627** in additional federal income taxes. When we divide that by Estelle's gross income of $104,800, the combined effective tax rate from these two cons is only **1.55%**.

So, did traditional retirement accounts create quantifiable drawbacks for Estelle in retirement? Yes. But are those drawbacks significant enough to make Roth contributions more appealing in hindsight? Hardly!

One more striking figure: the IRS collected just 1.16% of Estelle's $1 million traditional IRA in 2025 income taxes. That's a remarkably low percentage—especially given how onerous RMDs are often portrayed. And remember, this isn't the RMD of a 75-year-old—it's for someone who's 85.

Finally, note that even with a $62,500 RMD, Estelle isn't subject to IRMAA (Medicare premium surcharges).

Here's a second example—this one checks all the boxes of common RMD worries:

- A $4 million traditional IRA? Check.
- An 80-year-old widow subject to an RMD? Check.
- The Widow's Tax Trap? Check.
- IRMAA? Check.

Bethany is a widow who turns 80 in 2025. On December 31, 2024, her traditional IRA was worth $4 million. Using the IRS Uniform Lifetime Table's factor of 20.2 for age 80, her 2025 RMD is $198,020.

Bethany also holds a domestic equity index fund worth $1 million in a taxable account. It generates $15,000 of dividends: $13,000 are qualified dividend income, $1,000 are Section 199A dividends (ordinary income eligible for a 20% deduction), and $1,000 are other nonqualified dividends. She also has $50,000 in a bank account generating $2,500 of interest income. Her 2025 Social Security benefit is $50,000. Assume the traditional 401(k) contributions made by Bethany and her late husband were deducted at a 24% marginal federal income tax rate.

Before we dive into Bethany's numbers, it's important to acknowledge that she's something of a unicorn. She has over $5 million in financial assets and very high Social Security benefits as an 80-year-old widow. A $4 million traditional IRA and a $198,020 RMD (both measured in 2025 dollars) are well beyond what most Americans planning for early retirement will achieve.

We offer Bethany's extreme example to help you evaluate just how challenging the combination of RMDs, the Widow's Tax Trap, and IRMAA might be.

Here is what Bethany's 2025 federal income tax return looks like:

Item	Amount
Social Security	$42,500
Qualified Dividends	$13,000
199A Dividends	$1,000
Nonqualified Dividends	$1,000
Interest Income	$2,500
RMD	$198,020
Adjusted Gross Income	**$258,020**
Standard Deduction	$15,750
Additional Standard Deduction	$2,000
Share of Senior Deduction	$0
Qualified Business Income Deduction	$200
Total Deductions	**$17,950**
Taxable Income	**$240,070**
Federal Income Tax	$51,676
Net Investment Income Tax	$665
IRMAA (Estimated)	$6,000
Total Tax	$58,341
Overall Effective Tax Rate on Income	**21.97%**
Effective Income Tax Rate for IRA Distributions	23.47%
Rate Assigning All Tax to IRA Distributions	29.46%
Marginal Federal Income Tax Rate	32%
Percent of Traditional IRA Paid in Taxes & IRMAA	**1.46%**

Here's how Bethany's 2025 federal income tax breaks down:

Amount Received	Type of Income	Deducted At	Taxed At	Federal Income Tax	Assessment
$7,500	Excluded Social Security	N/A	0%	$0	
$17,950	Taxable Social Security Against Deduction	N/A	0%	$0	
$11,925	Taxable Social Security Against 10% Bracket	N/A	10%	$1,193	Con 2
$12,625	Taxable Social Security Against 12% Bracket	N/A	12%	$1,515	Con 2
$4,500	Non-RMD Ordinary Income Against 12% Bracket	N/A	12%	$540	Con 5
$19,425 RMD	RMD Against 12% Bracket	24%	12%	$2,331	Bethany defeats the IRS
$54,875 RMD	RMD Against 22% Bracket	24%	22%	$12,073	Bethany defeats the IRS
$93,950 RMD	RMD Against 24% Bracket	24%	24%	$22,548	Tie
$29,770 RMD	RMD Against 32% Bracket	24%	32%	$9,526	The IRS defeats Bethany
$13,000 QDI	QDI Against 15% LTCG Bracket	N/A	15%	$1,950	Con 5
Total **$265,520**	24%		**Effective Rate 19.46%**	**Total** **$51,676**	

There's a lot to observe about Bethany's situation. Yes, a $4 million traditional IRA leads to substantial federal income taxes in her 80s. But how bad is it, really?

Even with a large RMD, single filing status, IRMAA, and the Net Investment Income Tax (NIIT), Bethany keeps 78 cents on the dollar, resulting in over $200,000 of after-tax income to live on. A massive traditional IRA leads to a rather good tax outcome from a cash flow perspective. The supposedly onerous RMD rules have practically no adverse impact on Bethany's lived experience.

We trotted out all of the "boogeymen" of taxes in retirement, and **the federal government still couldn't take a quarter of every dollar of income.** That makes contributing to traditional 401(k)s—and not looking back—appealing.

At a minimum, it supports our third reason why RMDs aren't ugly: in many cases, RMDs are taxed rather lightly. As we saw with Estelle, and again with Bethany, most of the RMD faces an income tax rate of 24% or lower.

In Bethany's case—with a $4 million traditional IRA at age 80—only 15% of her feared RMD faces negative tax rate arbitrage. *Wow!*

Cons 2 and 5 cost Bethany an estimated $5,863 in federal taxes, which is nearly identical to her proportionately modest IRMAA surcharges.

Dividing that $5,863 by Bethany's income of $265,520 shows that Cons 2 and 5 imposed an effective tax rate of just 2.21%. Is that a drawback of using traditional retirement accounts? Yes. But is it enough to justify switching to Roth contributions instead? No!

Despite encountering many tax rules and tax "traps"—RMDs, the Widow's Tax Trap, and IRMAA—Bethany pays just 1.46% of her traditional IRA balance in the form of federal income tax, NIIT, and IRMAA.

Could some planning have helped Bethany avoid the 32% tax bracket? Sure. Before reaching their 80s, retirees like Bethany and her late husband should consider tactics to reduce taxes on large RMDs. But let's not overstate the case. The tax cost of neglecting some beneficial planning may be far less daunting than many fear.

In Real Life: It took over $5 million in financial wealth, IRMAA, the Widow's Tax Trap, and an RMD for an 80-year-old to end up with a Rate Assigning All Tax to IRA Distributions of 29.46%—a statistic suggesting our favored approach is suboptimal by 5.5 cents on the dollar. Based on that metric alone, it would appear that Bethany and her husband took the wrong path by prioritizing traditional over Roth contributions at work.

*This highlights the limitations of statistics. Bethany's financial outcome and lived experience are incredible, yet the statistic tells us she has a bad tax outcome. To us, being financially successful in retirement—with traditional 401(k) contributions as the primary driver, even with minor tax inefficiencies—does not strike us as a bad outcome. Quantitative analysis is important, of course, but **tax planning** statistics must be viewed in the proper context—one that considers broader **financial outcomes and success.***

We're pretty sure most Americans would gladly sign up for Bethany's outcome of being fabulously wealthy in her 80s with a tax inefficiency of just 6 cents on the dollar.

***Extra Credit:** We conservatively assumed Bethany and her husband deducted traditional 401(k) contributions at a 24% marginal rate. But what if it was actually 32%? That change in the facts alters how we assess Bethany's outcome in retirement.*

What's the Risk of Traditional Retirement Accounts?

Bethany's case reveals the real "risk" of traditional retirement accounts: **if your traditional retirement accounts grow too large, you'll be wealthy—and you'll face some tax inefficiencies.**

That's it!

Too often in personal finance, we focus on the trees and miss the forest. The trees here are IRMAA, some Social Security taxation, some investment income taxation, and 15.03% of an RMD experiencing negative tax rate arbitrage—to the tune of 8 cents on the dollar.

The forest? Bethany is rich!

Why should Bethany be upset about this outcome? She's wealthy and still receives favorable tax arbitrage on a large portion of her RMD. In a country where the median adult wealth in 2024 was under $125,000, Bethany's outcome—being more than financially secure with some modest tax inefficiencies—is a tremendous blessing.

For all the concerns about taxation in retirement, one truth stands out: higher tax rates tend to correlate with greater **financial success**!

If the worst-case scenario of contributing to traditional retirement accounts requires you to be financially successful in retirement, is it really a worst-case scenario?

RMD Mitigation Opportunities Abound

Fortunately, for those approaching or in retirement with significant retirement account balances like Bethany, there are plenty of opportunities to mitigate RMDs. The good news? Several strategies are relatively easy to implement.

Asset Location

As we discuss in Chapter 18, traditional retirement accounts are well-suited for holding the bond portion of a portfolio. This approach can help slow the growth of the account relative to others, which may in turn reduce future RMDs.

Qualified Charitable Distributions

For those who are charitably inclined and have traditional IRAs, qualified charitable distributions (QCDs) are a great way to give to charity and reduce the impact of RMDs. We discuss QCDs in more detail in Chapter 32.

QCDs combat RMDs in two ways. First, they reduce the traditional IRA balance. Starting at age 70½, an account owner can instruct their IRA custodian to send money directly to a qualified charity. These gifts are excluded from the IRA owner's income and permanently reduce the size of the traditional IRA—lowering all future RMDs.

Second, QCDs made after reaching RMD age reduce the tax on this year's RMD. The QCD will be part of the RMD, as long as it is made before distributions that already cover the RMD. Even if the owner is uninterested in reducing the taxable amount of the current year's RMD, he or she could make a QCD after taking their full taxable RMD for the year.

Here's an example of a QCD that reduces the taxable amount of an RMD:

Jordan, who turns 76 in 2025, has a $70,000 RMD from his traditional IRA. He instructs his custodian to transfer $1,000 per month (a total of $12,000) directly to his church, a qualified 501(c)(3) charity. That $12,000 is excluded from Jordan's gross income and counts toward his RMD. As a result, he only needs to withdraw an additional $58,000 from his IRA to fully satisfy his $70,000 RMD—and only that $58,000 will be taxable.

Strategic Roth Conversions

Many retirees will experience years when they can do Roth conversions and have the converted amounts taxed at favorable rates—or possibly tax-free against the standard deduction. This strategy moves money out of traditional retirement accounts, reducing future RMDs.

It's worth repeating that two key tactics can help retirees create more runway for advantageous Roth conversions before RMDs begin: keeping ordinary income low and delaying claiming Social Security.

Early Withdrawal Planning

Did you read Chapter 12 and think, "Sign me up for the Rule of 55," or "Looks like I'll need to set up one of those 72(t) payment plans"? Perhaps you're planning to retire in your 50s and live off distributions from a governmental 457(b) plan.

If so, you already have a significant head start on mitigating RMDs. By planning to draw from your traditional retirement accounts before age 59½, you're reducing their size well in advance—more than a decade and a half before RMDs begin.

Living Expenses Prior to RMD Age

You have our permission to splurge on the NFL Sunday Ticket package in retirement. If you pay for it with traditional retirement account withdrawals, you're reducing your future RMDs!

Jokes aside, **most early retirees are likely to draw from their traditional retirement accounts before age 75.** From an RMD perspective, that's a feature—not a bug. Living expenses in retirement serve to reduce the balance of traditional retirement accounts, which in turn lowers the amount of all future RMDs.

RMDs

To a degree, RMDs are a self-correcting problem. Each year's required distribution reduces the traditional retirement account balance—thereby lowering the RMD for the following year relative to what it would have been otherwise.

Your Own Mortality

If you're concerned about RMDs, a quick look at the actuarial tables in the Social Security Trustees' Report (available at https://www.ssa.gov/oact/STATS/table4c6.html) may help ease your mind.

For those who reach age 75—which, unfortunately, is not guaranteed—the expected remaining life expectancy is 10.92 years for men and 12.68 years for women. In other words, most early retirees will have more retirement years without RMDs than with them. Some will live into their 90s, but others may not get far into their 70s.

Our own mortality, while sobering, limits the number of years RMDs apply and reduces the likelihood they will be harmful from a tax planning perspective.

Implication of the Available Planning Techniques

Few people worry about diseases with cures that are cheap and readily available. It should be the same with RMDs. We've just outlined seven factors that mitigate RMDs—many of which are accessible to retirees, especially early retirees.

The availability of these factors is our fourth reason for believing that RMDs are not a significant tax or retirement planning problem.

Conclusion

We have outlined the four reasons RMDs typically have minimal adverse tax and retirement planning effects. They are:

1. The RMD rules require distributions that are relatively small, given the account size and the owner's age.
2. RMDs affect only a narrow portion of one's life and retirement—especially for early retirees.
3. RMDs tend to be taxed at relatively low rates.
4. Retirees can use effective, accessible techniques to reduce the negative impacts of RMDs.

Does this mean we ignore RMDs in tax and retirement planning? No. But it does mean that RMDs are not a compelling reason to avoid traditional 401(k) contributions for the vast majority of aspiring early retirees. Likewise, RMDs are often not a compelling reason to pursue large-scale Roth conversions.

That said, Tailored Taxable Roth Conversions (TTRCs)—as discussed in Chapter 17—are likely to be advantageous in many cases, and other Roth conversions may be beneficial.

16 – The Widow's Tax Trap

The Widow's Tax Trap strikes when the first spouse dies. While taxable income may decline slightly, it often remains similar—especially if the couple was already taking required minimum distributions (RMDs).

However, the tax treatment of that income changes, and not for the better. Taxable income that previously benefited from the larger standard deduction and wider tax brackets for married couples filing jointly is now subject to the lower thresholds for single filers. As a result, the widow(er) is likely to face a higher effective tax rate.

In Chapter 8, we saw Jane experience a 2.8% increase in her effective federal income tax rate due to the Widow's Tax Trap. We also saw her subject to IRMAA—a 1.9% nuisance tax in her case—due to the Widow's Tax Trap.

The Widow's Tax Trap is real, but is it enough to derail tax or retirement planning? Not likely.

Recall Estelle and Bethany from the previous chapter. Both were affected by the Widow's Tax Trap. Estelle had a favorable federal income tax situation, even though she had to take an RMD from a $1 million traditional IRA at age 85 as a single filer.

Even with a $4 million traditional IRA, Bethany's Effective Income Tax Rate for IRA Distributions was 23.47%—lower than the 24% marginal rate at which she and her husband deducted their traditional 401(k) contributions. It's remarkable that this is true for Bethany, even with a $4 million traditional IRA in the Widow's Tax Trap.

The Widow's Tax Trap can be mitigated by all seven of the factors we discussed in the previous chapter for mitigating RMDs.

Let's add two additional considerations:

1. **For the Widow's Tax Trap to be a significant problem, there needs to be a significant amount of time between the spouses' deaths.** In many cases, the surviving spouse passes away not long after their spouse. This likelihood inherently reduces the risk presented by the Widow's Tax Trap.

2. The IRS Uniform Lifetime Table helps mitigate the Widow's Tax Trap when the older spouse dies first—the most common fact pattern. That's because the younger surviving spouse inherits the account and uses their own (higher) RMD factor—resulting in smaller RMDs. As noted in Chapter 30, a surviving spouse can simply roll over retirement accounts they inherit from their spouse into their own IRA.

Consider this example: In 2025, Ned turns 81 and is married to Loretta, who turns 76. Ned has a $1.3 million traditional IRA as of December 31, 2024, and must take an RMD of **$67,010** ($1.3 million ÷ 19.4, the age-81 factor from the IRS Uniform Lifetime Table).

Ned dies in August 2025. Loretta transfers his traditional IRA into a traditional IRA in her own name. Assuming the traditional IRA is still worth $1.3 million as of December 31, 2025, Loretta's 2026 RMD from the account will be **$56,769** ($1.3 million ÷ 22.9, the age-77 factor from the IRS Uniform Lifetime Table).

As you can see, the surviving younger spouse's increased life expectancy factor reduces the required distribution—partially mitigating the Widow's Tax Trap. And if the surviving spouse has not yet reached RMD age, RMDs may be delayed.

Extra Credit: IRMAA is one component of the Widow's Tax Trap. As long as both spouses are alive, IRMAA tends to rarely affect retired couples—unless they have substantial income. After the first spouse dies, the likelihood of IRMAA increases. Still, as we've seen, when IRMAA does apply, it often acts as a minor nuisance tax, with little impact on financial success or quality of life in retirement.

Conclusion

The Widow's Tax Trap sounds scary. But when we break it down with actual numbers, the concern often begins to fade.

Does this mean we completely ignore it? No. Roth conversion planning during both spouses' lives can help reduce the potential impact of the Widow's Tax Trap. This is especially true when Roth conversion income can be offset by the standard deduction, the additional standard deduction for those age 65 and older, and the new senior deduction.

Is the Widow's Tax Trap a compelling reason to avoid traditional 401(k) contributions for most aspiring early retirees? Not in our opinion.

17 – Taxable Roth Conversions

Mike Piper has stated that the primary beneficial effects of Roth conversions are generally to reduce tax drag on taxable portfolios (by using taxable account funds to pay the conversion tax) and to address the challenges of required minimum distributions (RMDs) by lowering traditional retirement account balances. He also stated, "Roth conversions do not typically improve financial security in retirement."

When we combine our analysis with Mike Piper's perspective, it becomes clearer why Roth conversions may not always have a significant impact. In Chapter 10, we showed that the tax drag from taxable accounts can be minimal in early retirement. In Chapter 15, we demonstrated that RMDs are often not particularly harmful—especially for those born in 1960 or later, who begin RMDs at age 75.

At a minimum, we should ask: how many early retirees won't spend any traditional retirement account money before age 75? Even most conventional retirees will likely need to withdraw significant amounts before then. It will be rare for traditional retirement accounts to grow without some diminution for living expenses, qualified charitable distributions, and/or Roth conversions prior to RMDs starting at age 75.

If the problems Roth conversions are meant to solve—tax drag on taxable accounts and the burden of RMDs—aren't particularly problematic, then many Roth conversions may not be especially beneficial.

When do taxable Roth conversions make sense?

In this chapter, we review five situations where Roth conversions may make sense. We particularly favor the first three. The latter two are more subjective and may apply in specific circumstances, though those situations are less than common.

Here is our list:

1. Disruptions of income during the accumulation years. Think grad school, a layoff, a mini-retirement, or launching self-employment.

2. Roth conversions to create income sufficient to qualify for a Premium Tax Credit (PTC) during early retirement.

3. Roth conversions up to the level that both (1) keep total ordinary income within available deductions and (2) keep taxable income within the 0% long-term capital gain (LTCG) tax bracket. We call

these "Tailored Taxable Roth Conversions," or "TTRCs."

4. For the very financially successful, Roth conversions that reduce or eliminate inefficiencies during RMD years.

5. For the very financially successful, Roth conversions intended to improve the future tax situation of beneficiaries.

While we shy away from absolute statements, we believe that if you don't clearly fall into one of these five categories, taxable Roth conversions are unlikely to provide significant benefits.

Before we continue, let's be clear about what we are not discussing in this chapter: Backdoor Roths. When implemented properly, they're mostly nontaxable due to basis recovery. We cover Backdoor Roths in Chapter 9. Here, we're focused solely on taxable Roth conversions that generate material adjusted gross income—something a properly executed Backdoor Roth does not do.

Income Disruption Years

The world is changing. Accumulation is becoming less linear, and that opens the door to low- or no-tax Roth conversion opportunities.

Consider John, who worked at a consulting firm for four years before starting law school. With little or no taxable income during law school, he could convert his old traditional 401(k) to a Roth IRA. The resulting income would likely be sheltered from federal income tax thanks to the combination of the high standard deduction and the Lifetime Learning Credit.

Or take Jillian, who is taking a 12-month mini-retirement. If most or all of those months fall within a single calendar year, Jillian has a great opportunity to do Roth conversions sheltered from federal income tax by the standard deduction.

The takeaway for anyone considering or experiencing a significant income disruption is to evaluate whether a taxable Roth conversion makes sense during that time. Of course, it's important to consider whether any resulting federal or state income tax is affordable.

Premium Tax Credit Qualification

As discussed in Chapter 13, early retirees must meet a minimum income threshold to qualify for a Premium Tax Credit (PTC). This income must satisfy two requirements:

1. Modified Adjusted Gross Income (MAGI) must be at least 100% of the federal poverty level, and

2. Income must not be so low that the individual qualifies for their state's version of Medicaid.

This can be a challenge when retirees rely on low-yield taxable assets, recover basis when selling taxable assets, or spend primarily from cash reserves.

The solution? A taxable Roth conversion before year-end!

If income is too low to qualify for a PTC, a Roth conversion often makes sense from a federal income tax perspective. In many cases, the conversion is fully sheltered by the standard deduction. At worst, a small portion may be taxed in the 10% bracket. That modest cost—plus any applicable state income tax—is often well worth it, considering the thousands of dollars in PTCs that a Roth conversion can unlock.

Tailored Taxable Roth Conversions

Roth conversions tailored to fit within two parameters—what we call TTRCs—are often advantageous.

The **first parameter** of the TTRC is to keep total ordinary income at or below the standard deduction, plus any additional available deductions. The goal is to have the entire Roth conversion sheltered from federal income tax by these deductions.

Here are two examples:

Example 1: Willie and Mae, both 58, have $10,000 of qualified dividends, $60,000 of LTCG income, $3,000 of interest income, and $2,000 of nonqualified dividends. If they take no other action, their only ordinary income will be the interest and the nonqualified dividends. Before year-end, Willie and Mae should consider executing a **$26,500 TTRC**. Adding $3,000 + $2,000 + $26,500 equals $31,500—the exact standard deduction they qualify for in 2025.

They may also want to consider rounding up or down slightly. For instance, if they underestimate their other ordinary income by $1,000 (i.e., it's $6,000 instead of $5,000), and they do a $26,500 Roth conversion, it's not a big issue. The final $1,000 of the conversion would fall into the 10% federal income tax bracket, resulting in just $100 of federal tax for 2025.

Example 2: Robert and Natasha, both 66, have $2,000 of interest income, $4,000 of nonqualified dividends, $10,000 of qualified dividends (QDI), and $85,000 of long-term capital gains (LTCG) in 2025. They qualify for a $34,700 standard deduction plus a $12,000 senior deduction, for total deductions of $46,700. Since their existing ordinary income is $6,000, they can execute a **$40,700 TTRC** by year-end—fully sheltered by their available deductions.

Quick Aside: *Robert and Natasha can have $141,700 of adjusted gross income, pay no federal income tax, and move $40,700 tax-free from their traditional IRA to a Roth IRA. Why do people worry about taxes in retirement?*

Notice the main limitation on the ability to do tax-free Roth conversions: other ordinary income. The more interest and nonqualified dividend income retirees have, the less room there is for tax-free Roth conversions.

This is a key reason behind our drawdown principle of keeping ordinary income as low as possible during retirement.

Social Security benefits also count as ordinary income for this purpose. That's part of why we generally favor delaying Social Security—doing so helps maintain lower ordinary income for a longer period, creating more room for strategic Roth conversions when appropriate.

The **second parameter** of the TTRC is that the Roth conversion should keep taxable income within the 0% LTCG bracket. If it doesn't, the conversion can effectively be subject to a de facto 15% tax. This happens when the Roth conversion pushes LTCG and qualified dividend income (QDI) into the 15% tax bracket. Additionally, the conversion could reduce the benefit of the senior deduction, creating another layer of de facto taxation.

Let's revisit Robert and Natasha's example. As originally illustrated, their $40,700 Roth conversion is tailored to fit within this second parameter. Even with the large conversion, they still qualify for the full senior deduction, and none of their QDI or LTCG is taxed at the 15% rate.

But what happens if we increase their LTCG income?

Example 3: Imagine Robert and Natasha have all the same numbers as in Example 2 (before the Roth conversion)—except now they have $134,000 of LTCG in 2025 instead of $85,000. Let's call this Example 3, Scenario 1.

What might their federal tax return look like?

Item	Amount
Interest	$2,000
Nonqualified Dividends	$4,000
QDI	$10,000
LTCG	$134,000
Roth Conversion	$0
AGI	$150,000
Standard Deduction	$31,500
Additional Standard Deduction	$3,200
Senior Deduction	$12,000
Total Deductions	$46,700
Taxable Income	$103,300
Federal Income Tax	**$990**

Not bad at all: $150,000 of AGI and just $990 of federal income tax. They pay 15% on the portion of their taxable income that exceeds the top of the 0% long-term capital gains bracket ($96,700 in 2025). The $990 is derived from taxing the $6,600 excess ($103,300 – $96,700) at 15%.

You might be thinking: *Wait a minute—they still have $28,700 of unused standard deduction remaining. Shouldn't they "top up" their ordinary income to make full use of it?* By adding a Roth conversion of $28,700 to their $6,000 of interest and nonqualified dividends, they would soak up the entire available standard deduction.

Let's explore that. Imagine Robert and Natasha do a $28,700 Roth conversion just to soak up the rest of their standard deduction (we'll call this Example 3, Scenario 2).

Here's what their tax return would look like with the added Roth conversion:

Item	Amount
Interest	$2,000
Nonqualified Dividends	$4,000
QDI	$10,000
LTCG	$134,000
Roth Conversion	$28,700
AGI	$178,700
Standard Deduction	$31,500
Additional Standard Deduction	$3,200
Senior Deduction	$8,556
Total Deductions	$43,256
Taxable Income	$135,444
Federal Income Tax	**$5,812**

Whoa—that tax skyrocketed based on a relatively modest amount of additional income.

Technically, the $28,700 Roth conversion itself isn't taxed—it's fully sheltered by the standard deduction. However, the conversion indirectly triggers tax by pushing $28,700 of QDI/LTCG income out of the 0% bracket and into the 15% bracket, resulting in $4,305 of additional federal income tax.

Further, the increase in AGI caused by the Roth conversion reduces the senior deduction from $12,000 to $8,556. That reduction pushes another $3,444 of QDI/LTCG from the 0% bracket into the 15% bracket, creating $517 of additional tax. That's effectively a 1.8% additional tax on the Roth conversion, bringing the effective federal tax rate on the conversion to 16.8%.

If Robert and Natasha continued converting, they'd eventually hit the 10% ordinary income tax bracket—at which point their Roth conversions would (1) be taxed at 10%, (2) push more LTCG/QDI into the 15% bracket, and (3) further reduce the senior deduction.

These variations in Robert and Natasha's situation show why it's important to fit within both parameters of a TTRC.

Extra Credit: *There's a certain magic to the 12% tax bracket in retirement. Keeping annual taxable income near the top of the 0% LTCG bracket ($48,350 single / $96,700 MFJ in 2025), which closely aligns with the top of the 12% ordinary income bracket ($48,475 single / $96,950 MFJ), achieves three powerful objectives:*

1. *Keeps ordinary income tax low or nonexistent,*
2. *Eliminates federal income tax on LTCG and QDI, and*
3. *Optimizes for the new senior deduction for those age 65 and older.*

Lifetime Timing

TTRCs are most likely to make sense during the Golden Years—ages 66 through 69—but can also be beneficial earlier. They tend to be less attractive during years when the Premium Tax Credit (PTC) is a key planning factor. In those years, retirees should carefully weigh the benefits and costs before executing a TTRC.

After the Golden Years, TTRCs become less feasible, as most retirees will have begun collecting Social Security benefits, making it harder to meet the first TTRC parameter (keeping ordinary income within the standard deduction).

Charitable Contributions Starting in 2026 Can Increase TTRCs

The One Big Beautiful Bill (OBBB) introduces a helpful provision beginning in 2026: taxpayers who do not itemize deductions—which includes the vast majority of retirees—can deduct up to $1,000 per person for cash contributions to charity.

Starting in 2026, retirees should pay close attention. The available deduction for many—especially Golden Years retirees—will include the standard deduction, the senior deduction, and the new $1,000 per person charitable deduction. Assuming (for simplicity) no inflation adjustments for 2026, a married couple in the Golden Years making $2,000 in cash charitable contributions would have **$48,700** in available deductions to apply toward Roth conversions (or, alternatively, to support spending from the Hidden Roth IRA).

Reduce or Eliminate Future RMD Inefficiencies

This is where things become more subjective. Taxable Roth conversions beyond our three favored scenarios can still make sense—but it depends on the size of the deferred accounts and one's outlook on the future.

In 2025, the introduction of the senior deduction changed the landscape for taxable Roth conversions beyond TTRCs in two key ways. First, for some retirees, it altered the upfront cost of the conversion. Second, it affected the back-end taxation of future RMDs by lowering the tax burden many retirees will face.

For the very financially successful, Roth conversions can help reduce or even eliminate inefficiencies related to future RMDs. That said, these conversions can quickly trigger current-year trade-offs—such as reducing eligibility for PTCs, pushing more LTCG income into the 15% bracket, and reducing the senior deduction.

Recall Mike and Christine from Chapter 11. At age 71, they live on $80,000 per year of Social Security and withdraw $64,000 from their traditional retirement accounts. They also make $12,000 of qualified charitable distributions (QCDs) from those accounts.

Should they consider Roth conversions? **The size of their traditional retirement accounts is a key factor.** Let's assume Mike and Christine are "five percenters," withdrawing 5% of their retirement accounts annually. With $76,000 of total withdrawals, that implies traditional IRA balances of approximately $1.52 million.

We don't view a 71-year-old married couple with $1.52 million in traditional retirement accounts as having a tax problem. Born in 1954, Mike and Christine will begin taking required minimum distributions (RMDs) at age 73. Do you know how much their first RMD will be? Assuming the same account value, it would be around $57,400—even less than they're already withdrawing!

According to the IRS Uniform Lifetime Table, their RMD withdrawal rate won't exceed 5% until age 81.

So, why would Mike and Christine do Roth conversions to reduce RMDs that, for the first eight years, are already smaller than what they plan to withdraw anyway?

Further, taxable Roth conversions increase the taxable portion of Social Security benefits (due to the Tax Torpedo) and eventually reduce the senior deduction. These are two more reasons why a Roth conversion is unlikely to be advantageous in their case.

Mike and Christine are in a great position from a tax perspective. Why accelerate and increase their tax liability with Roth conversions? They've landed in a favorable spot in their tax planning journey, and there's simply no need to rock the boat.

But what about the future—specifically, when one of them passes away? Elaine's example in Chapter 11 is helpful here. At age 82, with a $2.4 million traditional retirement account, Elaine has no RMDs subject to a federal income tax rate greater than 24% and pays less than 20 cents on the dollar of her income to the federal government.

It's hard to justify exposing Mike and Christine to the Tax Torpedo and a reduced senior deduction today in order to mitigate a Widow's Tax Trap that isn't all that harmful—and may not last very long. In our view, the wiser move is to preserve their excellent current outcome: a sub-6% effective federal tax rate.

The fact that a couple with $1.52 million in traditional retirement accounts at age 71 is well-advised not to pursue Roth conversions is quite instructive.

Does that mean taxable Roth conversions beyond TTRCs are always a bad idea? Not necessarily.

Let's imagine Mike and Christine had $4 million in traditional retirement accounts instead. In Chapter 15, we saw that Bethany—while in the Widow's Tax Trap and with a $4 million traditional retirement account—faced a 32% tax rate on about 15% of her RMDs.

In that case, some Roth conversions may make sense, with the primary goal of reducing tax inefficiencies for the surviving spouse.

Additionally, a 71-year-old couple with $4 million in deferred accounts withdrawing just $76,000 screams out "underspending!"—drawing less than 2% annually. They might be better served by (1) spending more while they're young enough to enjoy it and/or (2) significantly increasing their highly tax-efficient QCDs.

Before doing taxable Roth conversions in retirement beyond TTRCs, it's worth remembering that taxable Roth conversions beyond TTRCs often require a high level of financial success to be truly beneficial.

As we've seen, even a rather successful retired couple—like Mike and Christine with $1.52 million in deferred accounts—may be better off avoiding taxable Roth conversions.

Cody's Take: *There are typically only four parties that will spend your wealth:*

1. *You*
2. *Your family*
3. *Charities*
4. *The government*

I encourage retirees who acknowledge they're underspending to consider having deeper conversations about how their wealth will be used—and by whom. This conversation is beyond the scope of this book, but it's a topic I'm deeply passionate about.

Sean's Take: I disfavor Roth conversions for most retirees living primarily on traditional retirement accounts prior to RMD age. First, any Roth conversion income stacks on top of other income, exposing the Roth conversion income to potentially higher marginal tax rates. Second, living primarily on traditional retirement accounts reduces any potential future RMD problem. There's generally little need to employ a second significant tactic to address RMDs. Remember, as we discussed in Chapter 15, RMD concerns tend to be overstated.

Lifetime Timing

Taxable Roth conversions beyond TTRCs are most likely to make sense during the Golden Years—especially if the retiree is still living off taxable accounts. Outside of that window, they may still be appropriate, but the likelihood decreases.

Additionally, as discussed, these conversions are generally only beneficial if the retiree has been very successful in building substantial traditional retirement account balances.

Tax Planning for Beneficiaries

Our final potentially advantageous taxable Roth conversion is also the most subjective. It addresses a second-order planning priority: managing the tax situation of someone other than yourself or your spouse.

Beneficiaries pay income taxes on distributions from inherited traditional retirement accounts. One way to avoid that outcome is for the account owner to "prepay" those taxes through Roth conversions.

Intergenerationally, this can absolutely make sense. For example, a retiree in the 22% or 24% marginal tax bracket may have a child in the 35% or 37% bracket. In such a case, the retiree doing Roth conversions can save significant income taxes across generations.

That said, we need to ask a fundamental question: What is the purpose of your retirement account? In our view, the primary purpose is to support you (and your spouse) to and through retirement—not to manage your adult children's future tax situation.

Of course, choosing to pay tax on Roth conversions for the benefit of the next generation is a personal decision. Some may prioritize reducing intergenerational tax exposure and choose to convert more, even though the primary benefit goes to their heirs.

Before doing any taxable Roth conversions primarily designed for the benefit of heirs, account owners should carefully assess their own needs. It makes little sense to accelerate taxes if doing so could jeopardize financial security in retirement.

For the extremely wealthy, Roth conversions can offer an additional benefit: reducing federal estate taxes by removing the income tax liability from the taxable estate. However, given today's high exemption levels, federal estate tax planning is unlikely to be relevant for most readers.

Paying Tax on Taxable Roth Conversions

There are two primary ways to pay the tax on taxable Roth conversions: estimated tax payments and IRA withholding. We cover both methods in detail in Chapter 14.

For Roth conversions during "income disruption" years, we strongly favor paying the tax using estimated tax payments—meaning the tax comes from taxable accounts or cash, not from a traditional retirement account. There are two key reasons for this approach:

1. Most income disruption years occur before the account owner turns 59½. Paying the tax from a traditional retirement account would generally trigger a 10% early withdrawal penalty.

2. If a person doesn't have enough in taxable accounts to comfortably pay the tax on a Roth conversion during an income disruption year, that's a strong sign they can't afford the conversion and shouldn't be doing it.

What about Roth conversions done to qualify for a PTC or executed as a TTRC? In most of those cases, no federal income tax should be due. There may be a minor state income tax liability, which can be handled with small estimated payments. Aside from a possible small state income tax liability, these conversions are typically structured to avoid triggering any significant federal income tax.

In most cases, taxes on Roth conversions designed to reduce or eliminate future RMD inefficiencies should also be paid via estimated tax payments. The same applies to Roth conversions done for the benefit of the next generation. These conversions are often most appropriate during the Golden Years, when affluent retirees often still have taxable accounts available. Paying the tax from taxable accounts may result in taxable income that is primarily long-term capital gains.

However, there are situations where paying the tax from the traditional retirement account may make sense—especially if the retiree is age 59½ or older and has largely exhausted their taxable accounts. In such cases, the retiree's overall financial situation should be carefully assessed. If paying the tax from the retirement account would significantly jeopardize their financial success in retirement, that's a clear indication that the Roth conversion should not be done.

Timing of Taxable Roth Conversions During the Year

Our favored timeframe for executing taxable Roth conversions is early to mid–fourth quarter. Why? Because knowledge is power. By October or November, retirees typically have a much clearer picture of their taxable income and deductions for the year, making it easier to "right-size" the conversion.

Additionally, Roth conversions are irreversible. So, why lock in additional income early in the year—when the full picture of that year's income and deductions is still uncertain?

Are Taxable Roth Conversions "Needed"?

People often worry: "I know I need to do a Roth conversion."

Need is a strong word. Let's revisit Mike Piper's insight: the primary benefits of Roth conversions are to reduce tax drag on taxable accounts and to minimize the harmful tax impact of RMDs. As we've shown, both of those issues may not be particularly harmful in retirement.

Calling Roth conversions a need often overstates things. Can all five types of taxable Roth conversions we've discussed in this chapter be beneficial under the right circumstances? Absolutely! But are they needed?

The one that comes closest to being a true need is the taxable Roth conversion done to qualify for a Premium Tax Credit. Early retirees with very low income should pay close attention—failing to do such a conversion could cost thousands of dollars in lost PTCs.

Beyond that, TTRCs often tend to be excellent opportunities. Still, even in those cases, we believe highly desirable is a better description than needed.

Sean's Take: Think about the necessity of a taxable Roth conversion during retirement in terms of "Would I disrupt a year-end Hawaii vacation to do a Roth conversion by December 31st?"

- *For a federal income tax–free "taxable" Roth conversion necessary to qualify for a PTC? Absolutely.*
- *For a TTRC (a) during the Golden Years or (b) prior to the Golden Years if I was not covered by an ACA medical insurance plan? Yes.*
- *For any other taxable Roth conversion? No.*

18 – Asset Location

Asset location has become increasingly important, especially for early retirees and those aspiring to retire early.

Asset **location** is not the same as asset **allocation**; it's the step that comes after. First, an investor decides which assets to invest in and in what proportions. Once that decision is made, asset location starts.

The idea is to hold the desired assets within the available tax categories—Roth, Traditional, Taxable, HSA—in a way that maximizes tax efficiency and supports broader tax planning objectives.

Sean's Take: My preferred term for the asset location concept is "tax basketing," but the world seems to have settled on asset location, which is the term we use throughout this book.

Early Retirees and Aspiring Early Retirees

To assess asset location for early retirees, we will need to make a few assumptions.

First, our avatars—the aspiring early retiree and the early retiree—want to hold three core assets: domestic equity index funds, international equity index funds, and domestic bond index funds. This is simply an assumption for the sake of analysis; it is not investment advice for you or anyone else.

Second, we assume these avatars hold at least 50% of their financial wealth in traditional retirement accounts. This aligns them with most Americans and, in our experience, with many people considering or already in early retirement.

Third, we assume their portfolios contain less than 50% in domestic bond index funds—again, just an assumption, not advice.

Lastly, we generally exclude HSAs from the analysis unless specifically noted. HSA balances are often modest, and much of the Roth-related analysis applies similarly to HSAs.

With those assumptions in place, let's explore where our avatars might hold their desired assets, given that they are either pursuing or living in early retirement.

Asset Yield

Asset location should consider many factors—chief among them is annual asset yield. Financial assets such as stocks, bonds, mutual funds, and exchange-traded funds (ETFs) typically generate interest and/or dividend income each year, often referred to as "yield."

The expected amount and type of that income help inform the most tax-efficient account in which to hold each asset.

Let's look at the three assets our avatars plan to hold, using Vanguard mutual funds as reasonable proxies for their annual income (yield) profile (not presented as investment advice):

Fund	Annual Dividend Yield	Est. Qualified Dividend Income %
VTSAX (domestic equities)	1.28%	95.17%
VTIAX (international equities)	2.88%	75.11%
VBTLX (domestic bonds)	3.79%	0%

All numbers are as of July 2025 and are subject to change. That said, they offer a useful guide for asset location decisions.

Let's begin with VTSAX, the domestic equity index fund. Notice two things:

First, its yield is quite low. For example, if an investor holds $1 million of VTSAX in a taxable account, it would generate just around $12,800 in annual taxable income.

Second, most of that income is tax-preferred qualified dividend income (QDI)!

Tax drag is a common concern when investing in taxable accounts, but asset location can significantly reduce its impact. Why worry about tax drag when it takes $1 million of VTSAX to generate just $12,800—most of which receives favorable tax treatment?

Now consider VTIAX, the international equity index fund. In today's environment, it yields more than twice as much dividend income as VTSAX, and only about 75% of that income qualifies as QDI. That means a greater portion of its income is taxed at ordinary income rates.

Finally, we turn to VBTLX, the domestic bond index fund. Bonds typically produce the highest yield among these three assets—and that yield is fully taxed as ordinary income. From an asset location perspective, bonds are generally the least desirable to hold in taxable accounts.

Asset Location Insights

Equities

Investors seek growth from equities, which makes both domestic and international equities ideal candidates for Roth accounts.

In today's environment, both domestic equities and international equities have low yields and can be good fits in taxable accounts. However, in 2025, domestic equity yields are particularly low, making them our generally preferred asset for taxable accounts in today's environment.

Recall our avatar holding $1 million in VTSAX. That position generates only about $12,800 in taxable income. If that were their only income, the standard deduction could offset it entirely—potentially eliminating the need to file a federal tax return.

That said, the distinction between domestic and international equities in taxable accounts is of marginal importance. There's no guarantee domestic equities will remain this low-yielding in the future.

An additional point: Many early retirees and aspiring early retirees will likely hold both domestic and international equities across all account types—Taxable, Traditional, and Roth. In our view, that's not a bad thing. Yes, when held in a traditional retirement account, qualified dividend income becomes tax-deferred and is eventually taxed as ordinary income. That's not ideal, but it's not a horrible outcome.

What About the Foreign Tax Credit?

It's true that holding international equities in a retirement account means sacrificing the foreign tax credit. In a world where yields and future returns were equal across asset classes, the foreign tax credit might tip the scales in favor of holding international equities in taxable accounts.

But we don't live in that world. And in practice, the foreign tax credit is often modest. For example, Japan withholds 10% when Japanese companies pay dividends to U.S. shareholders. It's not nothing, but given that international equities yield more than twice as much as domestic equities, the foreign tax credit isn't enough to make receiving that income in taxable accounts highly desirable from a tax standpoint.

Dividend withholding rates vary by country. In some cases, they're much lower—or even zero. For instance, most dividends paid by U.K. companies to American shareholders are not subject to withholding tax, meaning no foreign tax credit appears on the federal tax return.

At the margins, the foreign tax credit can slightly improve the after-tax performance of international equities held in taxable accounts.

Domestic Bond Funds

Domestic bonds and bond funds are generally well-suited for traditional retirement accounts. Why use up the tax-free growth space of Roth accounts on bond funds?

Because bonds tend to have lower expected returns, they're a good fit for traditional accounts. Holding the slower-growing assets in traditional accounts helps reduce future required minimum distributions (RMDs) and any potential need for large Roth conversions. We'll cover more on RMD mitigation later in this chapter.

Also, why place high-yield assets—producing income that's fully taxed as ordinary income—into taxable accounts? None of it qualifies as QDI.

So, the stage is set: it's often preferable to put all the bonds in traditional retirement accounts.

Tax-Exempt Bonds

High-income taxpayers often ask: "Should I hold tax-exempt bonds given my income level?"

In the early 1980s, the answer may have been yes. At that time, tax rates were higher, and many affluent Americans held most of their wealth in taxable accounts and pensions. Tax-exempt bonds, despite their lower yields, could make sense from a tax-planning perspective. The IRA and 401(k) era was just beginning, and few people had large balances in tax-deferred defined contribution accounts.

Fast forward to the mid-2020s, and the environment looks very different. Many pensions have disappeared, and today's affluent early retirees and aspiring early retirees often hold a substantial portion of their financial wealth in traditional IRAs and 401(k)s.

This shift makes traditional retirement accounts an ideal place to hold bonds. The income generated is tax-deferred, and these accounts usually offer ample space for the investor's entire bond allocation. If that's the case, why not hold all the desired bond allocation within traditional retirement accounts?

For most investors, there's little reason to adjust asset allocation just to include tax-exempt bonds—especially when doing so means sacrificing yield. Inside a traditional 401(k) or IRA, tax-exempt bonds offer no advantage over taxable bonds.

Measure Twice: As we mentioned in Chapter 13, tax-exempt interest is included in modified adjusted gross income (MAGI) when calculating Premium Tax Credits (PTCs) and Medicare IRMAA. Early retirees should consider this when aiming to increase PTC eligibility or reduce Medicare premiums. Just because municipal bond interest is federally "tax-free" doesn't mean it won't reduce other tax benefits.

Keeping Ordinary Income Low

Do you see what thoughtful asset location can do for the early retiree? If the only holdings in taxable accounts are domestic equity index funds, perhaps with a small savings account, taxable income remains low—and ordinary income is quite modest.

That opens the door for some great tax planning. For example, Roth conversions can be made against what would otherwise be an unused standard deduction—resulting in conversions taxed at a 0% federal income tax rate. Who's complaining about paying no tax?

Or consider the Hidden Roth IRA, where an early retiree draws from a traditional retirement account to cover living expenses, using the standard deduction to offset the income. Again, who's complaining about paying no income tax?

Finally, asset location can help keep qualified dividend income (QDI) and long-term capital gains within the 0% long-term capital gains (LTCG) tax bracket. In 2025, married couples with taxable income up to $96,700 qualify for a 0% federal tax rate on LTCGs and qualified dividends. Proper asset location helps maintain that desired outcome.

Higher-yielding bond funds can fill up taxable income space quickly, pushing QDI and LTCGs into the 15% LTCG bracket due to income stacking. Why not keep those high-yield, ordinary-income assets in traditional retirement accounts—and reserve taxable accounts for low-yielding domestic equities?

Keeping Ordinary Income Low Facilitates Roth Conversions

You may be wondering: "What if interest rates return to the low levels of 2020? Wouldn't it make sense to hold cash in taxable accounts during early retirement?

In our view, it's still not ideal. Why? Because of the importance of harvesting the standard deduction. Ordinary income crowds out Roth conversions in a way LTCGs and QDI do not.

Consider Ann and Aaron, a married early-retired couple in their 50s. They earn $5,000 in interest income and have a modest amount of LTCGs and QDI—say $50,000 total. How much federally tax-free Roth conversion space do they have in 2025? The standard deduction for a married couple under age 65 is $31,500. The $5,000 of interest uses up part of that space, leaving only **$26,500** available for tax-free Roth conversions before they enter the 10% tax bracket.

Now compare that to Brenda and Bart, also early retirees in their 50s. They have no interest income, but instead earn $60,000 in LTCGs and QDI. How much can they convert to a Roth IRA without paying federal income tax in 2025? **$31,500!**

Brenda and Bart have more total income than Ann and Aaron, yet they can do more tax-free Roth conversions. Why? Because of the **character of their income**. Here, character matters more than amount. By avoiding ordinary income in their taxable account, Brenda and Bart preserve their full standard deduction for strategic tax-free Roth conversions.

Less ordinary income = more room for Roth conversions!

A similar concept applies to retirees who partially rely on the Hidden Roth IRA. The more ordinary income reported on a tax return, the smaller the annual Hidden Roth IRA opportunity becomes.

Few early retirees will be able to keep their ordinary income at exactly $0—but the closer they get, the better their potential for tax-free Roth conversions.

Extra Credit: Let's say you enter early retirement and look at your taxable account thinking, "Wow, that's not great from an asset location perspective." Guess what can help out: your own living expenses! Consider funding your initial retirement years by selling taxable assets you aren't as fond of. This can gradually improve your asset location over time.

Keeping Ordinary Income Low and Nonqualified Annuities

Nonqualified annuities can make it more challenging to keep ordinary income low. These are annuities held in taxable accounts—outside of retirement accounts.

Distributions from nonqualified annuities include a portion of the annuity's earnings, which are taxed as ordinary income. As you can see, maintaining flexibility with income sources is helpful for retirement tax planning—and nonqualified annuities are inherently inflexible. Once annuitized, they produce ordinary income each year, limiting your ability to control taxable income and implement other tax planning tactics.

For many retirees, tax planning is a compelling reason to avoid nonqualified annuities.

Aspiring Early Retirees

For still-working aspiring early retirees, holding taxable investments that generate low and tax-preferred yield (QDI) can help reduce taxes during peak earning years.

A high earner would generally prefer receiving less QDI (from domestic equities) rather than more ordinary income (from bond funds). Keeping taxable income lower can also reduce or eliminate exposure to the 3.8% Net Investment Income Tax (NIIT).

Premium Tax Credit Considerations

Remember the fairy tale character Goldilocks searching for the "just right" bowl of porridge? She can also teach us something about asset location and the PTC in early retirement.

In theory, an early retiree could fund their living expenses entirely from one of three sources: traditional retirement accounts, Roth accounts, or taxable accounts. Testing these extremes can help reveal which account type is most favorable from a PTC perspective.

If Goldilocks starts by withdrawing from traditional IRAs and 401(k)s, it's too hot—every dollar spent shows up as household income, reducing or even eliminating her PTC.

If she relies only on Roth IRAs, it's too cold—her withdrawals of Roth basis don't count as income, which may leave her with too little income to qualify for the PTC at all. That can be a big problem in early retirement.

But if Goldilocks funds her early retirement from taxable accounts, it can be *just right* from a PTC perspective. Suppose she needs $60,000 to cover expenses. That won't create $60,000 of income—it'll be reduced by the tax basis of the assets she sells. That gives her a strong chance of keeping income low enough to qualify for a substantial PTC. And if her basis is too high and she ends up with too little income, she could make strategic Roth conversions before year-end to bring gross income up to the desired threshold.

The takeaway? It's very helpful to enter early retirement with substantial assets in taxable accounts. While it's still possible to manage the PTC without them, doing so usually requires more careful planning.

RMD Mitigation

As discussed in detail in Chapter 15, concerns about required minimum distributions (RMDs) are often overstated. That said, RMD mitigation is still a legitimate concern.

What can help mitigate RMDs? Asset location!

As mentioned earlier, holding all of one's domestic bond investments in traditional IRAs and 401(k)s can help keep future growth in those accounts modest. Bonds have lower expected returns than equities, which leads to lower expected future balances in traditional accounts. In turn, this reduces future RMDs and lessens the need for Roth conversions.

Remember, RMDs are calculated using the prior year's account balance as the numerator. Keeping that balance smaller naturally results in smaller future RMDs.

Sequence of Returns Risk and Asset Location

Some worry about sequence of returns risk: What if I retire and the stock market crashes—like in 1987 or 2008—right as I stop working? This is a concern for retirees at any age, and early retirement magnifies that risk.

Let's say Maury, age 50, is preparing to retire and is concerned about sequence of returns risk. He wants to fund his first three years of retirement exclusively by spending cash. Since cash generates interest income, it's typically tax-inefficient. Can Maury use asset location to implement his strategy while remaining tax efficient? Absolutely.

Imagine Maury retires with the following portfolio:

- $500,000 in a domestic equity index fund in a taxable brokerage account
- $240,000 in cash or money market funds in a traditional IRA (three years of expenses)
- $500,000 in domestic bonds in a traditional IRA
- $1 million in domestic and international equities in a traditional IRA

Maury can use the combination of his taxable account and his traditional IRA to synthetically live off the cash (residing in his traditional IRA) while actually selling assets in his taxable brokerage accounts to fund living expenses. This sounds counterintuitive, but it's actually quite simple.

Each year, Maury sells $80,000 of the domestic equity index fund in his taxable account, realizing mostly long-term capital gains and modest qualified dividend income. Meanwhile, inside the traditional IRA, he "spends down" the cash by rebalancing and using $80,000 annually to buy more of his desired asset mix—domestic equities, international equities, or bonds.

Since rebalancing inside a retirement account doesn't generate taxable events, this strategy allows Maury to live off almost a quarter of a million dollars without reporting a penny of interest income to the IRS!

Retirement portfolios are fungible. It's quite possible to "live on cash" and still maintain tax efficiency by applying asset location principles.

Cheat Code for Early Retirement

We're often asked: "What's the ideal balance between taxable, traditional, and Roth accounts?" As you know from our Compelling Three, we generally prefer some assets in each of the three tax locations going into early retirement.

But there's no mythical "optimal proportion" across the three for everyone. That said, in our view, there is an "optimal" tax return in the early years of retirement.

Ideally, the early retiree's tax return includes just three income items—maybe a fourth:

1. A small amount of interest income from an emergency fund
2. Dividends, mostly qualified, mostly from domestic equity mutual funds or ETFs
3. Capital gains from selling shares of equity funds to cover living expenses
4. (Optional) Roth conversions, usually "taxed" against the standard deduction.

Having just these three (or four) income sources in early retirement can:

1. Result in very low federal income taxes
2. Create eligibility for valuable PTCs for those covered by an ACA medical insurance plan
3. Set up the retiree to move money from traditional retirement accounts to Roth retirement accounts without incurring federal income tax.

In our view, holding most taxable assets in domestic equity index funds heading into early retirement is a cheat code for a low-tax federal income tax return and exceptional planning flexibility.

The more ordinary income (e.g., from interest or nonqualified dividends) that shows up on the early retiree's tax return, the more tax they're likely to pay—and the more challenging tax planning becomes.

What if an early retiree already holds high-yielding ordinary-income assets in a taxable account? That presents a planning opportunity. They might begin retirement by selling those assets to fund living expenses while rebalancing within retirement accounts. With thoughtful planning, future years can bring much lower ordinary income—and much greater flexibility.

Less Than Optimal Asset Location at Retirement

Jose, age 57, decides to retire. He has a combination of traditional retirement accounts, Roth retirement accounts, and taxable accounts.

In his taxable brokerage account, he has the following assets:

Fund	Value	Basis
VTSAX (domestic equities)	$300,000	$160,000
VTIAX (international equities)	$100,000	$80,000
VBTLX (domestic bonds)	$100,000	$96,000

Jose plans to draw from his taxable accounts first in retirement but is concerned about his asset location—specifically, holding international equities and domestic bonds in his taxable account.

What can he do?

First, instead of reinvesting the dividends from VBTLX and VTIAX, Jose can direct them to his bank account to help fund living expenses. This reduces the capital gains he needs to realize each year.

Second, he can fund additional living expenses by first selling the least tax-efficient asset—VBTLX. That reduces ordinary income hitting his annual tax return and triggers very small capital gains.

Funding Jose's living expenses this way keeps his income very low, accomplishing two things:

1. Improving his eligibility for a PTC.
2. Opening the door for Roth conversions against the standard deduction.

If Jose is concerned that selling only VBTLX will throw off his desired asset allocation, he can rebalance within his traditional retirement accounts. For example, he could sell equities inside the traditional IRA (without tax consequences) and use the proceeds to buy more VBTLX there.

Once the VBTLX in his taxable account is depleted, Jose can shift to selling VTIAX.

Of course, yields can change over time. If the yield on VTSAX eventually exceeds that of VTIAX, Jose can pivot to drawing from VTSAX first. By spending down taxable assets early in retirement, Jose reduces the long-term impact of yield-related tax drag. Fewer taxable holdings in later retirement years means less exposure to dividend income that negatively impacts tax planning.

Rental Real Estate

Some investors are drawn to the idea of holding rental real estate in a "self-directed" IRA or 401(k). We strongly disfavor this approach. In our view, the more straightforward and tax-efficient option is to hold rental real estate in the investor's own name or in a revocable living trust—both of which effectively treat the property as being held in a taxable account.

Keep in mind that many people interested in rental real estate also plan to hold financial assets—such as stocks, bonds, mutual funds, and ETFs—for diversification. That brings up a key asset location question: "Should I hold my rental real estate in taxable accounts or retirement accounts?"

Let's explore how rental real estate works when "housed" (pun intended) in retirement accounts versus taxable accounts, based on several factors:

Depreciation: One of the biggest tax benefits of rental real estate is the ability to deduct depreciation, which helps shelter rental income from taxes—but only if the property is held outside of a retirement account. Real estate held in a retirement account forfeits this benefit!

Now compare this to financial assets, which don't generate depreciation deductions. Suppose you have one type of asset (rental property) that can reduce your taxable income through depreciation and another (stocks and bonds) that can't. Wouldn't it make sense to hold the depreciable asset in a taxable account?

Some might ask, "What about depreciation recapture when the residential rental property is sold?" Depreciation recapture is real—but it's also speculative. It only applies to the gain on the sale of the property, is subject to a maximum federal tax rate of 25%, and may never come into play if the owner never sells the property. If the owner holds the property until death, the depreciation recapture is eliminated through the step-up in basis.

Step-Up in Basis: "Hiding" rental real estate in a retirement account forfeits the step-up at death—hardly an ideal tax planning outcome.

Now consider how valuable that step-up can be for rental real estate compared to financial assets. If a beneficiary inherits rental property held in a taxable account, they receive a step-up in basis. They can immediately take advantage of the step-up through depreciation deductions! As rental income begins to roll in, they can offset that income with depreciation, thanks to the higher depreciable basis.

How about financial assets? The beneficiary still happily receives a step-up in basis, but initially, that benefit sits dormant. There's no depreciation deduction, and as interest and dividends are received, they're reported as taxable income—regardless of the step-up.

The step-up in basis is particularly valuable for depreciable assets. So why go out of one's way to hold such an asset in a retirement account and forfeit the step-up in basis?

Flexibility and Complexity: Owning rental real estate in a taxable account can provide flexible cash flow. That cash flow is readily accessible for reinvestment or personal spending. Thanks to depreciation deductions, that cash flow is often lightly taxed—or even tax-free—along the way.

Owning the same rental property in a traditional retirement account, however, turns flexible, potentially tax-advantaged income into a more complex cash flow challenge. Whenever the owner wants to access the rental income, the distributions trigger ordinary income tax. And if the owner is under age 59½, they may also incur a 10% early withdrawal penalty.

Now consider RMDs from traditional retirement accounts. With publicly traded financial assets, it's easy to determine the prior year's ending balance to calculate the RMD. Not so with rental real estate. Valuing real property each year to calculate the RMD adds another layer of administrative burden and complexity.

Rental Real Estate Losses: Rental real estate can generate significant tax losses—if it's held outside of a retirement account. When the property is held in a taxable account, and the owner meets the relatively low "active participation" standard, up to $25,000 of rental real estate losses can be deducted against other income, provided the adjusted gross income (AGI) is below $100,000. Between $100,000 and $150,000 of AGI, the allowable deduction phases out at 50 cents per dollar.

Could an early retiree have a tax return showing less than $150,000 of income? Less than $100,000? Absolutely. If that's a possibility, why lock away valuable rental losses in a retirement account where they can't be used?

Compare that to financial assets. While they can produce capital losses, the ability to deduct them is much more limited—generally capped at $3,000 per tax return, per year. So yes, net losses from financial assets can help, but not nearly to the same degree as rental real estate losses for taxpayers within the right income range.

Fees: Self-directed retirement accounts that hold rental real estate often come with higher fees—typically more than what you'd pay to hold assets of any kind in a taxable account or to hold financial assets within a retirement account.

Compliance Risk: Do you own rental real estate in your name or in a revocable living trust and want to paint the walls or replace windows between tenants? No problem!

But what if that same property is held in your IRA or 401(k)? Suddenly, that paint job or window replacement becomes a prohibited transaction—one that could disqualify the entire account or trigger a prohibited transaction tax.

Holding rental real estate in a self-directed retirement account means subjecting yourself to even more tax rules. Why add this risk when rental real estate is already a tax-advantaged asset when held in the owner's name?

For all these reasons, we generally prefer that rental real estate investors hold those properties in taxable accounts rather than retirement accounts.

Cryptocurrencies

We could debate cryptocurrencies until we're blue in the face—but one thing is clear: they're volatile in 2025.

"Volatile" is a financial planner's ten-dollar word for "more likely than other assets to either go way up or way down."

Let's consider the downside first. Big losses in a crypto position are a real possibility. So, where do you want those losses to occur—from a tax perspective? In a retirement account or a taxable account?

Losses in retirement accounts (traditional, Roth, or HSA) have no tax value. In contrast, losses in a taxable account can be useful. Capital losses can offset capital gains, and up to $3,000 in net losses per year can be deducted against ordinary income. Even better, the wash sale rule—which normally disallows a loss if you repurchase the same or a "substantially identical" asset within 30 days—does not currently apply to cryptocurrencies. That allows for harvesting a loss and repurchasing the same cryptocurrency soon after.

Measure Twice: *Consider the important distinction of direct cryptocurrency ownership vs. regulated securities (such as ETFs that hold cryptocurrencies) when determining whether the wash sale rule applies. More details are included in Chapter 23.*

Now you might be thinking, "That's great if I lose money, but I'm investing to make money!" Okay, now picture a 100x gain on a cryptocurrency. Would a 30-year-old rather have that in a Roth retirement account or in a taxable account?

In a taxable account, assuming a holding period of over one year, the worst-case federal tax rate is 23.8% (20% long-term capital gains plus the 3.8% NIIT. And there's no early withdrawal penalty to worry about.

But in a Roth account, unless the 30-year-old investor waits until age 59½, the distribution of gain could be subject to ordinary income tax (up to 37%) and a 10% early withdrawal penalty.

The bottom line: volatile assets like cryptocurrency generally don't pair well with retirement accounts. In taxable accounts, losses can offer tax benefits, and gains—though taxable—can be accessed with much more flexibility.

Conclusion

Asset location can be a powerful driver of financial success to and through early retirement. Generally speaking, high-yielding assets such as taxable bonds sit well in traditional retirement accounts, while Roth and taxable accounts benefit from holding low-yield, potentially high-growth equities.

Alternative assets—such as rental real estate and cryptocurrency—tend to sit better in taxable accounts rather than in retirement accounts.

PTC considerations also tend to favor maintaining some assets in taxable accounts during early retirement. Thoughtful asset location can help keep taxable income low and facilitate highly effective early retirement tax planning.

A previous draft version of this chapter was originally published on Sean's FITaxGuy.com blog on March 4, 2025.

19 – 2025 Tax Law Changes

In July 2025, President Trump signed the reconciliation bill, commonly referred to as the One Big Beautiful Bill. For brevity, we'll refer to it as **OBBB**.

OBBB changes tax planning to and through early retirement in several ways.

The individual tax provisions in OBBB did not emerge in a vacuum. Their origins can largely be traced back to the 2017 tax law commonly known as the Tax Cuts and Jobs Act (TCJA). TCJA lowered tax brackets and increased the standard deduction. To help "pay for" TCJA tax cuts, most of the individual tax provisions—including the lower tax brackets and higher standard deduction—were scheduled to expire at the end of 2025.

This created an interesting dynamic: If Congress took no action in 2025, many Americans would face a substantial tax increase starting in 2026.

As a result, there was significant pressure to pass new tax legislation that, at a minimum, extended the TCJA tax brackets and standard deduction for several more years.

Tax Brackets and Standard Deduction

OBBB permanently extends the lower TCJA tax brackets. When we write "permanently," we mean those lower brackets (adjusted for inflation) will apply annually until a future enacted law changes them.

OBBB not only extended the TCJA's increased standard deduction but also slightly increased it. For 2025, the standard deduction will be $15,750 for single filers and $31,500 for those married filing jointly. This is an increase from the previously scheduled 2025 amounts of $15,000 and $30,000, respectively.

The standard deduction will continue to be adjusted annually for inflation.

Several tactics discussed in this book benefit from the extension and slight increase in the standard deduction—including living on 0% long-term capital gains in early retirement, the Hidden Roth IRA, and Tailored Taxable Roth Conversions (TTRCs).

The New Senior Deduction

OBBB introduces a valuable new deduction for those age 65 or older by year-end. Each qualifying individual receives a $6,000 annual deduction, as long as they do not file as married filing separately.

The senior deduction is subject to relatively high income phaseouts. It phases out at six cents per dollar of modified adjusted gross income (MAGI) above $75,000 for single filers and $150,000 for those married filing jointly.

This results in a phaseout range of $75,000 to $175,000 for singles and $150,000 to $250,000 for joint filers. As you can see, single retirees are more likely to lose some or all of the senior deduction compared to married couples.

Note that individuals who are still employed at age 65 or older also qualify for the deduction—but are more likely to be phased out due to higher income.

Taxpayers can claim the senior deduction whether they take the standard deduction or itemize.

Under OBBB, the senior deduction applies for tax years 2025 through 2028. It does not apply in 2029 or later.

Senior Deduction Examples

The book includes several examples where a retiree loses part or all of their senior deduction.

Recall Joe and Jane from Chapter 8. Both were age 66. We showed two examples:

In the first, Joe and Jane had an AGI of $253,000. Since their AGI exceeded the top of the MAGI phaseout range, they received no senior deduction.

In the second, we showed them with $200,000 of AGI. They received a combined senior deduction of $6,000. Here's how that was calculated:

Joe's Senior Deduction Calculation

- Potential Maximum Senior Deduction (A): $6,000
- Amount MAGI Exceeds $150,000 (B): $50,000
- Excess Amount as a Percentage of $100,000 (B ÷ $100,000) (C): 50%
- 100% Less Excess Percentage (100% − C) (D): 50%
- Joe's Senior Deduction (A × D): **$3,000**

Jane's Senior Deduction Calculation

- Potential Maximum Senior Deduction (A): $6,000
- Amount MAGI Exceeds $150,000 (B): $50,000
- Excess Amount as a Percentage of $100,000 (B ÷ $100,000) (C): 50%
- 100% Less Excess Percentage (100% − C) (D): 50%
- Jane's Senior Deduction (A × D): **$3,000**

Adding both deductions together, Joe and Jane receive a total senior deduction of **$6,000** when their MAGI is $200,000.

We also saw how the senior deduction is affected after Joe's death. Jane, now a widow, has an AGI of $144,600 and files as a single taxpayer. Her senior deduction is calculated as follows:

Jane's Senior Deduction as a Widow

- Potential Maximum Senior Deduction (A): $6,000
- Amount MAGI Exceeds $75,000 (B): $69,600
- Excess Amount as a Percentage of $100,000 (B ÷ $100,000) (C): 69.6%
- 100% Less Excess Percentage (100% − C) (D): 30.4%
- Jane's Senior Deduction (A × D): **$1,824**

Extra Credit: For senior deduction purposes, MAGI will usually equal AGI. However, there are three additions to AGI when calculating MAGI for this deduction:

1. *Foreign earned income*
2. *Income from several U.S. territories, and*
3. *Income from Puerto Rico.*

Optimizing for the Senior Deduction

Our favorite tactic for optimizing the senior deduction is to delay Social Security. This accomplishes two things:

1. It reduces income between ages 65 and 70, increasing the likelihood of staying below the senior deduction phaseout thresholds during those years.

2. It often leads the retiree to live on traditional retirement accounts or implement TTRCs during the Golden Years. This allows the senior deduction to increase either the size of the Hidden Roth IRA or the amount of tax-free Roth conversions.

Our second-favorite tactic is to keep ordinary income low. The lower a retiree can keep other taxable income, the more likely they are to qualify for the maximum senior deduction.

Temporary Nature of the Senior Deduction

You may be wondering about the future of the senior deduction. As currently written in OBBB, it expires at the end of 2028.

We're not overly concerned about its temporary nature. Like its cousins—the TCJA tax rate cuts and the expanded standard deduction—the senior deduction may start out temporary but become permanent through future legislation. Additionally, when the senior deduction is up for potential renewal, so are the tax cuts on tips and overtime pay. This alignment could improve the senior deduction's chances of being extended for political reasons.

Finally, this book is full of examples showing excellent tax outcomes for retirees—many of whom receive little or no senior deduction due to age or income. Even without the senior deduction, retirees can still achieve great tax results.

New Non-Itemizers' Charitable Deduction

Starting in 2026, non-itemizers—taxpayers who don't itemize deductions—can claim a $1,000 per person deduction for cash charitable contributions.

This is great news for many aspiring and current early retirees, as retirees often take the standard deduction in retirement. Now, there is an ability to deduct at least some cash charitable contributions while still claiming the standard deduction.

This new deduction supports tactics like living on 0% long-term capital gains income in early retirement, the Hidden Roth IRA, and TTRCs.

New Haircut on Itemized Charitable Deductions

Starting in 2026, taxpayers who itemize deductions will lose 0.5% of their MAGI as a reduction to their allowable charitable deduction.

Good news for retirees: qualified charitable distributions (QCDs) are not affected by the new haircut.

*In Real Life: The new tax law strengthens the case for accelerating large **donor-advised fund (DAF)** contributions into 2025.*

Consider this example: Jake has $300,000 of AGI in both 2025 and 2026. He's considering a $20,000 contribution of appreciated stock to a DAF in either year. If he makes the contribution in 2025, he can claim the full $20,000 tax deduction—assuming he itemizes his deductions.

If he waits until 2026, his deduction will be reduced to $18,500 due to the new charitable deduction haircut of $1,500 ($300,000 × 0.5%).

State and Local Tax Deduction Increase

OBBB includes a five-year increase in the state and local tax (SALT) deduction cap—from $10,000 to $40,000 per tax return—beginning in 2025, with slight adjustments over the following four years. The increase to the SALT cap is phased out at higher income levels. Note that the SALT deduction is capped at half that amount for married taxpayers filing separately.

The increased SALT cap will be irrelevant for many retirees who are likely to (1) continue to claim the standard deduction and (2) pay little in state income taxes due to their ability to control taxable income. However, the $40,000 SALT cap can benefit retirees in states with high property taxes.

The retiree profile most likely to benefit is a single retiree or widow in a high property tax state like New Jersey. Picture Sophia, an 80-year-old widow in New Jersey who pays $25,000 in property taxes in 2025. She can now deduct the full amount as an itemized deduction and will itemize instead of claiming the lower combined standard deduction of $17,750.

Extra Credit: *Recall that Sophia also qualifies for some or all of the $6,000 senior deduction as long as her MAGI is below $175,000.*

All Bronze Plans Qualify as High Deductible Health Plans

Starting in 2026, all ACA Bronze plans will qualify as high deductible health plans. This opens the door for many retirees to make deductible HSA contributions—potentially reducing their income tax liability and increasing their Premium Tax Credit (PTC).

OBBB made no changes to the previously scheduled 2026 expiration of the suspension of the 400% of federal poverty level (FPL) cliff for PTC eligibility. While we're writing this in mid-2025—and anything is theoretically possible—we suspect Congress will not pass legislation to extend this provision.

The combination of two factors—(1) the likely return of the 400% FPL cliff and (2) automatic HSA contribution eligibility—makes Bronze plans more attractive for many early retirees. Starting in 2026, Bronze plans will offer lower premiums and the potential for higher PTCs by enabling income reduction through HSA contributions.

We discuss tactics for early retirees to improve their chances of qualifying for the PTC in Chapter 13.

20 – Planning for Uncertainty

Taxes are going up! National debt and deficit! Everyone panic!

As you can imagine by now, we're "glass half-full" types. Cody rarely panics. Sean usually saves his panics for the fourth quarter of New York Jets football games.

We suggest you join us in not panicking when it comes to the future taxation of traditional retirement accounts.

This book aims to replace anxiety about taxes in retirement with analysis, reason, and logic. Until now, we've considered the current tax and retirement planning environment.

In this chapter, we look to the future. Unlike Doc Brown and Marty McFly, we don't have access to a DeLorean, 1.21 gigawatts of electricity, and a flux capacitor. Instead, we rely on logic, reason, and history to offer our glimpse into what lies ahead.

Can we predict the future with 100% accuracy? Of course not. Our conclusions are likely—but not guaranteed—as you'll see. And while likely conclusions don't always pan out, uncertainty doesn't invalidate the lessons that logic, reason, and history can teach us about retirement tax planning.

The future we discuss here is the **"relevant future"**—the reasonable remaining life expectancy of most readers reading this book. And we believe that the relevant future will be favorable when it comes to the taxation of retirees. We have three main reasons for that view.

First, it's uncommon for retirees to have more income (on an inflation-adjusted basis) than they did during their working years. That may seem obvious, but it often gets lost in the inchoate fear of taxes in retirement prevalent in personal finance media.

Why would you have more income when you're no longer working for income?

Second, we cannot ignore the history and motivations of those who write our tax laws: the President and Congress. As we'll explore, their incentives tend to align with the interests of retirees—as recent history repeatedly shows.

Third, even if we're wrong about the first two points, we'll demonstrate that politically untenable tax increases are still unlikely to make relying on a traditional 401(k) (and its positive tax arbitrage) a bad decision. In fact, in a future high-tax environment, many retirees will still come out ahead by using traditional retirement accounts instead of Roth retirement accounts through work.

This chapter discusses our approach to managing uncertainty in tax and retirement planning.

Pay Tax When Income is Lower

When are you likely to have more income? During your career, when you're **working for income**, or during retirement, when you're not?

As we mentioned in Chapter 7, personal spending tends to create a ceiling on taxable income in retirement. That's not the case during your working years.

For most retirees in most years, the upper income limit is their personal spending level.

In fact, in many retirement years, income may be much less than spending. Consider basis recovery when living on taxable assets, tax-free distributions from Roth IRAs and HSAs, and qualified charitable distributions (QCDs) — all of which fund spending without creating taxable income.

Even if a retiree lives entirely on taxable distributions from traditional retirement accounts, their annual income is still likely to match their spending.

Congress can increase taxes all they want. But unless they choose to increase required minimum distributions (RMDs), they can't force retirees to increase their income.

Also, recall our Central Thesis: for most Americans, the marginal tax rate benefit received when contributing to traditional retirement accounts will equal or exceed the tax rate applied to most distributions from those accounts.

Retirees benefit from the ability to run up the tax brackets. Even high-income retirees get to fill the lower brackets first when taking distributions from traditional retirement accounts — especially if they don't have pension income. In contrast, traditional 401(k) contributions typically reduce income at the worker's top marginal rate.

This nuance is often missed by those hyper-focused on future tax rates. Even if tax rates increase, many retirement distributions will still be taxed at low brackets — resulting in low effective tax rates — or even be absorbed by the standard deduction (as we saw with Justin and Rachel's example in Chapter 11).

The progressive nature of American income tax brackets helps reduce the uncertainty around taking a tax deduction for traditional 401(k) contributions at one's highest marginal rate and later including the distributions in retirement, when they may be offset by the standard deduction and taxed in lower brackets.

Tax Hikes on Retirees are Unlikely

Do you trust politicians?

You probably said, "No!"

Alright, let's try a different question.

Do you trust politicians to act in their own best interests?

"Absolutely!" may have just gone through your mind.

Now we're building trust.

More importantly, we're building a framework for planning for an uncertain future.

When it comes to the question of how to tax retirees, what aligns with politicians' best interests?

The Elderly Vote

Some insight into that question comes from the 2024 presidential election. Retirees and near-retirees tend to vote at higher rates than workers—based on the age composition of non-voters and voters.

Did you know that most American voters are 50 or older?

According to PRRI, in the 2024 election, adults aged 18 through 49 comprised an incredible 70 percent of all non-voters. Those same working-age adults comprised only 41 percent of voters.

In contrast, **adults aged 50 and older comprised just 30% of non-voters but a whopping 58% of voters.**

Aging is strongly correlated with both retirement and voter turnout. Why would Congress be eager to raise taxes on retirees when the elderly are the ones showing up at the polls?

Right, wrong, or otherwise, retirees and near-retirees vote more than workers—and their federal income tax treatment reflects that reality. This includes, but is certainly not limited to, the new senior deduction.

Politicians like to get re-elected. Retirees like to vote. That combination doesn't exactly scream "tax hikes on retirees!"

But it goes deeper than that. Let's take a closer look at how workers and retirees pay taxes.

The Implications of Payroll Withholding and Lack Thereof

While writing this book, we noticed an Instagram Story from lawyer and commentator Molly McCann Sanders. Commenting after Tax Day on April 16, 2025, she wrote:

If we did away with employers withholding income tax, and people had to pay the government an eye-watering check every April 15–along with all the 1099s–we'd all have lower taxes, because no one would stand for it.

Let's unpack that statement:

When W-2 **workers** pay their income taxes, as Mrs. Sanders notes, they never see the money. It never hits or comes out of their bank account. Instead of writing a check to the IRS, workers have taxes withheld by their employers each pay period and sent directly to the IRS. This **payroll withholding** softens the psychological blow of paying income tax.

Payroll withholding makes it difficult for workers to realize how much they're actually paying. As a result, they're less likely to feel overtaxed, complain about taxes, or vote based on their tax burden.

Now contrast that with how retirees—especially early retirees—pay taxes. By definition, retirement comes with no employer withholding. But the taxes still have to be paid.

As we discussed in Chapter 14, early retirees typically pay income taxes in two ways:

1. By making four quarterly estimated payments to the IRS, and/or
2. Through tax withholding on distributions from IRAs, 401(k)s, and other retirement accounts.

In both cases, the money sits in the retiree's account until it's paid to the IRS. Retirees "see" the tax when they write the check, set up the direct payment online, or elect withholding from IRA distributions—often in large, infrequent chunks. Paying taxes through these methods forces retirees to feel the financial burden.

Why would Congress increase taxes on the very voters who most directly feel those taxes?

Mrs. Sanders' observation illustrates that the risk of potential future tax hikes is more likely to fall on workers than on retirees.

If you were a member of Congress and wanted to raise revenue while minimizing political backlash, wouldn't you lean toward taxing workers—who don't notice it as much—over retirees, who do?

Translating this political risk into the current income tax system, perhaps the brackets at 24% and above are most at risk for a tax hike. Many retirees have most, if not all, of their income taxed against the standard deduction, the 10% bracket, the 12% bracket, and perhaps the 22% bracket. Raising the 24% bracket and higher brackets would affect many workers while leaving many retirees unscathed or minimally impacted.

Said differently: it's possible to design tax hikes that target workers more than retirees. Future politicians seeking to raise revenue without upsetting older, more reliable voters may find that option politically attractive.

The Politicians are Addicted to Tax Cuts for Retirees

We've heard it for years: commentators warning that taxes will increase on retirees in the future.

Fortunately for us, the future keeps showing up—so we can assess how accurate those predictions have been. And it turns out, there's a problem with those predictions: time and again, the future has brought tax cuts, not tax hikes, for retirees.

The past decade has been filled with one tax cut after another aimed at retirees. We keep looking for the tax hikes commentators predicted, and we still can't find them.

There have been so many recent tax cuts for retirees that we had to list them in a concise summary table to fit them all in.

Litany of Recent Tax Cuts for Retirees

Year	Act	Tax Cuts for Retirees	President	Congress	Prior Year Sept. 30 Federal Debt
2015	PATH Act	Made QCDs permanent	Democrat	Republican	$17.82 Trillion
2017	Tax Cuts and Jobs Act	For eight years: greater standard deduction, lower tax brackets	Republican	Republican	$19.57 Trillion
2019	SECURE Act	Delayed RMDs from age 70½ to 72	Republican	Democrat House / Republican Senate	$21.52 Trillion
2020	CARES Act	Suspended 2020 RMDs; allowed already taken RMDs to be rolled back in	Republican	Democrat House / Republican Senate	$22.72 Trillion
2020	U.S. Treasury Increases RMD Factors	Effective in 2022: increased RMD factors, lowering RMD amounts	Republican	N/A – Treasury Regulations	$22.72 Trillion
2022	SECURE 2.0 Act	Delays RMDs from 72 to 73 for some, to 75 for those born in 1960 and later	Democrat	Democrat	$28.43 Trillion
2025	The One Big Beautiful Bill	Makes TCJA tax cuts permanent; temporary senior deduction; all Bronze ACA plans become HDHPs in 2026	Republican	Republican	$35.46 Trillion

We highlight three important aspects of this table:

1. Notice that tax cuts for retirees are not tied to one political party. Both major parties have enacted tax cuts for retirees. In the past decade, neither party has significantly increased taxes on retirees.

2. Notice the national debt figures. These are included to show that ever-increasing debt has not been a barrier to continued tax cuts for retirees. We'll return to this point below.

3. Do you notice what's missing from the table? Tax hikes on retirees! That's because there haven't been any significant ones over the past decade.

What politicians do matters. But what they don't do can matter just as much. Let's consider two recent episodes.

First is the 0% long-term capital gains (LTCG) tax rate. A Republican president and Republican Congress enacted this remarkably favorable rule in 2003, effective in 2008. As we saw in Chapter 10, the 0% LTCG rate can be especially powerful for retirees—particularly early retirees.

In the 2008 election, Democrats swept into power with President Barack Obama, 257 out of 435 House seats, and 57 Senate seats.

So, in 2009, did Democrats repeal the 0% LTCG rate passed by Republicans? No!

Next up: the Tax Cuts and Jobs Act (TCJA), enacted by Republicans in 2017. After the 2020 election, Democrats again controlled the presidency and both chambers of Congress. In 2021, did they repeal the TCJA's lowered brackets and increased standard deduction? No!

That tax cuts for retirees have survived multiple political transitions tells us something about what future shifts in power may mean for retiree tax rates.

When predicting the future, we can't ignore the past. Politicians are motivated by re-election. And the past decade has shown that politicians in both parties have concluded it's in their best interest not to raise taxes on retirees—and to occasionally cut retirees' taxes instead.

Why do we expect future politicians to turn on a dime against both their own past behavior and their own best interests?

Do politicians ever change? Yes—though infrequently.

But do politicians radically change course when it's clearly against their own interests? Rarely, if ever.

Where's the Voting Bloc for Increasing Taxes on Retirees?

Sure, Congress and the President can increase taxes on any group in the future. But major tax increases require a voting bloc that supports the increase.

Let's look at a recent tax policy change in American politics: tariffs.

In 2025, President Donald Trump implemented significant tariffs. Compared to previous Republican policy—and many Democrat policies—these tariffs represented a significant change.

But were these tariffs against Trump's own best interests? No.

What proof do we have that tariffs were in Trump's best interests?

Trump himself believed tariffs were in his own best interests! He campaigned on raising tariffs. In fact, Trump's pro-tariff stance was so central to his 2024 campaign that, in an October appearance on The Joe Rogan Experience, he said: "To me, the most beautiful word... in the dictionary... is the word tariff."

Right, wrong, or otherwise, that rhetoric didn't cost him the election. He won all seven commonly recognized swing states.

Trump ran on tariffs, in part, because they appealed to a key voting bloc: certain blue-collar voters—including current and former autoworkers in Michigan, a crucial swing state.

Where's the key voting bloc that supports tax hikes on retirees?

Can you imagine a Democrat or Republican presidential candidate in 2028, 2032, or 2036 campaigning on "I'm going to increase taxes on retirees!"? The difficulty of imagining that scenario is revelatory about future tax policy as it applies to retirees.

Tax hikes on retirees don't appeal to any major voting bloc. Combine that with the fact that a significant portion of the electorate is age 50 or older, and it's clear that the political environment needed to support major tax increases on retirees is unlikely to exist in the relevant future.

Absent both an influential politician who sees increasing taxes on retirees as aligned with their own best interests and a key voting bloc that supports and/or benefits such a policy, it's difficult to see how significant tax increases on retirees would gain enough support to be enacted.

What About the National Debt?

Some commentators claim that the national debt guarantees retirees will face increased taxes.

We don't share that concern to any significant degree—for three reasons:

First, it's clear that retirees vote, and politicians understand that staying in their good graces is critical for re-election. Doubt that politicians understand the political importance of retirees? Their repeated actions over the past decade prove they are keenly aware of the political importance of retirees and their tax liabilities.

Second, let's not forget that many different cohorts are potential targets for tax hikes. A tax increase doesn't have to hit everyone equally.

Retirees were big winners in 2025 with the TCJA extension and the new senior deduction. Other groups weren't as fortunate. For example, according to one analysis, between January 1 and June 23, 2025, the United States collected $95.6 billion in tariffs—a 134.9% increase over the same period in 2024. If you import foreign goods, you know that not everyone received a tax cut in 2025.

Others saw tax increases too. The One Big Beautiful Bill includes tax hikes on several groups other than retirees. Large university endowments, individuals sending money to foreign countries, and those using clean energy tax credits all faced tax increases.

Yes, the federal debt is too big.

No, increasing taxes on politically powerful retirees is not a required solution to that problem. There are many alternative sources of revenue for politicians to consider for financial stability.

Third, if the national debt truly pointed to higher taxes on retirees, why hasn't it happened yet? Review the *Litany of Recent Tax Cuts for Retirees* table. Each time retirees received a tax cut, the national debt was already sky-high.

Are Future Tax Rates on Retirees Really Unknown?

Do we precisely know what tax rates retirees will face in 2037? Absolutely not.

But here's what we do know:

- Today's tax rates on retirees
- Retirees and near-retirees like to vote
- Politicians like to win elections
- There's no key voting bloc that supports tax hikes on retirees
- Other groups can absorb tax increases, as demonstrated by developments in 2025

When we put those five data points together, a reasonable conclusion emerges: the most likely tax environment for retirees in the relevant future will look a lot like the one retirees face in 2025.

Sure, there's a small risk that future tax rates on retirees will increase. But based on the available evidence, any such increases are likely to be modest.

And we should also acknowledge the possibility of movement in the other direction—politicians may continue giving retirees more tax cuts!

We can't know precisely what future tax rates on retirees will be. But to claim "retirees are surely headed for significant tax hikes" ignores readily available facts.

Fairness of Increasing Taxes on Retirees

Retirees have one final card to play against future tax hikes: fairness. Their plans are often more set in stone than those of younger workers—and going back to work isn't easy.

Setting aside the politics, it's fundamentally unfair to allow someone to retire and then face a dramatic increase in their federal income tax rate. Adjusting to higher tax rates is more difficult for those who are both retired and elderly.

Stress Testing Future Tax Hikes on Retirees

Is this book guaranteed to be right about the future? Absolutely not.

When planning a path for the future, it's wise to ask: "What if I'm wrong about the assumptions I'm baking in?"

Recall Joe and Jane from Chapter 8. They're both 66 in 2025. At a $200,000 retirement spending level, it appeared they were well advised to deduct at 24% into a traditional 401(k) during their working years. In retirement, even if every dollar of taxable income came from traditional retirement account distributions, their effective tax rate was just 12.44%. And none of their income was taxed above 22%, making traditional 401(k)s a winning strategy for Joe and Jane.

But what if tax rates increase by 50%? Let's stress test that with Joe and Jane and see what happens.

Under this scenario, the 10% bracket becomes 15%, the 12% bracket becomes 18%, and the 22% bracket becomes 33%. These hikes are politically unrealistic today—and likely tomorrow—but again, we're stress testing.

To push it further, we'll throw in another politically untenable tax hike: cutting the standard deduction in half. We'll also assume that the 2025 OBBB senior deduction is never extended.

Here's how Joe and Jane's tax picture looks under those aggressive assumptions:

Amount Withdrawn	Deducted At	Taxed At	Federal Income Tax	Win
$17,350	24%	0%	$0	Joe and Jane
$23,850	24%	15%	$3,578	Joe and Jane
$73,100	24%	18%	$13,158	Joe and Jane
$85,700	24%	33%	$28,281	The IRS
Total $200,000	24%	**Effective Rate 22.51%**	**Total $45,017**	Joe and Jane

Even under politically untenable tax hikes, Joe and Jane—withdrawing $200,000 of income from traditional retirement accounts—still win against the IRS by having used traditional 401(k)s instead of Roth 401(k)s on their path to retirement. It's remarkable that this remains true even with a 50% increase in tax rates and $200,000 of retirement income.

And remember: if Joe and Jane followed the Compelling Three, they likely have Roth accounts available in retirement. They could use those to avoid the hypothetical 33% bracket. So the worst-case scenario might not even be as "bad" as illustrated—and it still favors the traditional 401(k) contributions.

Also, do you really think Joe and Jane wouldn't notice a $20,000 tax hike? Few things signal "political backlash" like retirees who were accustomed to sending the IRS $25,000 annually suddenly sending $45,000.

Might that alone make Washington politicians think twice about raising taxes significantly on retirees?

The Senior Deduction

The new senior deduction is currently set to expire after 2028. When it comes to future planning, we're not overly concerned—for three reasons:

1. Temporary tax cuts often pave the way for permanent ones. The country just saw a clear example of this: the One Big Beautiful Bill (OBBB) made the TCJA's lower tax brackets and larger standard deduction permanent.

2. Consider the political ramifications if several temporary OBBB tax cuts expire in 2029. The resulting tax increases wouldn't hit the wealthy—they'd fall on waiters' and waitresses' tips, blue-collar workers' overtime pay, and seniors. An overnight tax hike on these three groups is exactly the kind of thing politicians will have every incentive to avoid.

3. The light tax treatment of retirees doesn't depend on the continued existence of the senior deduction. Throughout this book, we share examples of affluent retirees who receive little or no senior deduction but still enjoy strong tax outcomes.

Compelling Three Roth Flexibility

Building a strong Roth IRA balance—through annual contributions and/or Backdoor Roth IRAs over the years—gives retirees a tax-free pool to draw from if we're wrong about future tax rates. Perhaps our outlook holds for the 10% and 12% brackets, but not for the 22% bracket.

Imagine a future Congress increases the 22% bracket to 30%!

Likely no. Possible, yes.

Could a Compelling Three retiree live off traditional retirement account distributions through the 12% bracket, then switch to Roth IRA withdrawals for their remaining income needs to avoid the hypothetical 30% bracket? Absolutely.

The Compelling Three includes an entire pillar—Roth IRA contributions—that serves as insurance against future tax hikes. The Compelling Three does not put all its eggs in the "politicians are unlikely to raise taxes on retirees" basket.

Living First Off Taxable Assets

Drawing down taxable assets first offers a strong hedge against uncertainty. It allows early retirees to quickly capture the benefit of the 0% LTCG tax bracket.

While we don't believe favorable tax rules—like the 0% LTCG rate—are likely to disappear anytime soon, they're not guaranteed.

By taking advantage of the 0% LTCG bracket early in retirement, the retiree reduces uncertainty around the future taxation of taxable accounts and makes the first phase of retirement incredibly tax-efficient.

Uncertain Future Asset Yields

So far, we've mostly discussed political risk and how to approach that uncertainty.

But politics isn't the only unknown in the future. Consider asset yields.

Those planning for early retirement have benefited—at least from a tax perspective—from a low-yield environment. But that hasn't always been the case. On December 31, 1981, the yield on 10-year U.S. Treasury securities was nearly 14%! On that same date, the S&P 500 dividend yield was over 5%.

Could we return to that sort of environment? Absolutely.

Fortunately, those following the principles in this book would have some protection against the negative tax effects of a higher-yield future.

Holding bonds and bond funds in traditional retirement accounts shields the resulting interest income from current-year taxation.

Likewise, spending down taxable accounts first in early retirement reduces the amount of future uncontrolled income that could hit the tax return. If domestic equities begin yielding 5%, the higher income tax impact is largely mitigated by our favored approach of drawing down taxable assets first in retirement.

Tactics that work well in today's retirement planning landscape can also serve as a hedge against uncertainty.

Delay Social Security

Our favored tactic of having the higher-earning spouse (or a single person) delay claiming Social Security retirement benefits until age 70 also helps reduce uncertainty. Why? Because by spending down portfolio assets in one's 60s and delaying Social Security, the retiree is drawing from volatile (i.e., uncertain) assets while increasing a nonvolatile (i.e., more certain) asset: future Social Security payments.

We appreciate when effective tax planning also brings the added benefit of reducing uncertainty.

Social Security Uncertainty

Worried about the future of Social Security? Did you catch the fact that 58% of the 2024 electorate was age 50 or older? Social Security claimants (and soon-to-be claimants) represent a powerful voting bloc that protects current and future beneficiaries.

Does the combination of "retirees vote" and "politicians like to get re-elected" scream, "They won't pay 100 cents on the dollar of Social Security benefits"?

Those predicting cuts to Social Security are essentially saying that politicians with the power to borrow—and even print money—will choose to do neither, even when doing neither could be disastrous to their own political futures.

That's quite a prediction.

Sequence of Returns Risk

Those concerned about sequence of returns risk in early retirement should be drawn to our favored principle of spending taxable accounts first. As illustrated in Chapter 10, doing so can significantly reduce income tax liability during those early years. In fact, it's often possible to draw down taxable accounts and pay little or no federal income tax, thanks to the combination of the standard deduction, basis recovery, and the 0% LTCG tax bracket.

Sequence of returns risk is magnified by higher expenses early in retirement. The more that's spent in those early years, the greater a retiree's exposure to that risk. By reducing income tax expense early in retirement, our favored approach helps mitigate sequence of returns risk—and reduces uncertainty.

Conclusion

The next time someone worries about potential future tax hikes for retirees, ask them these two questions:

1. Why do you expect politicians to act against their own interests?
2. Why do you believe politicians will reverse course after repeatedly favoring tax cuts over tax hikes for retirees?

When planning around the uncertainty of future political behavior, our approach is grounded in logic: we don't expect politicians to suddenly act against their own best interests. And we won't change that expectation until there's evidence that their behavior is changing—specifically when it comes to taxing retirees.

That said, no amount of historical precedent or logic can fully eliminate uncertainty. But our favored planning approach accounts for that uncertainty in several meaningful ways:

1. Stress testing demonstrates that a couple earning $200,000 in retirement can weather even politically unrealistic tax hikes well.

2. Roth IRA contributions provide flexibility and serve as insurance against future tax increases.
3. Spending taxable brokerage accounts first with LTCG tax treatment can lead to years of little or no federal income tax in early retirement.
4. Thoughtful asset location helps mitigate the tax impact of potential increases in asset yields.
5. Delaying Social Security while drawing from volatile assets reduces future uncertainty.
6. Lower income tax liability early in retirement helps mitigate the harmful effects of sequence of returns risk.

21 – Pensions

For many Americans, the idea of a pension feels like a relic of the past. Yet for millions—including educators, public safety workers, federal employees, and some private-sector workers—defined benefit pensions continue to play a central role in retirement planning.

Throughout this book, we've emphasized what we call the Compelling Three:

1. Traditional retirement account contributions at work
2. Roth IRA contributions (direct or Backdoor)
3. Taxable account contributions

But a pension introduces a fourth variable—one with unique implications on the path to and through early retirement.

In Chapter 6, we discussed a common decision for those with pensions: whether to leave the pension as-is or roll it into a traditional IRA. In this chapter, we focus on considerations for those who choose to leave the pension as a pension.

How Pensions Affect Traditional vs. Roth Contribution Decisions

Pensions can provide a stable income floor in retirement, are often employer-funded, and help reduce longevity risk. However, compared to IRA and qualified plan distributions, pension payments tend to be inflexible. They limit control over the timing of taxable income and do not offer the Roth conversion flexibility available with traditional IRAs and qualified plans.

Once pension payments begin, they continue—whether the income is needed or not. Most or all of this "guaranteed" income is taxed as ordinary income and can quietly fill up the standard deduction and the lower marginal tax brackets (10% and 12%). This limits the effectiveness of tactics like Roth conversions and tax-gain harvesting in early retirement.

For example, suppose an employee contributes to a traditional 403(b) while in the 22% marginal federal income tax bracket. That contribution provides an immediate 22% federal tax deduction, along with potential state income tax savings. But if their pension in retirement fills up much of their standard deduction and lower tax brackets, they may find there's little or no room left for the tax-efficient strategies they had planned. If the pension pushes them into a higher bracket than the one in which they made their traditional contributions, they may experience negative tax rate arbitrage, as mentioned in Chapter 7.

This creates a planning dilemma: Should they continue contributing to a traditional 403(b), or shift some or all of their contributions to a Roth 403(b)?

There's no one-size-fits-all answer. If the pension is modest and begins later in retirement, a multi-year Roth conversion window may be available in early retirement. But if the pension is substantial and begins immediately upon retirement, it may crowd out those opportunities entirely.

Survivor Pensions

Another layer of complexity: 100% survivor pensions. These benefits continue at the same monthly amount after one spouse dies. While the surviving spouse benefits from the income stability, they will typically file as a single taxpayer in future years. This means facing compressed tax brackets and half the standard deduction they were used to—which limits the available space for planning tactics, such as Roth conversions.

When Traditional Contributions Still Make Sense

It's also worth noting that pension income in retirement is often much lower than a worker's income during their career—especially for early retirees or those who changed employers frequently.

Even if a pension fills the standard deduction and lower tax brackets in retirement, traditional contributions made during higher-earning years may still benefit from favorable tax rate arbitrage. In other words, expecting a pension doesn't automatically make Roth 401(k) and 403(b) contributions the right answer. It simply means the trade-offs are worth modeling—not fearing.

The Health Insurance Connection

Another planning wrinkle: pension income is often tied to eligibility for retiree health benefits. Many public sector and union workers receive subsidized health insurance in retirement—but only once they begin drawing their pension.

This connection can influence when retirees choose to begin their pension. It can also offer a valuable tax planning benefit: there's no need to manage income to qualify for Premium Tax Credits (PTCs) when a retiree is covered by their former employer's medical plan.

Timing Matters

Some pensions offer retired workers the option to delay benefits in exchange for higher future monthly income. Others require benefits to begin immediately upon separation of service. Those eligible for a pension should consider how the pension start date affects tax planning opportunities. For example, it may be beneficial to delay collecting the pension to spend down taxable assets first in early retirement.

Keep Finance Personal®

While this chapter outlines a few key considerations, it's important to emphasize that every pension plan is unique. The rules governing benefit formulas, payout options, survivor benefits, cost-of-living adjustments (COLAs), and retiree health coverage vary widely by employer, union, and state. When assessed alongside a retiree's personal circumstances, these differences can significantly impact decisions such as when to start a pension, how to balance traditional versus Roth contributions, and which tax strategies will be most effective. Please don't rely on rules of thumb alone—read your plan documents carefully, run the numbers, and revisit your strategies over time.

22 – Health Savings Accounts (HSAs)

Health Savings Accounts (HSAs) offer tax advantages for those covered by a high-deductible health plan (HDHP). They help pay for current and future qualified medical expenses on a tax-advantaged basis—for the account holder, their spouse, and eligible dependents.

HSA Contributions

To contribute to an HSA, a person's only medical insurance must generally be an HDHP. Medical insurance having a "high deductible" does not guarantee HDHP qualification. See IRS Publication 969 for details.

Contributions made through payroll withholding at work are the most tax-efficient. They are excluded from both income and FICA taxes (Social Security and Medicare). Combined employee and employer contributions appear on Form W-2, Box 12, Code W.

Alternatively, direct HSA contributions from a bank or brokerage account are also allowed until April 15 of the following year, similar to IRA contributions. These are deducted as Adjustments to Income (Schedule 1, Part II), not as itemized deductions.

Extra Credit: California and New Jersey do not recognize HSAs for state income tax purposes. Contributions are included in W-2 income, and earnings (interest, dividends, and capital gains) inside the HSA are taxed on the state income tax return.

Annual contribution amounts are based on whether the HDHP provides self-only coverage (one person) or family coverage (two or more people).

For 2025, the HSA contribution limits are:

- $4,300 for self-only coverage
- $8,550 for family coverage

For 2026, the HSA contribution limits are expected to be:

- $4,400 for self-only coverage
- $8,750 for family coverage

Spouses covered by a family HDHP share the family coverage contribution limit. They have flexibility in how they divide the total annual family contribution amount between themselves. That said, as a practical matter, the spouse whose employer provides the HDHP coverage often contributes the full amount to their own HSA ($8,550 for 2025, $8,750 for 2026). This leaves no remaining contribution room for the other spouse.

Those age 55 or older by year-end can contribute an additional $1,000 catch-up. There's an odd rule requiring each spouse to make their own $1,000 catch-up contribution to their own HSA. This rule is so odd that the original

House of Representatives version of the OBBB repealed it. The repeal did not make it into the final version of the bill, however.

Here is an example of how catch-up contributions work for a married couple:

Katrina (62) and Carlos (58) are covered by an HSA-eligible HDHP through Katrina's employer for all of 2025. To reduce taxable income and avoid FICA tax, Katrina contributes the family maximum of $8,550 (including employer contributions) to her family HSA through payroll, plus her $1,000 catch-up. Since Carlos is also over 55, he contributes his $1,000 catch-up to his own HSA by April 15 of the following year. Katrina's $9,550 contribution is excluded from her W-2 income, and Carlos deducts his $1,000 catch-up contribution on Schedule 1, Part II via Form 8889, Part I.

HSA contribution limits are typically prorated monthly based on HDHP coverage. For example, you cannot contribute to an HSA for any month you are covered by any part of Medicare.

Extra Credit: *The "last-month rule" allows those enrolled in an HDHP as of December 1 to make full-year HSA contributions as if they had HDHP coverage all year—if they maintain HDHP coverage through the end of the following year. This rule is detailed in IRS Publication 969.*

Another Planning Opportunity: *If a child is covered by a parent's HDHP but is not claimed as a tax dependent, they may be eligible to contribute to their own HSA—up to the family contribution limit! This scenario often applies to young adults under 26 who provide more than half of their own support but remain on a parent's health plan.*

HSA Distributions

HSA earnings grow tax-deferred, and distributions are tax-free if used to pay for (or reimburse) qualified medical expenses. Nonqualified distributions are taxed as ordinary income—and subject to a 20% additional tax ("penalty") if taken before age 65.

In Real Life: *To avoid tax and penalties, HSA owners can reimburse themselves for previously unreimbursed qualified medical expenses (PUQME)—as discussed in Chapter 9. These expenses can date back to when the owner's first HSA was established (opened and funded). For example, someone might reimburse themselves in early retirement for medical expenses paid 20 years ago—and use the tax-free cash to cover normal retirement expenses.*

Beyond the Scope: *IRS Publication 502 discusses qualified medical expenses, including COBRA insurance premiums, long-term care insurance premiums (limited), and Medicare premiums (not Medigap).*

Unlike Flexible **Spending** Accounts (FSAs), Health **Savings** Account (HSA) balances roll over year to year. Many owners choose to pay current medical expenses out of pocket from other sources, allowing HSA balances to grow and be used later to reimburse PUQME.

Measure Twice: *No documentation is required to receive an HSA distribution, but you must report it correctly on Form 8889, Part II, and retain reasonable proof in case of an IRS audit. As long as the distribution was used to pay a qualified medical expense or reimburse PUQME, it should be tax- and penalty-free.*

Particular Importance to Early Retirees

Financial planning constantly evolves. Two recent changes make HSAs particularly important for many early retirees:

1. OBBB—enacted in July 2025—deems all Bronze ACA plans to be HDHPs starting in 2026.
2. Barring unexpected Congressional action, the 400% federal poverty level (FPL) cliff returns in 2026. This means households with ACA coverage and income above the 400% FPL cliff will no longer qualify for Premium Tax Credits.

Together, these changes significantly increase the appeal of Bronze plans for early retirees. Bronze plans offer lower premiums, and starting in 2026, they'll also allow plan holders to contribute to an HSA. These tax-deductible contributions provide a federal (and potentially state) income tax deduction and reduce household income—helping retirees stay below the 400% FPL cliff.

Additionally, an HSA can serve as a nontaxable source of funds for qualified medical expenses, allowing retirees to avoid taxable distributions.

Many retirees with ACA coverage will want to strongly consider signing up for a Bronze plan for 2026 and beyond. The open enrollment period for 2026 coverage begins November 1, 2025.

HSA Asset Location

According to the Employee Benefit Research Institute (EBRI), as of 2022, only about 13% of HSA accounts were invested in something other than cash. This appears to be a missed opportunity for many HSA owners.

While we can't give you investment advice, we can say that HSAs are often best suited with assets that have significant long-term growth potential, such as equities. From an asset location perspective, it's odd to park low-growth assets in HSAs, particularly when one might have higher-growth assets in something like a traditional 401(k) or traditional IRA.

Cody's Take: HSAs are portable. I often recommend rolling over HSAs from an employer-sponsored custodian to a lower-fee provider after leaving a job. Most employer-sponsored HSAs require minimum cash balances and charge ongoing administrative fees. Transfers are initiated by the receiving custodian, and investments must be sold within the HSA by the owner before the transfer. Try to limit the number of transfers, as the delivering custodian may charge an outgoing transfer fee each time.

HSA Downside

A key downside of HSAs is their treatment at death. If the account owner's spouse is the designated beneficiary, they can simply treat the HSA as their own, allowing for continued tax-deferred growth and tax-free qualified distributions. But for nonspouse beneficiaries, the account immediately ceases to be an HSA, and the remaining balance becomes taxable to the beneficiary in the year of the owner's death, minus any qualified medical expenses the beneficiary paid for the decedent's care within one year after the date of death. If the estate is the beneficiary, the HSA balance is included on the owner's final income tax return. Naming a qualified charitable organization as the HSA beneficiary avoids taxation upon death.

We generally prefer to start reimbursing and paying for qualified medical expenses from HSAs when Medicare coverage begins (typically the month the owner turns 65). Medicare Part B and Part D premiums may also be reimbursed tax-free from an HSA.

However, PUQME distributions can also help fund early retirement years, especially for those trying to keep taxable income low and the Premium Tax Credit high.

23 – Tax Loss Harvesting

Tax loss harvesting is a tactic investors use to reduce their tax liability by selling securities in taxable brokerage accounts that have unrealized capital losses. An unrealized capital loss exists when the share's current price is less than its purchase price (cost basis).

As mentioned in Chapter 2, realized capital losses can offset realized capital gains, lowering taxable income. When total losses exceed total gains, taxpayers may deduct up to $3,000 of the net capital loss against ordinary income (such as W-2 wages or pre-tax retirement account distributions). Any unused capital loss exceeding $3,000 can be carried forward to future tax years, creating an ongoing tax benefit until the loss is fully used.

"But shouldn't I sell high and buy low?"

It may seem counterintuitive to sell investments when they're down, but tax loss harvesting doesn't have to negatively impact an investment plan. An investor can sell an investment to trigger a capital loss and immediately reinvest the proceeds into a similar (but not substantially identical) investment—even within the same asset category.

Wash Sale Rule

To prevent investors from creating artificial losses, Congress enacted what's known as the **wash sale rule**. This rule disallows a realized capital loss if the same or a "substantially identical" security is purchased within 30 days before or after the sale. The rule applies only to the number of shares purchased within a 61-day window (the day of the sale and the 30 days before and after).

Example 1: Meredith purchased 200 shares of ABC Mutual Fund on January 1, 2025, at $100 per share. On March 31, 2025, she bought an additional 30 shares at $120 per share. Then, on April 14, 2025, she sold 50 of her original shares for $90 per share, triggering what appears to be a $10 per share loss. However, because she repurchased 30 shares of the same fund within the 61-day wash sale window, the loss on 30 of the 50 shares sold is disallowed. That disallowed loss is added to the cost basis of the 30 newly purchased shares. Meredith can still claim the $10 per share loss on the remaining 20 shares sold.

Rather than waiting 31 days before repurchasing the same security (ticker), an investor can purchase similar but not substantially identical securities. For example, selling a Total U.S. Stock Market Index Fund and then immediately purchasing an S&P 500 Index Fund is a common substitution. These are not substantially identical because they track different indices, and, as of this writing, the Total U.S. Stock Market Index holds over 3,600 stocks, which is thousands more than the S&P 500 Index.

Extra Credit: *The wash sale rule does not currently apply to cryptocurrencies. However, it does apply to crypto-related securities, such as ETFs.*

Beyond the Scope: *Investment custodians must report wash sales for transactions involving the same CUSIP number/ticker symbol. The IRS has not clearly defined "substantially identical," so a prudent approach is to purchase another security within the same asset category but tracking a different index, such as switching from a U.S. stock market fund that tracks the CRSP U.S. Total Market Index to another that tracks the S&P 500 Index. Other asset categories offer similar opportunities.*

Example 2: Rebecca buys 100 shares of XYZ stock at $5 per share ($500 total). A few months later, the stock drops to $4 per share ($400 total value), and she sells all shares to harvest a $100 short-term capital loss. The next day, she uses $200 of the proceeds to repurchase XYZ stock. Rebecca has triggered a wash sale, disallowing $50 of her $100 loss, which is added to the new shares' cost basis.

Example 3: Instead of repurchasing XYZ stock, Rebecca buys shares of ABC stock. Because ABC is not substantially identical to XYZ, she retains the full $100 realized loss to offset other capital gains (and up to $3,000 of other income). She accomplishes this without attempting to "time the market."

Measure Twice: *Those selling an investment at a loss with automatic dividend reinvestment enabled could unknowingly repurchase shares within the wash sale window. In that case, only the reinvested shares trigger a wash sale, and the disallowed loss is added to the basis of those new shares. Investors focused on tax loss harvesting may consider turning off auto-reinvestment for that specific security and monitoring their account to ensure excess cash does not sit idle on the sidelines unintentionally.*

Sean's Take: *I can think of fewer tactics I favor more than automatically reinvesting dividends during the accumulation phase. This tactic builds up taxable accounts, one of the Compelling Three, without the investor thinking about it. During the accumulation phase, I disfavor turning off auto-reinvestment with the idea of potentially opening up tax loss harvesting opportunities. Note that during the drawdown phase, there can be good reasons to turn off auto-reinvestment to live off dividends and reduce sales of assets that can trigger capital gains.*

Aspiring Early Retirees

Tax loss harvesting can be quite valuable for the aspiring early retiree. Deducting up to $3,000 of capital losses annually against W-2 income can provide meaningful tax savings at the taxpayer's marginal income tax rate.

Applications in Early Retirement

For most early retirees, tax loss harvesting will be a rarely applicable tactic. Many reach retirement with significant unrealized capital gains due to several years of investing.

When available, tax loss harvesting can reduce gross income and lower income tax liability. This can unlock significant benefits, including:

- Increased eligibility for the Premium Tax Credit (PTC)
- Reduced taxation of Social Security benefits
- Tax gain harvesting within the 0% long-term capital gains (LTCG) tax bracket
- Avoidance or reduction of the Net Investment Income Tax (NIIT) for higher-income retirees
- Offsetting capital gains from the sale of real estate or other appreciated assets

Measure Twice: Don't overlook capital loss carryovers from the prior year when calculating current-year income for various benefits!

Sean's Take: I've yet to meet the person who reached their financial goals because they took $3,000 in tax loss harvesting deductions every year on their tax return. I believe Americans should invest based on risk-managed total return, not based on tax loss harvesting considerations. Yes, on occasion, why not tax loss harvest as an opportunistic tactical move? But in my view, that's about the limit of tax loss harvesting's role for most people's tax planning to and through early retirement.

Cody's Take: I use tax loss harvesting primarily to offset realized capital gains, with the $3,000 annual deduction as a secondary benefit. In taxable accounts, reinvested dividends create new tax lots. Using the Specific Identification (Spec ID) disposal method, an investor can harvest losses from select lots—even if the overall holding has a significant unrealized gain. This flexibility allows investors to strategically harvest losses to reduce household income or harvest gains on purpose within the 0% LTCG bracket. Tax harvesting won't make or break a financial plan, but it may be worth the hassle. We discuss this concept further in Chapter 29.

Don't Give Securities at a Loss

Avoid gifting securities with unrealized capital losses to individuals or qualified charitable organizations. The recipient does not receive the ability to harvest the donor's capital loss. To preserve the tax benefit, the donor can sell the security, realize the loss, and then give the cash proceeds instead. Don't let a loss go to waste!

Direct Indexing: Is It Worth the Noise?

Direct indexing involves owning individual securities or sector funds rather than a single index fund, which creates more tax loss harvesting opportunities. While it may work very well in niche cases, it also introduces complexity.

Commentator Rick Ferri has noted that direct indexing is oversold. It can be useful for someone with a large one-time capital gain—such as selling a private business—who wants to offset that gain with harvested losses. For example, the investor might utilize direct indexing by purchasing most of the individual stocks in the S&P 500 as fractional shares. Statistically, some of those stocks are likely to decline in value during the year. By selling the losers, the investor can offset a portion of the large capital gain with the resulting losses.

But what if there's no one-time large capital gain to offset? Managing possibly hundreds of stocks just to capture a $3,000 annual deduction is likely not worth it—especially for early retirees who may already pay a 0% federal income tax rate on long-term capital gains.

Complexities of direct indexing include:

- **Administrative Burden:** Managing multiple securities may require significant time, temperament, and talent (or costs if outsourced).

- **Rebalancing/Unwinding:** After using direct indexing to offset a one-time gain, the investor may be left with an unbalanced portfolio and numerous positions with embedded capital gains.

- **Drawdown Complexity:** In retirement, funding living expenses from a portfolio made up of dozens or hundreds of securities can make it more challenging to decide which shares to sell and in what proportions.

Weigh the potential tax benefits against the added complexity and costs before implementing optimized investment strategies like this. Direct indexing could be worth it, but as Rick Ferri has noted, the ideal use case is rare.

Cody's Take: There's a lot of hype around direct indexing. Some say it's the next evolution in tax-efficient investing, and others say it's a solution for a problem that doesn't exist. I say, don't let the "product" lead the planning. Direct indexing may help in specific situations, like offsetting significant, one-time capital gains, managing concentrated employer stock, or aligning portfolios with personal convictions (ESG). The potential benefits should be weighed against the complexity and its potential distraction from more impactful planning opportunities. I'd guess it's appropriate for fewer than 5% of investors.

24 – Tax Gain Harvesting

Unlike tax loss harvesting, which involves offsetting capital gains with losses to reduce taxable income, tax gain harvesting involves intentionally selling appreciated securities within taxable brokerage accounts to realize capital gains within the 0% long-term capital gains (LTCG) tax bracket. This tactic allows investors to access cash or reinvest with a reset cost basis while incurring little to no tax liability.

There are two flavors of tax gain harvesting. The first, which we previously covered in depth, involves **harvesting gains to fund living expenses in retirement.** We have seen how impactful this can be. Recall the examples of several affluent retirees such as Frank & Dana in Chapter 10, or Morty & Helen and Rich & Pat in Chapter 8. Each paid no federal income tax, thanks in large part to the 0% LTCG tax bracket.

The rest of this chapter focuses on the second flavor of tax gain harvesting: **basis resetting with possible reallocation.** The first is the primary planning objective, and the second is an optional additional planning objective.

Here are two examples to illustrate this second flavor of tax gain harvesting:

Henry and Deborah are early retirees who own $50,000 worth of JKL stock with a tax basis of $15,000. On Monday, they sold all of their JKL stock for $50,000 in cash. On Friday, they used that cash to purchase $50,000 of JKL stock. They keep their taxable income low enough this year that the $35,000 gain on the sale qualifies for the 0% LTCG tax bracket. This is a **basis reset**. Henry and Deborah own roughly the exact same amount of JKL stock, but now it has a tax basis of $50,000 instead of $15,000.

George and Lucille are early retirees. They own $60,000 of Banana Stand, Inc. stock with a tax basis of $20,000. On Tuesday, they sold all of the Banana Stand stock for $60,000 in cash. On Friday, they used that cash to purchase $60,000 of MNO Domestic Equity Index Fund, a diversified mutual fund. They keep their taxable income low enough this year that the $35,000 gain on the sale qualifies for the 0% LTCG tax bracket. This is a **basis reset with a reallocation**. George and Lucille now own $60,000 of MNO Domestic Equity Index Fund with a $60,000 tax basis.

When to Implement Tax Gain Harvesting

Tax gain harvesting is a potentially powerful planning tool in years with low to modest income. Here are common situations where it can make sense:

- **Early Career Years:** Young professionals often have lower taxable income, making them eligible for the 0% LTCG tax bracket.

- **Income Disruptions:** Periods of reduced income due to grad school, mini-retirements, career changes, or other temporary income reductions can create windows of opportunity for tax gain harvesting.

- **Early Retirement:** Retirees can manage their taxable income intentionally by distributing assets in a specific order, especially before Social Security, pensions, or Required Minimum Distributions (RMDs) begin.

Understanding the 0% LTCG Bracket

Tax gain harvesting is available when taxable income (including net capital gains) falls within the 0% LTCG bracket. In 2025, the limits are:

- **Single and Married Filing Separately:** Up to $48,350
- **Head of Household:** Up to $64,750
- **Married Filing Jointly:** Up to $96,700

The 0% LTCG bracket is a major reason we usually favor drawing from taxable accounts first in early retirement. It gets better: don't forget basis recovery—the portion of your withdrawal that isn't capital gain! For example, if you need to withdraw $120,000 from a taxable brokerage account, you almost certainly will not have $120,000 of adjusted gross income (AGI).

Example: Mary and Mark, both age 55, need to withdraw $120,000 from their taxable brokerage account. They sell $120,000 of ABC Mutual Fund, which has a $50,000 cost basis, generating $70,000 in long-term capital gains. Their taxable investments also produce $13,000 in dividends ($12,000 qualified and $1,000 nonqualified) throughout the year.

Mary and Mark's adjusted gross income (AGI) totals $83,000 ($70,000 in realized gains plus $13,000 in dividends). After subtracting the $31,500 standard deduction, their taxable income is $51,500—well within the 0% LTCG bracket. As a result, they owe $0 in federal income tax. They also have room to realize additional gains at the 0% tax rate. With the proceeds, they can either repurchase the same fund (with a reset cost basis) or diversify into other investments.

Measure Twice: Taxable income is a technical term, calculated by subtracting the standard/itemized and QBI deductions from AGI. Assuming taxpayers claim the standard deduction in 2025 and are under age 65, the 0% LTCG bracket applies when AGI is within:

- **Single and Married Filing Separately:** $64,100
- **Head of Household:** $88,375
- **Married Filing Jointly:** $128,200

Here is an example of a working couple using tax gain harvesting:

Married taxpayers Wilma (52) and Warren (50) earn $100,000 in W-2 wages as their only income source in 2025. After the $31,500 standard deduction, their taxable income is $68,500. With $28,200 of space left in the 0% LTCG bracket, and after evaluating potential state taxes and other implications, they sell $78,200 of appreciated stock with a $50,000 cost basis, realizing $28,200 in long-term capital gains—all taxed at 0% federally.

The Potential Impact on Other Areas

Even though federal income tax on capital gains may be 0%, tax gain harvesting can affect other areas:

- **State Taxes:** Most states tax capital gains at ordinary income rates, which means the capital gains realized may not be entirely tax-free.

- **Premium Tax Credit Eligibility:** Even if taxed at 0%, net realized capital gains are still included in modified adjusted gross income (MAGI), which is used to calculate subsidies when covered by an ACA medical insurance plan through the Health Insurance Marketplace. Increased realized gains could reduce the Premium Tax Credit (PTC).

- **Social Security:** Net capital gains are counted toward provisional income, which affects the amount of Social Security included in gross income (up to 85%). This can be a reason to delay claiming Social Security.

- **Financial Aid:** Higher income can reduce eligibility for needs-based college financial aid.

Staying Invested

There is no wash sale rule to consider when tax gain harvesting. Investors can immediately repurchase the same security after selling it for a gain without triggering adverse tax consequences. The 30-day waiting period requirement only applies to tax loss harvesting. By harvesting capital gains in low-income years, investors can gradually unwind appreciated assets and reset their cost basis tax-free—making taxable brokerage accounts behave more like Roth IRAs!

Roth Conversion Versus Tax Gain Harvesting

We often get asked: "Should we prioritize Roth conversions or tax gain harvesting?"

There's no one-size-fits-all answer, but we can consider two poles to frame the conversation:

One pole: An early retiree with a modest taxable account and a large traditional retirement account. They're satisfied with their taxable brokerage investments and have no urgent need to sell. In this situation, we favor Roth conversions over tax gain harvesting.

The other pole: An early retiree with a large taxable account holding investments they are not entirely satisfied with, such as old employer stock with significant unrealized gains. In this case, tax gain harvesting can be more beneficial than Roth conversions, allowing the retiree to sell and reinvest in more diversified assets.

We understand many readers won't fall neatly at either pole. The best approach considers how closely one's situation aligns with one pole or the other.

When push comes to shove, we usually favor Roth conversions over tax gain harvesting in many situations for three reasons:

1. **You might never owe tax on your taxable holdings**. Let's revisit Mary and Mark, who live off $120,000 per year from their taxable brokerage account. Thanks to basis recovery and the 0% LTCG bracket, they may be able to deplete their taxable assets without ever owing tax on those gains. **Why tax gain harvest if they'll never owe tax on those gains simply by living off the account?**

   Instead, Mary and Mark might focus on annual Roth conversions up to the standard deduction to reduce the long-term impact of their traditional retirement accounts. Under the assumptions provided, they could convert approximately $30,500 annually to Roth IRAs while continuing to withdraw $120,000 from taxable accounts tax-free (including their basis recovery). In this case, Roth conversions are likely to be the more effective long-term strategy.

2. **Traditional retirement accounts often present a more persistent tax issue**. Many retirees will deplete their taxable accounts within 5 to 10

years, but traditional retirement accounts are likely to last for the rest of their lives. Roth conversions in early retirement can help reduce future required minimum distributions (RMDs) and spread out tax liability more efficiently.

Extra Credit: We hope you have now learned that the problem of taxing traditional retirement accounts is often overstated, but it's still a meaningful planning consideration worth managing. In cases like Mary and Mark's, Roth conversions in early retirement up to the amount necessary to make ordinary income approximately equal the standard deduction can be a powerful tool in this regard.

3. **Roth conversions may benefit your heirs**. Unless you plan to leave your traditional retirement accounts to charity, someone will pay tax on them—whether it's you, your spouse, or your heirs. While we can't predict whose tax return those withdrawals will appear on, we are pretty sure they will be taxed eventually.

On the other hand, built-in gains in taxable brokerage accounts may never be taxed. If the assets are passed to heirs, they typically receive a step-up in cost basis, eliminating the unrealized capital gain. Since death wipes out capital gains but not the income tax liability associated with traditional retirement accounts, those concerned with the taxation of the next generation may prefer Roth conversions over tax gain harvesting.

25 – Special Opportunities for the Self-Employed

In this chapter, we explore two key planning tactics available to the self-employed: the Solo 401(k) and the SEP IRA. We begin by exploring the planning considerations for full-time self-employed individuals without employees—often referred to as "solopreneurs"—and then turn to considerations for side hustlers.

Full-Time Self-Employed

For full-time self-employed individuals, the Solo 401(k) is often the "go-to" tactic, assuming the solopreneur qualifies. In general, a self-employed person qualifies to contribute to a Solo 401(k) if they have no employees other than a spouse or any co-owners of the business.

If the business employs other individuals part-time, Solo 401(k) eligibility may still be possible, depending on both tax law and specific plan rules—details that are beyond the scope of this book.

Generally speaking, if the self-employed person employs an adult full-time who is neither a spouse nor an owner, the self-employed person will not qualify for a Solo 401(k).

With roughly 27 million nonemployer businesses in the United States, i.e., businesses that only employ the owner, this section focuses on the Solo 401(k) and assumes its qualification.

Note that Solo 401(k)s involve several technical nuances beyond the scope of this book. We'll focus on the high-level planning points.

Solo 401(k) Contributions

Schedule C Solopreneurs

Solopreneurs generally report income in one of two ways for tax purposes. For the vast majority, income and deductions are reported on Schedule C. The resulting net income from Schedule C is subject to self-employment (SE) tax, and solopreneurs can deduct half of their SE tax for federal income tax purposes.

To determine the maximum allowable employee deferral contribution and employer contribution to a Solo 401(k), the owner starts with Schedule C profit and subtracts the deduction for half the SE tax. The result—net self-employment income—is the computational base used to calculate Solo 401(k) contributions.

Let's look at a 2025 example:

Eli is 40 years old. His self-employment business is his only source of earned income:

- **Schedule C Profit:** $120,000
- **SE Tax:** $16,956 (i.e., $120,000 × 0.1412955)
- **Deduction for Half of SE Tax:** $8,478 ($16,956 × 50%)
- **Net Self-Employment Income:** $111,522 ($120,000 – $8,478)

Eli's maximum employee deferral contribution is the lesser of $23,500—the published 2025 limit—and his 2025 net self-employment income of $111,522. Therefore, his maximum employee deferral contribution (traditional and/or Roth) is **$23,500**.

Eli's maximum employer contribution is calculated as 20% of his net self-employment income of $111,522, which results in a 2025 employer contribution of **$22,304**.

There's one final contribution limit Eli must consider: the **all-additions limit**, which is the lesser of $70,000 (the 2025 number) or his net self-employment income of $111,522. Eli's combined employee deferral contributions of $23,500 and his employer contribution of $22,304 are $45,804—well within his $70,000 all-additions limit.

Note that, unlike traditional IRAs or Roth IRAs, a Schedule C solopreneur can't simply wake up on New Year's Day and "pre-fund" a Solo 401(k) for the new year on January 1. Employee deferral contributions must come from self-employment income as it's earned and received. In other words, the Schedule C solopreneur must collect the income before deferring it into the Solo 401(k) as an employee deferral contribution.

In Real Life: Those with Solo 401(k)s often benefit from working with a professional, but some prefer a DIY approach. Either way, it's smart to validate contribution calculations using helpful resources. Two we like:

1. *Deduction Worksheet for Self-Employed in IRS Publication 560, which helps calculate the maximum employer contribution.*
2. *Mike Piper's Schedule C Solo 401(k) calculator at obliviousinvestor.com, a useful tool for simpler situations like Eli's.*

Why not use multiple validation sources—potentially in conjunction with professional assistance?

S Corporation Solopreneurs

Some solopreneurs operate through an S corporation, which is either a corporation or limited liability company (LLC) that has elected "S corporation" status. This means the entity is generally not taxed on its own income. Instead, it passes income, deductions, credits, and other relevant information to its share-holders, who report them on their individual tax returns.

Here's the interesting wrinkle: the owner-employee must be paid "reasonable compensation" via W-2 wages for the services they perform for the S corporation. These W-2 wages form the computational base for any potential Solo 401(k) contributions.

Let's imagine Ross, age 45, owns XYZ LLC, which has elected to be taxed as an S corporation. In 2025, XYZ LLC pays Ross $80,000 in W-2 wages.

Ross's **maximum employee deferral contribution** is the lesser of two numbers: the published 2025 limit ($23,500) and his 2025 W-2 income ($80,000). Thus, Ross's maximum employee deferral contribution (traditional and/or Roth) is $23,500.

Ross's **maximum deductible employer contribution** is 25% of his W-2 income ($80,000). Thus, the employer contribution XYZ LLC can make to Ross's account for 2025 is $20,000.

There's one final contribution limit to apply to the total Solo 401(k) contributions. Ross must test his intended contributions against the all-additions limit, which is the lesser of $70,000 (the 2025 limit) and his W-2 income of $80,000. The sum of his employee and employer contributions is $43,500, which is less than his all-additions limit. If Ross makes the maximum employee deferral contribution of $23,500 and XYZ LLC makes the maximum deductible employer contribution of $20,000, the total fits within the overall additions limit.

Sean's Take: *In many cases, full-time solopreneurs will want to contribute to traditional Solo 401(k)s, including both employee and employer contributions. The Compelling Three also apply to solopreneurs, who benefit from the potentially higher contribution limits available through a Solo 401(k) compared to a large employer 401(k) plan.*

Extra Credit: *For those wanting to dive deeper into the Solo 401(k), Sean self-published a book on the topic: Solo 401(k): The Solopreneur's Retirement Account.*

Why Not the SEP IRA

Perhaps you're asking, "Why not use a SEP IRA instead of a Solo 401(k)?"

The SEP IRA is a viable alternative to the Solo 401(k). However, for most full-time solopreneurs pursuing early retirement, it's less advantageous than a Solo 401(k). The primary reason comes down to contribution limits. Solo 401(k)s allow for both employee and employer contributions, whereas SEP IRAs permit only employer contributions.

Eli and Ross could have used SEP IRAs instead of Solo 401(k)s, but their maximum contributions would have been significantly lower. For Eli, the maximum SEP IRA contribution would be just $22,304. For Ross, it would be $20,000.

It's worth noting that one can maintain both a Solo 401(k) and a SEP IRA, but this arrangement offers no real benefit. The two plans share the same contribution limits, so any employer contribution to a SEP IRA reduces the employer contribution that can be made to the Solo 401(k), and vice versa.

There's a second reason the Solo 401(k) may be preferable to a SEP IRA: For those using the Backdoor Roth IRA tactic (discussed in Chapter 9), SEP IRA balances are included in the Pro-Rata Rule calculation—potentially triggering unintended tax consequences. Solo 401(k) balances are excluded from that calculation.

Types of Solo 401(k) Plans

In our view, the simpler a Solo 401(k) plan is, the better. Bells and whistles tend to add unnecessary costs and compliance risks—including the risk of prohibited transactions.

We generally prefer prototype Solo 401(k) plans, also known as pre-approved Solo 401(k) plans. These are plans the IRS has already approved, typically offered by large financial institutions. They're usually straightforward and limited to investments like diversified mutual funds or ETFs.

To us, that's a feature, not a bug. While a Solo 401(k) can hold a broad range of investments, the further investors stray from "run of the mill" investments, the greater the risk of a prohibited transaction—potentially leading to adverse consequences.

Solo 401(k) plans that are not prototype plans can also invest in diversified mutual funds and ETFs, but they often come with higher fees. Some solopreneurs intentionally choose non-prototype plans to invest in alternative assets.

Sean's Take: Alternative investments in retirement accounts increase complexity and cost. They also encourage concentration of investments rather than diversification.

Form 5500-EZ

If a Solo 401(k) has more than $250,000 in assets at year-end—or if the plan is closed—the sponsoring employer must file Form 5500-EZ. This is currently a two-page form. While completing it is not our idea of fun, it is a manageable task.

Side Hustlers

For side hustlers, the Solo 401(k) and the SEP IRA can be effective savings options.

Should the side hustler choose the Solo 401(k) or the SEP IRA? Below, we outline two key factors that tend to support each option.

SEP IRA Factors

Maxed-Out Contributions at Work: Taxpayers have a single annual employee deferral contribution limit. For 2025, the limit for those under age 50 is $23,500. If a side hustler maxes out their employee deferral contributions through their main job's workplace retirement plan, they cannot make additional employee deferrals to a Solo 401(k). In that case, the Solo 401(k) contribution would be limited to the employer portion—making the contribution limit identical to that of a SEP IRA. That can make the SEP IRA the preferable path.

Simplicity: Managing a Solo 401(k) isn't rocket science, but opening and maintaining one is more complex than a SEP IRA. Furthermore, a SEP IRA does not have Form 5500-EZ filings.

Solo 401(k) Factors

Less Desirable Workplace Plan: If the side hustler dislikes the investment options and/or fees in their workplace plan, they might consider contributing only enough employee deferrals to capture the full employer match, then direct the remainder of the annual deferral contribution to a Solo 401(k) supported by their side hustle.

Backdoor Roth IRA: For side hustlers looking to utilize the Backdoor Roth IRA, the Solo 401(k) offers an advantage: its balance is excluded from the Pro-Rata Rule calculation. Keep in mind that all of the owner's pre-tax IRA balances—including traditional IRAs, SEP IRAs, and SIMPLE IRAs—are included in the calculation.

The Mega Backdoor Roth and the Solo 401(k)

Some solopreneurs ask, "Why not combine the Mega Backdoor Roth with the Solo 401(k)?"

It's possible, but we generally disfavor it for two reasons:

1. **Complexity and fees**. Prototype Solo 401(k) plans tend to have the lowest complexity and lowest fees. However, prototype Solo 401(k) plans typically do not allow after-tax contributions, which are required for the Mega Backdoor Roth. We generally disfavor eschewing a low-cost prototype plan just to enable the Mega Backdoor Roth.

2. **The numbers often don't justify it**. Many solopreneurs simply don't have the cash flow to make meaningful contributions to a Mega Backdoor Roth. Consider Eli from earlier, whose Schedule C income is $120,000. After maxing out his employee deferral contributions and employer contributions (about $45,000), he's left with only $75,000 to cover living expenses, $16,000 in self-employment taxes, and income taxes. That doesn't leave much room for a Mega Back-door Roth contribution.

What if Eli's Schedule C income is $175,000 instead of $120,000? He may have more cash flow, but how much space remains under his all-additions limit ($70,000) after maxing out his $23,500 employee deferral contributions and $32,527 employer contribution in 2025? Just $13,973.

If you're already contributing $56,000 to a Solo 401(k) without a Mega Backdoor Roth, is it worth the additional complexity to squeeze in another $14,000?

As you've likely gathered, we tend to favor simplicity in tax planning to and through early retirement—and Solo 401(k)s are no exception.

Caution

If you spend a bit too much time online—like Cody and Sean—you'll likely encounter a post like this:

"I have an old traditional IRA, but I want to do the Backdoor Roth IRA. My employer's 401(k) plan won't accept incoming rollover contributions from traditional IRAs. Should I drive Uber or Lyft for a few weekends so I can open a Solo 401(k) to get the traditional IRA out of the Pro-Rata Rule calculation?"

We encourage extreme caution in situations like the one contemplated above. Why? A Solo 401(k) requires a bona fide trade or business. It doesn't need to be the next Apple Computer Company, but it must be operated with a profit motive in a business-like manner. A short-lived activity—especially one that could reasonably be viewed as "born to die" and conducted with min-imal profit—may not qualify as a trade or business.

If the activity doesn't qualify as a trade or business, it doesn't qualify for a Solo 401(k). Rolling a traditional IRA into a "non-qualified" Solo 401(k) would effectively be treated as a taxable distribution—triggering income tax and a potential 10% early withdrawal penalty.

Aspiring early retirees and retirees must weigh the risks and rewards. Solo 401(k)s are a great fit for those operating a real business they'd pursue regard-less of the existence of the Solo 401(k). But using a brief side hustle solely to enable a Solo 401(k) should likely be avoided.

26 – Real Estate

We're fond of the Compelling Three. They primarily use diversified financial assets (mutual funds and ETFs) to get to and through early retirement in a tax-efficient manner.

Some, however, choose to add a wrinkle: investments in rental real estate.

Two Rental Real Estate Advantages

Below, we highlight the two primary tax advantages of investing in rental real estate.

Basis Utilization

Picture Shane. He has $100,000 in cash in a taxable brokerage account and invests it in a domestic equity index fund, ABC Index Fund. Suppose the fund pays Shane a 2% dividend, or approximately $2,000 for the year.

How much of that $2,000 dividend is taxable to Shane?

All $2,000!

Yes, Shane's basis in the ABC Index Fund is $100,000. But, generally speaking, none of that basis can be used to reduce the taxable dividend income.

Now consider a different investment. Shane uses the same $100,000 of cash to purchase 111 Happy Street, a rental property he plans to rent out. Each full year he owns the property (up to 27.5 years), he can depreciate the purchase price allocated to the building (not the land) and use that depreciation to reduce—or even eliminate—the taxable income generated by the property.

For illustration, let's assume $70,000 of the purchase price is allocated to the house and $30,000 to the land. Shane divides $70,000 by 27.5, resulting in a $2,545 annual depreciation deduction against his rental income.

Extra Credit: *What's the correct split between land and buildings? We have no idea. It can vary widely depending on the specific property and its location.*

With financial assets, basis sits dormant while the owner holds them—and even worse, its value erodes due to inflation. With rental real estate, basis goes to work for the owner, generating valuable tax deductions as soon as the property is placed in service.

Now, you may be thinking: "Cody and Sean, who is buying rental real estate for $100,000 in 2025?"

Great point.

In reality, most rental real estate investors use debt as leverage. So let's update the example: Shane puts in his $100,000 of cash and borrows $400,000 from the bank to purchase 222 Happy Street, a $500,000 rental property.

Assuming the same 70/30 building-to-land split, $350,000 is allocated to the building. Shane can now depreciate that amount over 27.5 years, producing $12,727 of annual depreciation deductions for each full year he owns the property (up to 27.5 years).

Leverage increases basis—and with it, tax deductions.

Given the same initial $100,000 investment, Shane can either:

1. Choose the ABC Index Fund and receive $0 in tax-deductible basis recovery, or
2. Choose 222 Happy Street and receive $12,727 per year in deductible basis recovery—in the form of depreciation.

Tax-Advantaged Cash Flow

The second major tax advantage of rental real estate is its potential to generate tax-advantaged cash flow.

Picture Amy, the owner of several rental properties. Each month, Amy collects $10,000 in gross rental income ($120,000 annually). She incurs cash expenses related to the properties, including HOA fees, plumber visits, and interest payments. In addition, she must make principal payments on any loans she has taken out.

If Amy is running a successful rental business, her gross rental income minus her cash expenses and principal repayments results in positive cash flow.

Then comes depreciation. Depreciation is not a cash expense—it's a "phantom" tax deduction. Ideally, Amy's depreciation deductions reduce her net rental income to near $0—or even create a net loss.

If that happens, Amy has created a positive cash flow stream that is lightly taxed—or possibly not taxed at all—in the current year.

Extra Credit: Amy may be able to claim limited or even potentially unlimited losses from her rental property. However, in our experience, most rental real estate investors are subject to the passive activity loss rules. For many early retirees, the maximum annual real estate losses allowable against other income are capped at $25,000, though the cap can be lower.

Losses that cannot be currently claimed under the passive activity loss rules are considered "suspended" losses and are reported annually on Form 8582. Suspended losses can be used in future years to offset future rental income and/or gains from the sale of rental property.

Disadvantages Compared to Financial Assets

Have we convinced you to invest in rental real estate? Before making any decisions, it's important to understand that there are significant disadvantages to investing in rental real estate when compared to financial assets.

Inflexibility and Friction

Want to buy a stock, bond, mutual fund, or ETF? Got a phone? In 2025, you can open a brokerage account in minutes. Once it's set up, buying and selling investments is easy—thanks to user-friendly online platforms.

Real estate? Not so simple. Buying property involves much higher transaction costs and far more friction.

What about small withdrawals? Let's say you want to spend $12,000 on a once-in-a-lifetime trip. It's easy to log in to an Internet portal and sell $12,000 of stock or a fund. But it's rather difficult to sell $12,000 worth of your rental property at 333 Happy Street.

Even more practical than a once-in-a-lifetime trip: consider rebalancing. Suppose your portfolio is 70% equities and 30% bonds, and you'd prefer a 75/25 split. With financial assets, it's straightforward: sell some bonds, buy some equities.

Now imagine you own five rental properties in the Southeast. You believe real estate in that region is overpriced and want to shift exposure to the Midwest. Rebalancing in real estate means selling properties, finding new ones, and managing the significant costs, time, and friction associated with this process.

Potential Negative Cash Flow

Mutual funds and ETFs never need a new roof or experience vacancies. Rental real estate, on the other hand, can generate negative cash flow—even if temporary—during retirement, in a way that mutual funds and ETFs do not.

Sector and Geographic Concentration

Compared to financial assets—particularly broad index mutual funds and ETFs—rental real estate is significantly more concentrated. Each property is inherently tied to a single sector (real estate) and a single geographic location.

Business Knowledge Required

You can invest in equity mutual funds and ETFs that own thousands of businesses across various sectors. No particular industry knowledge is required to invest in mutual funds and ETFs.

Rental real estate is different. While you don't need to master every aspect of property management, you do need a basic level of knowledge—at the very least, how to select a reliable property manager if you don't plan to manage the property yourself.

Success in rental real estate requires some understanding of property selection, tenant screening, and other day-to-day operations.

Tenant Rights

Stocks, bonds, mutual funds, and ETFs don't require tenants. Rental real estate does. Tenants have rights that may apply even if they don't pay rent on time.

When you rent out a property, you're creating a legal relationship in which someone else has rights against you with respect to your own investment.

Depreciation Deductions and the Investment Time Horizon

Consider an individual in their mid-40s planning for early retirement. They could have an investment time horizon of 40 years or more.

Depreciation deductions are valuable, but they don't last forever. For residential real estate, depreciation deductions effectively last 28 years, based on the tax code's 27.5 useful life. Once the basis has been fully depreciated, the owner may face years in retirement with little or no depreciation left to offset taxable rental income.

This can create taxable ordinary income later in retirement, well within the owner's investment time horizon. This is a tax drawback of investing in rental real estate during retirement.

Tax Environment on Financial Investments Has Improved

Yes, rental real estate offers some tax advantages. But so do financial assets.

The tax laws have evolved in ways that are highly favorable to financial asset income, especially for early retirees. Here are a few key developments:

First, most dividends paid by American companies, as well as many dividends paid by foreign companies, now qualify as qualified dividend income (QDI). Prior to 2003, QDI didn't exist, and all dividends were taxed as ordinary income.

Second, the 0% long-term capital gains tax bracket, introduced in 2008, applies to both long-term capital gains and QDI. We have seen that many early retirees can have years with no federal income tax liability due to the 0% long-term capital gains tax bracket.

Third, the higher standard deduction, in place since 2018, opens the door for planning opportunities, such as the Hidden Roth IRA.

Before these developments, the tax case for rental real estate was much stronger. In today's environment, the tax advantages enjoyed by real estate over financial assets are rather modest.

Conclusion

When selecting investments, investors should prioritize investment decisions over perceived tax benefits. Aspiring and current early retirees should first decide what they want to invest in, and then consider factors such as account type, asset location, and other tax-optimized tactics.

In our view, rental real estate does offer tax advantages. However, in the post-2025 tax planning environment, those advantages are much less compelling than they were thirty years ago, as tax rules have become increasingly favorable toward financial asset income.

27 – Late Starters

Tax planning to and through early retirement is possible whenever you start. If you're starting late, congratulations! At least you're starting.

The Profile of the Late Starter

Consider the profile of a late starter. They are typically further along in their career. With time often comes increased income due to promotions, experience, and tenure. As a result, many late starters are in their peak earning years.

At the same time, late starters tend to have lower balances in all types of retirement accounts. They may also plan to retire "less early" than those who began saving earlier.

These characteristics shape the tactics most late starters should employ.

Late Starter Tactics

Deduct, Deduct, Deduct!!!

Throughout the book, we've emphasized that traditional retirement accounts tend to be lightly taxed in retirement. This is especially true for the late starter. Most late starters would welcome a tax problem in retirement, because it means they've accumulated enough to have one!

Starting late makes it more difficult to build up large traditional retirement accounts. While that presents a sufficiency problem, it also reduces the risk of significant taxation in retirement.

When you're behind, you have to catch up. The fastest way to catch up is to maximize contributions to a traditional 401(k) or other workplace-qualified plan. For late starters, the future tax cost of those distributions is likely to be very manageable.

Consider a late-starting couple in their early 50s earning $220,000 after 25 years in their professions. That income puts them in the 22% federal marginal income tax bracket (based on 2025 brackets). A single filer with the same income would fall into the 32% bracket.

This couple is saving 22 cents on the dollar from the IRS for each dollar they contribute to a traditional 401(k) or other traditional qualified plan at work.

Why would late starters forgo a 22% tax deduction when, in retirement, most account distributions would be taxed at 0% (against the standard deduction and the senior bonus deduction), 10%, and 12%? As shown throughout this book, even many affluent retirees tend to face relatively low tax rates on their traditional retirement account distributions. This tends to be especially true for late starters.

Extra Credit: *As you may recall from Chapter 5, employee deferral contributions to traditional 401(k)s are excluded from income rather than taken as a tax deduction. In this chapter and elsewhere, we use the more common conversational term "deduct" rather than the more precise tax term "exclude" to describe these contributions.*

Invest the Traditional 401(k) Tax Savings at Home

The Compelling Three are particularly compelling for the late starter. The late starter can accelerate their path to retirement by implementing all three simultaneously.

What's the best way for the late starter to fund a Roth IRA and taxable accounts? Use the income tax savings from contributing to a traditional retirement plan.

In retirement, taxable accounts often benefit from the 0% long-term capital gains (LTCG) tax rate on both qualified dividends and realized capital gains. Asset location (as discussed in Chapter 18)—especially when primarily holding domestic equities in taxable accounts—can help keep dividend income low and taxable income within the 0% LTCG bracket.

Consider Deductible Traditional IRA Contributions

There are several reasons why some individuals start their retirement journey later in life. Some start saving late simply because they don't have access to a workplace retirement plan. While that's not ideal, it does present an opportunity.

Under current tax rules, individuals not covered by a workplace retirement plan during the year can deduct a traditional IRA contribution regardless of their modified adjusted gross income (MAGI). However, if one spouse is covered by a workplace plan, the ability to deduct a traditional IRA contribution phases out based on MAGI. Note, however, that the MAGI phaseout cap for the non-covered spouse is higher than the cap for the covered spouse. For late starters not covered by a workplace retirement plan, this often-overlooked deduction is well worth considering.

Another opportunity is a deductible traditional IRA contribution for a non-earning spouse. Even if one spouse has little or no earned income, they may still be eligible to make a fully deductible contribution to a traditional IRA, depending on MAGI for the year. IRS Publication 590-A provides additional details.

In 2025, the IRA contribution limits are $7,000 for those under age 50 and $8,000 for those turning age 50 or older during 2025.

Premium Tax Credit

Late starters might wonder: "If I build up large traditional retirement accounts, won't the future taxable distributions reduce my Premium Tax Credit (PTC) eligibility in retirement?"

This is a valid concern, but there are other factors to consider. Late starters typically have fewer years in retirement before turning age 65 and enrolling in Medicare. This alone significantly reduces the importance of the PTC as a tax-planning issue for late starters.

Those still concerned about the PTC should strongly consider building up taxable accounts and Roth IRAs in addition to traditional retirement accounts at work. Combining the Compelling Three gives late starters access to lightly taxed or untaxed distributions in retirement—helping to reduce MAGI and increase the PTC.

28 – Sudden Job Loss

The inspiration for this chapter came from YouTube and LinkedIn. Sean kept seeing videos of people in their 50s sharing their experiences with sudden layoffs at work. He also noticed LinkedIn headlines about well-known American companies laying off hundreds or thousands of workers.

Layoffs happen. Job losses happen. It's time to consider being prepared and the necessary action steps to take if you lose your job.

Traditional Retirement Accounts After a Sudden Job Loss

Some might question our fondness for traditional retirement account contributions in light of our admonition to be prepared in the event of a sudden job loss. "Isn't that money locked up until I'm 59½? Won't it be taxable to me at the worst possible time?"

The answers to these questions are: "Not really, but there are restrictions" and "Yes, but..." We will explain them in more detail.

But we guess that if you ever do experience job loss, you'll likely be glad you saved and invested significant amounts in retirement accounts, whether in traditional, Roth, and/or taxable accounts. Even traditional accounts can be beneficial for those experiencing a sudden job loss.

First Step: Do Nothing

People experience a wide range of emotions after a job loss. It's common to feel urgency and think, "Surely I have to do something with my money?"

The odds are you don't need to take action right away. What are your bills for the next month? How much is in your checking account? If your checking account balance exceeds your upcoming expenses, you likely have some time to figure things out.

Then ask yourself three questions:

1. Will I receive a severance payment?
2. What unemployment benefits am I eligible for?
3. How much is in my emergency fund?

Perhaps these amounts provide a month or more of runway before you need to make significant changes to your life or do any particular tax planning.

Second Step: Consider Sales of Taxable Assets

Now it's time to consider how long you might be without a job. Perhaps it will take a few or several months to find new employment. Or perhaps the layoff is the catalyst for a retirement you can already afford.

Once severance packages, unemployment benefits, checking accounts, and emergency funds are largely exhausted, selling taxable account assets often makes the most sense. These sales generate capital gain income with basis recovery, rather than the ordinary income created by traditional retirement account withdrawals.

Furthermore, it is generally better to leave money in traditional retirement accounts and Roth retirement accounts. Traditional retirement account withdrawals create ordinary income and may incur a 10% early withdrawal penalty. Roth withdrawals reduce future tax-free growth, which may be beneficial later in retirement.

Income Tax Refund

One matter to attend to after a sudden job loss is filing the tax return for the year of the job loss. These years often result in an income tax refund due to tax withholding and progressive tax rates.

Workplace withholding assumes you earn your entire salary for the year. But what if you don't because you were laid off in July? The months of salary you don't collect are, in effect, the higher taxed months, since our tax rates are progressive (i.e., they increase as you make more money during the year).

Since the withholding was done on the assumption that you would have a full year's salary and you ultimately did not, it is very possible that you will get a refund when you file your federal and state income tax returns. Thus, early in the following year, those facing a sudden job loss may want to file their tax returns as early as possible to receive the refund quickly.

Roth Basis

For needs during a temporary loss of employment, Roth basis can be a good answer. As discussed, withdrawals from Roth IRAs occurring prior to the owner turning 59½ are first deemed to be tax- and penalty-free distributions of annual contributions. That can be a great source of funds for a temporary unemployment situation, after emergency funds, other cash, and taxable accounts have been exhausted.

Roth basis planning might be a reason to roll a Roth 401(k) to a Roth IRA, as discussed in Chapter 6.

Roths can also be useful for those 59½ and older experiencing a sudden job loss. For individuals who are 59½ or older and meet the 5-year holding period for earnings, all Roth distributions are tax- and penalty-free qualified distributions. Even those age 59½ and older who haven't met the 5-year test still benefit from recovering old annual contributions first (tax- and penalty-free).

Rule of 55 / Governmental 457(b)

For those under age 59½ who need to access traditional retirement accounts after a job loss, the Rule of 55 or a government 457(b) plan are often the first two penalty-free options to consider. If available, they can provide flexible sources of cash flow to fund living expenses after a sudden job loss. We discussed both of these options in Chapter 12.

72(t) Payment Plan

Traditional retirement accounts can be accessed penalty-free prior to age 59½. However, it requires some structuring for those without flexible access to another 10% penalty exception—such as the Rule of 55 or a governmental 457(b).

From a traditional IRA, the owner can take a "series of substantially equal periodic payments," sometimes referred to as an SEPP or as 72(t) payments—the term we use. Our preferred method is the fixed amortization method, where the owner sizes a traditional IRA to produce equal annual payments using an amortization calculation. This calculation is essentially the same as a mortgage calculation. We explore 72(t) payment plans in much greater detail in Chapter 12.

A sudden job loss may ultimately necessitate a 72(t) payment plan, even if the owner hopes to return to work. In Chapter 12, we discuss how to significantly reduce 72(t) annual payments using a one-time change to the required minimum distribution (RMD) method.

Further, taking a smaller 72(t) payment while working a new job might not be a bad outcome. The extra cash flow can either (1) cover living expenses, freeing up income to contribute more to a workplace traditional 401(k) or other qualified plan, or (2) be invested into a Roth IRA or taxable accounts to support future retirement needs.

Extra Credit: After separating from service, a qualified plan account owner can establish a 72(t) payment plan from the qualified account. However, as discussed in Chapter 12, 72(t) payment plans are rarely established from 401(k)s and other qualified plans in practice.

Consider Paying the 10% Early Withdrawal Penalty

Some might suggest, "Why not just pay the 10% early withdrawal penalty and see what happens?" For short-term needs, this can absolutely be a viable tactic. That said, a 72(t) plan isn't the worst alternative—particularly for small amounts. If the owner returns to work, the annual payment can later be reduced through a one-time switch to the RMD method.

Consider Retirement Account Rollovers

Whenever you leave a job, review the retirement accounts held with your former employer. Does the plan offer good investments? Are the fees reasonable?

A job loss may present an opportunity to move the retirement account to a provider with better investment options and/or lower expenses.

That said, any potential rollover should consider how the owner plans to fund their unemployment or retirement needs. You can revisit rollover considerations in Chapter 6.

Conclusion

Job loss happens. In those moments, it's rare for someone to regret having accumulated financial assets in various accounts—taxable, traditional, Roth, and HSA.

Retirement planning should account for the possibility of a sudden job loss. Fortunately, the tax and retirement account rules are relatively friendly in this regard, allowing for flexible and tax-efficient options to help navigate periods of unemployment.

29 – Return on Hassle

When evaluating financial tactics, it's important to assess not only their potential benefits but also the effort, complexity, costs, and mental bandwidth required to implement and maintain them—a concept we call Return on Hassle (ROH). A tactic may offer marginal benefits, but the hassle involved can outweigh them.

In this chapter, we briefly evaluate several strategies through the lens of ROH to determine their practicality on the path to and through early retirement.

Insurance-Based Strategies

Indexed Universal Life (IUL) Insurance

IUL policies are permanent life insurance products often marketed as tax-free investment vehicles offering optimistic return projections and downside protection. However, actual performance is limited by participation rates, caps, spreads, and ongoing fees. IULs also come with high insurance costs, surrender charges, and the need for sustained premium payments to prevent policy lapse. While permanent life insurance may be suitable for a small subset of individuals with specific needs, the complexity and costs of IULs make them impractical for most investors.

Life Insurance Retirement Plans (LIRP)

LIRPs utilize permanent life insurance policies to accumulate cash value that can be accessed tax-free in retirement through policy loans. However, they often require high ongoing premiums to maximize cash value, and their benefits depend on policy performance and insurance costs. For most investors, LIRPs are less suitable than more straightforward and cost-effective retirement savings options, such as workplace retirement plans, Roth IRAs, and taxable brokerage accounts (the Compelling Three).

Annuities

Annuities can provide "guaranteed" retirement income but often come with high fees, complex structures, and surrender charges. While simple qualified annuities—such as single premium immediate annuities (SPIAs) and deferred income annuities (DIAs)—may help support a reliable income floor and provide longevity protection, variable and fixed indexed annuities often add unnecessary complexity, high fees, and liquidity constraints. It's essential to evaluate the specific type of annuity, its tax treatment, and whether it aligns with your specific retirement objectives—including your needs, risk capacity, and risk tolerance.

Furthermore, nonqualified annuity payouts create inflexible ordinary income in retirement. One of our favorite drawdown principles is to keep ordinary income low—and annuities in taxable accounts oppose that principle.

Retirees who delay claiming Social Security retirement benefits may reduce or eliminate any need for annuities by securing greater monthly Social Security payments in their 70s and beyond.

Sean's Take: Annuities subject retirees to single-entity creditor risk. Consider too the patchwork of state regulations applicable to insurance companies offering annuities. What happens to the retiree relying on an annuity if the issuing insurance company faces financial difficulties?

Retirement Account Strategies

Retirement Plan Loans

Borrowing from a 401(k) or other workplace retirement plan might seem like an easy way to access liquidity, but it comes with administrative hassle and significant risks—especially for those planning for early retirement.

Separation from service creates a problem. Repayment upon separation is typically required within a short window. Failure to repay on time results in the outstanding loan balance being treated as a taxable distribution, subject to ordinary income tax—and, for those under 59½, a potential 10% early withdrawal penalty.

Traditional IRA 60-Day Rollovers

The 60-day rollover rule allows individuals to temporarily access traditional IRA funds without tax or penalty, provided the funds are redeposited into a traditional IRA within 60 days of receipt. These interest-free 'loans' may sound appealing, but they are only allowed once per 12-month period. Further, failure to redeposit the funds within the 60-day window triggers a taxable distribution—plus a potential 10% early withdrawal penalty if under age 59½.

We generally disfavor 60-day traditional IRA rollovers unless absolutely necessary. Following a 60-day rollover, the once-every-12-months rule eliminates the 60-day rollover as a remedial measure if money is inadvertently withdrawn from an IRA during the next 12 months. We would rather have that tool available at all times.

One strategy we disfavor is using a 60-day rollover to pay income taxes in November or December. The idea is to take a late-year traditional IRA distribution, have it withheld for income taxes, and then redeposit the money into the traditional IRA in early January. This essentially creates a tax-free income tax payment from a traditional IRA.

Assuming the retiree is age 59½ or older—or otherwise qualifies for a penalty exception—we often favor retirees using withholding from traditional IRA withdrawals to pay taxes, especially when withdrawals are already funding living expenses. However, we strongly prefer this be done through standard taxable distributions—not through a distribution intended to be rolled back. Using a 60-day rollover for this purpose burns the one allowed 60-day rollover for the next 12 months.

What if money accidentally comes out of an IRA within that 12-month period? Accidents happen. In our view, it's best to preserve the 60-day rollover as a backup tool for genuine mistakes rather than using it to pay income taxes—a need that proper planning should have already addressed. If tax payments fall short, we think it's better to make up the difference with additional taxable IRA distributions or estimated tax payments.

Rollover Bonuses

Financial institutions sometimes offer cash incentives to attract rollovers of retirement accounts, with bonuses ranging from a few hundred to several thousand dollars, depending on the transferred balance. While these bonuses may seem like free money, they typically come with strings attached—such as maintaining large balances, paying platform fees, or being limited to specific investment options. It's important to weigh the short-term benefits against the potential long-term hassle.

Self-Directed Retirement Accounts

It is possible to hold alternative assets such as real estate, cryptocurrency, and private equity in retirement accounts. Colloquially, these are often called self-directed retirement accounts.

While self-directed retirement accounts offer access to alternative assets, they also require strict adherence to prohibited transaction rules to avoid disqualification and significant tax and penalties. Investors must also be mindful of fraud risks and the illiquid nature of certain alternative investments.

We discuss investing in real estate and cryptocurrency through self-directed retirement accounts in more detail in Chapter 25.

Real Estate & Investment Strategies

Real Estate Professional Status (REPS)

Qualifying for REPS allows rental real estate losses to offset other ordinary income—a potentially powerful tax benefit typically limited by passive activity loss rules. However, the strict material participation requirements make this status generally worth pursuing only as a primary business, such as for full-time real estate investors. It's not a casual election available for households with just a few rental properties; it requires a substantial time commitment.

Alaska Community Property Trust (ACPT)

Most states are not "community property" states. In the nine community property states, property acquired during marriage is typically considered property of the "community," not individually owned by each spouse.

Community property offers a unique federal income tax benefit: it receives a full step-up in basis at the death of the first spouse. In contrast, jointly owned property in non-community property states generally receives only a one-half step-up in basis at the first spouse's death.

By transferring property into a properly structured Alaska Community Property Trust, married couples living in non-community property states can access this full step-up in basis benefit. However, establishing and maintaining such a trust—subject to Alaska law—involves legal fees, compliance requirements, and administrative complexity. For many retirees, the hassle may outweigh the potential tax savings.

The "juice" of this planning concept depends on two key factors:

1. A meaningful amount of time between the spouses' deaths
2. Capital gains taxes being a significant concern

Here's a simplified example: Stan and Sarah live in New York and jointly own Acme Corp. stock purchased for $200,000, now worth $3,000,000. They establish an Alaska Community Property Trust and transfer the Acme stock into it. Sarah dies in late 2030. Stan sells some of the stock in 2031 with a full step-up in basis, incurring little or no tax. He then dies later that same year.

In their case, the trust provided just one year's worth of tax benefit.

Furthermore, as we've illustrated throughout this book, long-term capital gains are often taxed lightly. A one-half step-up in basis at the first death, combined with access to the 0% capital gains bracket, may be more than sufficient to allow a surviving spouse to sell appreciated assets while paying little to no federal income tax—without the hassle of utilizing an Alaska Community Property Trust.

Giving Securities to Minors

Transferring assets to a minor via a Uniform Transfers to Minors Act (UTMA) account may seem like an effective tax-saving strategy, as it shifts investment income to a dependent child with lower taxable income. However, the **kiddie tax** limits how much unearned income can be taxed at the child's lower rate, reducing the tax-saving potential.

Additionally, once the child reaches the age of majority (typically 18–21), their full control over the assets may not align with the donor's original intent. For these reasons, UTMA accounts are generally ineffective for significant long-term tax planning.

Giving Securities to Elderly Parents ("Upstream Gifting")

Some consider giving appreciated securities to elderly parents as a tax strategy. The idea is that the parent receives the assets with a carryover basis and holds them until death—at which point the securities are inherited by the adult child with a step-up in basis to fair market value.

We strongly disfavor this technique for several reasons.

First and foremost, transferring assets to potentially vulnerable individuals is a poor method for preserving and protecting wealth. Even if an elderly parent is not vulnerable today, will that still be true in two years? Five years?

Second, once the securities are in the elderly parent's name, there may be no safeguards. The assets could be transferred to other siblings, other relatives, scammers, or even a late-in-life romantic partner. Anything is possible.

Third, as mentioned throughout this book, appreciated securities may never be subject to federal income tax in retirement due to the 0% long-term capital gains (LTCG) tax rate. Why create additional risk through upstream gifting when capital gains taxes might not be a meaningful problem in the first place?

Direct Indexing

As mentioned in Chapter 23, direct indexing involves purchasing individual securities or sector funds to enhance tax loss harvesting opportunities within taxable brokerage accounts. While this approach can be useful for offsetting significant one-time capital gains, it adds complexity to portfolio management, tax reporting, and drawdown strategies—and involves higher costs when outsourced.

TreasuryDirect

While savings bonds and other Treasury securities purchased through the official TreasuryDirect platform offer tax-deferred growth, exemption from state and local income tax, and potential inflation protection, the platform comes with liquidity constraints and administrative limitations. Fortunately, many Treasury securities are also available on the secondary market and can be held within traditional IRAs—offering easier management and asset location flexibility.

ETFs Versus Mutual Funds

Some argue for holding exchange-traded funds (ETFs) in taxable accounts instead of mutual funds, primarily due to concerns about tax efficiency.

As discussed in Chapter 1, mutual funds tend to distribute more capital gains than ETFs. However, index funds—whether structured as mutual funds or ETFs—typically have minimal capital gains distributions due to their passive management. For most index fund investors, the difference between ETFs and mutual funds in taxable accounts is largely negligible.

Administrative & Cash Management Strategies

Income-Related Monthly Adjustment Amount (IRMAA)

IRMAA increases Medicare Part B and D premiums for higher-income retirees, based on Modified Adjusted Gross Income (MAGI) from two years prior. While it's helpful to be aware of IRMAA thresholds and surcharges, going to great lengths to avoid this "nuisance tax" can lead to minimal savings while distracting from more impactful tax and retirement planning strategies.

Cody's Take: Reviewing the thresholds in 2025, I noticed that total IRMAA for Medicare Parts B + D doesn't exceed 3% of a household's MAGI from two years prior—regardless of income level. While the premium amounts can feel significant, IRMAA is actually quite small relative to overall household income. It's also recalculated annually and may be reduced by filing Form SSA-44 if a qualifying life event occurs.

FDIC Coverage

Spreading cash across multiple banks to expand FDIC insurance coverage ($250,000 per depositor, per bank, per ownership category) increases security but also introduces administrative complexity. Managing multiple accounts requires additional coordination for transfers, account maintenance, and tracking across institutions.

Cody's Take: In my experience, retirees with enough cash to exceed FDIC limits at a single institution often hold more cash than is necessary for their financial objectives. It may be worth evaluating alternative investment options—including fixed income—to better align with those objectives.

High-Yield Savings Transfers

Some banks offer promotional high-yield savings rates that require large or frequent transfers. The incremental gain is often minimal compared to the hassle of opening new accounts and moving funds—especially if rates drop after the promotional period ends.

Cody's Take: *Most retirees I meet prefer to set up a simple financial system with no more than two financial institutions—one for investment accounts (IRAs, taxable brokerage, and HSAs) and another for everyday banking (checking and savings). I often say, "Become more passive with your investments and more active with your life." Don't underestimate the value of simplicity, especially during significant life transitions.*

Credit Card Bonuses

Opening new credit cards to earn sign-up bonuses can offer "free" travel points or cash back, but it requires managing multiple accounts, meeting spending thresholds, and keeping track of annual fees. The ongoing effort to track rewards, optimize redemptions, and evaluate card benefits also requires mental bandwidth—what we call "headspace premium." Consider whether the rewards and required spending meaningfully support your financial goals.

Conclusion

While this book explores a wide range of tax optimization tactics, we acknowledge that pursuing every opportunity can introduce complexity with minimal benefit. We recommend focusing on the 90% of your financial plan that truly moves the needle and assessing the ROH before fine-tuning the remaining 10%. Above all, avoid letting financial optimization become a form of procrastination and a distraction from what genuinely matters in your life.

30 – Inheriting Property

Those planning for early retirement may eventually inherit significant assets—many of which may be held in retirement accounts. This chapter explores tactics to consider when inheriting assets on the journey to and through early retirement.

A quick note on terminology before we proceed: The original owner of a retirement account is called the **owner**. The person designated to inherit the account—typically through a beneficiary designation form—is the **beneficiary**. The beneficiary never becomes the owner; they are always referred to as the beneficiary. If someone inherits a retirement account from a beneficiary, they are known as the **successor beneficiary**.

Traditional Retirement Accounts

Inheriting traditional retirement accounts is becoming increasingly relevant as the first generation to save primarily through defined contribution plans passes on and leaves unspent account balances to their Generation X and Generation Y children.

Most nonspouse beneficiaries of traditional retirement accounts will be subject to the 10-year rule. The traditional IRA will need to be fully depleted by the end of the 10th full year following the owner's death.

The challenge with the 10-year rule is that the full balance—minus any basis the owner had—must be reported as taxable income to the beneficiary within a 10-year period. This compression can be a problem, especially if the inheritance coincides with the beneficiary's peak earning years.

Beneficiaries who inherit sizable traditional retirement accounts need to plan proactively. One potential mistake is deferring withdrawals until the 10th year, creating a "Year 10 tax time bomb" that pushes large amounts of income into higher marginal tax brackets.

Instead, beneficiaries should estimate their projected taxable income without the inherited traditional retirement account and coordinate distributions accordingly to reduce the overall tax impact.

For example, someone who inherits a traditional IRA five years before retiring might consider taking only the required minimum distributions (RMDs) from the inherited traditional IRA while still working and then accelerating the remaining withdrawals during their first five years of retirement, when their taxable income is presumably lower.

Extra Credit: If the original owner had reached their required beginning date for taking RMDs, the beneficiary must take annual RMDs from the inherited traditional retirement account. In many years, the RMD amount will be significantly less than what the beneficiary might want to withdraw. To smooth out the tax impact and avoid entering higher tax brackets in a single year, beneficiaries often benefit from withdrawing more than the RMD amount.

Extra Credit: The 10-year rule began in 2020. Individual nonspouse beneficiaries inheriting from owners prior to 2020 are generally subject to RMDs unaffected by the 10-year rule.

Eligible Designated Beneficiaries

Not everyone will be subject to the 10-year rule, though most nonspouse beneficiaries reading this book likely will be.

Some beneficiaries will qualify to take RMDs over their lifetime—beginning in the year after the owner's death—instead of being subject to the 10-year rule. We refer to this as immediate RMD treatment. A person qualifying for immediate RMD treatment is known as an **eligible designated beneficiary**, a term defined in the Internal Revenue Code.

From a tax perspective, most beneficiaries will prefer immediate RMD treatment over the 10-year rule. Annual distributions under the RMD rules are usually smaller, and the funds can remain in the inherited retirement account much longer than 10 years.

Who qualifies as an eligible designated beneficiary? The list includes:

- A surviving spouse
- The owner's minor child (until they reach the age of 21)
- An individual not more than 10 years younger than the owner
- A chronically ill or disabled individual

Readers of this book are most likely to qualify as eligible designated beneficiaries **when inheriting retirement accounts from siblings or adult children.**

Although spouses are technically eligible designated beneficiaries, they rarely use immediate RMD treatment. Instead, surviving spouses commonly elect spousal rollover treatment, which we discuss later in this chapter.

Retitling

Whether traditional or Roth, inherited retirement accounts must be specially titled to indicate their inherited status and the beneficiary's status. The account title typically references the original owner, the date of the owner's death, and that the account is now held for the benefit of the named beneficiary.

When a traditional or Roth account is left to a nonspouse beneficiary, it must be retitled as an inherited retirement account. It cannot be rolled into the beneficiary's own retirement account.

Restrictions

One major advantage of inherited retirement accounts is that they typically have no early access restrictions and are not subject to the 10% early withdrawal penalty. While there are often good tax reasons to limit distributions in a given year, beneficiaries who need funds from inherited retirement accounts can generally access them without penalty.

Making the 10-Year Period 11 Years

A beneficiary can take a distribution from an inherited retirement account in the year of the owner's death. Practically speaking, the earlier in the year the death occurs, the easier this is to implement.

The year of death essentially becomes an eleventh year to begin drawing down the account. Beneficiaries should consider taking distributions in that year to reduce the amounts that must be withdrawn over the following ten calendar years—helping to spread out the tax impact.

Claiming the Owner's Final RMD

Any beneficiary inheriting from an owner subject to RMDs should ask, "Did the decedent take their RMD before death?" If not, the beneficiary must generally take that RMD by the end of the calendar year following the year of death. The RMD will be included in the beneficiary's taxable income in the year it is taken.

Three Great Uses for an Inherited Traditional Retirement Account

Too often, inherited traditional IRAs are seen as a problem. But let's consider them an opportunity instead.

Early Retirement

For those on the edge of early retirement, inheriting a traditional retirement account might be what finally tips the scale—for two reasons.

First, sufficiency. Prior to the inheritance, the beneficiary's financial wealth may not have supported an early retirement. But with the addition of the inherited account, sufficiency may be met.

Second, tax efficiency. The taxation of the inherited traditional retirement account could drop like a rock if the beneficiary retires. Imagine someone in the 24% marginal tax bracket due to significant W-2 income. If they inherit a traditional retirement account while still working, any distributions will be taxed at 24% or higher. But if that same person retires early, they could use distributions from the inherited account to fund living expenses—and those distributions might be taxed at much lower rates, including 0% (the standard deduction), 10%, and 12%.

Funding the "early" part of early retirement is a great use for an inherited traditional retirement account.

Holding Bonds

Many Americans include bonds in their investment portfolios for various reasons. In Chapter 18, we explored the concept of asset location and noted that bonds are often well-suited for traditional retirement accounts.

Bonds sit even better in inherited retirement accounts.

Most nonspouse inherited traditional retirement accounts must be depleted within 10 years. Because any growth is eventually taxed as ordinary income within that period, these accounts are generally not ideal for long-term growth assets.

From an expected return perspective, bonds typically grow less than equities. So why not prioritize holding equities in tax-free Roth accounts, lightly taxed taxable brokerage accounts, and even one's own traditional retirement accounts (which are subject to small RMDs later in life)—and hold bonds in inherited traditional retirement accounts, which are subject to taxation much sooner?

Paying Income Taxes

Inherited traditional retirement accounts can be a flexible source of funds to cover federal and state income taxes in early retirement.

Beneficiaries can take a distribution from the inherited traditional retirement account and elect to have most of it withheld to the IRS and/or their state taxing authority. This approach has three key advantages:

First, the timing is flexible. Withholding from retirement account distributions is treated as if it occurred evenly throughout the year, regardless of when the distribution happens. This means a distribution with withholding late in the year can help avoid underpayment penalties.

Second, distributions from inherited traditional retirement accounts are never subject to the 10% early withdrawal penalty, making this tactic penalty-free—even for beneficiaries under age 59½.

Third, the account needs to be depleted anyway. Some might object, "But that income tax payment is taxable!" Our response: Of course it is, but for most beneficiaries, all distributions will be taxable within 10 years anyway. If the beneficiary can use part of the account to pay taxes and avoid underpayment penalties, all the better.

Roth Retirement Accounts

Increasingly, Generation X and Generation Y will inherit Roth retirement accounts. This section outlines the rules and planning considerations when inheriting these accounts.

Inherited Roth IRAs

Most beneficiaries of inherited Roth IRAs will be subject to the 10-year rule, which requires the account to be fully depleted by the end of the 10th calendar year following the owner's death. However, there are no annual RMDs during the first nine years. Distributions are penalty-free and, in nearly all cases, income tax–free (discussed below).

From an income tax perspective, it's generally advantageous to leave assets in an inherited Roth IRA for the full 10-year period to maximize tax-free growth.

That said, there are two primary reasons beneficiaries might withdraw inherited Roth IRA funds sooner:

1. To cover large expenses. For example, a $50,000 home repair may be better funded with an inherited Roth IRA distribution than a traditional IRA withdrawal.
2. To optimize for Premium Tax Credits (PTCs). Using inherited Roth IRA distributions to fund living expenses can help keep household income low, thereby increasing PTC eligibility.

Extra Credit: Is it possible to owe income tax on an inherited Roth IRA distribution? Yes, but only in rare cases. Taxes apply to a distribution of earnings if it occurs before five tax years have passed since the owner established (opened and funded) their first Roth IRA. As detailed in Chapter 4, original contributions and conversions are withdrawn first, so it's uncommon for a beneficiary to tap into earnings before the five-year clock is satisfied—but it remains a theoretical possibility.

Inherited Roth IRA RMDs

"Roth IRAs never have RMDs, right?"

Well, usually right. If the inherited Roth IRA beneficiary qualifies as an **eligible designated beneficiary** (see earlier section), they can elect immediate RMD treatment—taking RMDs beginning the year after the owner's death, rather than being subject to the 10-year rule.

These RMDs are calculated using the beneficiary's life expectancy based on the IRS Single Life Table, starting the year after the original owner's death. They are generally not taxable and are never subject to the 10% early withdrawal penalty.

Immediate RMD treatment is generally preferable to the 10-year rule because it allows the beneficiary to preserve tax-free growth in the inherited Roth IRA for more than 10 years.

Inherited Roth 401(k)s and Other Qualified Plans

So long as the owner satisfies the five-year rule for their Roth 401(k) or other Roth qualified plan, the beneficiary's distributions will be fully tax- and penalty-free.

However, the five-year rule plays a more significant role in inherited Roth 401(k)s and other qualified plans than it does for Roth IRAs. If a beneficiary takes a distribution before the five-year rule is met, the portion attributable to earnings is subject to income tax.

At a minimum, beneficiaries should consider delaying distributions (other than RMDs) until they are certain the five-year holding period has been met.

Inheriting a Retirement Account from a Spouse

A surviving spouse will often choose a spousal rollover for an inherited employer plan account. When inheriting an IRA from a spouse, the surviving spouse may treat the inherited IRA as their own by rolling or transferring it to their own IRA.

However, this may not always be the best option for surviving spouses under age 59½. Taxable distributions from a spouse's own IRA before age 59½ are generally subject to the 10% early withdrawal penalty, whereas taxable distributions from an inherited IRA or inherited employer plan account are not. For this reason, a surviving spouse may benefit from keeping the inherited account until reaching age 59½, and only then rolling or transferring it to their own IRA.

Health Savings Accounts

When a nonspouse or noncharity beneficiary inherits a Health Savings Account (HSA), the entire balance becomes immediately taxable as ordinary income in the year of the owner's death. There is one narrow exception: if the beneficiary pays qualified medical expenses that the owner incurred before death, and does so within one year after death, those amounts can reduce the taxable amount.

If a spouse inherits an HSA, it simply becomes the surviving spouse's HSA.

Taxable Accounts and the Step-Up in Basis

Assets other than retirement accounts receive a step-up in basis upon the owner's death.

This makes portfolio reallocation after an inheritance relatively easy. When someone inherits a taxable account, they can sell the assets within it and realize capital gains or losses based only on the change in value after the original owner's death. Additionally, the holding period for inherited property is automatically considered long-term, regardless of how long the owner held or the beneficiary holds the assets. As a result, gains realized shortly after death are treated as long-term capital gains (LTCG) rather than ordinary income.

31 – Gifting Property to Family

In this chapter, we explore how to transfer wealth to the next generation.

Lifetime Transfers: Sufficiency Trumps

We love it when parents take care of their own financial lives. Doing so benefits both the parents and their children.

Too often, people ask, "How can I set my kid up to be a millionaire?" That's a fine question—if you're already financially independent. Notice we didn't say "on your way to financial independence." We mean that you are now **financially independent**. In our view, that's the most appropriate time to consider your children's future finances.

People often overlook this truth: **the greatest financial gift you can give your children is your own financial stability.** Want to create real stress in your adult child's life? Be an elderly parent with unstable finances. That instability creates pressure, stress, and often hardship for the next generation. By ensuring your own financial success, you support both yourself and your future adult children.

Gifts Go Well Beyond Tax Planning

Giving sizable financial assets to the next generation during your lifetime has implications that extend far beyond tax planning. How might receiving the gift affect the recipient? How could it change your relationship with them?

Gifting and Leaving Assets to Children with Disabilities

For families with minor or adult children with disabilities, special care should be taken when deciding if, when, and how to transfer money. It's important to consider how the funds would be managed in the recipient's hands—and whether the gift could impact their eligibility for aid programs. These decisions are complex and are best made in collaboration with an attorney experienced in disability and estate planning.

Strategic Gifting of Appreciated Securities

Parents who are sufficiently financially independent may want to consider gifting appreciated securities—rather than cash—to their adult children, particularly during their children's lower-earning years.

For example, instead of giving cash to help fund a home down payment, a parent could gift appreciated shares of stock or funds directly to their child. These appreciated assets transfer with a carryover basis and carryover holding period, meaning the child may be able to sell them and realize long-term capital gains at a 0% federal tax rate, depending on their income level and filing status.

Step-Up in Basis at Death for Taxable Accounts

It turns out death is a pretty effective time to transfer assets to the next generation—from a tax perspective.

Non-retirement assets transferred to the next generation receive a step-up in basis when the owner dies. In contrast, assets transferred during the owner's lifetime do not receive a step-up. Instead, the recipient generally takes on the carryover basis—the same basis the original owner had.

This makes a strong case for transferring appreciated assets at death rather than during life. Some of the best tax planning is both inevitable and free: the step-up in basis at death. It effectively wipes out unrealized capital gains in taxable brokerage accounts. Gifting those same assets during life forfeits that opportunity. Of course, this is just one of many factors to consider when planning gifts to the next generation.

Sean's Take: I disfavor transferring assets to minor children for a variety of reasons. A big one—why give assets to young kids when the owner can retain the assets, they can serve the owner's needs (if need be), and at death, adult children get a step-up in basis in the assets? Gifts to kids forgo a great (and free!) tax planning opportunity for children: the step-up in basis at their parent's death.

Beneficiary Designation Forms

It's essential to have beneficiary designation forms—sometimes referred to as payable-on-death (POD) or transfer-on-death (TOD) forms—on file with all financial institutions, including those holding retirement accounts. These forms should be carefully coordinated with the owner's overall estate plan.

Keep in mind: when it comes to financial assets, life insurance policies, and retirement accounts, it's the beneficiary designation form—not the will—that controls who receives the asset upon the owner's death.

Naming Spouses as Primary Beneficiaries

Those who are married will want to think very carefully before naming anyone other than their spouse as the 100% primary beneficiary on financial accounts, retirement accounts, and life insurance policies. Situations where it makes sense to name someone else are rare and often involve an incapacitated spouse or very high-net-worth scenarios, where it may be advantageous for some assets to bypass the surviving spouse to mitigate estate taxes.

Also, keep in mind that spouses are generally the most favored beneficiaries under tax law when it comes to inheriting retirement accounts—whether traditional or Roth accounts.

Secondary Beneficiaries

Consider who you'd want to inherit your financial assets after your spouse (if you're married). Are they capable of managing their finances responsibly? Are they in high-risk professions? Do they have current or anticipated issues with creditors?

In a perfect world, we would favor naming individuals directly as beneficiaries on financial and retirement accounts. This creates less legal complexity and administrative friction. However, there are situations where it may be more appropriate to name a trust as the beneficiary instead. In that case, the account is left to a revocable living trust, which generally becomes irrevocable upon the owner's death. Afterward, the trust is managed for the benefit of the named beneficiaries, with distributions made according to the trust's terms.

When it comes to tax-advantaged retirement accounts, the trust should be properly structured so that the individual beneficiary—not the trust—is treated as the beneficiary for tax purposes. This allows the inherited retirement accounts to maintain favorable distribution timelines.

In Real Life: We favor parents of one or more minor children consulting with an estate attorney regarding their retirement accounts. Why? Because if they pass away and minor children inherit the accounts directly, it can create administrative and legal challenges. An attorney can help design an estate plan—often involving a revocable living trust as the secondary beneficiary—that provides the appropriate structure and safeguards to pass retirement assets to minor children.

Traditional Retirement Accounts

Traditional retirement accounts are taxable to any noncharitable beneficiary who inherits them.

Those concerned about adult children inheriting traditional IRAs might consider doing Roth conversions beyond what benefits their own income tax situation. Of course, this should only be done if the additional tax liability does not jeopardize the retiree's own financial sufficiency in retirement.

Another tactic is to name one or more charitable organizations as partial or full primary beneficiaries of traditional retirement accounts. Section 501(c)(3) charities do not pay income taxes, so leaving traditional retirement accounts to them makes sense for those who are charitably inclined.

As we discussed in Chapter 30, inheriting traditional retirement accounts isn't all bad.

First, inherited traditional IRAs can be a useful source of income in early retirement. The role they play is similar to the role a "bridge quarterback" plays in the NFL: not elite, but capable of getting the job done in the short term. In the same way, inherited IRAs may not be the most tax-efficient asset, but they can serve a valuable, temporary role in an early retiree's income plan. Parents can do much worse than leaving adult children a bridge quarterback!

Second, inherited traditional retirement accounts are a great place to hold part or all of one's bond allocation.

Third, they are an excellent vehicle for paying federal and state income taxes.

While noncharity beneficiaries do pay income tax on inherited traditional retirement account distributions, it is certainly not a bad outcome to leave a loved one a traditional retirement account.

Sean's Take: Some people hesitate to build up traditional retirement accounts out of concern for the taxes the next generation might face when inheriting them. But this seems to miss the forest for the trees. The primary goal of a retirement account is to get the owner (and their spouse) to and through retirement—not to optimize for a future beneficiary's tax situation. Furthermore, inheriting a retirement account is a "good problem to have," even if the distributions push the beneficiary into a higher tax bracket.

The Church IRA

Some readers will have sizable traditional retirement accounts, even well into retirement. Charitably inclined widows, widowers, and other single retirees should consider naming a church or other charity as a partial primary beneficiary of those accounts. Sean refers to this concept as the "Church IRA."

Traditional retirement accounts are not very tax-efficient when inherited by individual beneficiaries. Those who are charitably inclined should consider directing a portion of their traditional IRA(s)—which would have been taxed most heavily if left to individual heirs—to a charitable organization instead. This reduces the taxable inheritance for adult children while maximizing the tax benefits of charitable giving.

Roth Retirement Accounts

Heirs appreciate inheriting Roth accounts. In most cases, adult children who inherit a Roth IRA from an elderly parent have 10 years to empty the account, and during that time, there are no RMDs.

This raises a common question: "Should I implement Roth conversions during retirement to leave more of the inheritance in Roth IRAs?" The answer is: maybe. It depends on the owner's financial needs and preferences.

For example, if the parent is in the 12% marginal tax bracket and their adult children are in the 37% bracket, converting traditional IRAs to Roth IRAs during the parent's lifetime reduces the multigenerational tax burden.

However, the first question is: "Can the parents afford to pay the additional federal and state income taxes during their lifetimes?"

If the answer is **No**, that ends the analysis. Roth conversions done solely to save adult children's taxes are unwise if the parent cannot comfortably cover the resulting tax bill—regardless of marginal tax rates.

But if the answer is **Yes**, it becomes a subjective decision. There's no moral imperative to minimize your adult children's future taxes on the assets you leave them.

Health Savings Accounts

Health savings accounts (HSAs) are immediately taxable as ordinary income to nonspouse, noncharity beneficiaries in the year of the owner's death. For this reason, married individuals should generally name their spouse as the 100% primary beneficiary on their HSA.

This also illustrates an important planning point: elderly individuals are often well advised to take HSA PUQME distributions (for previously unreimbursed qualified medical expenses) before death. These distributions are tax-free and can be a great source of funds for covering living expenses.

But what if the HSA owner doesn't need the funds for living expenses? They might still consider taking PUQME distributions and simply reinvesting the proceeds in a taxable brokerage account.

Why? Because the next generation would much rather inherit a taxable brokerage account, which is received income tax-free with a step-up in basis. That's far better than inheriting an HSA, which is fully taxable as ordinary income to the nonspouse beneficiary in the year of the owner's death.

Directing Assets When Leaving Money to Charities and Adult Children

If you are charitably inclined, it's worth considering which types of assets to leave to your children versus to charity.

Here's an oversimplified example to illustrate tax-efficient planning for the death of a charitably inclined individual:

Abe, age 80, rents an apartment and has $1,000,000 in financial wealth, as follows:

- $250,000 in a Roth IRA
- $400,000 in a traditional IRA
- $250,000 in a taxable brokerage account
- $100,000 in an HSA

At death, Abe wants to leave half of his wealth to his adult son, Barry, and the other half to his church.

Which accounts should Abe leave to Barry, and which to his church?

- Abe should leave the Roth IRA and taxable brokerage account to Barry. Barry will pay no income tax at Abe's death. He will receive a step-up in basis in the taxable account and will have a 10-year window (without RMDs) to deplete the Roth IRA.
- Abe should leave the traditional IRA and HSA to his church, since it will pay no income tax on the inherited assets.

Imagine Abe did the opposite: leaving the Roth IRA and taxable account to the church, and the traditional IRA and HSA to Barry. The church still pays no tax, but Barry now pays income tax on the entire HSA balance in the year of Abe's death, as well as on the traditional IRA over 10 years.

Why forgo the favorable inheritance attributes of Roth IRAs and taxable accounts on a charity if you also have individual beneficiaries?

32 – Tax-Optimized Charitable Giving

Giving to others through time, talents, knowledge, and financial resources can be a fulfilling lifelong practice. Generosity through charitable giving reflects that we've defined "enough" for ourselves and are fortunate to give to others without expecting anything in return.

This chapter focuses on tax-optimized methods for giving to qualifying Section 501(c)(3) organizations—aligning your values with intentional tax planning.

Measure Twice: *You can verify an organization's tax-exempt status and deductibility limits using the IRS Tax Exempt Organization Search Tool: https://www.irs.gov/charities-non-profits/search-for-tax-exempt-organizations.*

Tax Planning for Charitable Giving is Changing

Tax planning for charitable giving is changing. In 2026, many readers will see charitable gifts impact their tax return in a new way. In this chapter, we discuss how the landscape is shifting in 2025 and 2026.

Before 2026, the two primary charitable giving tactics were:

- Claiming charitable contributions as itemized deductions
- Making qualified charitable distributions (QCDs)

Starting in 2026, there will be three primary techniques:

- Itemized deductions
- A $1,000 per person deduction for cash charitable donations (available only to non-itemizers)
- QCDs

We tackle these three techniques below.

Itemizing Deductions

Prior to 2026, taxpayers most commonly benefit from charitable giving through itemized deductions, reported on Schedule A and subject to various limits. Itemized deductions include:

- Medical and dental expenses (rarely applicable due to the 7.5% of AGI floor)
- State and local taxes (SALT)
- Home mortgage interest
- Gifts to charity
- Casualty losses

Combined, these itemized deductions must exceed the standard deduction (based on filing status) to provide additional tax benefits. According to the Tax Policy Center, as of 2020, only about 10% of taxpayers itemize their deductions.

Three major changes over the past decade have reduced the number of itemizers:

1. 2018 ushered in the new, much higher standard deduction.
2. SALT deductions were capped.
3. Mortgage interest deductions declined as interest rates dropped—especially during the sub-3% refinance era.

> **Example:** A $500,000, 30-year mortgage with a 5% fixed interest rate provides approximately $24,800 in deductible interest in its first year. With a 2.75% interest rate, the deductible interest drops to approximately $13,600. In 2025, a married couple filing jointly (under age 65) would need combined itemized deductions exceeding $31,500 (their standard deduction in 2025) to benefit from giving cash to charity.

The decline in itemizing has been especially impactful for retirees. Most no longer have mortgage interest to deduct, which in recent years has taken deductible charitable contributions off the table for many retirees.

Starting in 2026, that changes, as we discuss below. Many Americans, including many early retirees, will begin receiving a federal income tax benefit for charitable contributions without itemizing. In addition, planning techniques can benefit charitably inclined accumulators and retirees alike.

Non-Itemizers' $1,000 Per Person Deduction

A notable change under the OBBB that will benefit many readers starting in 2026 is the new $1,000 per person deduction for cash charitable gifts available to non-itemizers. To qualify, the donation must be made in cash—contributions of property (e.g., goods, securities) are not eligible.

This deduction helps non-itemizers during the accumulation phase. In the drawdown phase, it enhances opportunities such as Tailored Taxable Roth Conversions (TTRCs) and the Hidden Roth IRA by increasing the available deduction by up to $1,000 for single filers and up to $2,000 for those married filing jointly.

Reduction in Charitable Itemized Deductions Starting in 2026

Beginning in 2026, taxpayers who itemize deductions will lose 0.5% of their modified adjusted gross income (MAGI) from their allowable charitable deductions. We colloquially refer to this as a haircut.

Example: Floyd has a MAGI of $180,000 in 2026. He contributes $12,000 to charity and itemizes his deductions. His allowable charitable deduction will be reduced by $900 (0.5% of $180,000), resulting in a deduction of $11,100.

In Real Life: For most modestly affluent accumulators and retirees, we suspect this new haircut will have a limited impact. However, for higher-income taxpayers, the reduction can be much more impactful. Very affluent donors may see substantial reductions in their allowable charitable deductions.

Donating Appreciated Securities

Charitable gifts aren't limited to cash. Donating capital gain property, such as long-term appreciated securities from a taxable brokerage account, can offer significant tax advantages—even if you don't itemize.

If you sell appreciated securities, realized long-term capital gains (LTCG) may be taxed at 15%, 18.8% or 23.8% federally (plus state taxes). But if you donate the shares directly to charity, the capital gain disappears—and the charity pays no tax either.

This tactic isn't necessarily market timing. You could repurchase the same investment with the cash you would have otherwise donated (no waiting period required).

*Measure Twice: Donating securities with unrealized **losses** is a missed opportunity. It's better to realize the capital loss to offset other gains and income, and then donate the settled cash.*

Measure Twice: Itemized charitable deductions are subject to MAGI limits based on the property type and qualified organization category. Excess contributions generally carry over for up to five years but are deductible only in years when you itemize.

Stacking Charitable Gifts

Another tax-efficient giving tactic is contributing to a donor-advised fund (DAF), which allows you to donate cash, securities, or other assets to a centralized charitable account.

A DAF enables taxpayers to increase the tax benefit of their gifts by stacking multiple years of deductible charitable donations into a single tax year. The owner can grant funds from the DAF to charitable organizations over time, including in future years when they might claim the standard deduction.

Here's an example:

Susan and Steve, both age 52, donate $1,000/month in cash to their church. Their adjusted gross income (AGI) is $180,000, and their standard deduction is $31,500. They have combined itemized deductions of *only* $25,000, including their state and local taxes, mortgage interest, and charitable gifts—unable to exceed the standard deduction and provide an additional tax benefit.

Back in 2007, they bought $1,000 of Apple stock in their taxable brokerage account. Fast forward to 2025, their shares are worth $48,000—with $47,000 in unrealized capital gains.

Rather than selling the stock (which would trigger a $7,050 tax bill at a 15% LTCG rate), they donate it directly to a DAF late in 2025 and continue their monthly giving from there over the next four years.

Beyond eliminating future realized capital gains, they can now itemize deductions—reducing their federal income tax liability by $9,130 in 2025. Dividing that $9,130 in tax savings by the $48,000 value of stock donated reveals a 19-cents-per-dollar current-year tax benefit for contributing to the DAF.

Donor-advised funds, in addition to accelerating and increasing tax deductions, help normalize the donor's relationship with their favorite charities. Few donors—like Susan and Steve—want to give $48,000 to their favorite charity this year and then absolutely nothing for the next three or four years. Instead, many donors prefer making relatively level annual donations. The donor-advised fund mechanism facilitates that level of giving while also offering the donor a potential significant upfront tax deduction for multiple years' worth of donations.

2025 Donor-Advised Fund Contributions

For those on the fence about making a DAF contribution in 2025 or 2026, the OBBB and its new haircut suggest you make it in late 2025.

Qualified Charitable Distributions (QCDs)

Traditional IRA owners age 70½ and older can donate IRA funds directly to qualified charitable organizations. These QCDs are excluded from gross income and from IRMAA calculations (which determine Medicare surcharges), and they can satisfy a portion or all of the RMDs.

Many in their 70s and 80s will use QCDs while claiming the high standard deduction. It's essentially a double benefit: exclude the "distribution" from income and still get the standard deduction.

QCDs also reduce future RMDs by lowering traditional IRA balances.

Even inherited IRAs qualify for QCDs, but only if the beneficiary is age 70½ or older.

Note that the new charitable deduction haircut does not apply to QCDs, since QCDs are not claimed as itemized deductions.

QCDs are one of the most effective ways to give in retirement.

Extra Credit: *Unlike itemized charitable deductions, QCDs are not subject to AGI limits. As of 2025, the QCD limit is $108,000 per person. This limit is adjusted for inflation annually.*

33 – 529s and Other Child Savings Options

Many families with young children seek clarity on how best to save for their children's future education and other objectives, including which accounts to use and how to balance flexibility with tax optimization.

529 Education Savings Accounts

One of the most popular vehicles for saving for a child's education is the 529 education savings account. These accounts offer the dual benefit of tax-deferred investment growth and tax-free distributions when funds are used for qualified education expenses, including tuition, fees, room and board, supplies, and more. Funds are also available for K-12 tuition and student loan repayments, subject to certain limitations.

However, if funds are not used for qualified expenses, the earnings portion of 529 account distributions is subject to ordinary income tax and an additional 10% tax (the "10% penalty").

Flexibility and Penalties

Many parents worry about what happens if their child receives a scholarship or decides not to pursue a traditional college education. Fortunately, the 10% penalty is waived for distributions up to the amount of a scholarship; only income tax applies to the earnings. Additionally, unused funds can be transferred to another eligible family member by changing the beneficiary. This flexibility is especially valuable for families with multiple children or those planning to support future generations.

Key Distinction: Only the earnings portion of nonqualified distributions is subject to federal income tax and the 10% penalty—not the contributions. Distributions generally take out proportionate shares of contributions and earnings.

Planning Point: One drawback of the 529 plan is that the earnings portion of a nonqualified distribution is taxed as ordinary income and is generally subject to the 10% penalty. By contrast, if invested in a taxable brokerage account, those earnings might have received more favorable long-term capital gains (LTCG) tax treatment.

Cody's Take: In our family, we prefer to divide contributions for future educational expenses between a 529 account and a taxable brokerage account held in our names. This combination offers both tax-free qualified education funding and flexibility to address future unknowns. As we've noted throughout this book, taxable brokerage accounts are underrated for their flexibility and income tax control.

Sean's Take: *From a planning perspective, the 529 has three significant problems. First, it solves a problem that is not much of a problem: the taxes on investment income. Outside of (usually) small state tax savings, the 529's main tax benefit is avoiding taxes on investment income. We've discussed how lightly taxed many taxable investments are. In a world of preferred long-term capital gains and qualified dividend income tax rates, as well as sub-2% yields on domestic equity index funds, the taxation of taxable investments can be quite modest, even for very affluent parents. Second, Mom and Dad restrict their money by putting it into a 529. If it were instead in a taxable brokerage account, the money could flexibly support Mom & Dad today, Mom & Dad's retirement, and/or Junior's college education. In a 529, it is highly constrained in terms of serving any objective other than Junior's college education. Third, I would be very hesitant to sign up for an account where the primary tax-efficient out is to send the money to American higher education. Are you familiar with the administrative bloat and six-figure student debt burdens that industry has created during this century? I question feeding the beast. While there can be some good use cases for the 529, they tend to be limited and apply only when Mom & Dad have achieved financial independence or are very close to it. Further, the most readily available alternative, the taxable brokerage account, is excellent.*

State-Specific 529 Plans

When choosing a 529 plan, families often compare state-specific plans based on the availability of state income tax credits or deductions, as well as differences in investment options and administrative fees. Most plans function similarly to workplace retirement accounts, offering age-based target-date funds and static options, including low-cost index funds.

Coordination with Education Tax Credits

Education tax credits—such as the American Opportunity Tax Credit and the Lifetime Learning Credit—incentivize paying at least a portion of qualified education expenses out of pocket, instead of from a 529 account. There are no education tax credits for amounts paid using tax-free 529 distributions. No double-dipping!

529-to-Roth IRA Rollover

SECURE 2.0, passed in late 2022, introduced a bailout option for overfunded 529 plans: the ability to roll up to $35,000 (a lifetime limit) of a 529 to the beneficiary's own Roth IRA, via a trustee-to-trustee transfer. This allows the money to move into the beneficiary's Roth IRA without the earnings being subject to federal income taxes or the 10% penalty.

This provision is subject to three key restrictions:

1. The annual rollover amount is limited to the Roth IRA contribution limit for that year, and the rollover counts toward that year's contribution (again, no double-dipping!).
2. The rollover amount must be attributable to contributions (and the earnings on those contributions) that have been in the 529 for at least five years.
3. The 529 account must be at least 15 years old.

We view this as a very limited bailout opportunity rather than a strategy to be planned into. Parents who want to fund their young adult child's Roth IRA don't need a 529 to do so. They simply need that amount of money available from their own wealth. Furthermore, our favorite overfunded-529 bailout technique—changing the beneficiary to a younger sibling—entirely avoids these 529-to-Roth rollover restrictions.

That said, families with overfunded 529s should still consider this opportunity. Note that some states, including California, do not recognize the federal treatment of 529-to-Roth IRA rollovers. In those states, the earnings portion of the rollover is treated as a nonqualified distribution, subject to state income tax and a potential state level penalty.

UTMA and UGMA Accounts

Some parents use custodial accounts, such as Uniform Transfers to Minors Act (UTMA) or Uniform Gifts to Minors Act (UGMA) accounts, to build up assets for their children's financial futures. However, these accounts have some potential drawbacks, including:

1. Contributions are irrevocable gifts for the child's benefit, and the child gains full control of the account at the age of majority (typically 18 or 21).
2. Unearned income may be subject to the "kiddie tax," which applies to children's unearned income over certain thresholds to prevent parents from shifting significant taxable income into lower tax brackets.
3. The child's assets are assessed more heavily in financial aid calculations—with up to 20% of their value considered in the Student Aid Index (SAI), compared to just 5.64% for parental assets.

Sean's Take: Children need many things. Financial assets are not among them. For the vast majority of readers, it is most logical to keep financial assets with the parents. Later in life, it can make sense to transfer financial assets to children with a specific intention, such as funding their honeymoon or helping to fund a grandchild's college education. But financial assets owned by a minor child have little to do with the child's lived experience—and put those assets beyond the parents' use.

Cody's Take: Some parents have told me they set up a UTMA account to hold monetary gifts from family members—like birthday money—or to help their child learn how the stock market works by investing and realizing small tax-free capital gains. It's a thoughtful idea, and the educational intent is commendable. That said, I think it's simpler to track a child's funds and teach investing with an account titled in the parent's name—without involving legal ownership changes.

Other Savings Options

Roth IRAs for Minors

If the child has earned income, they can contribute to a Roth IRA and invest for tax-free growth. While contributions can be withdrawn penalty-free at any age for any reason, we generally prioritize Roth IRAs for long-term retirement savings over short-term objectives during the accumulation phase. Also note that "tax-free" withdrawals from a child's Roth IRA may still count as income on the FAFSA, potentially reducing financial aid.

Some self-employed parents ask, "Should I hire my child in my business so they can contribute to a Roth IRA?"

Our view: if it would make sense to hire your child in a world with no income tax system, it's likely a wise move. If removing the income tax incentive would eliminate your desire to hire your child, you probably have your answer.

Extra Credit: Before hiring your child, consider state and local legal issues (such as working papers), potential payroll tax issues, and Solo 401(k) plan rules and your own plan eligibility as they relate to hiring your own child in your business.

Savings Bonds

Interest earned from U.S. Series EE and I bonds may be tax-free when used for qualified tuition and fees. However, the ability to exclude this interest income is subject to income-based phaseouts. For more details, see IRS Publication 970, Tax Benefits for Education.

529 Accounts Owned by Someone Else

529 plans owned by grandparents or others are not counted as parent or student assets in financial aid formulas. As of the 2024-2025 school year,

distributions from 529s owned by grandparents and others no longer count as the student's income for FAFSA purposes. Previously, such distributions could have been treated as student income for financial aid calculations (up to 50%).

Note that 529s owned by a parent and dependent student are reported as assets on the FAFSA, with up to 5.64% of their value considered available to fund education. Beyond the scope of this book, some families explore shifting 529 ownership based on the timing of financial aid applications.

34 – Estate and Gift Taxes

We've spent the vast majority of this book discussing federal income taxes. Now, let's spend a few pages on estate and gift taxes. To be fair, these are not major concerns for most readers. But it is helpful to understand what they are and how they might impact financial and tax planning.

Estate Tax

The estate tax applies to assets left to nonspouse, noncharity beneficiaries. However, it is rare for an American estate to owe estate tax.

Why?

Each individual receives a lifetime exclusion from estate and gift tax. As of 2025, the exemption is $13,990,000. In 2026, it will be $15,000,000. The lifetime exclusion is indexed for inflation annually.

You can see how this sizable exclusion shields even very affluent estates from taxes. To illustrate, if Mitch dies in 2025 and leaves his entire $12 million estate to his son Logan, Mitch's estate pays no federal estate tax because the assets fall below the exclusion. If Mitch instead leaves $16 million, then $2,010,000 (the amount above the exclusion) would be subject to federal estate tax.

The federal estate tax rate is generally steep for the relatively few estates subject to it. Taxable amounts above $1 million are subject to a 40% rate.

There are two major exceptions to the estate tax:

1. Assets left to a spouse.
2. Assets left to a qualified charitable organization.

You could leave $1 billion to a spouse and $1 billion to charity at your death, and your estate would owe no estate tax on those amounts.

Estates file **Form 706** to report and pay estate taxes. While most estates won't need to file Form 706, in today's planning environment, it can be beneficial for estates of first-to-die spouses to file—even if no estate tax is due. We discuss this filing in more detail later in the chapter.

Gift Tax and the Annual Exclusion

The gift tax exists in theory to protect both the income tax and the estate tax. Without it, the wealthy could reduce or eliminate income taxes by transferring significant assets to family members with lower taxable income. The gift tax steps in to potentially tax those transfers. Further, the estate tax would collect very little revenue if wealthy individuals could simply gift away their assets to younger family members with no tax consequences.

Thus, enter the gift tax.

The gift tax shares the lifetime exclusion with the estate tax, which is why it is often referred to as a unified lifetime exclusion. If you make a $1 million "taxable gift" during your lifetime, your $13,990,000 exclusion is reduced by that amount for both gift and estate tax purposes.

In practice, the gift tax is largely academic in everyday situations. Say you treat a friend to brisket at a Texas barbecue restaurant. Is that a "taxable gift" that reduces your $13,990,000 unified lifetime exclusion? No.

Why not? Because of the **annual exclusion**. As of 2025, the annual exclusion is $19,000 per giver per recipient. Gifts below the annual exclusion amount do not reduce the giver's unified lifetime exclusion.

This provision also allows for efficient wealth transfers among families. A married couple could jointly give $38,000 to their son and $38,000 to their daughter-in-law ($76,000 total) in a single year—all within the annual exclusion.

But what happens if gifts during the year exceed the annual exclusion limit? The giver must file **Form 709** to report the gift and reduce their lifetime exclusion accordingly.

In Real Life: Anyone making a five-figure gift should discuss it with their income tax return preparer. Among other considerations, Form 709 is not necessarily intuitive. For example, it's important to determine whether a married couple needs to elect gift-splitting on the return.

A reader of this book will only owe gift tax after fully using up their entire lifetime exclusion. Even among the very wealthy, few Americans will ever pay a penny in gift tax to the IRS.

Portability

Recall that when someone leaves property to their surviving spouse, no estate tax is owed. Their unified lifetime exclusion goes unused to the extent that they only left property to their surviving spouse at death.

Fortunately, the tax rules create an opportunity for the surviving spouse to utilize the deceased spouse's unused unified lifetime exclusion. To do this, the deceased spouse's estate can file Form 706 (the federal estate tax return) with the IRS. There's no estate tax owed, assuming everything was left to the surviving spouse. But the filing of that return allows for "portability," allowing the surviving spouse to claim the unused portion of their deceased spouse's exclusion.

Here's an example: Marv dies in 2025 and leaves all his assets to his wife, Marge. He never made any taxable gifts (above the annual exclusions) during his lifetime. As long as Marv's estate files Form 706 with the IRS, his unused $13,990,000 unified lifetime exclusion becomes portable and transfers to Marge. When Marge dies, her own unified lifetime exclusion is $13,990,000 plus the applicable unified lifetime exclusion for the year of her death.

Portability allows a wealthy couple to potentially pass $30 million (2026 number) or more estate-tax-free to the next generation. For many families, portability will be the most effective estate tax planning they can employ, and its cost is the fee to prepare Form 706.

Bunch 529 Gifts

Tax rules allow for "bunching" up to five years' worth of annual exclusion gifts into a single year when contributing to a 529 plan. This enables significant contribution amounts ($19,000 × 5 years per parent) in one year without reducing the donor's unified lifetime exclusion. Implementing this tactic requires filing Form 709 to report the election.

Sean's Take: As you saw in Chapter 33, I'm not too fond of 529s. Thus, I'm not too fond of bunching contributions to a 529. Yes, there are people for whom bunching 529 contributions might make sense. But I'd argue there are not too many of those people. The people for whom bunching 529 contributions could make sense are those who are already at a point where they could elect to retire early today, if not already retired.

State Estate and Inheritance Taxes

Several states impose estate and/or inheritance taxes. For whatever reason, these states tend to be located in the northern United States, with Kentucky being the southernmost on the mainland—though Hawaii also imposes an estate tax. The Tax Foundation, a nonprofit organization focused on tax policy, provides a helpful map of states with estate and inheritance taxes: https://tax-foundation.org/data/all/state/estate-inheritance-taxes/

State estate and inheritance taxes typically have lower asset exclusions and lower tax rates than the federal estate tax.

For early retirees, these state-level taxes are typically not a concern. In early retirement, **sufficiency is paramount**—and there's little reason, including state estate or inheritance tax, to transfer assets to the next generation in a way that could compromise a financially successful retirement.

While state estate and inheritance taxes are a second-order planning priority for early retirees—since the burden falls on the next generation—retirees may want to start planning for these taxes later in life.

If the retiree is financially successful later in life, sufficiency becomes less of a concern. Thus, the retiree can consider asset transfer strategies to help mitigate the potential impact of state estate and inheritance taxes. In many cases, this planning should be considered only after the first spouse passes, since sufficiency for one person is typically less of a concern than for a couple.

Connecticut is currently the only state that imposes a gift tax.

Those considering strategies to reduce or eliminate potential state estate or inheritance taxes should consult with a qualified estate attorney in their home state.

35 – Trusts

When it comes to **tax planning** to and through early retirement, trusts often play a surprisingly unimportant role.

However, when it comes to **estate planning**, trusts often play an incredibly important role.

This chapter highlights the roles trusts can play in estate planning and the tax treatment they receive.

Kinds of Trusts and Their Uses

Trusts are generally categorized as either revocable or irrevocable, depending on their terms and the laws of the jurisdiction where they are established.

For prospective early retirees and retirees, revocable living trusts are typically the most relevant. It's rare for someone in this group to create an irrevocable trust during their lifetime.

Probate Avoidance

Early retirees should consider trusts for two reasons—the first being probate avoidance. **Probate** is a ten-dollar financial planning term for the court-supervised process that governs how assets pass upon death. It involves lawyers and courts, which means incurring costs and dealing with administrative hassle.

But there's good news: probate can be avoided for many financial accounts by using beneficiary designation forms. These forms—not the probate process—generally control what happens to those assets upon death.

One big exception is the primary residence, which lacks a beneficiary designation option in most states. While it can be passed via will, doing so often requires probate. To avoid this, many owners choose to transfer their primary residence to a revocable trust. During life, the trust has little impact on the owner's lived experience; they still pay the mortgage and property taxes, and deduct the mortgage interest and property taxes on Schedule A (if applicable).

At death, instead of going through probate, the home passes according to the terms of the revocable living trust—a private legal instrument.

In addition to beneficiary designations and revocable trusts, other mechanisms—such as titling property in joint tenancy with rights of survivorship (JTWROS) and using transfer-on-death (TOD) designations—can help avoid probate.

Trusts as a Beneficiary

The second potential use of revocable living trusts is as a named beneficiary of accounts. This can be valuable when you want to leave assets to individuals whom you might not want to inherit directly, such as:

- Minor children
- Very elderly individuals
- Incapacitated individuals
- Beneficiaries with creditor issues
- Individuals who are unable to successfully manage their financial affairs
- Those in high-risk professions

In these cases, the account owner may prefer to name a revocable trust as the beneficiary to establish guardrails ("control from the grave") for the end-beneficiary's benefit.

Trusts add some administrative friction, but it can be worth the trade-off in certain situations. The friction tends to be less when leaving taxable accounts, personal property, and life insurance benefits through revocable living trusts.

However, naming a trust as a beneficiary of a retirement account tends to increase friction and risk. The trust must meet requirements listed in Treasury Regulation Section 1.401(a)(9)-4(f)(2) in order for the beneficiary to receive the longest possible payout period. Otherwise, the account may need to be fully distributed within five years of the owner's death. This issue is best discussed with an attorney when drafting a trust.

Sean's Take: When it comes to retirement accounts, most married early retirees should name their spouse as the 100% primary beneficiary. In terms of secondary beneficiaries or primary beneficiaries for single individuals, if the people you want to receive the retirement accounts are competent adults without creditor protection issues, you should strongly consider naming them directly and not using a trust. Administering trusts with respect to retirement accounts can unnecessarily introduce friction after the owner's death.

Revocable Living Trust Taxation

Fortunately, revocable living trusts don't pay income taxes. Their income is reported directly on the grantor's personal federal income tax return.

You might wonder, "Isn't that bad? Shouldn't we try to keep that income off the grantor's tax return?" Generally, no—because trusts, when taxed, are subject to very high tax rates on relatively low levels of income. Keeping the income on the grantor's return avoids the steep trust tax rate. And practically speaking, the grantor isn't any worse off with a revocable living trust—the income would have been reported on their tax return anyway if the asset had remained in their name.

Irrevocable Trusts

In most cases, Americans avoid forming irrevocable trusts during their lifetime unless advised by an estate attorney in very specific circumstances.

Here are two reasons to avoid forming irrevocable trusts during one's lifetime:

1. **Inflexibility:** Once created, the grantor generally can't change or revoke the trust.
2. **Tax Inefficiency:** In 2025, irrevocable trusts reach the 37% federal tax rate at just $15,651 of taxable income.

That said, irrevocable trusts may still be appropriate in certain situations, such as high-net-worth estate planning or asset protection—beyond the scope of this chapter.

Conclusion

Revocable living trusts can play a meaningful role in estate planning to and through early retirement, even if they're not tax-advantaged. They help avoid probate, protect beneficiaries, and offer customized asset transfers.

That said, trusts should be used carefully when dealing with retirement accounts, where tax rules add complexity and risk. Work with a qualified attorney to manage the details in your specific state.

36 – Early Retirement Implementation

The "flip of the switch" transition from a career to retirement can be daunting. Early retirees often get into the groove of working, saving, and investing for decades. For those who have implemented the Compelling Three, the investing piece can be nearly on autopilot by the end of their career.

You've also spent years surrounded by friends and colleagues on a similar path. Whether it was a coworker down the hall or a quick message on the company chat app, it was easy to find someone to bounce ideas off of.

Early retirement is different. The planning process is different. Your tax return and the way you pay taxes look different. And since most people retire at home rather than in an office, your day-to-day environment shifts. Aside from your spouse, there may be no one else around navigating a similar situation.

In this chapter, we explore key aspects of implementing tax planning during early retirement.

Early Retirement Tax Planning

By the time you reach early retirement, you'll hopefully have an initial game plan. Maybe it's "optimize for Premium Tax Credits until age 65, then do Tailored Taxable Roth Conversions (TTRCs) during the Golden Years." Or perhaps the approach is, "use 72(t) distributions before age 59½, then draw from traditional retirement accounts without restriction after that." Or maybe it's "spend from taxable accounts first, consider Roth conversions at year-end, then shift to a mix of traditional and Roth distributions once taxable assets are depleted." These are just a few examples of how an early retiree might structure their drawdown strategy.

As discussed in Chapter 11 on "practical ideal" drawdown paths, there's no single right "answer." It depends on where you are today and what's possible between now and early retirement.

Once in early retirement, executing on your overall strategy often involves year-end decisions. Some will want to pull the trigger on a Roth conversion or tax gain harvest. Others might want to make a large charitable contribution before year-end.

Timing

From a tax planning perspective, we generally prefer executing Roth conversions, tax gain harvesting, and large charitable contributions in the fourth quarter—for a couple of reasons. First, all these tactics are irreversible—once completed, you're locked in. Second, by the fourth quarter, you have a clearer picture of your capital gains, interest, dividends, taxable retirement account distributions, and other income—making it easier to estimate your year-end tax situation.

Process

We strongly recommend that early retirees track any capital gains or losses whenever they sell stocks, bonds, mutual funds, or ETFs. Keeping a detailed record makes it easier to prepare a spreadsheet estimating annual income in October or November. Start by listing estimated income, adjustments to income (such as HSA contributions), the senior deduction (if applicable), and the standard deduction (or itemized deductions).

This exercise helps you estimate your adjusted gross income (AGI) and taxable income, which forms the baseline to project your income tax if you make no further moves. From there, you can layer in alternative scenarios—such as adding a $10,000 Roth conversion or a $20,000 realized capital gain from tax gain harvesting—and compare the tax impacts.

Can you estimate your federal income taxes for the year? We believe you can. This book includes numerous examples of federal income tax calculations and explains the steps in detail. For instance, Chapter 1 includes five examples, Chapter 8 has three, Chapter 11 offers five, Chapter 15 has two, and this chapter provides two more. We think you can learn enough from those examples to reasonably estimate your own tax liability for planning purposes. Of course, this book is just one resource among many available for helping you estimate your federal income taxes in the fourth quarter.

You can also estimate your Premium Tax Credit (PTC). One great approach is to prepare a mock Form 8962, perhaps using a spreadsheet. The idea is to project your PTC under a "do nothing" scenario, then adjust the inputs (e.g., for a proposed Roth conversion) to see how your PTC amount might change.

New for 2025, retirees age 65 and older should estimate their senior deduction. In Chapter 19, we discuss how to compute the senior deduction and include two examples.

Distribution Planning

Controlling the tax impact of year-end distributions can be one of the most effective early retirement tax planning strategies. Sometimes the goal is simply to keep income low enough to qualify for a larger PTC or to avoid creeping into the 22% federal income tax bracket.

When optimizing distribution planning is a priority, the spreadsheet we recommended preparing in the fourth quarter should be maintained throughout the year. The goal is to monitor taxable income and use that information to guide future distribution decisions.

Consider the following example:

Roland, age 67 and single, tracks his income throughout the year. In November, he determines that he has withdrawn $70,000 from his traditional IRA in 2025 and estimates he'll have $1,000 of taxable interest from his savings account. He wants to withdraw an additional $10,000 from his retirement accounts to cover his expenses for the remainder of the year. Based on his $71,000 AGI so far, he applies the ordinary income tax brackets:

- The first $23,750 will be taxed at 0% due to the $15,750 standard deduction, the $2,000 additional standard deduction, and the new $6,000 senior deduction.
- The next $11,925 will fall into the 10% bracket.
- That leaves $35,325 to be taxed in the 12% bracket.

Roland realizes that if he takes the additional $10,000 from his traditional IRA, most of it will be taxed at the 22% rate, as he's already close to the top of the 12% bracket. Further, he will start to slightly reduce his senior deduction by increasing AGI over $75,000. To avoid these two outcomes, Roland instead takes the final $10,000 from his Roth IRA tax-free.

Working with an Advisor

Should you work with a financial planner before and/or during early retirement? The answer depends on many personal factors, making it impossible for us to offer a one-size-fits-all recommendation in a book intended for a broad readership.

That said, we acknowledge our own bias—we're both advice-only financial planners. For those considering working with a financial planner, we generally favor working with one who offers only their advice. Advice-only financial planners don't sell products or investment management services to financial planning clients. Instead, they provide advice to help you make informed decisions. While investing is a valuable component of a financial plan, we believe its implementation should come *after* understanding where you are, where you want to go, and how best to get there—whether you choose to validate or delegate your investment management. Regardless of the products and services an advisor provides, they must first understand your interests before offering advice in your best interest.

In Real Life: An educated client gets the best value from working with a professional. Good for you for reading this book and getting educated!

Computer Software

In our view, early retirees tend to consider two types of computer software to help plan their drawdown strategy and optimize for taxes.

The first type is current-year tax planning software, which is especially helpful for exploring year-end tax strategies. For example, it can project federal income taxes under different scenarios—such as planning with or without various amounts of Roth conversions.

The second type is long-term projection software, often called retirement calculators. These tools typically include dozens of inputs and toggles for modeling distribution strategies, investment returns, expenses, and more. Once all the data is entered, the software runs simulations to estimate the likelihood of not running out of money over your lifetime.

Sean's Take: I believe that there can be real value in using software that accurately projects current-year taxes with and without certain tactics, such as Roth conversions. That said, I think it is a real challenge to fold in PTC calculations, considering how variable they are based on geography.

Long-term planning software does not appeal to me. Computer software is simply someone else's judgment about the future reduced to computer code. Who is that someone? What is their judgment? How does the end user assess the validity of that judgment?

If you hire a financial planner, you can assess their judgment in the content they've put online, their meetings with you, their emails to you, etc. Based on these interactions, you can evaluate how they think and the validity of their conclusions and recommendations. You can assess the views, judgment, and reasoning of commentators such as Cody and me based on this book and the other personal finance content we have shared. How do you assess the judgment of a computer software program making assessments and recommendations about your financial future?

Cody's Take: Financial planning software can be a useful tool, but most people—including professionals—use it incorrectly. Its purpose is to provide general direction, not certainty. I find it most valuable for visualizing variable cash flows over time and estimating the potential impact of Roth conversions. However, it's just as important to step back and focus on what's right in front of you—especially the factors within your control.

The accuracy of any financial projection is only as strong as its inputs—many of which are inherently uncertain. As Sean noted, planning software is just a mechanical engine, based on someone else's interpretation and judgment of historical assumptions about market returns, inflation rates, tax laws, healthcare costs, and life expectancy. Even small miscalculations or unexpected life changes can significantly affect the reliability of long-term projections.

"Plan" is both a noun and a verb. Create a plan to establish general direction and spot opportunities, but embrace planning as an ongoing process that adapts as life unfolds.

A note on Monte Carlo analysis: I encourage financial planning clients and DIY planners to rethink how they interpret the "Probability of Success" commonly displayed in Monte Carlo simulations. It's not a grade like you received in school, and a "100% Probability of Success" doesn't mean your plan is perfect. Instead, think of it as the "Probability of Not Needing to Make Adjustments." More often, a "100% Probability" reflects chronic under-spending, missed opportunities for generosity toward family and causes you care about, and a reluctance to use your wealth to amplify memorable experiences while you're alive.

Paying Taxes

Where you stand determines where you sit when it comes to paying taxes in early retirement. Your overarching plan for funding early retirement informs how you pay your federal and state income taxes.

Living on Taxable Accounts First

Perhaps your flavor of early retirement involves selling taxable brokerage investments to fund the first few years. Some using this approach will find they owe no federal income tax for the year—while others will. In that case, the primary way to pay your taxes is by making four quarterly estimated payments at directpay.irs.gov.

"How do I make a first quarter payment on April 15 when I have no idea what the capital gains will be from my May, June, and July sales—much less from December sales?"

In most years, the answer is simple for early retirees living off taxable capital gains: pay 100% of the prior year's tax liability to the IRS in four equal estimated payments. Doing so qualifies the early retiree for the safe harbor. Even if they win the lottery in December, they're protected from underpayment penalties as long as those four payments are made on time—by April 15, June 15, September 15, and the following January 15.

Later in this chapter, we present two examples of retirees using the 90% current-year safe harbor. In each case, they could consider the 100% of prior-year safe harbor if it results in lower required payments throughout the year. We covered the safe harbors in more detail in Chapter 14.

Note that if the prior year's AGI was more than $150,000 ($75,000 if married filing separately), the prior year safe harbor applies using 110% of the prior year's tax liability instead of 100%. That said, many affluent early retirees funding their lifestyle by selling taxable assets will not exceed $150,000 of AGI due to significant basis recovery embedded in those sales.

72(t) Payment Plan

Let's consider an extreme case: someone funding early retirement using a 72(t) payment plan. In most cases, this person (or couple) has one primary source of income: the annual 72(t) payment. There might be a small amount of interest income, but the 72(t) payment accounts for the lion's share of their income—making it relatively easy to calculate and manage their federal income tax liability.

Example: Keisha and Marcus, both age 57, are living off a $100,000 72(t) payment in 2025. Their only other income is $2,000 in interest. With an AGI of $102,000, all from ordinary income, estimating their federal income tax is straightforward:

Income	Rate	Tax
$31,500	0% (Standard Deduction)	$0
$23,850	10%	$2,385
$46,650	12%	$5,598
Total **$102,000**	**Effective Rate** 7.83%	**Total** **$7,983**

To simplify tax payments, Keisha and Marcus elect to withhold 8% from their $100,000 72(t) payment—resulting in a net annual payment of $92,000. This approach covers their full federal income tax liability in one step and eliminates the need for quarterly estimated tax payments. Although they are younger than 59½, the withheld portion is not subject to the 10% early withdrawal penalty, since the tax withholding is part of the 72(t) payment.

Paying $8,000 to the IRS through withholding will easily satisfy their 90% safe harbor requirement. There is no underpayment penalty for estimated taxes when a taxpayer pays at least 90% of the current year's federal income tax liability through four equal estimated tax payments or through tax withholding (such as W-2 withholding, and, for retirees, 1099-R withholding from IRA and qualified plan distributions).

Because all tax withholding is treated as if it occurred equally throughout the year, it doesn't matter when Keisha and Marcus take their annual 72(t) payment with taxes withheld.

Extra Credit: Prior to establishing a 72(t) payment plan, retirees should consider the available income tax withholding percentages at each financial institution. As of this writing, Fidelity and Schwab allow flexible withholding elections, including single-digit percentages. Vanguard, however, only permits withholding at a rate of 10% or higher. All three institutions allow owners to opt out of income tax withholding entirely, but Vanguard does not permit single-digit percentage withholding elections.

Inherited IRA

Picture Nick and Nancy, both 57 in 2025, early retirees. Nancy inherited a $1 million traditional IRA from her mother in 2024. Nancy is subject to the 10-year rule. Nick and Nancy have decided to live primarily off the inherited IRA during the early years of retirement, even though they also hold sizable taxable accounts.

In 2025, they withdraw $120,000 from the inherited IRA. Separately, they receive $11,000 in qualified dividends, $2,000 in nonqualified dividends, and $1,000 in interest income—resulting in $134,000 of AGI and $102,500 of taxable income. So, what does their federal income tax liability look like?

Income	Rate	Tax
$31,500	0% (Standard Deduction)	$0
$23,850	10%	$2,385
$67,650	12%	$8,118
$5,200	0% (Long-Term Capital Gain)	$0
$5,800	15% (Long-Term Capital Gain)	$870
Total **$134,000**	**Effective Rate** **8.49%**	**Total** **$11,373**

How do they pay the estimated $11,373 in federal income taxes? By electing income tax withholding on one or more of Nancy's inherited IRA distributions. This approach is flexible: as long as at least 90% of their estimated liability is paid through withholding, they avoid underpayment penalties.

In Real Life: We favor rounding up when making tax payments.

Nick and Nancy might consider withholding nearly all taxes from one large inherited IRA distribution (possibly later in the year) and opt for no withholding on earlier distributions.

Because the tax withholding is from an inherited IRA, it is not subject to the 10% early withdrawal penalty—even though Nancy is under age 59½.

Extra Credit: The table above illustrates how long-term capital gains are taxed after ordinary income. In this example, ordinary income (from $1 to $91,500 of taxable income) is taxed at the 10% and 12% brackets. Long-term capital gains are then "stacked" on top, occupying the range from $91,501 to $102,500. In 2025, for married couples filing jointly, the first $96,700 of taxable income is taxed at 0% for long-term capital gains. In Nick and Nancy's case, $5,200 of their $11,000 in qualified dividends falls into that 0% bracket, and the remaining $5,800 is taxed at the 15% LTCG rate.

Extra Credit: Nancy is subject to annual required minimum distributions (RMDs) on the inherited IRA if her mother had already begun RMDs. **For many early retirees, including Nancy, the inherited IRA RMD is mostly academic.** *To avoid a large tax bill in year 10, Nancy and Nick take substantial distributions earlier—well above Nancy's 2025 inherited RMD of $33,557.05 (calculated as $1,000,000 ÷ 29.8, using the IRS Single Life Expectancy Table for age 57). By living off the inherited IRA first, they keep the effective tax rate on those distributions quite low.*

Premium Tax Credit Considerations

For early retirees enrolled in an ACA health insurance plan, there are additional factors to consider. When signing up for an ACA plan, the household estimates its annual income to determine eligibility for the PTC. When filing the tax return, Form 8962 serves two purposes:

1. It calculates the actual PTC based on modified adjusted gross income (MAGI).
2. It reconciles the actual PTC with the advance premium subsidies received based on the original income estimated during the enrollment period.

As a result, the tax return can show a refund or balance due, depending on how the PTC estimate compares to the actual PTC.

This reconciliation can be a reason to adjust tax payments, either through estimated tax payments or IRA withholding. However, for those who meet the 100% of prior year tax safe harbor (or 110% for higher-income taxpayers), there's typically no need to adjust withholding specifically for the PTC. Any required repayment can be made when filing the return or extension—without triggering an underpayment penalty.

Filing Tax Returns

Should you hire a professional to prepare your tax return? For early retirees, it depends.

Resources like this book can certainly help you build tax knowledge. We didn't set out to write a tax preparation training manual, but we hope the insights shared throughout offer helpful context and education.

That said, comfort levels with tax rules and software vary widely. For some, outsourcing tax prep is well worth the cost, saving time and frustration. For others, preparing the return themselves is a manageable task that doesn't justify hiring a professional.

If you choose to work with a tax return preparer, consider this tactic: Filing on extension to improve the client experience. Tax season is an absolute grind for most preparers. So, why compete for their attention in late February or March when they're at their busiest? Filing on extension allows you to work with your tax preparer after April 15, when they're more rested and less rushed.

This approach does require estimating your tax liability before April 15 to ensure you've paid enough to avoid penalties. But preparing an extension is less work for the tax pro than completing a full return under time pressure—and it can lead to a better, more thoughtful filing experience later.

37 – A Critique and a Response

Trade-offs are inherent in any lifetime tax planning strategy. Our favored approach is no exception.

Our favored approach generally shifts the tax burden away from high-income years towards lower-income years. For many, this means prioritizing traditional 401(k) contributions during working years, followed by rather moderate Roth conversions during the early part of retirement. Beyond Tailored Taxable Roth Conversions (TTRCs), we tend to be rather conservative when it comes to aggressive early retirement Roth conversions.

This opens our favored approach to some criticism. Doesn't it expose widow(er)s and single individuals to higher taxes later in retirement, more so than other planning strategies?

That is a legitimate criticism.

Some might say we shift too many taxes to the later years of widow(er)s' and singles' retirements. In response, we observe that these later years are often the shortest span of one's adult life from accumulation through retirement. Further, even for affluent widow(er)s, we believe the resulting tax burden is unlikely to be onerous. The examples of Elaine in Chapter 11 and Estelle and Bethany in Chapter 15 illustrate this outcome. That said, both our argument and opposing views in this regard are speculative.

Extra Credit: Our approach does not leave elderly widow(er)s and singles as sitting ducks for taxes later in life—far from it! We generally favor tactics such as qualified charitable distributions, asset location, TTRCs, and selective Roth conversions beyond TTRCs to reduce taxation later on. But yes, when compared to other strategies, ours tends to place more tax risk later in life.

Tax Planning To and Through Early Retirement and Risk

Measuring the future tax burden of elderly widow(er)s and singles is inherently speculative. What's less speculative is where a tax strategy shifts tax risk. Our favored approach tends to shift risk into a period we believe the affluent retiree is best positioned to bear it.

A high tax burden in later widowhood typically requires significant financial success. Recall Estelle's example—an 85-year-old widow who is moderately affluent. Her tax burden is quite light. This illustrates that the true risk of a high tax burden in widowhood generally applies only to the very wealthy.

We believe an affluent widowhood is an appropriate place to park risk. Yes, our approach contains a risk shift with a downside. But in our view, that downside is more than compensated for by the accompanying reduction in risk during one's accumulation years and the early and middle stages of retirement.

Consider a strategy that emphasizes Roth 401(k) contributions during working years. That approach increases tax expense during one's high-earning years—often when workers are supporting a spouse and/or children, and the success of their financial future is still uncertain.

Now consider a strategy that emphasizes more aggressive Roth conversions in early or mid-retirement. This can increase income taxes precisely when sequence of return risk is most impactful and may also reduce eligibility for the Premium Tax Credit.

There is no lifetime tax strategy entirely free from trade-offs—not even ours. We prefer to shift the tax burden later into retirement. For most Americans, this reduces total lifetime taxes. Estelle's case in Chapter 15 demonstrated this. Even with an RMD from a $1 million traditional IRA at age 85, her marginal tax rate didn't exceed 22%, with most of the RMD taxed at 12%.

For Estelle—and many Americans—shifting tax risk to later years reduces both tax burden and tax risk.

Where the risk magnifies is in the case of the **very financially successful widow(er)**. We saw this with Elaine in Chapter 11 and Bethany in Chapter 15. Yes, they both paid a healthy amount in federal income tax and IRMAA. But each kept more than 75 cents on the dollar of their significant income annually.

Perhaps you believe our approach unfavorably exposes affluent widows like Elaine and Bethany to higher tax risk. Our response: the materialization of tax risk in these cases has little, if any, impact on their lived experience.

Why not park tax risk in a time period where its realization does little to affect a retiree's lived experience?

Very financially successful widow(er)s and singles are in a position where sufficiency concerns and sequence of returns risk are no longer significant to their financial futures. To varying degrees, these risks still matter for early retirees. And for those still saving for retirement, sufficiency concerns are paramount to their future retirement planning.

So why elect a greater tax burden when sufficiency concerns and sequence risk are magnified? Why not—to the extent tax planning can—shift that risk to a period when sufficiency is largely met and sequence risk has diminished?

Long-Term Care

You may be asking, "Why shift risk to a period when long-term care expenses can be significant?"

Traditional IRAs and other pre-tax retirement accounts can be excellent vehicles for funding long-term care. Many long-term care costs qualify for the itemized medical expense deduction. For example, an elderly retiree living in a long-term care facility may withdraw funds from a traditional retirement account to cover those significant expenses—and deduct 92.5 cents on the dollar as itemized medical expenses. The remaining 7.5 cents is generally taxed in the 10% and 12% income tax brackets.

Yes, spending the end of life in a long-term care facility is not an ideal outcome. However, from a tax perspective, long-term care expenses can help draw down traditional retirement accounts with minimal tax cost. There is generally less tax risk when qualified medical expenses account for a significant portion of end-of-life spending.

Conclusion

All tax planning strategies involve trade-offs.

One trade-off of the approach we generally favor is a reduction in tax risk during accumulation and early-to-mid retirement in exchange for a potential increase in tax risk later in life. We believe that this later-life tax risk is very manageable—and rarely, if ever, materially harmful.

For many Americans, shifting tax risk to later years actually reduces overall risk. As we saw with Estelle, taxation late in life tends to be rather light for those who are moderately successful.

For the very financially successful, increased tax risk later in life tends to have little to no impact on their lived experience. Even when facing RMDs, IRMAA, and the Widow's Tax Trap, individuals like Elaine and Bethany still enjoyed strong after-tax cash flow.

38 – The Lessons of This Book

"I feel like I just gave birth . . . to an accountant!"
Rodney Dangerfield as Thornton Melon in Back to School (1986)

We've gone from pillar to post when it comes to tax and retirement planning—exploring many nooks and crannies along the way. While individual planning concepts and tax rules matter, they don't matter as much as having a good plan.

As we conclude the book, we want to restate the key lessons and leave you with a few final thoughts.

Absolutely No Fear

It's time to put the vague and often exaggerated fears about IRMAA, RMDs, the Widow's Tax Trap, the Tax Torpedo, and taxes in retirement to bed.

Do these issues present costs for some American retirees? Sure.

But for any of these trees in the retirement forest to meaningfully impact a retiree's plan, that retiree must already be quite financially successful.

Throughout this book, we've shown that distributions from traditional retirement accounts are often lightly taxed in retirement. On the relatively rare occasions when they are significantly taxed, it's typically in the context of great financial success and substantial after-tax income.

Does this mean retirement tax planning is unnecessary? Hardly. But it should be guided by quantitative analysis, logic, and reason.

Tax planning to and through early retirement should not be motivated by fear.

The Big Picture

The details are important, but don't get bogged down in them. Always return to the big picture of tax planning to and through early retirement.

1. Traditional retirement account contributions tend to provide a tax benefit at the owner's highest marginal federal income tax rates during their lifetime.
2. For most Americans, most traditional retirement account distributions are lightly taxed.
3. Premium Tax Credit considerations tend to favor traditional retirement account contributions. Their resulting current tax savings help fund taxable accounts and Roth IRAs—two assets that help early retirees keep income low and thus Premium Tax Credits higher prior to Medicare enrollment.

Assets Become Income Very Efficiently

In the United States, financially successful early retirement boils down to one thing: translating accumulated assets into income.

Fortunately, for retirees, assets can become income in a very tax-efficient way. In fact, turning assets into income is a much better way to fund living expenses than going to work for W-2 wages.

Consider an early retiree living off the sale of taxable assets. They have two incredible advantages:

1. Basis recovery – Selling $100,000 of taxable assets does not generate $100,000 of taxable income. The taxable portion is only the amount above the cost basis—perhaps $30,000, $40,000, or $50,000.

2. Favorable tax rates – That capital gain may be taxed at the 0% long-term capital gains bracket.

How does that compare to going to work for a W-2 paycheck?

Even retirees living on traditional IRA withdrawals often benefit from favorable tax treatment. They can benefit from the high standard deduction, the 10% and 12% federal income tax brackets, and—new for 2025—the $6,000 per person senior deduction (subject to income limits). In many cases, retirees can cap their annual income at or below their annual spending, giving them greater control over taxable income than many workers have over theirs.

When In Doubt, Simplify

This book shows that many retirees can achieve outstanding tax results with some thoughtful planning. Does it suggest anything wildly complicated? No!

In fact, complexity in our financial lives often leads to higher fees, confusion, and friction—and can even result in higher taxes. While it's tempting to seek complexity when facing uncertainty, simplicity is often the effective strategy.

Pay Tax When You Pay Less Tax

We strongly question tactics that accelerate and increase federal income tax. For many Americans, choosing a Roth 401(k) contribution over a traditional 401(k) contribution does exactly that. Deferring tax to retirement is often a decision to pay tax when you pay less.

Congress has repeatedly shown a preference for lightly taxing retirees. Politicians have known motivations, reflected by their legislative behavior.

Why not take advantage of that reality to reduce your total lifetime taxation?

Keep Ordinary Income Low in Retirement

Aspiring and current early retirees have many opportunities to structure their finances in a way that keeps ordinary income low during retirement. This opens a valuable planning window for potential Roth conversions or living several years off substantial Hidden Roth IRAs.

Holding bonds inside a traditional retirement account isn't revolutionary, but it can support years of effective tax planning. Delaying Social Security can also help keep ordinary income low while providing additional long-term benefits for retirees.

Enjoy Retirement!

There's so much to appreciate about retirement planning in 2025. While we refer to the years from ages 66 through 69 as the Golden Years, you have the power to make every year of your retirement golden.

Focus on faith, family, and fun in retirement. Tax planning is great, but remember what truly counts. In conversation after conversation with retirees, a common desire emerges: fewer things, more memories.

We hope your financial and tax planning sets you up to enjoy the remaining chapters of your life.

<u>Acknowledgments</u>

I am first and foremost grateful to God for putting me in the position to co-write Tax Planning To and Through Early Retirement. It has been a privilege to work on this project. Thank you, God, for the opportunity.

Someone else who deserves much credit for enduring this project is my wonderful wife, Catherine Mullaney. She has been patient as I have been highly focused on this writing, even enduring my working on this project during the early morning hours of a Memorial Day weekend vacation. Many thanks to Catherine for all you do for me and for supporting me throughout this project in particular.

My family has supported me and given me the upbringing to be able to go out on my own into self-employment. Many thanks to my parents, Thomas & Colleen Mullaney, and my brothers Tom and Jim Mullaney for all their support throughout the years.

I have been privileged to get to know the financial independence community during my journey as both a financial planner and as a personal finance content creator. There are too many people to state by name, but three people who have contributed greatly to my journey are Brad Barrett and Jonathan Mendonsa, the co-founders of the ChooseFI podcast, and Stephen Baughier, the founder of CampFI. They provide forums to deepen both relationships and knowledge of financial independence concepts. Brad, Jonathan, and Stephen have been great to me during my own journey in the world of personal finance.

Many thanks to Denise Appleby, MJ, APA, CISP, CRC, CRPS, *The IRA Whisperer*, for reviewing our technical IRA and qualified plan discussions in this book. It is a better book for her having been involved.

Lastly, to a friend and one of the best co-authors in the world of personal finance, Cody Garrett. This book is the latest of Cody's many contributions to improve the lives of both financial planners and financial planning "end users." I'm honored to be a part of it.

Sean Mullaney
Woodland Hills, California
August 2025

First, I thank God for guiding my steps and giving me the gifts, opportunities, and calling to serve others through education. I am deeply grateful to my family and church family for their encouragement, prayers, and example of living with faith, purpose, and generosity.

I want to thank my wife, Marissa, for her unwavering support throughout my personal and entrepreneurial journey. She has been incredibly generous and encouraging as we've built Measure Twice®. Her patience, wisdom, and belief in my work have sustained me through long stretches and the many demands of running multiple businesses. Marissa's faith, kindness, and care are invaluable, and I am deeply grateful for the joy she brings to life.

I am deeply grateful to my first financial planning mentor, Joe Birkofer. In 2018, Joe saw potential in a 30-year-old musician with no financial credentials—just curiosity and drive. He invited me into client meetings, encouraged me to accelerate my education and experience ("drinking from the firehose"), and poured his time, energy, and wisdom into my growth. His generosity and transparency shaped not only my career but also the way I serve others today.

I also want to thank the Measure Twice Planners community. You are a remarkable group of financial planners who value generosity, transparency, and curiosity. Your thoughtful questions, willingness to share openly, and openness to let me teach (and learn twice!) have sharpened my understanding and fueled my passion for financial education.

I am grateful to Brad Barrett, Jonathan Mendonsa, and the ChooseFI community; Andy Panko and the Retirement Planning Education community; and the many other personal finance content creators who serve their audiences with integrity.

To you, the reader: thank you for your commitment to going beyond the basics while remembering to Keep Finance Personal®. Your desire to align your finances with your unique values and desired outcomes inspires my work every day.

Lastly, I want to thank my co-author, Sean Mullaney. Writing this book together has been both an honor and a joy. I once believed "the only ship that doesn't sail is a partnership," but now I know that teamwork truly makes the dream work. Sean's steady collaboration, shared passion for helping others, and depth of knowledge have made this a far better book than I could have written alone. I am grateful for his friendship and for the many ways he has contributed to the unique communities we serve.

Cody Garrett
Houston, Texas
August 2025

Bibliography

Introduction

Vanguard, How America Saves 2024, available at https://corporate.vanguard.com/content/dam/corp/research/pdf/how_america_saves_report_2024.pdf.

Danielle Wallace, Schumer forces name change for 'big, beautiful bill' moments before it passes, available at https://www.foxnews.com/politics/schumer-forces-name-change-big-beautiful-bill-moments-before-passes.

Employee Benefit Research Institute (EBRI) and Greenwald & Associates 2023 Retirement Confidence Survey Fact Sheet, "Expectations About Retirement." 2023.

Employee Benefit Research Institute/Greenwald Research, "2025 EBRI/Greenwald Retirement Confidence Survey Summary Report," April 24, 2025.

Michael Lombardi, Bill Walsh's NFL draft philosophies: Six lessons from the master, available at https://www.nfl.com/news/bill-walsh-s-nfl-draft-philosophies-six-lessons-from-the-master-09000d5d82857c66.

Sean Mullaney, Solo 401(k): The Solopreneur's Retirement Account, 2022.

1 – The Federal Income Tax Formula

Publication 17 - Tax Guide for Individuals: https://www.irs.gov/pub/irs-pdf/p17.pdf.

IRS, Form 1040, U.S. Individual Income Tax Return, available at https://www.irs.gov/pub/irs-pdf/f1040.pdf.

Jeff Levine, https://x.com/CPAPlanner/status/1940856699872858202.

2025 Reconciliation bill, available at https://www.congress.gov/119/bills/hr1/BILLS-119hr1eas.pdf.

Section 302 of the Jobs and Growth Tax Relief Reconciliation Act of 2003, available at https://www.congress.gov/108/plaws/publ27/PLAW-108publ27.pdf.

Sabrina Parys, 2024-2025 Tax Brackets and Federal Income Tax Rates, available at https://www.nerdwallet.com/article/taxes/federal-income-tax-brackets.

Sabrina Parys, Capital Gains Tax: How It Works, Rates and Calculator, available at https://www.nerdwallet.com/article/taxes/capital-gains-tax-rates.

Sabrina Parys, Child Tax Credit: Eligibility, How to Claim in 2024-2025, available at https://www.nerdwallet.com/article/taxes/qualify-child-child-care-tax-credit.

Publication 550 - Investment Income and Expenses: https://www.irs.gov/pub/irs-pdf/p550.pdf.

Publication 525 - Taxable and Nontaxable Income: https://www.irs.gov/pub/irs-pdf/p525.pdf.

Publication 554 - Tax Guide for Seniors: https://www.irs.gov/pub/irs-pdf/p554.pdf.

Arielle O'Shea, Saver's Credit: What It Is and How It Works, available at https://www.nerdwallet.com/article/taxes/can-you-take-the-savers-credit.

2 – Taxable Accounts

Publication 551 – Basis of Assets: https://www.irs.gov/pub/irs-pdf/p551.pdf.

Sean Mullaney, Understanding Your Form 1099-DIV, available at https://fitaxguy.com/understanding-your-form-1099-div/.

IRS, Schedule D Capital Gains and Losses, available at https://www.irs.gov/pub/irs-pdf/f1040sd.pdf.

IRS, 2024 Instructions for Schedule D, Capital Loss Carryover Worksheet--Lines 6 and 14, page 11, available at https://www.irs.gov/pub/irs-pdf/i1040sd.pdf.

IRS, Topic no. 559, Net investment income tax, available at https://www.irs.gov/taxtopics/tc559.

Jobs and Growth Tax Relief Reconciliation Act of 2003 Section 302, available at https://www.congress.gov/108/plaws/publ27/PLAW-108publ27.pdf.

Michael Kitces, Mechanics Of The 0% Long-Term Capital Gains Tax Rate And Harvesting Capital Gains For A Free Step-Up In Basis!, available at https://www.kitces.com/blog/understanding-the-mechanics-of-the-0-long-term-capital-gains-tax-rate-how-to-harvest-capital-gains-for-a-free-step-up-in-basis/.

Sean Ross, A History of the S&P 500 Dividend Yield, available at https://www.investopedia.com/articles/markets/071616/history-sp-500-dividend-yield.asp.

Michael Kitces, IRS Issues Guidance For New 3.8% Medicare Tax On Net Investment Income, available at https://www.kitces.com/blog/irs-issues-guidance-for-new-3-8-medicare-tax-on-net-investment-income/.

Section 1411, available at https://www.law.cornell.edu/uscode/text/26/1411.

3 – Tax-Advantaged Accounts

Publication 571 - Tax-Sheltered Annuity Plans (403(b) Plans): https://www.irs.gov/pub/irs-pdf/p571.pdf.

4 – The Basics of IRAs

Section 408: https://www.law.cornell.edu/uscode/text/26/408.

Sean Mullaney, Solo 401(k)s and the Rule of 55: Does the Answer Lie in 1962?, available at https://fitaxguy.com/wp-content/uploads/2024/06/Solo-401ks-and-the-Rule-of-55FINAL.pdf.

IRS, Form 8880 Credit for Qualified Retirement Savings Contributions, available at https://www.irs.gov/pub/irs-pdf/f8880.pdf.

Sean Mullaney, 2025 IRA Contributions for Beginners, available at https://fitaxguy.com/2025-ira-contributions-for-beginners/.

IRS, Notice 2024-80, available at https://www.irs.gov/pub/irs-drop/n-24-80.pdf.

IRS, Are You Covered By An Employers Retirement Plan, available at https://www.irs.gov/retirement-plans/are-you-covered-by-an-employers-retirement-plan.

IRS, Schedule 1, Additional Income and Adjustments to Income, available at https://www.irs.gov/pub/irs-pdf/f1040s1.pdf.

IRS, Rollovers of retirement plan and IRA distributions, available at https://www.irs.gov/retirement-plans/plan-participant-employee/rollovers-of-retirement-plan-and-ira-distributions.

2025 Reconciliation bill, available at https://www.congress.gov/119/bills/hr1/BILLS-119hr1eas.pdf.

Ben Henry-Moreland, Analyzing The Individual Tax Provisions Of The House Republicans' 2025 Proposed Tax Bill, available at https://www.kitces.com/blog/republican-proposed-tax-bill-2025-tax-cuts-and-jobs-act-tcja-sunset-salt-deduction-cap-child-tax-credit-qbi-deduction-maga/.

Franchise Tax Board, Early distributions, available at https://www.ftb.ca.gov/file/personal/income-types/early-distributions.html.

Greenbush Financial, Secure Act 2.0: RMD Start Age Pushed Back to 73 Starting in 2023, available at https://www.greenbushfinancial.com/all-blogs/secure-act-2-rmd-age-73.

IRS Publication 590-B: Distributions from Individual Retirement Arrangements (IRAs), available at https://www.irs.gov/pub/irs-pdf/p590b.pdf.

Natalie B. Choate, Life and Death Planning for Retirement Benefits (8th Ed. 2019), pages 46 and 164.

Treasury Decision 9930, available at https://www.taxnotes.com/research/federal/treasury-decisions/final-regs-provide-guidance-on-rmd-calculations/2d5f9.

Fidelity, IRS Uniform Lifetime Table, available at https://www.taxnotes.com/research/federal/treasury-decisions/final-regs-provide-guidance-on-rmd-calculations/2d5f9.

National Society of Tax Professionals, SECURE Act 2.0 – When Does the RMD Start?, available at https://www.nstp.org/article/secure-act-2-0-%E2%80%93-when-does-the-rmd-start.

Sections 6654(g), 31, and 3405, available at https://www.law.cornell.edu/uscode/text/26/6654#g, https://www.law.cornell.edu/uscode/text/26/31, and https://www.law.cornell.edu/uscode/text/26/3405.

Fidelity, Federal and State Tax Withholding—IRA Withdrawals, available at https://clearingcustody.fidelity.com/app/proxy/content?literatureURL=/964543.PDF.

Fidelity, IRA Notice of Withholding, available at https://institutional.fidelity.com/app/literature/view?itemCode=704656&renditionType=pdf.

Section 408A: https://www.law.cornell.edu/uscode/text/26/408A.

Sean Mullaney, The Pro-Rata Rule, available at https://fitaxguy.com/the-pro-rata-rule/.

Sean Mullaney, The Taxation of Roth IRA Distributions, available at https://fitaxguy.com/the-taxation-of-roth-ira-distributions/.

IRS, Form 8606 Nondeductible IRAs, available at https://www.irs.gov/pub/irs-pdf/f8606.pdf.

5 – The Basics of 401(k)s and Other Qualified Plans

Sean Mullaney, Solo 401(k)s and the Rule of 55: Does the Answer Lie in 1962?, available at https://fitaxguy.com/wp-content/uploads/2024/06/Solo-401ks-and-the-Rule-of-55FINAL.pdf.

IRS, Form 8880 Credit for Qualified Retirement Savings Contributions, available at https://www.irs.gov/pub/irs-pdf/f8880.pdf.

Sean Mullaney, Understanding Your 401(k), available at https://fitaxguy.com/understanding-your-401k/.

IRS, Notice 2024-80, 2025 Amounts Relating to Retirement Plans and IRAs, as Adjusted for Changes in Cost-of-Living available at https://www.irs.gov/pub/irs-drop/n-24-80.pdf.

Kelley R. Taylor, New SECURE 2.0 Super 401(k) Catch-Up Contribution for Ages 60-63, available at https://www.kiplinger.com/taxes/super-catch-up-contribution-for-age-60-63.

IRS, Notice 2024-2, Miscellaneous Changes Under the SECURE 2.0 Act of 2022, pages 73–74, available at https://www.irs.gov/pub/irs-drop/n-24-02.pdf.

IRS, Topic no. 751, Social Security and Medicare withholding rates, available at https://www.irs.gov/taxtopics/tc751.

IRS, Rollovers of retirement plan and IRA distributions, available at https://www.irs.gov/retirement-plans/plan-participant-employee/rollovers-of-retirement-plan-and-ira-distributions.

IRS, Rollover Chart, available at https://www.irs.gov/pub/irs-tege/rollover_chart.pdf.

Thrift Savings Plan, Annual Limit on Elective Deferrals, available at https://www.tsp.gov/publications/tspfs07.pdf.

Franchise Tax Board, Early distributions, available at https://www.ftb.ca.gov/file/personal/income-types/early-distributions.html.

Karen Roberts and Brian Baker, What is the rule of 55 and how does it work?, available at https://www.bankrate.com/retirement/rule-of-55.

Jacob Schroeder, The Rule of 55: One Way to Fund Early Retirement, available at https://www.kiplinger.com/retirement/the-rule-of-55-one-way-to-fund-early-retirement.

Fidelity, Federal and State Tax Withholding — Retirement Plan Withdrawals, available at https://clearingcustody.fidelity.com/app/proxy/content?literatureURL=/9585653.PDF.

Vanguard, Helping you make sense of tax withholding rules for your IRA, available at https://personal1.vanguard.com/pdf/s273.pdf?2210114361.

Dr. Jim Dahle, Mega Backdoor Roth IRA Conversion in Your 401(k) or 403(b), available at https://www.whitecoatinvestor.com/mega-roth-conversion/.

IRS, Guidance on Allocation of After-Tax Amounts to Rollovers, available at https://www.irs.gov/pub/irs-drop/n-14-54.pdf.

IRS, Form 1040 U.S. Individual Income Tax Return, available at https://www.irs.gov/pub/irs-pdf/f1040.pdf.

IRC Section 72(t)(2)(A)(v), available at https://www.law.cornell.edu/uscode/text/26/72.

Ed Slott & Company, LLC, Retirement Account RMD Aggregation Chart, available at https://ira-help.com/wp-content/uploads/2024/03/IRA-Advisor-RMD-Aggregation-Chart_2024.pdf.

Natalie B. Choate, Life and Death Planning for Retirement Benefits, 8th Edition 2019, page 140.

Sean Mullaney, Roth 401k Withdrawals, available at https://fitaxguy.com/roth-401k-withdrawals/.

Treas. Reg. Section 1.408A-10, available at https://www.law.cornell.edu/cfr/text/26/1.408A-10.

Mike Piper, Solo 401(k) Contribution Calculator, available at https://obliviousinvestor.com/solo-401k-contribution-calculator/.

IRS, Instructions to Form 5329, available at https://www.irs.gov/pub/irs-pdf/i5329.pdf.

IRS, Retirement Topics – Exceptions to tax on early distributions, available at https://www.irs.gov/retirement-plans/plan-participant-employee/retirement-topics-exceptions-to-tax-on-early-distributions.

Governmental and Non-Governmental 457 (457b) Retirement Plans for Physicians, available at https://www.physiciansidegigs.com/457-b-retirement-plans.

Jenny Kiffmeyer, Nongovernmental 457(b) Plans and Rollovers the Two Don't Mix, available at https://www.napa-net.org/news/2024/2/nongovernmental-457b-plans-and-rollovers--two-dont-mix/.

6 – Rollovers of Retirement Accounts

IRS, Rollovers of retirement plan and IRA distributions, available at https://www.irs.gov/retirement-plans/plan-participant-employee/rollovers-of-retirement-plan-and-ira-distributions.

Natalie B. Choate, Life and Death Planning for Retirement Benefits, 8th Edition, 2019, pp. 153, 157, 180-183, 185-188, 262-263, 266, 271.

Section 408(d)(3), enacted September 2, 1974, 88 Stat. 961-962, available at https://uscode.house.gov/statviewer.htm?volume=88&page=961# and https://uscode.house.gov/statviewer.htm?volume=88&page=962#.

Sean Mullaney, Solo 401(k)s and the Rule of 55: Does the Answer Lie in 1962?, available at https://fitaxguy.com/wp-content/uploads/2024/06/Solo-401ks-and-the-Rule-of-55FINAL.pdf.

Nina Lantz, SECURE 2.0: Mandatory cash-out limit increases in 2024, available at https://www.milliman.com/en/insight/client-action-bulletin-secure-2-mandatory-cash-out-limit.

Bankrate, Mortgage rate history: 1970s to 2025, available at https://www.bankrate.com/mortgages/historical-mortgage-rates/.

IRS, Retirement plans FAQs relating to waivers of the 60-day requirement, available at https://www.irs.gov/retirement-plans/retirement-plans-faqs-relating-to-waivers-of-the-60-day-rollover-requirement.

Fidelity, Federal and State Tax Withholding—Retirement Plan Withdrawals, available at https://clearingcustody.fidelity.com/app/proxy/content?literatureURL=/9585653.PDF.

Vanguard, Helping you make sense of tax withholding rules for your IRA, available at https://personal1.vanguard.com/pdf/s273.pdf?2210114361.

Internal Revenue Code Section 72(t)(2)(E), available at https://www.law.cornell.edu/uscode/text/26/72#_2_E.

Sean Mullaney, Roth 401(k)s and the Rule of 55, available at https://fitaxguy.com/roth-401ks-and-the-rule-of-55/.

IRS, Exceptions to tax on early distributions, available at https://www.irs.gov/retirement-plans/plan-participant-employee/retirement-topics-exceptions-to-tax-on-early-distributions.

Sean Mullaney, Traditional 401(k) Contributions are Fine for Most Americans (Really)!, available at https://fitaxguy.com/traditional-401k-contributions-are-fine-for-most-americans-really/.

Jeffrey Levine, How Safe From Creditors is Your 401(k) Money if You Roll it to an IRA?, available at https://irahelp.com/slottreport/how-safe-creditors-your-401k-money-if-you-roll-it-ira/.

IRS, Instructions to Forms 1099-R and 5498 (2024), Direct Rollovers, available at https://www.irs.gov/instructions/i1099r#en_US_2024_publink1000291938.

IRS, Instructions to Forms 1099-R and 5498 (2024), Transfers, available at https://www.irs.gov/instructions/i1099r#en_US_2024_publink1000291947.

Andy Ives, IRA Trivia: Missed RMD or Excess Contribution?, available at https://irahelp.com/slottreport/ira-trivia-missed-rmd-or-excess-contribution/.

IRS, Form 1040 U.S. Individual Income Tax Return, available at https://www.irs.gov/pub/irs-pdf/f1040.pdf.

Sean Mullaney, Rollover Distributions to Qualified Plans Should Not Take Basis, available at https://fitaxguy.com/wp-content/uploads/2021/08/Rollover-Distributions-to-Qualified-Plans-Should-Not-Take-Basis.pdf.

Sean Mullaney, The Basis Isolation Backdoor Roth IRA, available at https://fitaxguy.com/the-basis-isolation-backdoor-roth-ira/.

Pension Benefit Guaranty Corporation, Guaranteed Benefits, available at https://www.pbgc.gov/wr/benefits/guaranteed-benefits.

Franchise Tax Board, Early distributions, available at https://www.ftb.ca.gov/file/personal/income-types/early-distributions.html.

IRS Publication 590-B: Distributions from Individual Retirement Arrangements (IRAs), available at https://www.irs.gov/pub/irs-pdf/p590b.pdf.

Fidelity, Federal and State Tax Withholding—IRA Withdrawals, available at https://clearingcustody.fidelity.com/app/proxy/content?literatureURL=/964543.PDF.

Internal Revenue Code Section 408A: https://www.law.cornell.edu/uscode/text/26/408A.

Sean Mullaney, The Pro-Rata Rule, available at https://fitaxguy.com/the-pro-rata-rule/.

Sean Mullaney, The Taxation of Roth IRA Distributions, available at https://fitaxguy.com/the-taxation-of-roth-ira-distributions/.

IRS, Form 8606 Nondeductible IRAs, available at https://www.irs.gov/pub/irs-pdf/f8606.pdf.

7 – Pay Tax When You Pay Less Tax

Nick Maggiulli, Roth 401(k) vs. 401(k): Which is the Better Option?, available at https://ofdollarsanddata.com/roth-401k-vs-401k/.

Sean Mullaney, Accumulators Should Ignore the Conventional Wisdom, available at https://fitaxguy.com/accumulators-should-ignore-the-conventional-wisdom/.

8 – Moving To Early Retirement: The Compelling Three

Quotefancy, https://quotefancy.com/quote/909730/Stephen-R-Covey-To-begin-with-the-end-in-mind-means-to-start-with-a-clear-understanding.

IRS, Publication 590-B, available at: https://www.irs.gov/publications/p590b.

Kamaron McNair, Here are the new federal income tax brackets for 2025 — the standard deduction is now up to $30,000, available at https://www.cnbc.com/2024/10/22/new-federal-income-tax-brackets-for-2025.html.

Jeff Levine, https://x.com/CPAPlanner/status/1940856699872858202.

2025 Reconciliation bill, available at https://www.congress.gov/119/bills/hr1/BILLS-119hr1eas.pdf.

Ben Henry-Moreland, Analyzing The Individual Tax Provisions Of The House Republicans' 2025 Proposed Tax Bill, available at https://www.kitces.com/blog/republican-proposed-tax-bill-2025-tax-cuts-and-jobs-act-tcja-sunset-salt-deduction-cap-child-tax-credit-qbi-deduction-maga/.

Kate Ashford, CSA, IRMAA Brackets 2025: What They Are and How They Work, available at https://www.nerdwallet.com/article/insurance/medicare/what-is-the-medicare-irmaa.

John Waggoner, 13 States That Won't Tax Your Retirement Distributions, available at https://www.aarp.org/money/taxes/states-that-do-not-tax-your-retirement-distributions/.

U.S. Bank, New tax laws 2025: Tax brackets and deductions, available at https://www.us-bank.com/wealth-management/financial-perspectives/financial-planning/tax-brackets.html.

Tina Orem, California State Income Tax Guide for 2024-2025, available at https://www.nerdwallet.com/article/taxes/california-state-tax.

Sean Mullaney, 2025 IRA Contributions for Beginners, available at https://fitaxguy.com/2025-ira-contributions-for-beginners/.

Wikipedia, Lifestyles of the Rich and Famous, available at https://en.wikipedia.org/wiki/Lifestyles_of_the_Rich_and_Famous.

Sean Mullaney, The MAGI Limits on Roth IRA Contributions, available at https://fitaxguy.com/the-magi-limitation-on-roth-ira-contributions/.

9 – Moving To Early Retirement: Additional Tactics

Sean Mullaney, 2025 IRA Contributions for Beginners, available at https://fitaxguy.com/2025-ira-contributions-for-beginners/.

Sean Mullaney, The Timing of the Backdoor Roth IRA, available at https://fitaxguy.com/backdoor-roth-ira-timing/.

Sabrina Parys, 2024-2025 Tax Brackets and Federal Income Tax Rates, available at https://www.nerdwallet.com/article/taxes/federal-income-tax-brackets.

The White Coat Investor, Rollovers, Roth, and Investing - WCI Podcast #423, available at https://youtu.be/6wyCU5pIfoM?si=Db3lqAZXiaSNZNoS&t=945.

IRS, Notice 2004-2, Q&A 26, available at https://www.irs.gov/pub/irs-drop/n-04-2.pdf.

Section 223(f)(4)(A), available at https://www.law.cornell.edu/uscode/text/26/223#f_4_A.

Governmental and Non-Governmental 457 (457b) Retirement Plans for Physicians, available at https://www.physiciansidegigs.com/457-b-retirement-plans.

Section 72(t)(1), available at https://www.law.cornell.edu/uscode/text/26/72#t_1.

Section 4974(c), available at https://www.law.cornell.edu/uscode/text/26/4974#c.

Barbara Weltman, How Non-Qualified Deferred Compensation Plans Work, available at https://www.investopedia.com/articles/personal-finance/052915/how-nonqualified-deferred-compensation-plans-work.asp.

Kaye A. Thomas, Consider Your Options: Get the Most from Your Equity Compensation, Fairmark Press, 2023 Edition.

10 – Drawdown Principles

Sean Mullaney, The Advantages of Living on Taxable Assets First In Early Retirement, available at https://fitaxguy.com/the-advantages-of-living-on-taxable-assets-first-in-early-retirement/.

JL Collins, The Simple Path to Wealth, 2025, p. 231.

Sabrina Parys, Capital Gains Tax: Long and Short-Term Rates for 2024-2025, available at https://www.nerdwallet.com/article/taxes/capital-gains-tax-rates.

Kamaron McNair, Here are the new federal income tax brackets for 2025—the standard deduction is now up to $30,000, available at https://www.cnbc.com/2024/10/22/new-federal-income-tax-brackets-for-2025.html.

Sean Mullaney, Why I Don't Worry Much About Sequence of Returns Risk, available at https://fitaxguy.com/why-i-dont-worry-much-about-sequence-of-returns-risk/.

Ben Henry-Moreland, Breaking Down The "One Big Beautiful Bill Act": Impact Of New Laws On Tax Planning, available at https://www.kitces.com/blog/obbba-one-big-beautiful-bill-act-tax-planning-salt-cap-senior-deduction-qbi-deduction-tax-cut-and-jobs-act-tcja-amt-trump-accounts/.

IRS, Publication 915 Social Security and Equivalent Railroad Retirement Benefits, available at https://www.irs.gov/pub/irs-pdf/p915.pdf.

Covisium, Taxable Social Security Benefit Calculator, available at https://www.covisum.com/resources/taxable-social-security-calculator.

11 – Moving Through Retirement

Section 36B, available at https://www.law.cornell.edu/uscode/text/26/36B.

2025 Poverty Guidelines: 48 Contiguous States (all states except Alaska and Hawaii), available at https://aspe.hhs.gov/sites/default/files/documents/dd73d4f00d8a819d10b2fdb70d254f7b/detailed-guidelines-2025.pdf.

2025 Reconciliation bill, available at https://www.congress.gov/119/bills/hr1/BILLS-119hr1eas.pdf.

Ben Henry-Moreland, Analyzing The Individual Tax Provisions Of The House Republicans' 2025 Proposed Tax Bill, https://www.kitces.com/blog/republican-proposed-tax-bill-2025-tax-cuts-and-jobs-act-tcja-sunset-salt-deduction-cap-child-tax-credit-qbi-deduction-maga/.

IRS, Revenue Procedure 2025-19, available at https://www.irs.gov/pub/irs-drop/rp-25-19.pdf.

Sabrina Parys, Capital Gains Tax: Long and Short-Term Rates for 2024-2025, available at https://www.nerdwallet.com/article/taxes/capital-gains-tax-rates.

Mile High FI Podcast, Buy Borrow Die for FI and Mailbag Questions - Rusty | MHFI 270 | Mile High FI Podcast, available at https://www.youtube.com/watch?v=6D4OlMhXVNs.

Jeff Levine, https://x.com/CPAPlanner/status/1940856699872858202.

Kamaron McNair, Here are the new federal income tax brackets for 2025—the standard deduction is now up to $30,000, available at https://www.cnbc.com/2024/10/22/new-federal-income-tax-brackets-for-2025.html.

Ward Williams, Social Security Payment Schedule 2025, available at https://www.investopedia.com/social-security-payment-schedule-5213627.

IRS, Publication 915 Social Security and Equivalent Railroad Retirement Benefits, available at https://www.irs.gov/pub/irs-pdf/p915.pdf.

Covisium, Taxable Social Security Benefit Calculator, available at https://www.covisum.com/resources/taxable-social-security-calculator.

Sean Mullaney, Traditional 401(k) Contributions Are Fine for Most Americans (Really!), available at https://fitaxguy.com/traditional-401k-contributions-are-fine-for-most-americans-really/.

William Reichenstein and William Meyer, Understanding the Tax Torpedo and Its Implications for Various Retirees, available at https://www.financialplanningassociation.org/sites/default/files/2020-09/July2018_Contribution_Reichenstein.pdf.

Fidelity, IRS Uniform Lifetime Table, available at https://www.fidelity.com/bin-public/060_www_fidelity_com/documents/UniformLifetimeTable.pdf.

Kelley R. Taylor, 2025 Tax Deduction Change for Those Over Age 65, available at https://www.kiplinger.com/taxes/tax-deduction-change-for-those-over-65.

Kate Ashford, IRMAA Brackets 2025: What They Are and How They Work, available at https://www.nerdwallet.com/article/insurance/medicare/what-is-the-medicare-irmaa.

Larry David: A Pretty Good Tribute, available at https://www.youtube.com/watch?v=O_05qJTeNNI.

Sean Mullaney, How Much Income Tax on an $80,000 72(t) Payment Plan?, available at https://www.youtube.com/watch?v=NtG0m-qOlsw.

Sean Mullaney, Accumulators Should Ignore the Conventional Wisdom, available at https://fitaxguy.com/accumulators-should-ignore-the-conventional-wisdom/.

12 – Your Money Isn't Locked Up: The 10% Additional Tax "Penalty"

Internal Revenue Code Section 72(t), available at https://www.law.cornell.edu/uscode/text/26/72#t.

Sean Mullaney, Accessing Retirement Accounts Prior to Age 59½, available at https://fitaxguy.com/accessing-retirement-accounts-prior-to-age-59-%c2%bd/.

Natalie B. Choate, Life and Death Planning for Retirement Benefits, 8th Edition 2019, pages 97, 223, 361–362, 372, 595–597, 600, 603–605.

Karen Roberts and Brian Baker, What is the rule of 55 and how does it work?, available at https://www.bankrate.com/retirement/rule-of-55.

Jacob Schroeder, The Rule of 55: One Way to Fund Early Retirement, available at https://www.kiplinger.com/retirement/the-rule-of-55-one-way-to-fund-early-retirement.

IRS, Instructions for Form 5329, available at https://www.irs.gov/pub/irs-pdf/i5329.pdf.

Equity Trust, Tax Brackets Announced for 2025: What's Changing, available at https://www.trustetc.com/blog/federal-tax-bracket-changes/.

IRS, Rollover Chart, available at https://www.irs.gov/pub/irs-tege/rollover_chart.pdf.

Internal Revenue Code Section 457(a)(2), available at https://www.law.cornell.edu/uscode/text/26/457#a_2.

Kamaron McNair, Here are the new federal income tax brackets for 2025—the standard deduction is now up to $30,000, available at https://www.cnbc.com/2024/10/22/new-federal-income-tax-brackets-for-2025.html.

IRS, Notice 87-13, available at https://www.taxnotes.com/research/federal/irs-guidance/notices/advance-notice-provides-temporary-guidance-for-deferred-compensation-plan-distributions/1frrr.

Sean Mullaney, The Taxation of Roth IRA Distributions, available at https://fitaxguy.com/the-taxation-of-roth-ira-distributions/.

Treas. Reg. Section 1.408A-6, available at https://www.law.cornell.edu/cfr/text/26/1.408A-6.

Internal Revenue Code Section 72(t)(8), available at https://www.law.cornell.edu/us-code/text/26/72#t_8.

Sean Mullaney, Roth IRA Withdrawals (Prior to Age 59½), available at https://fitaxguy.com/wp-content/uploads/2020/09/Roth-IRA-Withdrawals-Prior-to-Age-59-%C2%BD.pdf.

Sean Mullaney, Roth 401(k) Withdrawals, available at https://fitaxguy.com/roth-401k-withdrawals/.

Treas. Reg. Section 1.408A-10, available at https://www.law.cornell.edu/cfr/text/26/1.408A-10.

IRS, Notice 2022-6, available at https://www.irs.gov/pub/irs-drop/n-22-06.pdf.

IRS, Substantially equal periodic payments, available at https://www.irs.gov/retirement-plans/substantially-equal-periodic-payments.

Sean Mullaney, Retire on 72(t) Payments, available at https://fitaxguy.com/retire-on-72t-payments/.

IRS, Revenue Ruling 2025-1, available at https://www.irs.gov/pub/irs-drop/rr-25-01.pdf.

IRS, Revenue Ruling 2025-6, available at https://www.irs.gov/pub/irs-drop/rr-25-06.pdf.

IRS, Revenue Ruling 2025-8, available at https://www.irs.gov/pub/irs-drop/rr-25-08.pdf.

IRS, Section 7520 interest rates, available at https://www.irs.gov/businesses/small-businesses-self-employed/section-7520-interest-rates.

My Florida Retirement System, 72(t) Calculator, available at https://www.myfrs.com/calculators/Retire72T.html.

Fidelity, 72(t) Calculator, available at https://calculators.ssnc.cloud/Fidelity/c72t.

Treas. Reg. Section 1.408A-4 Q&A 12, available at https://www.law.cornell.edu/cfr/text/26/1.408A-4.

Treas. Reg. Section 1.401(a)(9)-9, available at https://www.ecfr.gov/current/title-26/chapter-I/subchapter-A/part-1/subject-group-ECFR6f8c3724b50e44d/section-1.401(a)(9)-9.

IRS, Notice 2004-2, Q&A 26 and Q&A 28, available at https://www.irs.gov/pub/irs-drop/n-04-2.pdf.

IRS, Notice 2004-50, Q&A 39, available at https://www.irs.gov/pub/irs-drop/n-04-50.pdf.

IRS, Publication 502 Medical and Dental Expenses, page 3, at https://www.irs.gov/pub/irs-pdf/p502.pdf.

IRS, Form 8889, available at https://www.irs.gov/pub/irs-pdf/f8889.pdf.

13 – Health Insurance Before Medicare and the Premium Tax Credit

U.S. Department of Labor, FAQs on COBRA Continuation Health Coverage for Employers and Advisers, available at https://www.dol.gov/sites/dolgov/files/EBSA/about-ebsa/our-activities/resource-center/faqs/cobra-continuation-health-coverage.pdf.

Publication 974 - Premium Tax Credit (PTC): https://www.irs.gov/pub/irs-pdf/p974.pdf.

IRS, 2024 Instructions for Form 8962, pages 1, 3–6, 8, available at https://www.irs.gov/pub/irs-pdf/i8962.pdf.

Healthcare.gov, How to pick a health insurance plan, available at https://www.healthcare.gov/choose-a-plan/plans-categories/.

Healthcare.gov, Catastrophic health plans, available at https://www.healthcare.gov/choose-a-plan/catastrophic-health-plans/.

KFF, Health Insurance Marketplace Calculator, available at https://www.kff.org/interactive/subsidy-calculator/.

CMS.gov, Second Lowest Cost Silver Plan Technical FAQs, available at https://www.cms.gov/cciio/resources/fact-sheets-and-faqs/downloads/second-lowest-cost-silver-plan-technical-faqs12162016.pdf.

IRS, Form 1040, U.S. Individual Income Tax Return, available at https://www.irs.gov/pub/irs-pdf/f1040.pdf.

KFF, Medicaid Income Eligibility Limits for Adults as a Percent of the Federal Poverty Level, available at https://www.kff.org/affordable-care-act/state-indicator/medicaid-income-eligibility-limits-for-adults-as-a-percent-of-the-federal-poverty-level/?currentTimeframe=0&sortModel=%7B%22colId%22:%22Location%22,%22sort%22:%22asc%22%7D.

KFF, Medicaid and CHIP Income Eligibility Limits for Children as a Percent of the Federal Poverty Level, available at https://www.kff.org/affordable-care-act/state-indicator/medicaid-and-chip-income-eligibility-limits-for-children-as-a-percent-of-the-federal-poverty-level/?currentTimeframe=0&sortModel=%7B%22colId%22:%22Location%22,%22sort%22:%22asc%22%7D.

Healthcare.gov, Count income & household size, available at https://www.healthcare.gov/income-and-household-information/how-to-report/.

2024 Poverty Guidelines: 48 Contiguous States (all states except Alaska and Hawaii), available at https://aspe.hhs.gov/sites/default/files/documents/7240229f28375f54435c5b83a3764cd1/detailed-guidelines-2024.pdf.

KFF, Medicaid in Texas, available at https://files.kff.org/attachment/fact-sheet-medicaid-state-TX.

American Council on Aging, 2025 Federal Poverty Levels / Guidelines & How They Determine Medicaid Eligibility, available at https://www.medicaidplanningassistance.org/federal-poverty-guidelines/.

Internal Revenue Code Section 36B, available at https://www.law.cornell.edu/uscode/text/26/36B.

World Population Review, US County Populations 2025, available at https://worldpopulationreview.com/us-counties.

Healthcare.gov, Special enrollment opportunities, available at https://www.healthcare.gov/coverage-outside-open-enrollment/special-enrollment-period/.

Healthcare.gov, A quick guide to the Health Insurance Marketplace®, https://www.healthcare.gov/quick-guide/dates-and-deadlines/.

Healthcare.gov, Health benefits & coverage, available at https://www.healthcare.gov/coverage/pre-existing-conditions/.

Healthcare.gov, Out-of-pocket maximum/limit, available at https://www.healthcare.gov/glossary/out-of-pocket-maximum-limit/.

CMS.gov, Affordable Care Act Implementation FAQs - Set 18, available at https://www.cms.gov/cciio/resources/fact-sheets-and-faqs/aca_implementation_faqs18.

Healthcare.gov, Cost-sharing reductions, available at https://www.healthcare.gov/lower-costs/save-on-out-of-pocket-costs/.

2025 Reconciliation bill, available at https://www.congress.gov/119/bills/hr1/BILLS-119hr1eas.pdf.

IRS, Revenue Procedure 2025-19, available at https://www.irs.gov/pub/irs-drop/rp-25-19.pdf.

14 – Paying Taxes in Early Retirement

Natalie B. Choate, Life and Death Planning for Retirement Benefits, 8th Edition 2019, page 164.

Section 6654(g), available at https://www.law.cornell.edu/uscode/text/26/6654#g.

Section 31, available at https://www.law.cornell.edu/uscode/text/26/31.

Section 3405, available at https://www.law.cornell.edu/uscode/text/26/3405.

Treas. Reg. Section 1.6654-1(a)(3), available at https://www.law.cornell.edu/cfr/text/26/1.6654-1.

IRS, Publication 505 - Tax Withholding and Estimated Tax: https://www.irs.gov/pub/irs-pdf/p505.pdf.

IRS, Form 1040, available at https://www.irs.gov/pub/irs-pdf/f1040.pdf.

IRS, Form 1040-SR, available at https://www.irs.gov/pub/irs-pdf/f1040s.pdf.

IRS, Form W-4V, available at https://www.irs.gov/pub/irs-pdf/fw4v.pdf.

15 – Tackling Required Minimum Distributions (RMDs)

JL Collins, The Simple Path to Wealth, 2025, pp. 155-156.

Treasury Decision 9930, available at https://www.taxnotes.com/research/federal/treasury-decisions/final-regs-provide-guidance-on-rmd-calculations/2d5f9.

Natalie B. Choate, Life and Death Planning for Retirement Benefits, 8th Edition 2019, page 46.

Fidelity, IRS Uniform Lifetime Table, available at https://www.fidelity.com/bin-public/060_www_fidelity_com/documents/UniformLifetimeTable.pdf.

The White Coat Investor, Getting to Know Jim: His Past, Present, and Future Relationship with Money, available at https://youtu.be/5ap0UXoW9-A?si=wdbXE2giTZKdkpYU&t=2184.

Section 401(a)(9)(C)(v), available at https://www.law.cornell.edu/uscode/text/26/401#a_9_C.

Social Security Actuarial Life Table, available at https://www.ssa.gov/oact/STATS/table4c6.html.

IRS, Publication 915 Social Security and Equivalent Railroad Retirement Benefits, available at https://www.irs.gov/pub/irs-pdf/p915.pdf.

Covisium, Taxable Social Security Benefit Calculator, available at https://www.covisum.com/resources/taxable-social-security-calculator.

Kamaron McNair, Here are the new federal income tax brackets for 2025—the standard deduction is now up to $30,000, available at https://www.cnbc.com/2024/10/22/new-federal-income-tax-brackets-for-2025.html.

Kate Ashford, IRMAA Brackets 2025: What They Are and How They Work, available at https://www.nerdwallet.com/article/insurance/medicare/what-is-the-medicare-irmaa.

Sean Mullaney, Widow's Tax Trap Crushes $1M Traditional IRA?, available at https://www.youtube.com/watch?v=z0h8_gul-Ns.

Sean Mullaney, Widow's Tax Trap! IRMAA! A $4M Traditional IRA Will Get Crushed by Taxes! . . . Or Maybe Not, available at https://www.youtube.com/watch?v=vyiDhQvd9do.

UBS, Global Wealth Report 2025, page 18, available at https://www.ubs.com/us/en/wealth-management/insights/global-wealth-report.html.

16 – The Widow's Tax Trap

Fidelity, IRS Uniform Lifetime Table, available at https://www.fidelity.com/bin-public/060_www_fidelity_com/documents/UniformLifetimeTable.pdf.

17 – Taxable Roth Conversions

Bogleheads® Conference 2024 Roth Conversion Deep Dive with Mike Piper, available at https://www.youtube.com/watch?v=Wjbf9KVSG7s.

IRS, Lifetime Learning Credit, available at https://www.irs.gov/credits-deductions/individuals/llc.

Sabrina Parys, Capital Gains Tax: Long and Short-Term Rates for 2024-2025, available at https://www.nerdwallet.com/article/taxes/capital-gains-tax-rates.

Kamaron McNair, Here are the new federal income tax brackets for 2025—the standard deduction is now up to $30,000, available at https://www.cnbc.com/2024/10/22/new-federal-income-tax-brackets-for-2025.html.

2025 Reconciliation bill, available at https://www.congress.gov/119/bills/hr1/BILLS-119hr1eas.pdf.

Ben Henry-Moreland, Breaking Down The "One Big Beautiful Bill Act": Impact Of New Laws On Tax Planning, available at https://www.kitces.com/blog/obbba-one-big-beautiful-bill-act-tax-planning-salt-cap-senior-deduction-qbi-deduction-tax-cut-and-jobs-act-tcja-amt-trump-accounts/.

Internal Revenue Code Section 170(p), available at https://www.law.cornell.edu/uscode/text/26/170#p.

IRS, 2021 Form 1040 U.S. Individual Income Tax Return, available at, https://www.irs.gov/pub/irs-prior/f1040--2021.pdf.

Fidelity, IRS Uniform Lifetime Table, available at https://www.fidelity.com/bin-public/060_www_fidelity_com/documents/UniformLifetimeTable.pdf.

18 – Asset Location

Yahoo Finance, https://finance.yahoo.com/quote/VTSAX/, https://finance.yahoo.com/quote/VTIAX/performance/, https://finance.yahoo.com/quote/VBTLX/.

Vanguard, Qualified dividend income, available at https://investor.vanguard.com/investor-resources-education/taxes/qdi-yearend-qualified-dividend-income?year=2025.

S&P 500 Dividend Yield by Month, available at https://www.multpl.com/s-p-500-dividend-yield/table/by-month.

PwC, Japan Corporate – Withholding Taxes, available at https://taxsummaries.pwc.com/japan/corporate/withholding-taxes.

PwC, United Kingdom Corporate – Withholding Taxes, available at https://taxsummaries.pwc.com/united-kingdom/corporate/withholding-taxes.

Sean Mullaney, Three Great Jobs for Inherited IRAs, available at https://www.youtube.com/watch?v=fxTDRmo-DtQ.

Sean Mullaney, Tax Basketing for a 72(t) Payment Plan, available at https://fitaxguy.com/tax-basketing-for-a-72t-payment-plan/.

Sean Mullaney, How Much Tax on a Roth Conversion, available at https://www.youtube.com/watch?v=vXboMKuemAw.

Sean Mullaney, Do You Have a Hidden Roth IRA?, available at https://www.youtube.com/watch?v=NXN7kfmqWY0.

Sabrina Parys, Capital Gains Tax: How It Works, Rates and Calculator, available at https://www.nerdwallet.com/article/taxes/capital-gains-tax-rates.

Goldilocks and the Three Bears, available at https://americanliterature.com/childrens-stories/goldilocks-and-the-three-bears#google_vignette.

Eric Reed, What Is an Annuity and How Are They Taxed?, available at https://smartasset.com/retirement/non-qualified-annuity-taxation.

IRS, Eligibility for the Premium Tax Credit, available at https://www.irs.gov/affordable-care-act/individuals-and-families/eligibility-for-the-premium-tax-credit.

Sean Mullaney, Tax Basis for Beginners, available at https://fitaxguy.com/tax-basis-for-beginners/.

Sean Mullaney, Rental Real Estate in Retirement Accounts, available at https://fitaxguy.com/real-estate-in-an-ira/.

Thomson Reuters, Depreciation recapture tax, available at https://tax.thomsonreuters.com/en/glossary/depreciation-recapture-tax.

Internal Revenue Code Section 469(i), available at https://www.law.cornell.edu/uscode/text/26/469#i.

Sean Mullaney, Rental Real Estate Losses, available at https://fitaxguy.com/rental-real-estate-losses/.

Internal Revenue Code Section 4975, available at https://www.law.cornell.edu/uscode/text/26/4975.

IRS, Retirement topics - Prohibited transactions, available at https://www.irs.gov/retirement-plans/plan-participant-employee/retirement-topics-prohibited-transactions.

Kali McGuire, Biden Administration 2025 FY budget proposes Wash Sale Rule for digital assets and crypto mining tax, available at https://www.dlapiper.com/en/insights/publications/blockchain-and-digital-assets-news-and-trends/2024/biden-administration-2025-fy-budget-proposes-wash-sale-rule-for-digital-assets-and-crypto-mining-tax.

IRS, Instructions for Schedule D (2024), available at https://www.irs.gov/instructions/i1040sd.

19 – 2025 Tax Law Changes

Danielle Wallace, Schumer forces name change for 'big, beautiful bill' moments before it passes, available at https://www.foxnews.com/politics/schumer-forces-name-change-big-beautiful-bill-moments-before-passes.

Jeff Levine, https://x.com/CPAPlanner/status/1940856699872858202.

2025 Reconciliation bill, available at https://www.congress.gov/119/bills/hr1/BILLS-119hr1eas.pdf.

Andy Panko, https://www.linkedin.com/posts/andypanko_taxes-taxplanning-retirementplanning-activity-7346897576824041472-4FB3?utm_source=share&utm_medium=member_desktop&rcm=ACoAAADSfwMBsB8x1E-Wh4OmdVu2M7W3qtn0UuE.

Jeff Levine, https://x.com/CPAPlanner/status/1940993500105044075.

Sean Mullaney, https://x.com/SeanMoneyandTax/status/1940998855040159805.

Internal Revenue Code Section 911, available at https://www.law.cornell.edu/uscode/text/26/911.

Internal Revenue Code Section 931, available at https://www.law.cornell.edu/uscode/text/26/931.

Internal Revenue Code Section 933, available at https://www.law.cornell.edu/uscode/text/26/933.

Internal Revenue Code Section 170(p), available at https://www.law.cornell.edu/uscode/text/26/170#p.

Internal Revenue Code Section 170(b)(1)(H), available at https://www.law.cornell.edu/us-code/text/26/170#b_1_H.

Internal Revenue Code Section 408(d)(8)(C), available at https://www.law.cornell.edu/us-code/text/26/408#d_8_C.

Internal Revenue Code Section 170(b), available at https://www.law.cornell.edu/us-code/text/26/170#b.

IRS, IRS releases tax inflation adjustments for tax year 2025, available at https://www.irs.gov/newsroom/irs-releases-tax-inflation-adjustments-for-tax-year-2025.

IRS, Revenue Procedure 2024-40, available at https://www.irs.gov/pub/irs-drop/rp-24-40.pdf.

Ben Henry-Moreland, Breaking Down The "One Big Beautiful Bill Act": Impact Of New Laws On Tax Planning, available at https://www.kitces.com/blog/obbba-one-big-beautiful-bill-act-tax-planning-salt-cap-senior-deduction-qbi-deduction-tax-cut-and-jobs-act-tcja-amt-trump-accounts/.

Internal Revenue Code Section 36B(b)(3)(A), available at https://www.law.cornell.edu/us-code/text/26/36B#b_3_A.

20 – Planning for Uncertainty

Sean Mullaney, The Tax Hikes Are Coming!!! Or Maybe Not, YouTube video, available at https://www.youtube.com/watch?v=mCgRSCPuR-k.

Sean Mullaney, Accumulators Should Ignore the Conventional Wisdom, available at https://fitaxguy.com/accumulators-should-ignore-the-conventional-wisdom/.

U.S. Treasury, Historical Debt Outstanding, available at https://fiscaldata.treasury.gov/datasets/historical-debt-outstanding/historical-debt-outstanding.

Public Debt of the United States from 1990 to 2023, available at https://www.statista.com/statistics/187867/public-debt-of-the-united-states-since-1990/.

Hiranmayi Srinivasan, U.S. National Debt by Year, available at https://www.investopedia.com/us-national-debt-by-year-7499291.

Murphy Desmond S.C., PATH Act Places Additional Restrictions on Claims for Certain Credits, available at https://www.murphydesmond.com/path-act-places-additional-restrictions-on-claims-for-certain-credits.

H.R.2029 - Consolidated Appropriations Act, 2016, available at https://www.congress.gov/bill/114th-congress/house-bill/2029/all-actions?overview=closed&q=%7B%22roll-call-vote%22%3A%22all%22%7D.

Consolidated Appropriations Act, 2016, available at https://www.congress.gov/114/plaws/publ113/PLAW-114publ113.pdf.

2014 United States elections, available at https://en.wikipedia.org/wiki/2014_United_States_elections.

2018 United States elections, available at https://en.wikipedia.org/wiki/2018_United_States_elections.

Treas. Reg. Section 1.401(a)(9)-9, available at https://www.ecfr.gov/current/title-26/chapter-I/subchapter-A/part-1/subject-group-ECFR6f8c3724b50e44d/section-1.401(a)(9)-9.

Jobs and Growth Tax Relief Reconciliation Act of 2003, Section 301, available at https://www.congress.gov/108/plaws/publ27/PLAW-108publ27.pdf.

2002 United States elections, available at https://en.wikipedia.org/wiki/2002_United_States_elections.

Voting bloc, available at https://en.wikipedia.org/wiki/Voting_bloc.

Joe Rogan Experience #2219 - Donald Trump, available at https://youtu.be/hBMoPUAeLnY?si=7Zs3tsTrUOCAOl7u&t=2445.

2008 United States elections, available at https://en.wikipedia.org/wiki/2008_United_States_elections.

2008 United States Senate elections, available at https://en.wikipedia.org/wiki/2008_United_States_Senate_elections.

Fidelity, IRS Uniform Lifetime Table, available at https://www.fidelity.com/bin-public/060_www_fidelity_com/documents/UniformLifetimeTable.pdf.

Kamaron McNair, Here are the new federal income tax brackets for 2025—the standard deduction is now up to $30,000, available at https://www.cnbc.com/2024/10/22/new-federal-income-tax-brackets-for-2025.html.

PRRI, Breaking Down the Differences Between Voters and Non-Voters in the 2024 Election, available at https://www.prri.org/spotlight/breaking-down-the-differences-between-voters-and-non-voters-in-the-2024-election/.

Politico Interactives Staff, Are Trump's tariffs making money? Watch this chart, available at https://www.politico.com/interactives/2025/trump-tariff-income-tracker/.

Jeff Levine, https://x.com/CPAPlanner/status/1940856699872858202.

H.R.1 - One Big Beautiful Bill Act, available at https://www.congress.gov/bill/119th-congress/house-bill/1/text.

Don Lonczak, Elina Teplinsky, David McCullough, M.C. Hammond, and Baylee Beeman, Congress Sends Big, Beautiful Bill for President's Signature: Status of Clean Energy Tax Credits, available at https://www.pillsburylaw.com/en/news-and-insights/renewable-energy-tax-credits-big-beautiful-bill-IRA.html.

Federal Reserve Bank of St. Louis, Market Yield on U.S. Treasury Securities at 10-Year Constant Maturity, Quoted on an Investment Basis, available at https://fred.stlouisfed.org/series/DGS10.

S&P 500 Dividend Yield by Year, available at https://www.multpl.com/s-p-500-dividend-yield/table/by-year.

22 – Health Savings Accounts (HSAs)

IRS, Publication 969 Health Savings Accounts and Other Tax-Favored Health Plans: https://www.irs.gov/pub/irs-pdf/p969.pdf.

IRS, 2025 Form W-2, available at https://www.irs.gov/pub/irs-pdf/fw2.pdf.

IRS, Form 8889, Health Savings Accounts (HSAs), available at https://www.irs.gov/pub/irs-pdf/f8889.pdf.

IRS, Schedule 1, Additional Income and Adjustments to Income, available at https://www.irs.gov/pub/irs-pdf/f1040s1.pdf.

Internal Revenue Code Section 223, available at https://www.law.cornell.edu/uscode/text/26/223.

IRS, Revenue Procedure 2024-25, available at https://www.irs.gov/pub/irs-drop/rp-24-25.pdf.

IRS, Revenue Procedure 2025-19, available at https://www.irs.gov/pub/irs-drop/rp-25-19.pdf.

Ben Henry-Moreland, Analyzing The Individual Tax Provisions Of The House Republicans' 2025 Proposed Tax Bill, available at https://www.kitces.com/blog/republican-proposed-tax-bill-2025-tax-cuts-and-jobs-act-tcja-sunset-salt-deduction-cap-child-tax-credit-qbi-deduction-maga/.

2025 Reconciliation bill, available at https://www.congress.gov/119/bills/hr1/BILLS-119hr1eas.pdf.

Publication 502 - Medical and Dental Expenses: https://www.irs.gov/pub/irs-pdf/p502.pdf.

Sean Mullaney, 2026 Premium Tax Credits and the One Big Beautiful Bill, available at https://www.youtube.com/watch?v=o1gZgUTpjXo.

Healthcare.gov, When can you get health insurance?, available at https://www.healthcare.gov/quick-guide/dates-and-deadlines/.

2022 HSA Findings, available at https://www.ebri.org/content/health-savings-account-balances--contributions--distributions--and-other-vital-statistics--evidence-from-the-ebri-hsa-database.

23 – Tax Loss Harvesting

Section 1091(d), available at https://www.law.cornell.edu/uscode/text/26/1091#d.

Treas. Reg. Section 1.1091-1(h) Examples 1 & 2, available at https://www.law.cornell.edu/cfr/text/26/1.1091-1.

Treas. Reg. Section 1.6045-1(d)(6)(iii)(A)(1), available at https://www.law.cornell.edu/cfr/text/26/1.6045-1.

Excess Returns YouTube Channel, The Fastest Market Selloff Since 2020: Rick Ferri on Tactics to Survive and Thrive, available at https://youtu.be/pERcEpGZ-P0?si=csCmnxLCEUEkF_n&t=1214.

24 – Tax Gain Harvesting

Sabrina Parys, Standard Deduction for 2024 and 2025: Amounts, When to Take, available at https://www.nerdwallet.com/article/taxes/standard-deduction.

Sabrina Parys, Capital Gains Tax: How It Works, Rates and Calculator, available at https://www.nerdwallet.com/article/taxes/capital-gains-tax-rates.

25 – Special Opportunities for the Self-Employed

Fed Small Business, 2023 Report on Nonemployer Firms: Findings From the 2022 Small Business Credit Survey, page 5, available at https://www.fedsmallbusiness.org/reports/survey/2023/2023-report-on-nonemployer-firms.

Mike Piper, Solo 401(k) Contribution Calculator, available at https://obliviousinvestor.com/solo-401k-contribution-calculator/.

Treas. Reg. Section 1.401(k)-1(a)(6)(iv), available at https://www.law.cornell.edu/cfr/text/26/1.401(k)-1.

IRS, One-participant 401(k) plans, available at https://www.irs.gov/retirement-plans/one-participant-401k-plans.

Sean Mullaney, The Odd 403(b) Rule for Side Hustlers, available at https://fitaxguy.com/section-415k4-and-the-self-employed/.

IRS, Instructions for Form 5500-EZ, available at https://www.irs.gov/pub/irs-pdf/i5500ez.pdf.

IRS, Form 5500-EZ, Annual Return of A One-Participant (Owners/Partners and Their Spouses) Retirement Plan or A Foreign Plan, available at https://www.irs.gov/pub/irs-pdf/f5500ez.pdf.

Sean Mullaney, Solo 401(k) Mega Backdoor Roth? 2025 Numbers, available at https://www.youtube.com/watch?v=ULlEcKEKD9c.

Section 401(c)(2)(A), available at https://www.law.cornell.edu/uscode/text/26/401#c_2_A.

IRS, Here's how to tell the difference between a hobby and a business for tax purposes, available at https://www.irs.gov/newsroom/heres-how-to-tell-the-difference-between-a-hobby-and-a-business-for-tax-purposes.

IRS, Know the difference between a hobby and a business, available at https://www.irs.gov/newsroom/know-the-difference-between-a-hobby-and-a-business.

26 – Real Estate

IRS, Form 8582, Passive Activity Loss Limitations, available at https://www.irs.gov/pub/irs-pdf/f8582.pdf.

Jobs and Growth Tax Relief Reconciliation Act of 2003 Section 302, available at https://www.congress.gov/108/plaws/publ27/PLAW-108publ27.pdf.

Michael Kitces, Mechanics Of The 0% Long-Term Capital Gains Tax Rate And Harvesting Capital Gains For A Free Step-Up In Basis!, available at https://www.kitces.com/blog/understanding-the-mechanics-of-the-0-long-term-capital-gains-tax-rate-how-to-harvest-capital-gains-for-a-free-step-up-in-basis/.

27 – Late Starters

Sabrina Parys, 2024-2025 Tax Brackets and Federal Income Tax Rates, available at https://www.nerdwallet.com/article/taxes/federal-income-tax-brackets.

Sean Mullaney, 2025 IRA Contributions for Beginners, available at https://fitaxguy.com/2025-ira-contributions-for-beginners/.

28 – Sudden Job Loss

IRS, Notice 2022-6, Determination of Substantially Equal Periodic Payments, available at https://www.irs.gov/pub/irs-drop/n-22-06.pdf.

Fidelity, IRS Single Life Expectancy Table, available at https://www.fidelity.com/retirement-ira/irs-single-life-expectancy-table.

Internal Revenue Code Section 72(t)(3)(B), available at https://www.law.cornell.edu/uscode/text/26/72#t_3_B.

29 – Return on Hassle

"Return on Hassle": Term heard initially from Mitchell Baldridge, CPA, CFP®.

FINRA. "Insurance." FINRA Investor Insights, https://www.finra.org/investors/investing/investment-products/insurance.

Thomas E. Lambert and Christopher B. Tobe, "Safe" Annuity Retirement Products and a Possible US Retirement Crisis, available at https://papers.ssrn.com/sol3/papers.cfm?abstract_id=4761980.

IRS, Rollovers of retirement plan and IRA distributions, available at https://www.irs.gov/retirement-plans/plan-participant-employee/rollovers-of-retirement-plan-and-ira-distributions.

Forge Trust, Private Equity IRA, available at https://forgetrust.com/private-equity-ira/.

Internal Revenue Code Section 469, available at https://www.law.cornell.edu/uscode/text/26/469.

IRS, Publication 555 Community Property, available at https://www.irs.gov/pub/irs-pdf/p555.pdf.

Tim Parker, Community Property States, available at https://www.investopedia.com/personal-finance/which-states-are-community-property-states/.

Cody Garrett, CFP®, Medicare + IRMAA | Create Your Own Financial Plan (24/38), YouTube, https://www.youtube.com/watch?v=xkcMetKWDVE.

TreasuryDirect, Tax information for EE and I bonds, available at https://www.treasurydirect.gov/savings-bonds/tax-information-ee-i-bonds/.

TreasuryDirect, Treasury Inflation Protected Securities (TIPS), available at https://treasurydirect.gov/marketable-securities/tips/.

"Headspace Premium": Term originally discussed with Shane Sideris, CFA.

30 – Inheriting Property

Jeffrey Levine, Untangling The IRS's New Finalized (And Proposed) Regulations On RMDs: The 10-Year Rule, Trust Beneficiaries, Spousal Beneficiaries, Annuities, And More!, available at https://www.kitces.com/blog/secure-act-2-0-irs-regulations-rmd-required-minimum-distributions-10-year-rule-eligible-designated-beneficiary-see-through-conduit-trust/.

Internal Revenue Service, Treasury Decision 10001, available at https://www.federalregister.gov/documents/2024/07/19/2024-14542/required-minimum-distributions.

Treasury Regulation Section 54.4974-1(g)(3), available at https://www.law.cornell.edu/cfr/text/26/54.4974-1.

Sean Mullaney, Inherited Roth IRAs, available at https://fitaxguy.com/inherited-roth-iras/.

Natalie B. Choate, Estate Planning for Retirement Benefits Under SECURE and Proposed Treasury Regulations, page 12, available at https://ataxplan.com/wp-content/uploads/2022/09/Estate_Planning_for_Retirement_Benefits_post_SECURE_and_Prop_Regs-OCT-1-2022.pdf.

Natalie B. Choate, Life and Death Planning for Retirement Benefits, 8th Ed. 2019, p. 70.

Treas. Reg. Section 1.402A-1, available at https://www.law.cornell.edu/cfr/text/26/1.402A-1.

Section 223(f)(8)(B), available at https://www.law.cornell.edu/uscode/text/26/223#f_8_B.

Section 1223(9), available at https://www.law.cornell.edu/uscode/text/26/1223#9.

IRS, Publication 544 - Sales and Other Dispositions of Assets: https://www.irs.gov/pub/irs-pdf/p544.pdf.

31 – Gifting Property to Family

Treas. Reg. Section 1.401(a)(9)-4, available at https://www.ecfr.gov/current/title-26/chapter-I/subchapter-A/part-1/subject-group-ECFR6f8c3724b50e44d/section-1.401(a)(9)-4.

Natalie B. Choate, Estate Planning for Retirement Benefits.

Under SECURE and Proposed Treasury Regulations, page 42, available at https://ataxplan.com/wp-content/uploads/2022/09/Estate_Planning_for_Retirement_Benefits_post_SECURE_and_Prop_Regs-OCT-1-2022.pdf.

32 – Tax-Optimized Charitable Giving

Urban Institute & Brookings Institution Tax Policy Center, What are itemized deductions and who claims them?, available at https://taxpolicycenter.org/briefing-book/what-are-itemized-deductions-and-who-claims-them.

IRS, Publication 502 - Medical and Dental Expenses, available at https://www.irs.gov/pub/irs-pdf/p502.pdf.

IRS Publication 936 - Home Mortgage Interest Deduction: https://www.irs.gov/pub/irs-pdf/p936.pdf.

Calculator.net, Mortgage Calculator, available at https://www.calculator.net/mortgage-calculator.html.

2025 Reconciliation bill, available at https://www.congress.gov/119/bills/hr1/BILLS-119hr1eas.pdf.

Internal Revenue Code Section 170(b)(1)(H), available at https://www.law.cornell.edu/uscode/text/26/170#b_1_H.

IRS, 2025 Amounts Relating to Retirement Plans and IRAs, as Adjusted for Changes in Cost-of-Living, available at https://www.irs.gov/pub/irs-drop/n-24-80.pdf.

Sarah Brenner, QCDs and RMD Requirements of Inherited IRAs: Today's Slott Report Mailbag, available at https://irahelp.com/slottreport/qcds-and-rmd-requirements-inherited-iras-todays-slott-report-mailbag/.

IRS Publication 526 - Charitable Contributions: https://www.irs.gov/pub/irs-pdf/p526.pdf.

Fidelity Charitable, What is a donor-advised fund (DAF)?, available at https://www.fidelitycharitable.org/guidance/philanthropy/what-is-a-donor-advised-fund.html.

33 – 529s and Other Child Savings Options

IRS, Publication 970 - Tax Benefits for Education, available at: https://www.irs.gov/pub/irs-pdf/p970.pdf.

Sean Mullaney, SECURE 2.0 529-to-Roth IRA Rollovers, available at https://fitaxguy.com/secure-2-0-529-to-roth-ira-rollovers/.

Internal Revenue Code 529(c)(3)(E), available at https://www.law.cornell.edu/uscode/text/26/529#c_3_E.

Ben Henry-Moreland, 529-To-Roth IRA Rollovers: Taking Advantage Of The New Option To Move Education Savings To Retirement Savings, available at https://www.kitces.com/blog/529-to-roth-ira-rollover-retirement-saving-education-planning-secure-2-0-backdoor-roth/.

ScholarShare529, Frequently asked questions, available at https://www.scholarshare529.com/resources/faq/.

Fidelity Viewpoints, Must-know facts about UGMA/UTMA custodial accounts, available at https://www.fidelity.com/learning-center/personal-finance/custodial-account-for-kids.

College Raptor Staff, What Counts As An "Asset" On The FAFSA?, available at https://www.collegeraptor.com/paying-for-college/articles/questions-answers/counts-asset-fafsa/.

Robert Farrington, How To Use A Roth IRA To Save For College, available at https://thecollegeinvestor.com/21215/roth-ira-save-for-college/.

New York State Department of Labor, Working Papers, available at https://dol.ny.gov/working-papers.

Vanguard, Understanding the 529 plan "grandparent loophole", available at https://investor.vanguard.com/investor-resources-education/education-college-savings/529-grandparent-loophole.

Schwab, Grandparent-Owned 529s Get a Boost, available at https://www.schwab.com/learn/story/grandparent-owned-529s-get-boost.

Saving for College Editorial Team, How Do 529 Plans Affect Financial Aid?, available at https://www.savingforcollege.com/intro-to-529s/does-a-529-plan-affect-financial-aid.

34 – Estate and Gift Taxes

IRS, IRS releases tax inflation adjustments for tax year 2025, available at https://www.irs.gov/newsroom/irs-releases-tax-inflation-adjustments-for-tax-year-2025.

2025 Reconciliation bill, available at https://www.congress.gov/119/bills/hr1/BILLS-119hr1eas.pdf.

Kay Bell, Estate Tax: Definition, Tax Rates and Who Pays, available at https://www.nerdwallet.com/article/taxes/estate-tax.

IRS, Instructions to Form 709, available at https://www.irs.gov/pub/irs-pdf/i709.pdf.

IRS, Form 709, , available at https://www.irs.gov/pub/irs-pdf/f709.pdf.

Dr. Jim Dahle, How to Superfund a 529 Plan, available at https://www.whitecoatinvestor.com/529-superfunding/.

Joseph Johns, Estate and Inheritance Taxes by State, 2024, available at https://taxfoundation.org/data/all/state/estate-inheritance-taxes/.

American Bar Association, Estate, Gift, and GST Taxes, available at https://www.americanbar.org/groups/real_property_trust_estate/resources/estate-planning/estate-gift-gst-taxes/.

35 – Trusts

Treas. Reg. Section 1.401(a)(9)-4(f)(2), available at https://www.ecfr.gov/current/title-26/chapter-I/subchapter-A/part-1/subject-group-ECFR6f8c3724b50e44d/section-1.401(a)(9)-4.

IRC Section 671, available at https://www.law.cornell.edu/uscode/text/26/671.

IRC Section 676, available at https://www.law.cornell.edu/uscode/text/26/676.

Eric Reed, Trust Tax Rates and Exemptions for 2024 and 2025, available at https://smartasset.com/taxes/trust-tax-rates.

36 – Early Retirement Implementation

IRS, Publication 505, available at https://www.irs.gov/publications/p505.

Internal Revenue Code Section 6654(d)(1)(A), available at https://www.law.cornell.edu/uscode/text/26/6654#d_1_A.

Sabrina Parys, 2024-2025 Tax Brackets and Federal Income Tax Rates, available at https://www.nerdwallet.com/article/taxes/federal-income-tax-brackets.

Sabrina Parys, Capital Gains Tax: How It Works, Rates and Calculator, available at https://www.nerdwallet.com/article/taxes/capital-gains-tax-rates.

Fidelity, IRA Notice of Withholding, available at https://institutional.fidelity.com/app/literature/view?itemCode=704656&renditionType=pdf.

Schwab, Tax Withholding Election Form for Individual Retirement Accounts, available at https://www.schwab.com/resource/tax-withholding-election-form.

Vanguard, Helping you make sense of tax withholding rules for your IRA, available at https://personal1.vanguard.com/pdf/s273.pdf?2210114361.

Fidelity, IRS Single Life Expectancy Table, available at https://www.fidelity.com/retirement-ira/irs-single-life-expectancy-table.

Fidelity, IRA Beneficiary Distribution Request, available at https://institutional.fidelity.com/app/literature/view?itemCode=B-IRA-BDIS&renditionType=pdf.

37 – A Critique and a Response

IRS, Publication 502, Medical and Dental Expenses, available at https://www.irs.gov/pub/irs-pdf/p502.pdf.

38 – The Lessons of This Book

Internet Movie Database, Back to School Quotes, available at https://www.imdb.com/title/tt0090685/quotes/.

Cambridge Dictionary, https://dictionary.cambridge.org/dictionary/english/from-pillar-to-post.